THE LONGEST NIGHT

DATE DUE

The University of California Press gratefully acknowledges the generous support of the Floersheimer Center for Constitutional Democracy at the Benjamin N. Cardozo School of Law.

THE **LONGEST NIGHT**

Polemics and Perspectives on Election 2000

EDITED BY

Arthur J. Jacobson and

Michel Rosenfeld

UNIVERSITY OF CALIFORNIA PRESS

Berkeley   Los Angeles   London

University of California Press
Berkeley and Los Angeles, California

University of California Press, Ltd.
London, England

© 2002 by the Regents of the University of California

The editors gratefully acknowledge the following publications: *London Review of Books,* vol. 23, no. 3, for Bruce Ackerman, "Anatomy of a Constitutional Coup"; The Green Bag, Inc., Copyright 2001, for Robert W. Bennett, "Popular Election of the President without a Constitutional Amendment"; and *New York Review of Books,* vol. 48, no. 1, for Ronald Dworkin, "A Badly Flawed Election," and vol. 48, no. 3, for Charles Fried, "A Badly Flawed Election: An Exchange" and "Reply by Ronald Dworkin."

Library of Congress Cataloging-in-Publication Data
  The longest night : polemics and perspectives on election 2000 / edited by Arthur J. Jacobson and Michel Rosenfeld.
      p. cm.
  Includes bibliographical references and index.
  ISBN 0-520-23373-5 (cloth : alk. paper)—ISBN 0-520-23549-5 (paper : alk. paper)
      1. Presidents—United States—Election—2000. 2. Election law—United States. I. Jacobson, Arthur J. II. Rosenfeld, Michel, 1948–
JK526 2002
324.973'0929—dc21   2001007758
                                                              CIP

Manufactured in the United States of America

  11 10 09 08 07 06 05 04 03 02

10 9 8 7 6 5 4 3 2 1

The paper used in this publication is both acid-free and totally chlorine-free (TCF). It meets the minimum requirements of ANSI/NISO Z39.48–1992 (R 1997) *(Permanence of Paper).*♾

For our children, Sam and Ben Jacobson
and Maia and Alexis Rosenfeld,
to whom we entrust the future of our democracy

CONTENTS

ACKNOWLEDGMENTS

The editors gratefully acknowledge the Floersheimer Center for Constitutional Democracy for its generous support.

The editors also wish to thank Andy Strauss (Benjamin N. Cardozo School of Law 2002) for taking a leading role in compiling the chronology and for his able research and editorial assistance. Mimi Yang (New York University School of Law 2003) also provided valuable research assistance.

Eric Smoodin, our editor at the University of California Press, deserves special thanks for showing us that our sharp differences concerning Election 2000 could be harnessed into a reasoned public discussion from a multitude of diverse perspectives.

Paul Verkuil, former dean of the Benjamin N. Cardozo School of Law, was a constant source of support and encouragement.

INTRODUCTION

Arthur J. Jacobson and Michel Rosenfeld

Quite unexpectedly, the American presidential election of 2000 has become the most remarkable and in many ways the most unsettling one that the country has yet experienced. The millennial election stretched for well over one month, and its repercussions are sure to be felt for a long time to come. It has raised fundamental questions not only about American democracy but also about the nation's more than two-hundred-year-old Constitution and about the legitimate role of American courts, state and federal and in particular the highest court in the land, the United States Supreme Court, which in effect put an end to the election in a bitterly divided 5–4 decision rendered on December 12, 2000.

As the polls began closing on the evening of election day, November 7, 2000, there was no reason to anticipate any of the remarkable developments that were about to unfold. True, there had been a closely fought and vigorous campaign and much heated rhetoric. The intensity of the candidates, however, by and large did not spill over to the great majority of the voters. The country was at peace and in the midst of a long period of unprecedented prosperity. Moreover, in spite of their sharp differences, Bush and Gore seemed to aim for the center of the American political spectrum.

The opinion polls had been fluctuating, but Bush had maintained a small but steady lead in all the major polls in the weeks leading up to the election. On the eve of the election, most pundits were confident that Bush would win the popular vote, although some speculated that there was a remote chance that Gore might win a majority in the Electoral College. If that were to happen, moreover, it might well rekindle the debate over abolition of the Electoral College, one of the seemingly most vulnerable institutions of America's eighteenth-century Constitution. With the completely unexpected sequence of events after election day, however, the debate about the Electoral College would turn out to be but one among many, and it would by no means rank at the top of the list.

There was nothing unusual until well into the evening of November 7. In the early evening after Bush and Gore were each predictably projected the winner in respectively solidly Republican and staunchly Democratic states, the television networks predicted that Gore would win key toss-up states like Michigan, Pennsylvania, and Florida. This was a little surprising but well within the possibilities envisaged by the experts. Based on this, moreover, the Democrats were beginning to think that they would keep the White House after all.

The Democrats' newly raised expectations would be short lived, however, as around 9:00 P.M. EST, in the first truly unusual moment of election day 2000, the networks retracted their projection that Gore would win Florida and placed the state in their too-close-to-call column. Although this retraction was unusual in terms of network coverage of presidential elections, it did not presage the highly unusual turn of events that would soon ensue. As a matter of fact, even the networks' later projection that Bush would win Florida followed by a second retraction as dawn was approaching did not necessarily foretell anything unusual about the election itself, though it made it quite clear that something had gone awry with the way the media were covering it. Even Gore's retraction of his concession to Bush after the networks took Florida from the latter's column—though highly unusual in the annals of television-age presidential election concessions—could readily be interpreted as caused by misplaced reliance on the media rather than by any problems with the election itself.

I

As the chronology that follows indicates, the magnitude of the problems posed by the 2000 presidential election in general and by controversies that developed in Florida, the state that would decide the final outcome of the election, would gradually emerge during the thirty-six days following November 7. The fierce polemic engendered by the election took shape during that period and has continued ever since. Moreover, what is perhaps most salient about the many perspectives that have emerged from the polemic is that for the most part they have remained divided along partisan lines.

The aim of this collection of essays is to provide a representative sampling of the polemics and perspectives generated to date as a consequence of the 2000 presidential election. Concerning the polemics, we have made a concerted effort to provide a balance between Bush and Gore sympathizers. With respect to perspectives, however, we have endeavored to provide a wide variety, in terms of both differences in time and differences in geography. Thus some of the essays included were produced during the heat of the postelection battle that preceded the December 12 Supreme Court decision or shortly thereafter. Others were written with somewhat greater temporal distance, up to six months after that fateful December date. Although six months may be hardly relevant from the standpoint of history, the political mood in the United States is palpably different at this writing in June 2001 than it was in December 2000.

In terms of geography, the contributors to this volume certainly range far and near. At least two of them, Henry Brady and Charles Fried, were directly involved in the Florida battles, the first as a political scientist working for Gore and the second as counsel of record for the Florida legislature in two cases relating to the election. Farthest removed geographically from Florida are the authors from Europe and the Middle East, who provide valuable foreign perspectives on America's millennial election. The authors differ among themselves but converge on two somewhat disparate points: (1) amazement at the arcane and archaic nature of the American electoral system and at the pitfalls deriving from reliance on local control and (2) admiration for the great resilience and stability of the American political system in the face of the long uncertainty concerning the outcome of the presidential election and of the heated disagreements over the propriety of Supreme Court intervention.

In addition, the perspectives included in this volume are divided among participants in the postelection controversies, contemporaneous observers, and those who have analyzed the events based on a review of the record. Moreover, among those who had no direct experience with the millennial election, some have had relevant involvements in other elections. Thus Shlomo Avineri has often been an official foreign observer in many national elections, and Justice Noëlle Lenoir, until recently a member of the French Constitutional Council, has had an official role in that capacity for the supervision of the French presidential election of 1995 and for monitoring the vote count in its aftermath.

II

Whereas the millennial election—in particular, the events surrounding the election in Florida—provides the main focus of this volume, the subjects addressed in the various essays are far ranging. As the essays amply demonstrate, the continuing fascination with the millennial election stems not only from the heated controversy it has unleashed but also from the crucial questions it has raised concerning subjects as diverse as the essential tenets and fault lines of American democracy; the relation between law and politics; the legitimate constraints on judicial interpretation; the virtues and vices of federalism as it relates to the tension between local control and uniformity of conditions for all voters and vote counters; the difficulties of achieving justice through law; the hurdles confronting the adaptation of social scientific statistical evidence for use in a legal proceeding; and the confrontations between liberty, equality, citizenship, and nationhood in the context of discrepancies between America's pre–Civil War constitutional heritage and its post–Civil War counterpart.

Among this wealth of diverse perspectives and subjects, certain issues and queries stand out and deserve brief mention here as they transcend the bounds of the individual essays. Chief among these are the fact that America's Constitution and laws are ill equipped to deal with problems such as those that arose in relation to the millennial election. As Richard Pildes, one of the foremost experts on election law, makes plain in his clearly nonpartisan overview of the legal framework available to deal with disputed elections, the combination of America's eighteenth-century Constitution and the patchwork of imperfect and incomplete state and federal laws relating to elections makes it virtually impossible to reach satisfactory or nonpartisan resolutions of serious election disputes. Consistent with this, whatever resolution of the 2000 election may have been reached in accordance with the Constitution and applicable law would inevitably have appeared unfair and partisan to about half the electorate. It follows that impressions of partisanship in the resolution of the disputes arising out of the Florida election were at least in part attributable to deficiencies in the relevant legal designs. That still leaves open the question of whether the resolutions at stake were unduly, excessively, or gratuitously partisan. Significantly, the various essays in this volume are quite divided on this latter question.

By and large, the assessments of the judicial opinions, both state and federal, contained in this volume can be sorted out along partisan lines. Those who sympathize with the Democrats tend to defend the legitimacy of the Florida Supreme Court decisions and attack that of the U.S. Supreme Court December 12 decision. Republican sympathizers tend to draw entirely opposite conclusions. This contrast is most vividly illustrated by the two longest essays dealing with the various state and federal judicial opinions, by Michel Rosenfeld and Nelson Lund respectively. Rosenfeld argues that the Florida Supreme Court acted well within the bounds of judicial legitimacy while the U.S. Supreme Court majority violated the fundamental principles of consistency and integrity. Lund maintains that the Florida Supreme Court "careen[ed] out of control," completely beyond the bounds of permissible legal interpretation, and the U.S. Supreme Court majority could not have done otherwise than it did without abandoning principle and precedent. What is one to make of this stark discrepancy? Can analysis rise above partisanship? And if it can, which of these two diametrically opposed positions is more consonant with any possible nonpartisan criteria?

Based on the U.S. Supreme Court's December 12 opinion and a reading of all the essays bearing on the relevant judicial opinions, readers will be able to answer these questions for themselves. Regardless of the conclusions one ultimately reaches, however, the justices who decided *Bush v. Gore* took positions that, at least on first impression, seem strongly at odds with their previously expressed views. This observation, moreover, is equally applicable to the justices in the majority as to those who dissented. Thus, for example, it seems odd that Chief Justice Rehnquist and Justices Scalia and Thomas who have traditionally espoused a narrow conception of equal protection limited to prohibiting discrimination on the basis of race, religion, or national origin, should have agreed to find a violation of equal protection (and possibly due process) based on discrepancies in the manner in which votes were recounted. Conversely, it seems surprising that Justice Ginsburg, who has championed equality for women as a civil rights attorney and who certainly ranks as one of the justices with the most expansive views of equal protection on the present Court, should have concluded that the discrepancies did not even raise a plausible constitutional claim. Furthermore, at least on the surface it seems particularly ironic that the Chief Justice, joined by Justices Scalia and Thomas, the fiercest defenders of the prerogatives of the states against federal encroachment, filed a concurring opinion raising objections against a state supreme court's interpretation of its own state's law. By the same token, it seems noteworthy that two of the dissenters, Justices Ginsburg and Stevens, should have embraced positions seemingly grounded on complete deference to state court action and on state law in the face of challenges under the federal Constitution and federal law. Are some or all of these apparent discrepancies equivalent? Can some or all of them be explained away after careful examination? Do they evince a surrender to politics? Or do they ultimately demonstrate steadfast adherence to principle notwithstanding impressions to the contrary?

Another important issue brought to the fore by Election 2000, but with important ramifications that spread far beyond it, concerns the continuing viability of the Electoral College and its role in relation to democracy. The Florida election raised questions about the desirability of the Electoral College in two different but equally dramatic ways. First, if it were not for the Electoral College, the vicissitudes surrounding the Florida election and its aftermath would have had but minor repercussions. Indeed, since Gore won the nationwide popular vote by more than five hundred thousand votes, absent the Electoral College the disputed events in Florida would have had no impact on the outcome of the national election. Second, even if the award of Florida's twenty-five electoral votes to Bush had been unanimously accepted as unquestionably warranted, it would still have been the case in 2000, for the first time since the nineteenth century, that the winner of the Electoral College majority happened to be the loser of the popular vote.

Underlying these issues concerning the Electoral College are questions of both substance and procedure. From a substantive standpoint, the key question is that of the relation between the Electoral College and democracy. Unlike in a unitary country such as France where democracy is envisioned as majority rule on a nationwide scale, in the United States democracy has been conceived in terms of competition among mutually constraining majorities operating at both the state and the federal level. Yet even in this scheme of "checks and balances" among diverse democratic majorities, the presidency occupies a special place: It is the only national office, and the president is the only elected official (with the vice president) who represents all the citizens on a nationwide scale. And hence the debate—made all the more heated and urgent by Election 2000—over whether it would be preferable to have a direct nationwide popular-vote-majority election for president or to stick to the present system, which is meant to give states an important mediating role through preservation of the Electoral College.

From a procedural standpoint, what the 2000 Florida election underscores is the lack of uniformity in how votes are cast and counted throughout the United States. Moreover, this lack of uniformity exists not only from one state to the next but also, as the focus on Florida amply demonstrated, within a single state. Indeed, as is now well known, each of Florida's sixty-seven counties was responsible for organizing the presidential election within its territory. This led to many glaring disparities, including the fact that a voter in a punch-card–ballot county was three times more likely not to have his or her vote counted than a voter in some of the optical-scan machine–ballot counties.

Procedural reform seems much more likely and less controversial than substantive reform. This is in part because the basic procedural goals—equal voting conditions for all eligible voters and an accurate count of the vote—are generally accepted and uncontroversial. Substantive goals do not enjoy any comparable level of uniform support, as they depend on different conceptions of democracy and of how democracy might best be promoted. Significantly, Florida and Georgia have already adopted important reforms regarding the conduct of future elections. At this writing, however, little has occurred at the federal level. It is within the powers of the federal government either to encourage state reforms through subsidies or to mandate that national standards apply to all federal congressional elections, for all practical purposes ensuring uniformity throughout the country. Indeed, although Congress cannot directly regulate presidential elections under the Constitution, it can do so with respect to congressional elections. Accordingly, if nationwide standards applied to the latter, it would be both impractical and costly for states to conduct completely separate voting procedures in presidential elections. Finally, even without movement on the federal front, all states may eventually be forced to adopt uniform systems throughout their territories to conform to plausible further elaborations of the Supreme Court's equal protection ruling in *Bush v. Gore.*

Many conceivable substantive changes, such as abolition of the Electoral College, confront not only a lack of consensus but also constitutional hurdles that are difficult to surmount. Even if a vast majority of Americans were to support abolishing the Electoral College, this would require a constitutional amendment. Before such an amendment could be adopted, however, three-fourths of the state legislatures (or specially organized conventions in three-fourths of the states) would have to ratify it. And this would be highly unlikely given the widespread belief that smaller states would lose much of their influence on presidential elections with the abolition of the Electoral College.

Arguments for and against the abolition of the Electoral College are found in the essays in part 6. In addition, several other possible reforms, some requiring a constitutional amendment, others not, have been formulated. Each of these has certain advantages and disadvantages and promotes a somewhat different kind of democracy. Two proposals deserve brief mention, for they both seek to preserve the role of states in the election of the president while eliminating—or at least greatly minimizing—the likelihood that the loser of the popular vote nationwide would be nonetheless the winner of an Electoral College majority.

The first proposal would retain the Electoral College as currently constituted but would replace its winner-take-all aspects by a more proportional system. Under the present system, each state has a number of electors in the Electoral College corresponding to the number of congressional districts into which that state is divided—each congressional district corresponding to a unit of population, with the proviso that each state shall have at least one congressional district no matter how sparsely populated—plus two corresponding to its two senators. Moreover, all states but two—Maine and Nebraska—operate a winner-takes-all system, such that the presidential candidate with the largest percentage of the popular vote in the state wins all the electors to which that state is entitled. Thus, for example, if a candidate wins California by a single vote, he or she is awarded all of that state's 54 electors, who represent 20 percent of the 270 needed to win a majority of the Electoral College and hence the presidency. Suppose further that the opponent of the California winner wins New York—the state that in 2000 had the largest number of electors after California—by a margin of two million votes, then that opponent would have 33 electors against the other candidate's 54, notwithstanding having won the combined California–New York popular vote by 1,999,999 votes.

Under the system currently in force in Maine and Nebraska, the electors can be split if different candidates win in different congressional districts. For example, Nebraska had five electoral votes in 2000 (all of which were awarded to Bush) and hence three electoral districts. If one candidate had won a large majority in one congressional district and an overall majority throughout the state but had narrowly lost in the two remaining congressional districts, then that candidate would have ended up with three electors (one corresponding to the congressional district the candidate had won plus the two corresponding to the state's two Senate seats that are awarded to the statewide winner) and his or her opponent would have ended up with two (corresponding to the two districts won by that opponent). Now, if all the states adopted the Maine-Nebraska formula, then the likelihood that the popular vote loser would win a majority of electors would be greatly diminished.

Another possibility along similar lines would be for states to apportion electors, not in relation to congressional districts, but according to a system based on the principle of proportionality. The focus would remain on the statewide vote, but instead of awarding electors on a winner-takes-all basis, they would be apportioned according to the respective percentages of the vote guaranteed by the various candidates. Returning to the example of California and New York, under such a proportional system, the winner in California by one vote would be awarded 28 electors and the loser 26. Furthermore, the winner in New York by two million votes would be awarded, say, 22 electors and the loser 11. Under this scheme, the winner of a large majority of the combined California–New York vote ends up with a majority of the electors from the two states: 48 to 39.

A shift from a winner-takes-all system to one based on the principle of proportionality would not require a constitutional amendment to the extent that such a change is within the existing powers of the several states. Another suggestion along similar lines, however, would require a constitutional amendment. According to this suggestion, the Electoral College ought to continue to function as it currently does, except that a bonus of an additional number of electors would be awarded to the nationwide winner of the popular vote. Proponents of this change can argue that it preserves the current role reserved for the states in presidential elections while virtually eliminating the possibility that the winner of the popular vote might lose in the Electoral College. This argument seems persuasive inasmuch as Bush pulled ahead of Gore by a margin of four electoral votes on being officially declared the winner in Florida.

The 2000 election rekindled the debate over the desirability of retaining the Electoral College—which is not only an eighteenth-century device but also one originally promoted to safeguard the interests of slaveholding states—and several of the essays provide useful insights and varied perspectives. In the end the conclusions one may draw from this debate depend on one's view of how federalism ought to be factored into presidential elections and to what extent the presidency ought to be linked to national majorities as opposed to the competition among a plurality of subnational majorities. Moreover, while it seems important that the president enjoy a mandate, it is debatable given the present set of circumstances *which* mandate or even whether any cogent mandate can be discerned or sustained over time. To some, winning the majority of votes cast on election day would give a president-elect a legitimate mandate to govern and to press for his or her political agenda. But how relevant is such a mandate in the face of constant polling concerning approval of the president and his or her policies throughout the entire duration of the presidential term? Or in the face of the current system of financing presidential elections? Or of the fact that fewer than half the eligible voters in the United States vote in presidential elections? In short, the 2000 election has raised many new questions and revived many old ones concerning presidential elections and democracy in the United States. The essays in this volume address many of these questions and concerns. They provide some answers and set a framework for further discussion. Given the urgency and complexity of the issues involved, however, it is hoped that the analysis provided in the following pages will spur further inquiry into the numerous fundamental questions brought to light by Election 2000.

III

This book is divided into six parts, preceded by a chronology of the most salient events during the extraordinary period between election day, November 7, 2000, and inauguration day, January 20, 2001. Part 1 contains two essays by a participant in the "battle for Florida," Henry E. Brady, a political scientist who worked as an expert on behalf of Gore. In chapter 1, "Equal Protection for Votes," Brady provides statistical evidence for his claim that the differences among different voting devices throughout Florida far outweighed—by a factor of ten to twenty—any variability attributable to inconsistencies found in manual vote recounts. In chapter 2, "Law and Data: The Butterfly Ballot Episode," Brady and several coauthors— other political scientists who joined him to provide expert testimony in Palm Beach County's "butterfly ballot" cases—recount their experiences as experts trying to reconcile the "facts" they found and the "law." In addition to providing a unique day-to-day account of their involvement as statisticians in the legal battle in Palm Beach, the chapter conveys its authors' frustrations resulting from what they conclude is the legal system's inability to cope with the scientifically provable fact that the voting system fails "to convert people's vote intentions into counted votes."

Part 2, "The Machinery of Democracy in America," contains a single chapter by Richard H. Pildes titled "Disputing Elections." As already noted, Pildes takes a nonpartisan approach as he analyzes the legal and institutional conditions that circumscribed the disputed 2000 election. Stressing that neither the Constitution, nor existing law, nor the prevailing institutional mechanisms are adequately equipped to deal fairly and efficiently with problems such as those that arose in Florida, Pildes concludes that no conceivable resolution of the controversies could have avoided the appearance of partisanship. He also notes that nearly all the scholarship on the election and court decisions seems palpably partisan, and that may be due, at least in part, to the absence of accepted canons of judicial interpretation of the Constitution or of federal laws. Pildes further indicates that the U.S. Supreme Court greatly contributed to the impression that its final decision regarding the election was partisan by not refraining from intervention, or from limited intervention designed to set appropriate constitutional standards, but leaving it to Congress to make the final decisions. Indeed, the Constitution clearly gives Congress a role in settling disputes in presidential elections, but it is silent about any such role for the Court. Pildes reminds us that resolution in Congress is also bound to be partisan and notes that regardless of whether the Court's intervention was appropriate, it was not an isolated occurrence or an aberration. Instead, it fit as part and parcel of the present Court's trend to "constitutionalize democracy" by making itself "the exclusive arbiter . . . of the most basic aspects of democratic politics itself." In Pildes's view, the relevant institutions designed to handle election disputes such as those that arose in 2000 can never transcend partisanship, but the goal should be to turn to institutions that would channel partisanship in less destructive directions.

Two U.S. Supreme Court decisions in effect settled Election 2000. The first of these, the grant of a stay on December 9, 2000, ordered that all vote counting in Florida be stopped until the Court could decide Bush's appeal on the merits. While commentators—including those whose essays are included here—disagree on whether the Court had a valid justification for granting the stay, the issuance of an opinion in the context of a stay is—as Justice Scalia, the opinion writer, himself noted—highly unusual. Moreover, both the short concurring opinion filed by Justice Scalia and the dissenting opinion signed by four justices provide a remarkably succinct account of the sharp battle lines drawn within the Court.

The December 12 decision is the Court's final decision on the merits. It consists of a per curiam opinion, a concurring opinion by three justices, and four dissenting opinions. The use of a per curiam opinion in what is ultimately a 5–4 decision seems odd, at least on first impression. In general, per curiam—that is, by the court—opinions appear to be used for unanimous decisions or for relatively unimportant or primarily procedural decisions. If this is the case, is the per curiam opinion in *Bush v. Gore* deceptive? Was it intended to convey the impression that the Court as a whole (or at least the seven justices who concluded either that there had been a violation of equal protection or that there might have been such a violation) was behind the decision when only five justices agreed with the result? Or was the "per curiam" label used because its presumptive authors, Justices O'Connor and Kennedy, did not want to append their names to the majority opinion? As demonstrated in Arthur J. Jacobson's essay on the origins and uses of per curiam opinions by the Supreme Court (chap. 8), matters are generally more complex. Nevertheless, speculation about the use of a per curiam opinion in *Bush v. Gore* is not likely to vanish any time soon.

Part 3, "The Decisions," contains six essays that deal with the decisions by the Florida courts and/or the U.S. Supreme Court. Chapter 5 consists of an exchange between Ronald Dworkin, the first leading legal academic to criticize the U.S. Supreme Court decision in the essay included here as chapter 4, and Charles Fried, another leading legal academic who represented the Republican-controlled Florida legislature in federal cases relating to the election. Dworkin's essay (chap. 4), written on December 14, 2000, two days after the Supreme Court decision, is particularly noteworthy for at least two distinct reasons. First, it is a reasoned contemporaneous reaction to the Supreme Court decision; and second, it frames both the liberal case against the Court's decision and the broader subsequent debate about the Court's intervention to put an end to the election. Dworkin emphasizes that the Supreme Court's December 12 decision is one of the least persuasive he has ever read and that the 5–4 split among the justices is most disturbing because it does not track the ordinary split between liberals and conservatives evident on such issues as federalism, abortion, or homosexual rights. According to Dworkin, no established conservative position justifies the decision reached by the Court's conservative majority. Therefore, one is left to wonder if the justices in the majority would have reasoned the way they did if that would have led to sealing a victory for Gore. In the second part of his essay, Dworkin advocates abolishing the Electoral College by adopting a constitutional amendment that would provide for election of the president by a plurality of the national vote in a direct election.

In his response to Dworkin, Fried acknowledges that the case was a difficult one but vigorously rejects any implication that the Court acted injudiciously or out of partisan zeal. Fried emphasizes that the Court did not seek to intervene in the election but that once it had the case before it, it did the best it could. Fried then argues that the Court's majority legal positions were plausible and defensible and that Dworkin's attack on the Court's conservatives is unwarranted. According to Fried, the Court's four liberal dissenters were no less partisan than their colleagues in the majority. Moreover, Fried maintains that two of the justices in the majority, O'Connor and Kennedy, are not really conservative, as they had voted to uphold abortion rights. Similarly, two of the "liberal" justices, Souter and Breyer, agreed with the majority that the vote recounts ordered by the Florida Supreme Court involved an equal protection violation. Although Fried acknowledges that the Court's majority statement that December 12 constituted the deadline for vote recounts in Florida was the weakest link in its decision, he strongly believes it had no practical effect on the outcome of the election. As he sees it, even if the Florida Supreme Court had ordered a new recount under constitutionally valid standards, such a recount could not have been concluded by December 18, the deadline for reporting electoral votes. In short, Fried concludes, the Court acted creditably in the face of unique and freakish circumstances. In his reply to Fried, Dworkin disputes several of Fried's arguments and states that Fried's essay has not convinced him that there can be a plausible principled defense of the majority's reasoning in *Bush v. Gore.*

Chapters 6 and 7, by Michel Rosenfeld and Nelson Lund respectively, come to dramatically opposed conclusions concerning the justifications for the decisions by the Florida Supreme Court and the U.S. Supreme Court. Rosenfeld finds the former justified because it falls within permissible bounds of judicial interpretation and the latter clearly unjustifiable under the same criterion. Placing the Florida and U.S. Supreme Court decisions in their broader context, Rosenfeld argues that the events that culminated with the U.S. Supreme Court's decision awarding the presidency to Bush are the result not only of a failure of the Court but also of serious shortcomings with the Constitution, federal and state laws, and the current state of American democracy. Because of all these factors, Rosenfeld maintains, no fully satisfactory solution of the problems raised by Election 2000 was likely. Nevertheless, according to Rosenfeld, none of this relieves the U.S. Supreme Court's majority of responsibility for having rendered an ill-advised decision that lacks both consistency and integrity. Rosenfeld stresses that the relevant legal and constitutional provisions that the Court had to interpret were neither complete nor transparent and that they were, accordingly, amenable to different judicial interpretations. This meant that certain liberal *and* certain conservative interpretations could be justified but that the Court's majority failed all tests of consistency or of integrity, be they liberal or conservative.

In contrast to Rosenfeld, Lund denies that the relevant legal and constitutional provisions were legitimately open to differing interpretations. According to Lund, based on precedent and the "plain meaning" of the legal texts at stake, the interpretations of the Florida Supreme Court were entirely without justification whereas those of the U.S. Supreme Court were the only legitimate ones. Specifically, Lund insists that the U.S. Supreme Court's finding that the vote recount ordered by the Florida court violated the Equal Protection Clause is not only justified but also compelled by the Court's previous voting rights jurisprudence. Furthermore, Lund argues that the ubiquitous attacks against the Court's pronouncement that since December 12 was the deadline for vote recounts, no time remained for any further recounts, consistent with the Court's equal protection ruling, were based on a widespread misconception. In Lund's reading, far from acting arbitrarily to ensure a Bush victory, the U.S. Supreme Court was simply following the Florida Supreme Court's interpretation of Florida law pursuant to the unanimously accepted principle that federal courts are bound by a state's highest court interpretation of that state's law. It is noteworthy, however, that one of the justices on the Florida Supreme Court stated, in the course of its dismissal of the Florida cases consistent with the U.S. Supreme Court's December 12 decision, that the U.S. Supreme Court had misinterpreted the Florida court's ruling on the state law in question. Does that undercut Lund's argument? Or should it be disregarded as an after-the-fact attempt by the justice in question to rehabilitate the reputation of his own court? Although most critics of the U.S. Supreme Court majority disagree, Lund's (and Jacobson's) answer to such objections is that the U.S. Supreme Court left the Florida court free to correct whatever misinterpretation the Supreme Court majority had made of Florida law or to change its mind about what Florida law required and proceed with a recount.

In chapter 8, "The Ghostwriters," Jacobson explores the origins and evolution of per curiam opinions to test the claims of certain liberals that the use of the per curiam decision in *Bush v. Gore* was misleading and designed to detract attention from the narrow 5–4 majority by giving the impression that they were speaking for the Court. Based on his historical research, Jacobson reports that the U.S. Supreme Court's use of per curiam decisions effectively began in 1883. Significantly, while such decisions were unanimous at first, that began to change in 1909, when Justice Holmes dissented from a per curiam opinion. Moreover, since the 1940s the number of per curiam opinions with dissents has greatly increased. According to Jacobson, what this means is that today "per curiam" does not stand for unanimity but is rather the equivalent of the Court's majority stating that "this case *ought to be* unanimous." When viewed in this light, Jacobson concludes, it is Justices Souter and Breyer and not their colleagues in the majority who may have acted questionably. Because Justices Souter and Breyer shared with the majority the belief that the recounts ordered by the Florida Supreme Court violated equal protection, they ought to have joined the majority's per curiam opinion. Their only disagreement with the majority was that they concluded that Florida law did not require completion of the count by December 12, the very day of the Supreme Court's decision in

Bush v. Gore. As to that issue, they could have done what five justices did in another celebrated case whose opinion was per curiam, *Buckley v. Valeo:* concur in part and dissent in part. With a 7–2 rather than a 5–4 majority, the rhetorical, hence political, effect of the *Bush v. Gore* per curiam, Jacobson argues, would have been very different.

The final chapter in part 3 is unlike all others in that it is in the form of fictitious opinions written as if they were penned by the U.S. Supreme Court justices who decided *Bush v. Gore.* Burt Neuborne, a leading civil rights advocate, wrote these opinions to demonstrate to his law students that although the various actual opinions filed in *Bush v. Gore* appear to be unprincipled, this by no means needed to be so. As a veteran champion of individual rights who has won many constitutional cases and who thus has firsthand experience on the important institutional role the Court has played over the years, Neuborne believes that it would be unfortunate if those disappointed by the Court gave up on the institution. Surmising that the actual opinions suffered from the extreme time constraints under which their authors labored, Neuborne imaginatively and artfully crafts as principled and well reasoned as possible a statement for each of the positions articulated by members of the Court.

Part 4, "American Perspectives," brings together four essays that explore the broader implications of Election 2000 and of the U.S. Supreme Court decision of December 12. Chapter 10, "Anatomy of a Constitutional Coup," by Bruce Ackerman, places in context the actions of Bush, his brother, Jeb, governor of Florida, Republican demonstrators, the Florida legislature, and the U.S. Supreme Court and concludes that collectively they mounted what is tantamount to a constitutional coup with disturbing and lasting implications for America's constitutional rule and democracy. Building on his widely disseminated thesis that America's Constitution is a living one— which evolves less through formal amendments than through transformations shaped by moments of widespread consensus on fundamental society-wide issues known as "constitutional moments"—Ackerman regards the resolution of Election 2000 as an illegitimate effort to reinstate the obsolete written Constitution. In Ackerman's view, the twentieth-century presidency shaped by such men as Wilson, Roosevelt, and Reagan had virtually nothing in common with the presidency envisioned by the authors of the 1787 written Constitution. By ignoring the fact that the legitimacy of modern presidents stems from the mandate they obtain from the American people rather than from the arcane preoccupations that led to constitutionalization of the Electoral College, the Republicans and their allies on the Court thus—consistent with Ackerman's analysis—pulled off a veritable coup. Ackerman also discusses what would have most likely happened had the Supreme Court refrained from deciding the election and had it allowed Congress to settle the matter as foreseen in the Constitution. Contrary to some conservative commentators, Ackerman is confident that the result would not have been worse or less legitimate.

Chapter 11, by George Fletcher, is titled "The Many Faces of *Bush v. Gore*." Specifically, Fletcher sees three distinct faces reflected in the Supreme Court decision. The first of these is the narrowest: the Court's decision could be distilled to an interpretation—albeit a disputed and perhaps erroneous one—of the Florida decision under review that asserts Florida law required vote recounts to be completed by December 12. The second face, according to Fletcher, is shaped by the assumption that federal courts should regulate state-run elections for the American presidency. This second face, moreover, calls for reconciliation of the Court's decision in terms of broader principles and more abstract arguments of justice. Fletcher finds the Court's decision wanting from the standpoint of these principles and arguments, in an analysis that echoes that of many of the other critics of the decision. Fletcher, however, provides an entirely novel approach, from the standpoint of the third face of the decision, which he characterizes as the product of the clash between the two distinct constitutional orders that have been implanted in the course of American history.

The first of these orders emanates from the 1787 Constitution and has as its cornerstones "We the People" conceived as a voluntary association, the pursuit of liberty, and political elitism envisioned as a New England town meeting where public issues were decided by the propertied few. In contrast, the second order, which originated during the Civil War, regards the country as a nation rather than a voluntary association, emphasizes that all men are created equal, thus imposing equality under law, and shifts from elitism to popular democracy. Fletcher goes on to argue that from the perspective of the third face, the Supreme Court's emphasis on federal control of state presidential elections and its insistence on equal protection can be regarded as consistent with deployment of the dictates of the second constitutional order. Fletcher concludes, however, that in thwarting rather than buttressing democracy, the Court ultimately failed to accommodate an essential component of the second constitutional order that has become firmly rooted since the Civil War.

Richard Brookhiser's essay, "Springtime for Rousseau"—a title that evokes the highly comical though designedly tasteless exploitation of a fictitious musical titled "Springtime for Hitler in Germany" in the musical comedy *The Producers*—raises an important question about democracy while ridiculing certain Democrats' complaints about Election 2000. Referring to a liberal Democrat who criticized Republican conduct in late November 2000 with the comment, "The whiff of fascism is in the air," Brookhiser proceeds to discredit the Democrats' call for new vote counts or a new vote. While Brookhiser portrays the Democrats as sore losers, he raises an important question by refusing to accept on faith the widely held proposition that the purpose of elections is to allow for the expression of the will of the people. Brookhiser argues that it is not clear what the will of the people or of the majority is, and even if it were, it is not clear what its relevance may be given that political majorities are prone to constant shifts. Consistent with these views, it is Rousseau, perhaps the fiercest defender of democratic self-government, who deserves the label "fascist." For Rousseau, democracy requires implementation of the "general will." But because according to Rousseau's logic everyone must be subjected to the general will, some have accused him of being a precursor of totalitarianism. Following that line of reasoning, Brookhiser suggests that Rousseau's democracy is fascist in at least two senses. First, the general will is oppressive and forces the individual to forgo his or her independence in order to serve democracy. Second, many oppressive regimes, including Hitler's, have been put or kept in power as a consequence of votes construed as expressing the will of the majority or of the people. Hence the reference to fascism and the link between Rousseau and Hitler. While Brookhiser's view of Rousseau and his intimation of the link between the latter and Hitler is, to say the least, controversial, the questions of how periodic voting relates to democracy and how democracy relates to good policies are serious ones, deserving of greater attention.

In chapter 13, "Machiavelli in Robes? The Court in the Election," Frank Michelman explores the implications of the fact, amply established in opinion polls, that a large percentage of Americans were relieved by the Supreme Court's decision in *Bush v. Gore* although they were convinced that the justices had acted out of political motivation rather than in accordance with legal principle and justice. Michelman does not labor under the hypothesis that the justices in the majority wanted Bush as president. Instead he works on the assumption that the justices decided as they did, knowing that there was no sound basis in law for their decision, because they felt it imperative that they save the nation from further strife and disruption. In short, the Court sacrificed law to order.

Michelman notes that the Court's decision was shrouded in hypocrisy and that a vast segment of the American people went along, thus becoming an accomplice in that hypocrisy. This conclusion brings Michelman to Machiavelli's Prince whose obligation is to lie and violate the law if necessary to safeguard the well-being and safety of his subjects. Although he acknowledges that it may be good for leaders in a republic to be Machiavellian sometimes, Michelman wonders whether it should ever be acceptable for the Court to be Machiavellian. Unlike the Prince, the Court has neither the power of the sword nor that of the purse. The Court must rely on its persuasiveness and reputation for integrity, and Michelman sets out to determine whether nonetheless the Court can, on rare occasions, afford to be Machiavellian.

Part 5, "Foreign Perspectives," consists of five essays by foreign authors that convey a strong sense of how Election 2000 was perceived beyond the shores of the United States. The authors in this part are not only from different countries, they also have different professional experiences. Two have been constitutional judges, two are political scientists, and one is a professor of law.

In chapter 14, "A Flawed yet Resilient System: A View from Jerusalem," Shlomo Avineri traces the principal systemic flaws that led to the difficulties encountered in the course of Election 2000 to the problem of running a twenty-first-century democracy within the framework of an eighteenth-century Constitution designed for a republic that was not meant to be democratic in any modern sense of the term. Avineri stresses that in spite of a patchwork of reforms since the eighteenth century, the current constitutional and legal apparatus is not up to the task. While Avineri admires the American system's resilience—he observes that at no time during the crisis was there any danger of a coup or a military takeover—he maintains that the crisis was more serious than most Americans thought. He finds it particularly disturbing that the system did not provide any clear exit strategy, leaving in limbo for well over a month the identity and legitimacy of the person about to become the most powerful political officeholder throughout the world.

Avineri points out how anomalous, in the context of modern democracies, it is for Bush, who lost the popular vote to Gore by more than five hundred thousand ballots, to have won the presidency. While similar situations may occur in certain parliamentary democracies, Avineri emphasizes that in no country with an executive presidency subjected to universal suffrage can any candidate who has won fewer votes than his or her opponent be the winner. Furthermore, Avineri also criticizes the constraints that federalism imposes on the fairness and efficiency of elections to national office. Finally, he reports how in his own country, Israel, where elections are centralized and voter registration made easy, the problems that chronically plague American elections—such as the exclusion of significant numbers of minority citizens as was the case in 2000 in Florida—are by and large avoided.

In chapter 15, Justice Noëlle Lenoir, until recently a member of the French Constitutional Council, discusses how disputed elections are handled in her country and considers whether disputes such as those involved in *Bush v. Gore* could arise in France. Lenoir possesses a unique perspective as the French Constitutional Council monitors and certifies all elections—including presidential ones—in addition to having the exclusive power to determine if the laws enacted by the French Parliament are constitutional. Moreover, as a member of the Constitutional Council from 1992 to 2001, Lenoir participated in monitoring and certifying the French presidential election in 1995.

Unlike the United States, France is a unitary and highly centralized state, and its national elections are conducted under uniform conditions throughout the national territory. Also, in contrast to its American counterpart, the French Constitution of 1958 and French law provide extensive unified guidelines, constantly updated to account for changing circumstances, for supervising elections and for dealing with electoral challenges. France does not have presidential primaries but, as Lenoir underscores, a nominating process followed by designation of candidates, a campaign, and one or two rounds of voting, depending on whether any candidate in the first round obtains a majority of the votes cast. The Constitutional Council, in turn, is involved throughout the process, from nominations to final certification of the winner. Because the Constitutional Council routinely deals with all elections, it does not risk raising partisan suspicions as the sporadic and highly unusual intervention by the U.S. Supreme Court in Election 2000 did. Nevertheless, Lenoir discusses whether, and to what extent, there may be a risk that the Constitutional Council would deal with election disputes in a partisan manner.

This discussion is particularly important, for on the surface at least, the Constitutional Council appears to be a more political institution than the U.S. Supreme Court. Members of the Constitutional Council are appointed for nine years. One-third of them are appointed by the president of the Republic, one-third by the president of the Senate, and one-third by the president of the National Assembly. Unlike in the United States where appointment to the Supreme Court often requires compromise by the president and a majority in the Senate, appointments to the French Constitutional Council can be—and often are—purely political.

Although Lenoir acknowledges that it would be possible for the Constitutional Council to resolve a contested election in a partisan manner, in practice it has remained above the political fray. As she suggests, since intervention is regular and routine under clear and comprehensive guidelines, the potential for partisanship is minimized. To that one may add that unlike in the United States, where Supreme Court intervention in a presidential election may not occur again for a long time, any partisan bias in favor of one candidate or party by the Constitutional Council may inevitably invite retaliation the next time around. In short, as the role of the Constitutional Council in elections is regular and clearly prescribed, paradoxically the political nature of its makeup may be the best antidote to partisan bias.

Justice Dieter Grimm was until recently a member of the German Constitutional Court. Although Germany is a parliamentary democracy and hence could have no experience akin to that of Election 2000, its experience is valuable for comparative purposes inasmuch as it has a federal system and its Constitutional Court is empowered to adjudicate certain disputes relating to elections. In chapter 16, Grimm indicates why *Bush v.*

Gore could not have occurred in Germany. In spite of Germany's federalism, elections to the Bundestag, the German Parliament, are entirely governed by comprehensive and detailed federal laws and regulations. Ballots are uniform throughout the country, and so are vote-counting procedures. Moreover, there is little danger of partisan bias in vote counts and recounts as they are organized under the supervision of nonpartisan bodies. Election disputes are first considered and settled by the Bundestag and can only go to the Constitutional Court thereafter. The court, therefore, cannot, as was the case in *Bush v. Gore,* decide the election. It can, however, order a new vote in whole or in part as the circumstances may warrant. Like France, Germany has a post–World War II constitution, and though it is not a unitary state, it has uniform elections throughout the country and a comprehensive scheme of regulations to deal with national elections.

In chapter 17, "*Bush v. Gore:* A View from Italy," Pasquale Pasquino assesses familiar aspects of Election 2000 and *Bush v. Gore* and some less familiar ones from the standpoint of an Italian scholar expert in European democracies and constitutional courts. Some American readers can certainly take comfort that Pasquino views some of the relevant events very much like they do. Beyond that, Pasquino offers a fresh perspective and focuses on aspects of the overall story largely ignored by American authors. Pasquino, for example, highlights a lower federal court decision by Judge Middlebrooks, dealing with and rejecting the kind of equal protection claims that would later prove critical to buttress the Supreme Court's majority in its December 12 decision. Judge Middlebrooks acknowledged that there could not be equal voting conditions under the current decentralized election system in the United States. But rather than regard this as a weakness or as constitutionally unacceptable, Judge Middlebrooks considered it a virtue, as he believed that decentralization was a guarantee against corruption. Also novel and undoubtedly surprising to most American readers is Pasquino's conclusion that the U.S. Supreme Court conducted itself more like a parliament than a court in its approach to the election dispute that culminated in its December 12 decision.

In the final essay of part 5, "Democracy in America: A European Perspective on the Millennial Elections," Mattias Kumm engages in a comparison between U.S. federalism as it emerges in the aftermath of Election 2000 and current projections of what may become the government of a unified European Union. Although American democracy and federalism may be characterized as exceptionalist, and so may any viable political union among the member countries of the European Union, Kumm draws many useful parallels and contrasts. Viewed from the standpoint of the European Union, where the member nations retain a strong political, cultural, historical, and linguistic identity, American state citizenship appears relatively insignificant. Accordingly, though the input of the states may have a positive impact on American democracy, the Electoral College and the problems unleashed by Election 2000 are best regarded as odd historical relics. The American example, on the other hand, underscores that the European Union is far from federalism and that there is no clear blueprint for a democracy on the scale of the Union.

Part 6, "Reform?" consists of four essays centered on the issue of retention or abolition of the Electoral College in view of the problems highlighted by Election 2000. These essays consider both the desirability and the feasibility of changes, particularly in light of the great unlikelihood of approval in the foreseeable future of a constitutional amendment to abolish or substantially modify the Electoral College.

Chapter 19, by Judith Best, one of the foremost U.S. experts on the Electoral College, is titled "Weighing the Alternatives: Reform or Deform?" Best discusses the various alternatives to the present system that have garnered the most interest over the years. These include the direct election plan, supported by 60 percent of Americans, under which the winner of the popular vote in a single nationwide election would become president; the national bonus plan, which would keep the Electoral College but add bonus points for the winner of the popular vote to avoid what happened in 2000, namely, that the winner of the popular vote was the loser of the electoral vote; the instant runoff voting plan, a variation on the direct election plan, which would ensure that the winner obtained a majority rather than a plurality of votes cast; the automatic plan, which would retain the Electoral College but eliminate the possibility that individual electors not cast their vote for the candidate to whom they are pledged—as was the case in 2000 with one of Gore's Washington, D.C., electors who decided to abstain to protest the District's lack of representation in Congress rather than cast her vote for Gore; the district plan, which retains the Electoral College but replaces its winner-take-all feature with an allocation of electors on a (congressional) district-by-district basis; and the proportional plan, another proposal that would retain the Electoral College while replacing its winner-takes-all aspect, in this case by allocating a state's electors proportionally to the percentage of the vote obtained by each candidate. Based on a thorough discussion of the arguments in favor of and against all these possible reforms, Best concludes that retention of the Electoral College with adoption of the automatic plan to eliminate the problem of the faithless electors is by far the preferable alternative.

Lawrence D. Longley, a longtime leading critic of the Electoral College, strongly argues for its abolition in his essay, "The Electoral College: A Fatally Flawed Institution." After considering the Electoral College at its best and at its worst, Longley concludes that it is dangerous because it distorts American democracy and threatens in certain cases to undermine the legitimacy of the president.

In chapter 21, "The Electoral College: A Modest Contribution," Keith E. Whittington argues that whereas the Electoral College is not among the most important constitutional institutions and whereas he would not advocate adopting it were the Constitution drafted today, he nonetheless believes it ought to be kept. Whittington regards the contribution of the Electoral College as narrow but worthwhile. According to him, the Electoral College contributes to encouraging compromise and consensus building and to minimizing the impact of narrow factions.

In the last essay in the book, "Popular Election of the President without a Constitutional Amendment," Robert W. Bennett provides a novel and ingenious suggestion. Bennett's proposal would require state legislation by as few as eleven large states whose total electoral votes equal 270, a majority in the Electoral College. While the legislation in question would require coordination among the relevant states, it would not require acquiescence by smaller states. Smaller states are generally considered obstacles to a constitutional amendment to abolish the Electoral College, as it is thought that they would refuse to yield the influence they can exert under the present system. Against this common wisdom, Bennett indicates that the Electoral College is actually more prone to favoring large states than small ones.

As the essays in this volume amply demonstrate, Election 2000 and *Bush v. Gore* were complex, controversial, and full of rich and varied implications. The essays provide multifaceted insights and perspectives on the various issues and controversies engendered or rekindled by Election 2000. Some of these may fade or intensify in the future, but it is unlikely that any of them will be exhausted or definitively settled. Perhaps what is most striking about all that has been unleashed by the millennial election is the number of paradoxes and ironies it has already produced. In this regard, the findings of one of the news media that conducted a vote recount throughout Florida after the presidential election had been officially settled is exquisite. Had Gore succeeded in having a recount under the standards he advocated in Court, Bush would have won. However, had a recount been conducted under the standards advocated by Bush during the period of protracted litigation, the winner would have been Gore.

CAST AND CHRONOLOGY

THE CAST

The Candidates

Albert Gore Jr., vice president of the United States and Democratic candidate for the U.S. presidency.

Joseph Lieberman, Democratic senator from Connecticut and Gore's running mate.

George W. Bush, governor of Texas and Republican candidate for the U.S. presidency.

Dick Cheney, secretary of defense under George H. W. Bush, George W. Bush's father, and George W. Bush's running mate.

Gore's Team

William M. Daley, Gore's campaign chairman.

Warren Christopher, secretary of state under Bill Clinton and head of Gore's legal team in Florida.

David Boies, a prominent lawyer and a member of Gore's legal team in Florida.

Bush's Team

James A. Baker III, secretary of state under George H. W. Bush and head of Bush's legal team in Florida.

The Florida Government

Jeb Bush, Florida's Republican governor, brother of George W. Bush, and co-chair of Bush's Florida campaign.

Katherine Harris, Florida's Republican secretary of state and co-chair of Bush's Florida campaign. She is also a member of Florida's Division of Elections and the state's chief election officer.

Robert A. Butterworth, Florida's Democratic attorney general and Gore's Florida campaign chairman.

Florida State Legislature, consisting of a House and a Senate, both Republican controlled.

The Florida Judiciary

Judge Nikki Ann Clark, Leon County Circuit Court, appointed by a Democratic governor. (Circuit courts are the primary trial courts in Florida's judicial system, although they also have limited appellate jurisdiction. Circuit court judges are placed on the bench either by appointment by the governor of Florida to fill vacancies in the circuits, the usual method, or by nonpartisan, contested elections for six-year terms. Typically, circuit judges appointed by the governor serve the duration of the term of the vacancy that was filled and then run—successfully—in the proceeding election.)

Judge Terry P. Lewis, Leon County Circuit Court, appointed by a Democratic governor.

Judge N. Sanders Sauls, Leon County Circuit Court, appointed by a Republican governor.

The Florida Supreme Court, composed of seven justices, all of whom were appointed by Democratic governors. One of the justices, Peggy A. Quince, was appointed by Governor Lawton Chiles (a Democrat) and then–Governor-elect Jeb Bush. (The justices of the Florida Supreme Court are appointed by the governor of Florida, then face an uncontested merit retention vote in the next general election that occurs more than one year after their appointment and then every six years, if retained in office. No justice has ever been removed by a merit retention vote.)

The Federal Judiciary

Judge Donald M. Middlebrooks, U.S. District Court for the Southern District of Florida, an appointee of Bill Clinton.

Eleventh Circuit Court of Appeals, a twelve-member panel sitting in Atlanta that hears appeals from federal district courts in Florida, Alabama, and Georgia. Seven of the twelve justices were nominated by Republican presidents (including four by President George H. W. Bush).

United States Supreme Court, composed of nine justices, seven of whom were nominated by Republican presidents: Chief Justice William H. Rehnquist (nominated by Richard Nixon), John Paul Stevens (Gerald Ford), Anthony M. Kennedy (Ronald Reagan), Sandra Day O'Connor (Reagan), Antonin Scalia (Reagan), David H. Souter (George H. W. Bush), and Clarence Thomas (Bush). The remaining justices, Stephen G. Breyer and Ruth Bader Ginsburg, were nominated by Democrat Bill Clinton. (U.S. Supreme Court justices are nominated by the president of the United States and then must be confirmed by the U.S. Senate. Supreme Court justices have life tenure.)

THE EVENTS

Tuesday, November 7

As exit poll projections and final results come in, it becomes apparent that the election is very, very close. Gore wins most of the states in the Northeast and on the West Coast. Bush wins most of the states in the South and Midwest, including Gore's home state of Tennessee. Several states—Iowa, Oregon, Michigan, New Mexico, Wisconsin, Pennsylvania, Florida—are too close to be firmly determined by early projections. Neither candidate is in a clear position to be declared the winner of the necessary 270 electoral votes.

AROUND 8:00 P.M.: The major networks declare Gore the winner in Michigan, Pennsylvania, and Florida based on exit poll projections. This most likely gives Gore enough electoral votes to win the election.

AROUND 9:00 P.M.: The major networks declare that Florida is too close to call and Florida's 25 electoral votes are up for grabs. At this point, it is clear that the winner in Florida will be the winner of the election.

Wednesday, November 8

SHORTLY AFTER 2:00 A.M.: Several news organizations declare that Bush has won Florida by around 50,000 votes and hence the presidency. Gore's aides state that he is preparing his concession speech.

2:30 A.M.: Gore telephones Bush at the Governor's Mansion in Austin, Texas, to congratulate him. Gore has already written his concession speech.

3:30 A.M.: After learning that the latest count in Florida has reduced Bush's lead to less than 1,000 votes, Gore telephones Bush a second time. He states that the election is too close to call, that there would be an automatic recount in Florida, and that he is withdrawing his concession. Bush replies incredulously, "You mean to tell me, Mr. Vice President, you're retracting your concession?" "You don't have to be snippy about it," Gore replies. Bush tells Gore that his brother, Jeb Bush, governor of Florida, had assured him that he won Florida. "Let me explain something," Gore responds. "Your younger brother is not the ultimate authority on this." The conversation ends shortly after.

According to the Florida Division of Elections, Bush leads Gore in Florida by 1,784 votes (2,909,135 to 2,907,351). This margin, representing three one-hundredths of one percent of the total votes cast, triggers by Florida law[1] a machine recount, which begins immediately.

Bush states that he expects the recount in Florida to confirm his victory. He announces that he has called on James A. Baker III to lead his legal team in Florida.

Gore states, "This matter must be resolved expeditiously, but deliberately and without any rush to judgment." He announces that he has called on Warren Christopher to head the team of lawyers representing him in Florida.

President Clinton, talking to reporters at the White House, attempts to reassure the nation that the undecided election does not amount to a national crisis.

Warren Christopher, at Gore's news conference, states, "I don't have any reason to think we're on the edge of a constitutional crisis. And we don't intend to try to provoke a constitutional crisis."

Democratic officials in Palm Beach County contend that the "butterfly" ballot used there was confusing and caused Democratic voters to vote mistakenly for Reform Party candidate Patrick Buchanan instead of for Gore. In this mainly Democratic and strongly Jewish county, Buchanan, who had been criticized in the past for anti-Jewish sentiments, received almost 2,700 votes more than he received in any other Florida county. Nearly 30,000 ballots were thrown out because they showed two or more votes for president ("overvotes") or no votes for president ("undervotes"). Robert Weisman, a Palm Beach County administrator, announces that many of the approximately 19,000 overvotes included votes for both Gore and Buchanan. Hundreds of voters picket outside the Board of Elections to complain, and three Palm Beach County residents file a lawsuit in state circuit court claiming that the design of the ballot violated state law and requesting a new presidential vote in the county.

Thursday, November 9

Florida's secretary of state and chief election officer, Katherine Harris, a Republican and onetime co-chair of the Bush campaign in Florida, declares that ballots received from absentee voters up to ten days after the election (November 14) would be counted, pursuant to Florida law.

The Gore campaign chairman, William M. Daley, calls for hand recounts in the counties of Miami-Dade, Broward, Volusia, and Palm Beach. (According to Florida law, any candidate, political committee, or political party may request that a county canvassing board perform a sample manual recount of at least three precincts and at least one percent of the votes cast for the candidate.[2] If the manual recount indicates an error in the vote tabulation that could affect the outcome of the election, the county canvassing board is required to correct the error, which may entail manually recounting all ballots.)[3]

The Volusia County Canvassing Board agrees to perform hand recounts in all precincts, and the Palm Beach County Canvassing Board agrees to perform hand recounts in three precincts.

Speaking of the unusually high vote count of 3,407 that he received in Palm Beach County, Pat Buchanan states that "most of those are probably not my vote." Although only 337 voters in Palm Beach County are registered members of the Reform Party, a Bush spokesman claims that the vote count is not unusual because Palm Beach County is a "Pat Buchanan stronghold."

Democratic elected officials from Broward and Miami-Dade Counties claim that many African Americans had been unfairly turned away from the polls. The NAACP states that there had been efforts to stop blacks from voting in several areas of Florida.

According to the Associated Press, Gore leads Bush nationally by 218,441 votes (49,244,746 to 49,026,305).

Friday, November 10

The automatic machine recount required by Florida law is completed, but no official result is released. According to the Florida secretary of state's office, Bush leads Florida by 960 votes with 66 of 67 counties reporting. According to the Associated Press's unofficial tally of all 67 counties, Bush leads Gore by 327 votes (2,910,198 to 2,909,871).

The Broward County Canvassing Board declares it will conduct sample manual recounts in three precincts on November 13. County officials also report cases of "hanging chads." (A "chad" is the piece of paper that gets punched through on a ballot. A "hanging" chad is one that has not been completely punched through a ballot. A "pregnant" or "dimpled" chad is an indentation created when a hole is not pierced.)

James Baker claims that Bush is the winner in Florida, and Bush announces that he is making transition plans.

Democratic Party lawyers in Tallahassee announce that they are considering a legal challenge to the butterfly ballot in Palm Beach County.

Saturday, November 11

Bush files a lawsuit in the U.S. District Court for the Southern District of Florida seeking a stay of the manual recounts, citing the "potential for mischief" and the unfair and subjective nature of hand counting as compared to machine counting.

Palm Beach County begins a sample manual recount of 4,000 votes. During the recount, teams of Republicans, Democrats, and election officials argue often over the interpretation of chads.

In anticipation of future lawsuits challenging the election results, hundreds of voters from Palm Beach County complete affidavits alleging that they voted for the wrong person for president or voted for two candidates because of confusion over the ballot.

A poll by *Newsweek* indicates that two-thirds of Americans believe that Al Gore did the right thing in withdrawing his concession and that 72 percent of those polled say it is more important to make certain the vote count in Florida is fair and accurate than to resolve matters quickly.

Sunday, November 12

The Palm Beach County Canvassing Board approves a full manual recount after the completed sample recount produces 19 new votes for Gore.

Volusia County begins a full manual recount.

Harry Jacobs, a lawyer and a member of the Democratic Executive Board, claims that Seminole County election official Sandra Goard allowed Republican Party workers to correct errors on thousands of applications for absentee ballots to be sent to Republicans. Democratic campaign officials claim that the actions of these workers, adding missing voter identification numbers to what otherwise would have been rejected absentee ballot applications, violated Florida law. Seminole County is heavily Republican.

In West Palm Beach, the Reverend Jesse Jackson, joined by local and national Jewish leaders, calls for a manual recount of Palm Beach County ballots and urges people to attend upcoming rallies.

Monday, November 13

After completing a sample recount that resulted in a gain of only 4 votes for Gore, Broward County officials reject a countywide recount.

Relying on an interpretation of Florida election law given in an advisory opinion by the Florida Division of Elections, Secretary of State Harris announces that she will ignore any results received after 5:00 P.M. on November 14, unless the lateness is caused by a hurricane or other natural disaster. (According to Florida law,[4] if election returns are not received by the Department of State by 5:00 P.M. on the seventh day after the election, the secretary of state may ignore such results in the certification of the statewide results.)

U.S. District Court Judge Donald M. Middlebrooks, a Clinton appointee, denies Bush's November 11 request for an injunction to stop the manual recounts, on the grounds that the state court, not the federal court, is empowered to resolve issues relating to state election laws.[5]

The Volusia County Canvassing Board, joined by Gore, the Florida Democratic Party, and the Palm Beach Canvassing Board, ask Judge Terry P. Lewis of the Leon County Circuit Court in the state's capital, Tallahassee, to overturn Harris's ruling and extend the certification deadline.

A *New York Times*/CBS News Poll shows that Americans, although divided on the issue of who should rightfully be president, are not concerned over the uncertainty.

Reverend Jackson leads a six-hundred-person march in West Palm Beach, protesting irregularities in the presidential election.

Tuesday, November 14

Judge Lewis rules that the counties must file their returns by the seven-day statutory deadline.[6] He also holds that Harris may ignore late-filed returns but may not do so arbitrarily.

Miami-Dade County conducts a sample recount of one percent of the precincts and decides not to proceed with a full manual recount.

The Palm Beach County Canvassing Board, a group of three Democrats, votes to begin a manual recount on Wednesday morning. The board then postpones the recount after receiving an advisory opinion from the Division of Elections declaring that the planned recount was not authorized because there was nothing wrong with the county's ballot machines. This opinion is contradicted by an advisory opinion issued by Florida's attorney general, Robert A. Butterworth (a Democrat who was Gore's Florida campaign chairman during the election), stating that the recount is legal.

At the request of county Democrats, Broward County Circuit Judge John A. Miller rules that the Broward County Canvassing Board does not have to abide by the 5:00 P.M. Tuesday deadline set by Harris.

Volusia County completes its manual recount, netting Gore an increase of 98 votes.

Harris announces that Bush leads by 300 votes with all 67 counties reporting. She also sets 2:00 P.M. as the deadline for written explanations of late returns from Broward, Palm Beach, and Miami-Dade Counties.

David Boies, a prominent lawyer who had been hired by the Justice Department to lead the government's successful antitrust action against Microsoft, joins Gore's legal team in Florida.

Florida Governor Jeb Bush publicly supports Harris's enforcement of the November 14 deadline. Speaking of the possible harmful effects on Florida's reputation resulting from the election controversy, Bush states, "I've been disheartened by the image of such a great state being focused on what is literally a handful of votes out of millions cast." He also acknowledges that the state's election laws may need to be reviewed after the election is decided.

Wednesday, November 15

Katherine Harris announces that she will deny requests from several counties to extend the deadline and that she plans to certify the final election results on November 18 after the overseas absentee ballots have been counted.

The Florida Supreme Court, all of whose justices are Democratic appointees, unanimously denies Harris's request that the Court stop the recounts[7] and accepts Palm Beach County's request for clarification of the dispute between Harris and the Florida attorney general on the legality of the recount.

The Broward County Canvassing Board votes to begin a countywide hand recount.

Bush files an appeal in the Eleventh U.S. Circuit Court of Appeals in Atlanta (which hears appeals from federal district courts in Florida, Alabama, and Georgia), seeking to have Judge Middlebrooks's decision to allow recounts overturned. Bush argues that recounts are unconstitutional because they treat some votes differently than others.

In a nationally televised address, Gore offers to end further legal challenges if Bush will either accept a statewide recount or accept the results of manual recounts in Broward, Miami-Dade, and Palm Beach Counties plus the uncounted overseas ballots. Bush rejects Gore's offer, reiterating his objection to "arbitrary and chaotic" manual recounts.

Republican congressman Tom DeLay sends a memorandum to congressional Republicans alerting them that the House and the Senate can reject a state's electoral votes should they decide the votes are tainted. Democratic congressman David E. Price introduces a resolution to have the United States Archivist provide the House with information about the Electoral College.

Thursday, November 16

The Florida Supreme Court, considering the conflicting advisory opinions from November 14 concerning the legality of recounts, unanimously rules that hand recounts in Palm Beach and Broward Counties can continue.[8] After days of uncertainty over its legality, a manual recount begins in Palm Beach County.

In front of Judge Lewis, Gore's lawyers seek an emergency ruling to find Harris in contempt of Lewis's November 14 order and to compel Harris to accept the amended returns, arguing that Harris's announcement that she would not consider any results past the deadline was an abuse of discretion.

Harry Jacobs sues the Seminole County Canvassing Board in county circuit court to have all 15,215 absentee ballots disqualified because of the alteration of absentee ballot applications by Republican election workers. Although only about 4,700 applications were altered, Jacobs argues for the disqualification of all absentee ballots as there is no way to separate those absentee votes that were cast from correct applications. If these ballots were thrown out, Gore would net 5,000 votes.

Friday, November 17

Judge Lewis denies Gore's November 16 request for an emergency ruling, stating that Harris did not abuse her discretion in excluding manually recounted ballots.[9]

The Florida Supreme Court agrees to hear Gore's appeal of Judge Lewis's ruling and bars Harris from certifying the results until the court rules on the case.

The Miami-Dade County Canvassing Board votes to begin a full manual recount of approximately 500,000 ballots.

In Broward County, Circuit Judge John Miller rules that officials can consider ballots on which voters did not perforate the punch cards. Lawyers for the Democratic Party had asked the judge to order the County Canvassing Board to reconsider its decision to count only ballots with chads separated from the ballot by two or more corners and also to order the board to count pregnant or dimpled chads as votes. Judge Miller notes that West Palm Beach Circuit Court Judge Jorge Labarga had earlier issued a ruling that the Palm Beach County Canvassing Board could not reject ballots that were not fully perforated.

The Eleventh Circuit denies Bush's request for an injunction to stop the recounts, stating that the "states have the primary authority to determine the manner of appointing Presidential Electors and to resolve most controversies concerning the appointment of Electors."[10]

Saturday, November 18

After completion of the statewide count of all overseas absentee ballots, Bush's lead increases to 930 votes. The Bush team accuses Democrats of targeting the most likely Republican military votes for disqualification. In response, the Gore team accuses Republicans of counting military votes that legally should have been thrown out.

In their brief to the Florida Supreme Court on appeal of Judge Lewis's November 17 decision upholding Harris's enforcement of the deadline, lawyers for Gore argue that the recounts should continue and should be included in the official vote because they are the most accurate method of objectively determining voter intent. The briefs emphasize abuse of discretion by Secretary of State Harris.

Republican leaders in the Florida state legislature announce that they are examining a federal law (Title 3, Section 2 of the U.S. Code) that they believe gives them the power to choose electors if the outcome of the state's popular vote is uncertain. The law, which had never been used, states, "Whenever any State has held an election for the purpose of choosing electors, and has failed to make a choice on the day prescribed by law, the electors may be appointed on a subsequent day in such a manner as the legislature of such State may direct."

Sunday, November 19

At the request of Democrats, the Broward County Canvassing Board announces its decision to adopt a broader standard for counting votes from punch cards, allowing the consideration of dimpled or one-corner chads as possible votes. The board had previously counted as votes only chads with two or more corners punched through. Republicans harshly criticize this decision, claiming that it significantly increases subjectivity.

Bush's legal team files its briefs with the Florida Supreme Court arguing that based on specific language in Florida's election statutes, the court should enforce the Tuesday, November 14, deadline set by Harris. Gore's reply brief stresses the importance of the determination of voter intent and urges the court to set a firm (and broad) standard for determining this intent.

Responding to Republican charges that Democrats were systematically trying to exclude absentee ballots from Florida voters in the military, Senator Joseph Lieberman, Gore's running mate, states that he and Gore "would not tolerate a campaign that was aimed specifically at invalidating absentee ballots from members of our armed services." He urges vote counters in Florida to "give the benefit of the doubt" to ballots coming in from military personnel.

Monday, November 20

The Florida Supreme Court hears oral arguments in the appeal of Judge Lewis's November 17 decision upholding Harris's enforcement of the November 14 deadline.

Judge Debra Nelson of the Seminole County Circuit Court agrees to hear the case concerning the corrected absentee ballot applications filed on November 16.

In a lawsuit brought by voters in Palm Beach County, West Palm Beach Circuit Court Judge Jorge Labarga concludes that he lacks the legal authority to order a revote in Palm Beach County, even if confusion over the butterfly ballot had made a difference in the outcome of the election.

Miami-Dade County begins its countywide manual recount.

In response to Republican complaints, Florida Attorney General Butterworth urges local officials to count previously disqualified overseas military ballots.

Tuesday, November 21

The Florida Supreme Court unanimously nullifies the November 14 deadline set by Harris and rules that hand recounts must be included in the official tally as long as they are submitted by 5:00 P.M. on Monday, November 26.[11]

James Baker accuses the court of changing the rules in the middle of the game.

Democrats claim that the court's ruling allows for a broad standard in counting votes.

Gore announces that it is time for him and Governor Bush to begin planning for transition to the presidency.

Wednesday, November 22

Bush petitions the U.S. Supreme Court to overturn the Florida Supreme Court's November 21 ruling allowing hand recounts to go forward, claiming that the Florida court "rewrote the laws" and "changed the rules."

Congressional Republicans call the Florida court's ruling an abuse of power and the result of partisanship. Representative Dick Armey of Texas, the majority leader, calls on the Florida legislature to act. Discussions continue in the Florida legislature about the possibility of the legislature choosing electors.

Republicans hold intense protests at the office of the Miami-Dade supervisor of elections, where the Miami-Dade County Canvassing Board is conducting the manual recount of approximately 654,000 ballots. When the board decides to close the proceedings to the public, the protests briefly become violent as protesters, led by staff workers from the offices of U.S. Senate Majority Leader Trent Lott and House Majority Whip Tom DeLay, pound on doors and even shove the Miami-Dade Democratic Party chairman as he leaves the tabulation room. Shortly after, the Canvassing Board decides to stop the manual recount, stating that because all of the county's ballots could not be counted by the Sunday, November 26, deadline, none of the ballots should be counted. Although the board members deny that the protest had anything to do with their decision, Democrats accuse Bush supporters of deliberately inciting the protest in the hope of forcing the board to halt the recount. Republicans deny the accusation of intimidation, saying that the protest was a natural expression of the voters' anger.

In Washington, Bush's running mate, Dick Cheney, is hospitalized after suffering a mild heart attack.

The Bush team files suit in the Leon County Circuit Court seeking to force the recount in thirteen counties of previously rejected overseas ballots.

Thursday, November 23

The Florida Supreme Court unanimously refuses to order Miami-Dade County to resume its manual recount.[12] The Gore team announces that on Monday, November 27, Gore will formally contest Florida's certified results. (According to Florida law,[13] an unsuccessful candidate, qualified elector, or taxpayer may contest in circuit court the certification of an election on particular grounds, including "the receipt of a number of illegal votes or rejection of a number of legal votes sufficient to change or place in doubt the result of the election.")

Gore's lawyers file their response with the U.S. Supreme Court, urging the Court to reject Bush's request to have the hand recounts declared unconstitutional and emphasizing the lack of an issue that can appropriately be heard by the Court.

The Broward County Canvassing Board begins a hand recount of 1,800 dimpled ballots, while the Palm Beach County Canvassing Board takes the day off for Thanksgiving.

Friday, November 24

The U.S. Supreme Court agrees to hear Bush's request to overturn the Florida Supreme Court's decision allowing the continuation of the manual recounts.[14] At the same time, the Court decides not to hear Bush's appeal of the Eleventh Circuit November 17 decision.[15]

The Palm Beach County Canvassing Board resumes its manual recount and votes not to count ballots with a single dimple in the column for president. The Gore team announces plans to contest the election results in Palm Beach County based on confusion over the butterfly ballot and failure to count dimpled ballots.

The Nassau County election board votes to use an election night tabulation instead of the machine recount tabulation, netting Bush 52 votes. David Boies announces that the Gore team will challenge this decision in the Nassau County courts.

The Florida legislature announces that it will join Bush's Supreme Court challenge to the hand recounts.

The campaign manager for Seminole County Circuit Judge Debra Nelson announces that volunteers for Nelson's 2000 campaign had corrected 3,000 returned absentee ballot forms from which the voter identification numbers had been left off. Judge Nelson is set to hear the case concerning the Seminole County corrected absentee ballot applications on Wednesday, November 29. (On November 27, at the request of both parties, Judge Nelson transfers the case to the Leon County Circuit Court.)

Saturday, November 25

Broward County completes its manual recount, netting Gore 567 votes. Palm Beach County continues to count.

Bush files separate suits against four counties (and plans another suit against a fifth county) to force the review of previously rejected overseas military ballots before the November 26 deadline. At the same time, Bush drops a similar suit against thirteen counties filed on November 22 in Leon County Circuit Court, just hours before the judge was prepared to rule. The judge had told Bush's lawyers on Friday that there was no evidence of wrongdoing by the counters who dismissed the ballots.

For the second straight day, hundreds of Republican demonstrators picket outside the Broward County Courthouse in support of Bush.

Sunday, November 26

Secretary of State Harris denies a request from Palm Beach County for more time to complete its recount and then refuses to accept an incomplete total (showing a gain by Gore of 180 votes) submitted before the 5:00 P.M. deadline. Palm Beach completes its recount shortly before 7:00 P.M.

The Florida Election Canvassing Commission (which includes Katherine Harris) certifies the final recount, which shows Bush leading Gore in Florida by 537 votes (2,912,790 to 2,912,253). At 7:30 P.M., Katherine Harris declares Bush the winner of Florida's 25 electoral votes.

Senator Lieberman announces that Gore will not concede.

In a televised address, Bush declares himself the winner in Florida and the winner of the presidential election. He urges Gore not to pursue the promised legal challenges.

Monday, November 27

Gore files suit in Leon County Circuit Court contesting the certification of the results on the grounds that they included some illegal votes and failed to include some legal votes. (According to Florida law,[16] cases involving the contestation of vote certification of elections covering more than one county are heard in Leon County Circuit Court.) In particular, Gore argues that he would have won the election in Florida had all the votes been counted in Nassau, Miami-Dade, and Palm Beach Counties. Gore asks Leon County Circuit Court Judge N. Sanders Sauls to recount approximately 12,000 ballots: about 3,300 ballots from Palm Beach County that had been manually recounted but considered not to be legal votes and about 9,000 ballots from Miami-Dade County that the counting machine registered as nonvotes and which have never been counted.

Gore supporters file suit in Palm Beach County alleging that the butterfly ballot was so confusing that it disenfranchised thousands of voters.

On national television, Gore states that his challenge to the vote count in Florida is an effort to preserve democracy and asks the American public to be patient while the recount is being completed.

Bush continues his transition planning, but the Clinton administration refuses to release $5.3 million in federal transition funds until a final winner is declared. Dick Cheney announces that he is opening a Bush transition office in Washington using private funds.

Palm Beach County announces that its completed recount—which was rejected by Secretary of State Harris—shows a net gain of 215 votes for Gore.

Tuesday, November 28

Three conservative constitutional consultants tell a committee of the Florida legislature that the legislature has a "constitutional duty" to name Florida's 25 electors should the continuing legal battles not definitively settle the election by December 12.

Judge Sauls denies Gore's request for an immediate recount of the 12,000 disputed ballots from Miami-Dade and Palm Beach Counties but orders that the ballots be delivered to the court. He schedules a hearing for Saturday, December 2, to decide the certification issue and to determine whether to count the ballots and the standards to be used in the count.

Officials in heavily Republican Martin County report the correcting of as many as 500 absentee ballot applications by Republican election workers, a situation similar to what was reported in Seminole County.

Gore suggests that the problems with punch card balloting disproportionately affected Florida's minority voters. Sixty-four percent of Florida's black voters live in punch-card counties, while only 56 percent of whites do.

An analysis by the *Miami Herald* shows that Gore's gains in a Miami-Dade County ballot recount would not be as significant as his legal campaign had suggested.

Wednesday, November 29

Judge Sauls orders all of the ballots from Palm Beach and Miami-Dade Counties—more than 1.1 million of them—delivered to his court. This action comes at the urging of Bush's lawyers, who argue, "If you recount any ballots, you have to recount all of them."

Jeb Bush announces that he supports the Florida legislature's plan to hold a special session to name Florida's electors.

The Bush transition team opens an office in McLean, Virginia. Bush invites General Colin Powell, a leading candidate for secretary of state, to his ranch.

Thursday, November 30

A special committee of Florida's legislature recommends that a special session be called to name Florida's presidential electors. Gore's lawyers ask the U.S. Supreme Court to block this possible action by Florida's legislature.

As the 1.1 million ballots begin arriving by truck in Tallahassee, Bush's lawyers announce their plan to subpoena nearly 1.7 million ballots from three other Florida counties.

As Bush's lawyers raise a host of new legal issues and state that thousands more ballots should be brought to Judge Sauls's courtroom, Gore's lawyers appeal to the Florida Supreme Court to immediately begin a hand count of the 12,000 disputed ballots from Palm Beach and Miami-Dade Counties.

Democrats in Martin County file suit seeking to disqualify almost 10,000 absentee ballots because of alleged tampering with absentee ballot applications by Republican election workers. If these ballots were thrown out, Gore would net 2,800 votes.

Friday, December 1

The U.S. Supreme Court hears arguments on Bush's November 22 appeal of the Florida Supreme Court's November 21 decision to allow recounts to continue. Outside the Court, supporters of Bush and Gore hold boisterous demonstrations.

The Florida Supreme Court rejects Gore's November 30 request to begin an immediate recount of 12,000 disputed ballots.[17] The court also refuses to order a new election in Palm Beach County to remedy the use of butterfly ballots.[18]

Judge Sauls announces that he plans to ensure that the trial to begin on Saturday moves quickly, predicting that it will be completed within twelve hours.

Saturday, December 2

Judge Sauls begins to hear testimony on Gore's contest of the Florida vote certification. After twelve hours, the case is continued to Sunday.

Bush is shown on television discussing the economy with congressional leaders.

Sunday, December 3

In Judge Sauls's courtroom, testimony continues, followed by closing arguments, which are completed shortly before 11:00 P.M.

Gore and Warren Christopher make it clear that Gore is not currently considering concession.

Cheney calls on Gore to concede. He invokes the possibility of an imminent recession and stresses the need for a new administration to begin dealing with it.

Monday, December 4

The U.S. Supreme Court nullifies the Florida Supreme Court's November 21 decision to extend deadlines in order to include manual recounts and sends the case back to the Florida court for clarification of the basis for its decision as it relates to federal law.[19]

Judge Sauls refuses to order a recount of the 12,000 disputed ballots and upholds the certification of Bush as the winner in Florida, concluding that there was no credible evidence that proved the election outcome would be altered by the recounts.[20] Gore's lawyers immediately appeal.

Several of Gore's advisers express pessimism about the possibility that the Florida Supreme Court will overturn Judge Sauls's ruling.

Tuesday, December 5

The Eleventh Circuit hears arguments on Bush's appeal of Judge Middlebrooks's November 13 decision to allow manual recounts.

Wednesday, December 6

Gore's lawyers ask the Florida Supreme Court to overturn Judge Sauls's decision rejecting a manual recount of 12,000 votes and upholding the certification of Florida's election results. Gore's lawyers state that this is the vice president's final appeal in his quest for the presidency.

Republican leaders of the Florida legislature schedule a special session on Friday, December 8, to select Florida's presidential electors. Florida Democrats label the action clearly partisan and claim that it was orchestrated by the Bush campaign. "The only thing missing from the proclamation was a postmark from Austin, Texas," said Lois Frankel, the leader of Florida's House Democrats.

A divided Eleventh Circuit rejects Bush's request to declare the manual recounts unconstitutional.[21]

Arguments begin in the trials concerning the Republican correction of absentee ballot applications in Martin and Seminole Counties. At stake is the possible disqualification of nearly 25,000 absentee votes (15,215 in Seminole County and 9,773 in Martin County), which would net Gore almost 8,000 votes.

Thursday, December 7

The Florida Supreme Court hears arguments on Gore's request to overturn Judge Sauls's December 4 decision denying manual recounts and upholding certification.

The *New York Times* reports that in 1998 the Florida Supreme Court had severely rebuked Judge Sauls for his efforts to dismiss a court administrator and had stripped him of his title as chief judge.[22]

Friday, December 8

In Leon County Circuit Court, Judges Nikki Ann Clark and Terry Lewis reject the requests to disqualify nearly 25,000 absentee ballots from Seminole and Martin Counties, finding that, despite the irregularities in the correction of absentee ballot applications, "the sanctity of the ballot and the integrity of the election were not affected."[23]

Judge Lacey A. Collier of the U.S. District Court for the Northern District of Florida rules at Bush's request that 337 overseas absentee ballots previously rejected by the canvassing boards of several Florida counties should be counted.[24]

A closely divided Florida Supreme Court (4–3) overturns Judge Sauls's ruling upholding certification, stating that "[o]nly by examining the contested ballots . . . can a meaningful and final determination in this election contest be made."[25]

The court declares that the recount of the 9,000 undervotes from Miami-Dade County, as well as all undervotes across the state, must begin immediately. The court also rules that 383 votes for Gore previously counted in Palm Beach and Miami-Dade Counties but not included in the certified results must be added to Gore's total, reducing Gore's deficit to less than 200 votes.

Bush asks U.S. Supreme Court Justice Anthony M. Kennedy to halt enforcement of the Florida Supreme Court's decision and asks for an emergency hearing with the Eleventh Circuit.

Pursuant to the Florida Supreme Court's decision, the Leon County Circuit Court is placed in charge of conducting the recount. Judge Sauls recuses himself and the task is assigned to Judge Terry Lewis. Judge Lewis states that he and other judges will oversee the recounts and orders all recounts to be concluded by 2:00 P.M. on Sunday, December 10.

Saturday, December 9

As a result of the Florida Supreme Court's December 8 decision, a statewide manual recount of approximately 45,000 undervotes begins.

The Eleventh Circuit rejects Bush's request for a rehearing on the issue of the constitutionality of the manual recounts, allowing the recounts to continue.[26]

Shortly before 3:00 P.M., the U.S. Supreme Court, in a 5 to 4 decision, agrees to hear Bush's appeal from the Florida Supreme Court's December 8 decision to allow the recounts and grants Bush's request to order a suspension of the Florida court's ruling.[27] Across Florida, the recounts, at various stages of completion, are halted.

Sunday, December 10

Lawyers for Bush and Gore file their briefs with the U.S. Supreme Court.

Monday, December 11

The U.S. Supreme Court hears arguments from Theodore B. Olson for Bush, Joseph P. Klock Jr. for Katherine Harris, and David Boies for Gore.

The Florida Supreme Court issues its rewritten decision overturning Harris's enforcement of the November 14 deadline, which had been vacated and remanded by the U.S. Supreme Court on December 4.[28] The Florida court states that its interpretation of Florida's election statutes "results in the formation of no new rules of state law but rather results simply in a narrow reading and clarification of those statutes."

House and Senate committees of Florida's legislature pass resolutions to appoint Florida's 25 electors. The House is set to vote on the resolution on December 12, with the Senate set to vote the following day.

Democrats file briefs with the Florida Supreme Court seeking to overturn the December 8 rulings allowing the counting of the 25,000 disputed absentee ballots from Seminole and Martin Counties.

Tuesday, December 12

Several newspapers report that Supreme Court Justice Antonin Scalia's son is a partner in Theodore Olson's law firm.

Judge Gilbert S. Merritt of the U.S. Court of Appeals for the Sixth Circuit calls for Supreme Court Justice Clarence Thomas to recuse himself because Thomas's wife is working for the Heritage Foundation, a conservative think tank, helping to recruit Republicans for a possible Bush administration.

In the Florida legislature, the House approves the resolution to appoint Florida's electors.

The Florida Supreme Court agrees with the lower courts that the 25,000 disputed absentee ballots from Seminole and Martin Counties should not be invalidated.[29]

In another 5 to 4 decision, the U.S. Supreme Court overturns the Florida Supreme Court's December 11 decision allowing manual recounts, on the grounds that the Florida court failed to provide a constitutional standard for counting votes.[30] The Court also tells the Florida court that there is no time left to implement an appropriate standard and bars further recounting of disputed ballots. The case is sent back to the Florida Supreme Court.

Wednesday, December 13

At 9:00 P.M., in an eight-minute televised speech, Gore concedes and urges unity.

At 10:00 P.M., Bush claims victory and speaks of reconciliation.

Thursday, December 14

The Florida Supreme Court dismisses the case remanded from the U.S. Supreme Court on December 12, stating that the Florida Election Code did not provide the elements necessary for a resolution of the disputed issues.[31]

Monday, December 18

In the Electoral College voting, Bush receives 271 votes to Gore's 266. One Gore elector, Barbara Lett-Simmons of the District of Columbia, leaves her ballot blank in protest of the District's lack of representation in Congress. (For final popular and electoral vote counts, see table 1 below.)

Saturday, January 20

In Washington, D.C., George W. Bush is inaugurated the forty-third president of the United States.

EPILOGUE

On April 4, 2001, the *Miami Herald* and *USA Today* issued the results of their reviews of the undervote recount. The papers found that had the statewide recount been allowed to continue using the most inclusive standard as advocated by Gore (counting partial punches and dimples on ballots), Bush would have won the election by 1,665 votes, a margin nearly three times greater than the official margin. Conversely, had the standard advocated by Bush (counting only clean ballot punches) been used to complete the recount, Gore would have won by a mere three votes. The *Herald* also reported that had the recount begun from scratch (instead of including the results of several counties that had already completed their recounts by the time the statewide recount was halted by the U.S. Supreme Court) using the most inclusive standard, Gore would have won the election by 393 votes.

TABLE 1   STATE-BY-STATE RESULTS

State	Bush			Gore		
	Popular Vote	%	Electoral Votes	Popular Vote	%	Electoral Votes
Alabama	943,799	57	9	696,741	42	
Alaska	136,068	59	3	64,252	28	
Arizona	715,112	51	8	635,730	45	
Arkansas	472,120	51	6	420,424	45	
California	4,437,557	42		5,721,195	54	54

TABLE 1 *(continued)*

State	Bush Popular Vote	%	Electoral Votes	Gore Popular Vote	%	Electoral Votes
Colorado	884,047	51	8	738,470	42	
Connecticut	545,954	39		795,861	56	8
Delaware	137,081	42		180,638	55	3
Florida	2,911,872	49	25	2,910,942	49	
Georgia	1,416,085	55	13	1,110,755	43	
Hawaii	137,785	38		205,209	56	4
Idaho	336,299	69	5	138,354	28	
Illinois	2,019,256	43		2,588,884	55	22
Indiana	1,242,372	57	12	899,836	41	
Iowa	634,225	48		638,355	49	7
Kansas	616,829	58	6	392,867	37	
Kentucky	869,946	57	8	637,518	41	
Louisiana	924,670	53	9	789,837	45	
Maine	284,724	44		316,109	49	4
Maryland	770,911	40		1,093,344	57	10
Massachusetts	876,906	33		1,610,175	60	12
Michigan	1,947,100	47		2,141,721	51	18
Minnesota	1,110,290	46		1,168,190	48	10
Mississippi	549,426	57	7	400,845	42	
Missouri	1,189,521	51	11	1,110,826	47	
Montana	239,755	58	3	137,264	34	
Nebraska	408,719	63	5	215,616	33	
Nevada	301,539	49	4	279,949	46	
New Hampshire	273,135	48	4	265,853	47	
New Jersey	1,253,791	41		1,747,445	56	15
New Mexico	286,417	48		286,783	48	5
New York	2,235,776	35		3,767,609	60	33
North Carolina	1,607,238	56	14	1,236,721	43	
North Dakota	175,572	61	3	96,098	33	
Ohio	2,294,167	50	21	2,117,741	46	
Oklahoma	744,335	60	8	474,326	38	
Oregon	712,705	47		719,165	47	7
Pennsylvania	2,264,309	47		2,465,412	51	23
Rhode Island	132,535	32		254,500	61	4
South Carolina	804,826	57	8	578,143	41	
South Dakota	190,515	60	3	118,750	38	
Tennessee	1,056,480	51	11	977,789	48	
Texas	3,796,850	59	32	2,429,329	38	
Utah	512,168	67	4	201,734	26	
Vermont	119,273	41		148,166	51	3
Virginia	1,431,654	52	13	1,221,094	45	

TABLE 1 *(continued)*

	Bush			Gore		
State	Popular Vote	%	Electoral Votes	Popular Vote	%	Electoral Votes
Washington	1,101,621	45		1,240,302	50	11
Washington, D.C.	17,020	9		162,004	86	3
West Virginia	329,708	52	5	291,088	46	
Wisconsin	1,235,035	48		1,240,431	48	11
Wyoming	147,674	69	3	60,421	28	

TOTAL RESULTS

Candidate	National Popular Vote	National Percentage	States Won	Electoral Votes
Gore	50,996,116	48	21	266
Bush	50,456,169	48	30	271
Other	3,874,040	4	0	0

SOURCE: http://www.cnn.com/ELECTION/2000/results/index.president.html. Results as of 1/6/01.

NOTE: The following states' returns consist of only 99 percent of all precincts reporting: Maine, Mississippi, New York, and Pennsylvania.

NOTES

1. Fla. Stat. § 102.141(4) (2000).

2. Fla. Stat. § 102.166(4) (2000).

3. Fla. Stat. § 102.166(5) (2000).

4. Fla. Stat. § 102.112 (2000).

5. See Siegel v. LePore, 120 F.Supp.2d 1041 (S.D. Fla. 2000), *aff'd,* 234 F.3d 1163 (11th Cir. 2000), *reh'g denied,* 234 F.3d 1218 (11th Cir. 2000).

6. See McDermott v. Harris, No. CV 00–2700, 2000 WL 1693713 (Fl. Cir. Ct. Nov. 14, 2000), *rev'd,* Palm Beach County Canvassing Bd. v. Harris, 772 So.2d 1220 (Fla. 2000), *vacated,* Bush v. Palm Beach County Canvassing Bd., 121 S. Ct. 471 (2000), *on remand,* Palm Beach County Canvassing Bd. v. Harris, 772 So.2d 1273 (Fla. 2000).

7. See Harris v. Circuit Judges, No. SC00–2345, 2000 WL 1702529 (Fla. Nov. 15, 2000).

8. See Palm Beach County Canvassing Bd. v. Harris, 2000 WL 1708520 (Fla. Nov. 16, 2000).

9. See McDermott v. Harris, No. 00–2700, 2000 WL 1714590 (Fl. Cir. Ct. Nov. 17, 2000), *rev'd,* Palm Beach County Canvassing Bd. v. Harris, 772 So.2d 1220 (Fla.

2000), *vacated,* Bush v. Palm Beach County Canvassing Bd., 121 S. Ct. 471 (2000), *on remand,* Palm Beach County Canvassing Bd. v. Harris, 772 So.2d 1273 (Fla. 2000).

10. See Touchston v. McDermott, 234 F.3d 1130 (11th Cir. 2000).

11. See Palm Beach County Canvassing Bd. v. Harris, 772 So.2d 1220 (Fla. 2000), *vacated,* Bush v. Palm Beach County Canvassing Bd., 121 S. Ct. 471 (2000), *on remand,* Palm Beach County Canvassing Bd. v. Harris, 772 So.2d 1273 (Fla. 2000).

12. See Gore v. Miami-Dade County, No. 00–2370, 2000 WL 1730879 (Fla. Nov. 23, 2000).

13. Fla. Stat. § 102.168(3)(c) (2000).

14. See Bush v. Palm Beach County Canvassing Bd., 121 S. Ct. 510 (2000); see also Bush v. Palm Beach County Canvassing Bd., 121 S. Ct. 471 (2000), *on remand,* Palm Beach County Canvassing Bd. v. Harris, 772 So.2d 1273 (Fla. 2000).

15. See Siegel v. LePore, 121 S. Ct. 510 (2000).

16. Fla. Stat. § 102.1685 (2000).

17. See Gore v. Harris, No. 00–2808, 1D00–4688, 2000 WL 1770382 (Fla. Dec. 1, 2000).

18. See Fladell v. Palm Beach County Canvassing Bd., 772 So.2d 1240 (Fla. 2000).

19. See Bush v. Palm Beach County Canvassing Bd., 121 S. Ct. 471 (2000), *on remand,* Palm Beach County Canvassing Bd. v. Harris, 772 So.2d 1273 (Fla. 2000).

20. See Gore v. Harris, No. CV-00–2808, 2000 WL 1770257 (Fl. Cir. Ct. Dec. 4, 2000), *rev'd,* Gore v. Harris, 772 So.2d 1243 (Fla. 2000), *cert. and stay granted,* Bush v. Gore, 121 S. Ct. 512 (2000), *rev'd,* Bush v. Gore, 121 S. Ct. 525 (2000), *on remand,* Gore v. Harris, 773 So.2d 524 (Fla. 2000).

21. See Siegel v. LePore, 234 F.3d 1163 (11th Cir. 2000), *reh'g denied,* 234 F.3d 1218 (11th Cir. 2000).

22. See David Barstow & Somini Segupta, *Sauls' Difficult History with Florida High Court,* N.Y. Times, Dec. 8, 2000, at A1.

23. Taylor v. Martin County Canvassing Bd., No. CV 00–2850, 2000 WL 1793409, at *5 (Fla. Cir. Ct., Dec. 8, 2000), *aff'd,* 773 So.2d 517 (Fla. 2000). See also Jacobs v. Seminole County Canvassing Bd., No. 00–2816, 2000 WL 1793429 (Fla. Cir. Ct., Dec. 8, 2000), *aff'd,* 773 So.2d 519 (Fla. 2000).

24. See Bush v. Hillsborough County Canvassing Bd., 123 F. Supp. 2d 1305 (N.D. Fla. 2000).

25. See Gore v. Harris, 772 So.2d 1243 (Fla. 2000), *cert. and stay granted,* Bush v. Gore, 121 S. Ct. 512 (2000), *rev'd,* Bush v. Gore, 531 U.S. 98 (2000), *on remand,* Gore v. Harris, 773 So.2d 524 (Fla. 2000).

26. See Siegel v. LePore, 234 F.3d 1218 (11th Cir. 2000).

27. See Bush v. Gore, 121 S.Ct. 512 (2000); see also Bush v. Gore, 531 U.S. 98 (2000), *on remand,* Gore v. Harris, 773 So.2d 524 (Fla. 2000).

28. See Palm Beach County Canvassing Bd. v. Harris, 772 So.2d 1273 (Fla. 2000).

29. See Jacobs v. Seminole County Canvassing Bd., 773 So.2d 519 (Fla. 2000); Taylor v. Martin County Canvassing Bd., 773 So.2d 517 (Fla. 2000).

30. See Bush v. Gore, 531 U.S. 98 (2000), *on remand,* Gore v. Harris, 773 So.2d 524 (Fla. 2000).

31. Gore v. Harris, 773 So.2d 524 (Fla. 2000).

Part One

IN THE HEAT
OF THE BATTLE

1

EQUAL PROTECTION FOR VOTES

Henry E. Brady

"Counting all the votes" and "fairness" are catchwords of the now more than five-week-long postelection campaign. These principles have collided repeatedly as the Gore campaign seeks manual recounts and the Bush campaign protests the unfairness of these recounts. "The lack of uniform standards for counting 'votes,'" the Bush campaign argued in its brief to the United States Supreme Court, "means that voters who cast identical ballots in different counties will likely have their ballots counted differently." The result, according to the Bush campaign's Supreme Court brief, is a violation of the Equal Protection Clause of the Fourteenth Amendment, which "forbids the state from treating similarly situated voters differently based merely on where they live." If the Bush campaign is right and the Supreme Court accepts their argument, then one outcome of our national exercise in electioneering will undoubtedly be a succession of Supreme Court cases that will change the way we vote in America.

We all agree voters should not be treated differently based merely on where they live. That is why the differences in the Broward County and Palm Beach County standards for hanging chads and dimples seems so disconcerting. But if these different standards upset us, then we should be even more troubled by the fact that the different voting devices used from one county to another have far greater impacts than different standards for manual recounts. Different voting devices not only lead to vastly different numbers of spoiled ballots, they also interact with personal characteristics such as education, infirmity, and voting experience to produce biases in our voting system.

Consider Florida. The Bush campaign is right in saying that there were different standards for counting undervotes (those ballots on which the tabulating machine does not detect a vote) in Broward and Palm Beach

Counties. In Broward County, about 20 percent of undervotes were considered real or "legal" votes, and the Bush campaign believes this is too high because it includes dimpled ballots. In Palm Beach County, about 10 percent of undervotes were considered legal votes. The Bush campaign has also objected to the Palm Beach County standard, but it was favorably compared to the Broward County standard by the Bush campaign's lawyer in his replies to questions at the Supreme Court on Monday. Because there are about 62,000 undervotes in Florida, the number of votes recovered if the Palm Beach standard is applied across the state would be 6,200 and the number recovered if the Broward standard is used would be 12,400. The difference is 6,200 votes, and the Bush campaign fears that these extra votes might give Al Gore even more chances to become president of the United States than just the 6,200 that would be recovered if the more restrictive Palm Beach County standard were used, although their preference is clearly to see none of the undervotes considered.

The increase in new votes that results from using the Broward versus the Palm Beach County standard is worrisome, but it pales in comparison with the difference in the undervotes from using the Accuvote optical scanning devices versus the older punch-card systems. The Accuvote devices (used in sixteen Florida counties) have an undervote rate of about three per thousand, which amounts to 18,000 undervotes statewide if Accuvote were used everywhere. The punch-card systems (used in twenty-four counties) have an undervote rate of about fifteen per thousand, which amounts to about 90,000 undervotes if applied statewide. The difference is 72,000 votes—more than ten times the difference between the Broward and Palm Beach County standards.

But that is not all. Different voting machines lead to different numbers of total overvotes (those ballots on which the tabulating machine detects two or more votes for the same office). The overvote rate for the Accuvote devices is about three to four per thousand, which amounts to 21,000 votes if applied statewide. The overvote rate for the punch-card machines is about twenty-five per thousand, which amounts to 150,000. The difference between these two vote recording systems would be 129,000 votes—more than twenty times the difference between the Broward and Palm Beach County standards.

By any reckoning, the machine variability in undervotes and overvotes exceeds the variability arising from different standards by factors of ten to twenty. Far more mischief, it seems, can be created by poor methods of recording and tabulating votes than by manual recounts.

Moreover, there is evidence that undervotes and overvotes are concentrated in areas with poor people, minorities, and older people. In Duval County, Florida, for example, the overvotes and undervotes were heavily concentrated in poor, black precincts. In Florida we know that the punch-card systems are concentrated in counties that went for Gore. The Gore fraction of the two-party vote in the twenty-four punch-card counties is 53 percent, while the fraction of the two-party vote in the sixteen counties using the Accuvote system tilted toward Bush (51.4 percent). Twenty-five of the remaining twenty-seven counties that lean heavily toward Bush (58 percent of the two-party vote) have undervote and overvote rates much closer to the Accuvote system than the punch-card devices. As a result, George Bush gained thousands of votes because his support came from counties with better voting devices that reduced both undervotes and overvotes. We know much less about the biases that come from manual recounts, despite a great deal of rhetoric on the topic. There may be biases from a manual recount of undervotes, but they must be much smaller than the biases from poor voting devices.

Although interesting, these results provide little guidance for the current impasse. Both Gore and Bush deserve the best possible results from an imperfect system. But if the Supreme Court decides to base its decision in *Bush v. Gore* on the need for equal protection of votes, then something good may come of this. Because the differences across voting devices is a much bigger problem than differences across manual recount methods— especially once the manual recount has been extended to the entire state of Florida—the next decade may see a flurry of legislation to equalize voting systems so that the promise of one person, one vote is realized.

2

LAW AND DATA:
THE BUTTERFLY BALLOT EPISODE

*Henry E. Brady, Michael C. Herron, Walter R. Mebane Jr., Jasjeet
Singh Sekhon, Kenneth W. Shotts, and Jonathan Wand*

On the television series *Law and Order* the police catch criminals and hand
them over to lawyers to get convictions. The program's dramatic tension
comes in part from the police operating under the scrutiny of a rigid and
unforgiving legal system. The suspense increases as the lawyers try to do
their job even though there is often a gap between justice and what the law
requires.

In "Law and Data," data analysts track down the facts and prove their
theories, but they often have trouble explaining them simply and clearly.
Lawyers find it hard to obtain, or even define, justice. And the law sometimes goes in odd directions, missing the biggest facts and emphasizing
seemingly trivial ones. Justice is not always done.

Our "Law and Data" episode involves political scientists from Cornell,
Harvard, Northwestern, and the University of California, Berkeley, who
came together through a series of accidents to become expert witnesses for
the "butterfly ballot" cases in Palm Beach County, Florida. In the first few
days after the 2000 election, our work was motivated solely by intellectual
curiosity, the importance of the issue, and the availability of data on the
Internet that made quick analysis possible. Our initial analysis of the surprisingly high Buchanan vote in Palm Beach County was completed and
posted to the Web by the Saturday after the election, and this led to a
telephone call and an e-mail message from a lawyer in Florida who asked
us to become involved in the butterfly ballot cases. Throughout the process,
our admiration grew for the lawyers' and judges' efforts to do their best,
but our doubts have increased over whether the legal process can effectively
digest statistical information and make the best use of it. We saw, up close,
a very significant problem—the failure of our voting system to convert peo-

ple's vote intentions into counted votes—chopped into lawsuit-sized pieces that obliterated the larger picture and led to legalistic solutions that often seemed to miss the point.

THE PALM BEACH COUNTY BUTTERFLY BALLOT

Through news stories and e-mail, each of us learned about the badly designed butterfly ballot the day after the election, Wednesday, November 8. We learned that some voters in Palm Beach County, many of them Jews and African Americans, believed that they had mistakenly voted for Pat Buchanan instead of Al Gore because of the design of the ballot, which had candidate names on both pages (the butterfly's "wings") and punch-holes down the middle. One look at the ballot suggested that it would be easy for Bush supporters, who only had to match the first name on the ballot with the first punch-hole, to cast their votes correctly. But it would be harder for Gore supporters, who had to match the second name on the left-hand side of the ballot with the third punch-hole in the center of the ballot. If a Gore supporter mistakenly punched the second hole, then he or she cast a vote for Pat Buchanan whose name was listed on the right-hand side of the ballot, somewhat higher on the page than Al Gore's name but somewhat lower than George Bush's name.[1] In addition, some Gore voters claimed that they had mistakenly punched the names of two candidates for president because the ballot said "vote for group" and there were punch-holes next to both Gore's and Lieberman's names. This mistake spoiled their ballots.

The election results in Palm Beach County suggested that a sizable number of people may have made these mistakes. Pat Buchanan received almost 20 percent of his total statewide support in Palm Beach County, which constitutes only about 7 percent of the voters in Florida.[2] A simple calculation reveals that more than 2,000 Gore supporters may have mistakenly voted for Buchanan. Furthermore, the number of multiply punched presidential ballots, called "overvotes," was more than 19,000. That seemed very high compared to other counties, leading to the possibility that thousands of Gore votes might have been lost because of the ballot form. With the presidential election result in Florida depending on a difference of less than 1,000 votes, the butterfly ballot might have made a big difference.

Although this evidence implicates the butterfly ballot, it is only circumstantial. Perhaps counties routinely have large "outliers" in votes for third-party candidates or in spoiled ballots. Perhaps there is a history of unusually strong Buchanan support in Palm Beach County, or perhaps there was some reason that he had strong support in 2000. Furthermore, perhaps Bush supporters were just as likely to make mistakes as Gore supporters so that the net effect on the presidential race was zero. These are the kinds of questions that sprang into our minds when we first heard about the butterfly ballot, and each of us chose to address them in his own way.[3]

HOW WE GOT INVOLVED AND WHAT WE FOUND

At Harvard University in Cambridge, Massachusetts, on Wednesday, November 8, Jasjeet Sekhon learned about the butterfly ballot and the large vote for Buchanan from Congressman Robert Wexler on CNN. Sekhon talked about it that day with Walter Mebane and Jonathan Wand of Cornell University. Although they thought it plausible that the ballot might have caused Gore supporters to vote for Buchanan, they did not believe that the evidence presented thus far made the case.

The basic statistical evidence that was circulating on Wednesday via e-mail and that was available on the Web by Thursday, November 9, had been done very quickly by Greg Adams and Chris Fastnow at Carnegie Mellon University.[4] Their analysis was also widely reported in the news media. They plotted the vote for Buchanan by total votes for Florida's sixty-seven counties and fitted a simple linear regression line to all counties but Palm Beach.[5] The plot showed that Palm Beach County appeared to be an extreme outlier with many more votes for Buchanan than might be expected given its size and partisanship. However, the statistical method used by Adams and Fastnow, ordinary least squares applied to votes instead of vote shares, was not well suited for detecting outliers, and their analysis used only Florida data. Perhaps every state in the country had such an outlier, and perhaps large counties such as Palm Beach tend to have substantial variability in their vote for third parties. After all, the total vote percentage for Patrick Buchanan in Palm Beach County was less than 1 percent (0.78 percent).[6]

Mebane, Sekhon, and Wand decided that none of the existing analysis could establish that Palm Beach County was an anomaly because of the butterfly ballot. Palm Beach County might just be one of many U.S. counties that had somewhat deviant but statistically understandable values for the Buchanan vote. They decided that a convincing analysis would require more data and better statistical methods. By late Wednesday night, they found that more sophisticated analysis using countywide regressions uncovered additional outliers, but none in counties as large as Palm Beach.

In Chicago at Northwestern University, Ken Shotts sent out an e-mail to colleagues and friends the day after the election with some very simple data analysis regarding the Buchanan vote in Palm Beach County. He also talked about the issue by telephone with his colleague Michael Herron who was visiting Harvard for the year. Herron agreed with Shotts that it seemed surprising to find so many Buchanan votes in a county with a large Jewish and African-American population, but he wondered whether there was some plausible explanation other than the ballot form. Perhaps there was some hidden source of Buchanan support in Palm Beach County. That evening, Shotts's father responded to his e-mail by saying that Shotts's analysis did not identify the source of the extra votes for Buchanan. Perhaps they were Bush voters who mistakenly voted for Buchanan. While thinking about his father's comments, Shotts realized that precinct-level data could be used to figure out where the votes came from.

At the University of California, Berkeley, Brady heard about the butterfly ballot on Wednesday through an e-mail, and he discussed the issue with his graduate students. The research that had been posted until that time had used only county-level data to establish that the Buchanan vote seemed anomalous, but Brady and his students agreed that precinct-level data were needed to determine whether the extra votes for Buchanan came from Bush or Gore supporters. One of Brady's graduate students, Laurel Elms, found Palm Beach County precinct-level data on the Internet and suggested that it looked like Buchanan votes were concentrated in liberal precincts. A convincing analysis, however, would require formulating and statistically estimating a model containing a behavioral parameter—the fraction of Gore voters who mistakenly voted for Buchanan. Moreover, the model would be even more convincing if it also estimated the proportion of Bush supporters who had mistakenly voted for Buchanan.

By shortly after noon on Thursday, Brady completed a paper that developed a statistical ("mixture") model that tested whether Bush or Gore voters were responsible for the unusually high Buchanan vote. He concluded, "Using data from the 67 Florida counties along with data from precincts in Palm Beach County, I find that there is a strong likelihood that over 2000 of the Buchanan votes in Palm Beach County were cast by Gore supporters who mistakenly punched Buchanan's name." Moreover, there was no evidence that Bush supporters had made the same mistake. In spare moments throughout the rest of the day, Brady sent out his paper via e-mail, and he posted it to his Website (http://ucdata.berkeley.edu).

At the same time, on Thursday, November 9, Wand was visiting Sekhon on the Harvard campus, and they ran into Michael Herron in Harvard Yard as they were going to lunch. Herron mentioned that he and Shotts were working on the Palm Beach County butterfly ballot. They decided that the five of them would work together to address three questions:

· Was Buchanan's vote in Palm Beach County really an outlier?
· Were the extra Buchanan votes from Gore supporters?
· Were the overvotes, those ballots with more than one candidate punched for president, Gore supporters?

After several days of intensive work, Wand, Shotts, Sekhon, Mebane, and Herron[7] posted a paper to the Web just before noon on Saturday, November 11, in which they concluded:

> We find that Buchanan's Palm Beach County vote total is not merely large but that in statistical terms it is extraordinary. Furthermore, we examine voting patterns within Palm Beach County and find strong statistical evidence that Buchanan voters are concentrated in the most liberal precincts of Palm Beach County. We also find that invalid, double-punched ballots—presumably double-punched for Gore and Buchanan—tend to come from relatively liberal precincts. These two findings are evidence for the claim that the ballot format in Palm Beach County led some Gore supporters mistakenly to vote for Buchanan and, in some cases, to vote for multiple presidential candidates.[8]

Three reporting units were identified in the paper as more irregular than Palm Beach County. Although we did not know it at the time, one of them (Mississippi County, Arkansas) turned out to be the result of an error in the data reported on the CNN Website. Another was a small New Hampshire township, Richmond, where over 10 percent of the presidential votes were for Buchanan (55 of 533 votes). The Republican voters in Richmond are very conservative judging by their votes in the 2000 presidential primary, but the total still appears high. The third anomaly was Jasper County, South Carolina, where one precinct, Tillman, accounted for 239 of Buchanan's 245 votes in the county, and in this precinct, there was only one vote for Gore, one for Bush, 111 for Nader (the next highest precinct had three votes for Nader), and 5 votes for the remaining candidates.[9] Affidavits collected from registered voters in Tillman eventually showed that many more registered voters actually voted for presidential candidates George Bush and Al Gore. On December 13, a new election was ordered for county offices in Jasper. These results confirm that in the November 11 paper we were finding true outliers.

Later work using even more sophisticated robust estimation methods has shown that Palm Beach County had the most anomalous Buchanan vote in 2000 among all of the 2,998 counties and independent cities (about 96.4 percent of all such units in the nation) that we were able to examine.[10] This work also shows that there is nothing anomalous about the Reform Party vote for other offices in Palm Beach County in 2000 or 1996. Consequently, Buchanan's support in 2000 cannot be attributed to Reform Party stalwarts.

By noon on Saturday, November 11, we had come to a common conclusion. For all six of us, the data told a very clear story. Palm Beach County was an extraordinary outlier even when compared to the entire nation. Gore supporters and not Bush supporters had mistakenly voted for Buchanan in Palm Beach County. Spoiled ballots came disproportionately from liberal precincts. Almost all of the other analyses posted to the Web came to the same conclusions, and the dissenters based their complaints on work that had not taken the precautions we had. Unlike most social science data that tell equivocal stories, these data told a very clear and consistent tale. Every analysis proclaimed that something very odd had happened in Palm Beach County.

GOING TO FLORIDA

On Saturday morning, a Fort Lauderdale attorney, David Krathen, contacted several of us. Krathen had filed a lawsuit in the Fifteenth Judicial Circuit on November 9 that contested the legality of the butterfly ballot on behalf of two Palm Beach County voters, Beverly Rogers and Ray Kaplan.[11] Krathen indicated that all the legal work was being done pro bono and that there was no money to pay airfares or expenses, much less any fees, for expert witnesses. But he needed help and hoped we would come to Florida. All of us decided to go.

Palm Beach and Fort Lauderdale — Monday, November 13

In Florida we faced the difficult task of translating our data analysis into terms that made sense to journalists and to the legal system. Our paramount concern was to ensure the integrity of our analysis. For each of us, our professional reputations as trustworthy and competent researchers mattered much more than anything else. At the same time, as teachers we recognized the need to explain our results in ways that were comprehensible to those who lacked our background and training.

On Monday afternoon, we were off to the Palm Beach County Courthouse, about forty miles north of Fort Lauderdale. After getting off the freeway, we encountered blocked roads, people holding protest signs about the butterfly ballot, and police everywhere near the courthouse. At least half a dozen helicopters were circling overhead. Later we learned that the demonstrators were going to a march led by Jesse Jackson and that he had been ushered away by police as Bush supporters came at his entourage chanting "Jesse, go home!"[12]

On entering the courthouse, one of our team explained our purpose to an African-American security guard and asked for directions. The guard courteously complied and volunteered the opinion that the butterfly ballot had been intentionally designed to harm African Americans in particular. All the evidence, including the fact that the ballot was approved by a Democratic commissioner of elections, suggests this is not true, but the security guard's comments and the demonstration outside suggested the depth of feeling about the issue.

After the hearing, which dealt with procedural matters, we walked out into a sea of cameras and a press conference. At this time, we began to realize that the press craved precise numbers and expressions of certainty that we were only partly prepared to provide. We felt confident that at least two thousand Gore supporters had mistakenly voted for Buchanan, but we did not know what to say about the spoiled ballots because we had very limited data on them.

Palm Beach and Fort Lauderdale — Tuesday, November 14

On Tuesday morning we had to prepare for a possible hearing. The trick, we realized, was that we needed pictures that told the story simply and clearly. But the simplest figures, such as those done by Greg Adams and Chris Fastnow, were not as acceptable technically as the figures in our papers. And the technically superior figures, for example, "Histogram of Discrepancies from Expected Vote for Buchanan—4481 Reporting Units in 46 States," from the paper by Wand and colleagues, suffered from using concepts such as "studentized residual" and having three reporting units that were even more extreme than Palm Beach County. All of this could be explained, of course, but the Adams picture was appealing because it had direct impact. Any child could plot Buchanan votes versus total votes, and in this picture Palm Beach County stood far apart from other Florida counties.

We also faced the problem of demonstrating why Buchanan's vote came from Gore supporters and not Bush supporters. Brady's mathematical argument, as satisfying as it was to us, would not do. The solution was to develop a hypothetical example that eventually found its way into Brady's affidavit, "Report on Voting and Ballot Form in Palm Beach County." In this example, we start from the fact that in Florida, and in Broward and Miami-Dade Counties just to the south of Palm Beach County, the fraction of Buchanan voters increased with the fraction of Bush voters in a precinct. Not surprisingly, Buchanan's support is usually greatest where there is strong Republican support. Then we show that the positive relationship between Buchanan's vote share and Bush's vote share becomes even stronger if Bush voters are mistakenly voting for Buchanan but becomes weaker if Gore voters are mistakenly voting for Buchanan. In fact, if enough Gore voters are mistakenly voting for Buchanan, then the percent of Buchanan voters in a precinct *decreases* with the fraction of Bush voters in a precinct: that is, the relationship between Buchanan votes and Bush votes becomes negative. Put another way, the fraction of Buchanan voters *increases* with the fraction of *Gore* voters. And that is exactly what we find in Palm Beach County but not in nearby Broward or Miami-Dade.

Finally, we faced the problem of explaining the overvotes. Because there

were more than nineteen thousand overvotes, the overvote story appealed
to the attorneys, who wanted the biggest possible number of affected
votes.[13] But it was the hardest story to tell. We knew that the fraction of
spoiled ballots increased with Gore support in a precinct, but there are
many reasons why ballots can be spoiled. While we were in Palm Beach
County we found data reported by Peter Orszag and Jonathan Orszag (at
http://www.sbgo.com/election.htm) that described the overvotes in the 1
percent sample of ballots hand counted by the Palm Beach County Elections Canvassing Commission on November 11. Based on that sample the
commission had decided to do a complete manual recount of all the Palm
Beach County ballots.

Of the 144 multiply punched ballots in the Palm Beach County sample,
132 had double punches and 114 (79 percent) had adjacent double
punches. Among the adjacent double punches, 80 were for Buchanan and
Gore and 21 were for Gore and McReynolds while 11 were for Bush and
Buchanan and one was for "blank two" (the box above the box for Bush)
and Bush. A simple projection might suggest that 70 percent (101 of 144)
of all the overvotes in Palm Beach County were intended to be votes for
Gore while 8 percent (12 of 144) were intended to be votes for Bush, but
it seemed dubious to allocate all the votes away from Buchanan, not to
allow that some proportion of the four key patterns of double punches
were meaningless errors, and to extrapolate to all of Palm Beach County
from a 1 percent sample comprising four nonrandomly selected precincts.[14] We felt confident that Gore had lost votes from double punching
caused by the poor ballot design, but it was hard to come up with a definitive minimum number for those votes. Eventually, in his affidavit completed very early Thursday morning, November 16, Mebane chose 3,400
as the minimum net number of votes that Gore certainly lost, although he
strongly believed the actual number was much higher than that.

As we went running out the door to go to Palm Beach County for another
court appearance, we were handed affidavits from Palm Beach County voters. We read them as we drove north and found confirmation for our theories about what was happening. One woman wrote:

> I had reviewed the sample ballot before going to the polling place, and had
> even gone through training to serve as a poll worker. Even though I was
> familiar with the sample ballot and had voted many times before, I found the
> ballot I received on November 7th very confusing. . . . Because I was so con-
> fused, though, I asked a poll worker for assistance lining up the holes on the
> ballot properly, and informed her that I was having trouble lining up the
> holes to see which hole I should punch to vote for Vice President Al Gore to
> be the next president. She did not provide me with the assistance I requested
> in lining up the ballot in the voting machine, and just told me I should "punch
> the hole" near Vice President Gore's name in order to vote for him. This was

not at all helpful to me, since my problem was that I could not tell which was the hole nearest to Vice President Gore's name. . . . I punched the second hole on the ballot, believing that to be the correct hole to punch in order to vote for the Democratic candidate for President since they were listed second on the ballot. . . . My husband, who was at the polls voting with me and had started filling out his ballot shortly after I did, noticed my confusion and told me that a poll worker had informed him that the proper way to vote for the Democratic candidates was to punch both the second and third holes on the ballot in order to vote for both Vice President Gore and Senator Lieberman. This seemed very unusual and surprising to me, but I believed it since I understood it was what the poll worker had instructed us to do.

This affidavit, one of thousands, shows how some voters mistakenly voted for Buchanan when they meant to vote for Gore and how other voters might have spoiled their ballot by punching two names because of the mysterious instruction to "vote for group" or the confusion of holes. Although only about 1 percent of the Gore supporters mistakenly voted for Buchanan and about 4 percent spoiled their ballots by making multiple punches for Gore and some other candidate, these numbers are very high for machine failures. Banking machines, cash registers, or telephones that failed in 5 percent of the total transactions would certainly be sent to the junkyard.[15]

The affidavits not only told us something about the problems that had bedeviled voters, they provided us with an unexpected finding. While reading an affidavit, Brady found a copy of the absentee ballot and realized that it did not have the same defects as the butterfly ballot. In effect, Palm Beach County had run a quasi-experiment. More than 45,000 absentee voters received a ballot without the problems of the butterfly ballot, and almost 400,000 people voted on election day with the butterfly ballot. We knew that absentees tended to be somewhat different from election day voters, but they were still a pretty good control group for the butterfly ballot "treatment" because they were not that different. In fact, absentee voters tend to be more conservative than election day voters, so that if we found a lower rate of voting for Buchanan among the absentees than among the election day voters in Palm Beach County, then we would have very strong evidence for the butterfly ballot's effects.

When we got back to Fort Lauderdale, we compared the vote for Buchanan among those who voted absentee with the Buchanan vote among those who voted on election day. We also looked at the same information for nearby Broward and Miami-Dade Counties. The results were striking, and they are summarized in figure 1. In Broward and Miami-Dade Counties, the absentee voters were slightly more likely to vote for Buchanan, but in Palm Beach County, the *election day voters* were almost four times more likely to vote for Buchanan.

This was the smoking gun we had been looking for. When combined

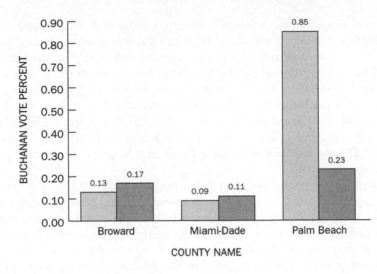

Figure 1. Buchanan vote by ballot type and county.

with the rest of our evidence, it seemed very hard to doubt that most of the Buchanan vote was not his. Moreover, the figure of 0.23 percent of absentee voters who voted for Buchanan provided a highly defensible upper bound for the "true" Buchanan vote percentage throughout Palm Beach County, and it led us to conclude that approximately 2,400 people cast their votes for Buchanan in error. Once again, the data were converging on the same answer.

We prepared for a possible court appearance until late into Tuesday night. By this time, a number of lawyers, led by George Badey, had appeared from the Philadelphia law firm that was connected to the case through one of the plaintiffs. The lawyers were smart and tough-minded, and the legal issues became clear and vexing. We had excellent evidence to show that the butterfly ballot had wreaked havoc with people's votes. But the case had to revolve on a clear point of law that was violated, and it had to seek a remedy that was legal and politically feasible as well.

The original brief filed by our lawyers noted that Florida law requires that the candidates for any office be listed on the ballot so that the candidate of the party that received the highest number of votes for governor in the last gubernatorial election is listed first and the candidate of the party that received the second highest number of votes is listed second. Jeb Bush, of course, won the last Florida gubernatorial election, so the presidential candidate of his party, George W. Bush, was listed first. The Democratic candidate, Al Gore should have been listed second. But was he? Al Gore was listed second in the left-hand column, but he was third on the ballot, with Patrick Buchanan clearly above him, if one considers vertical placement. Voting for Gore required punching the third, not the second, punchhole. The ballot assigned the number "3" to George W. Bush, "4" to Patrick Buchanan, and "5" to Al Gore. By this reckoning, Gore was second on the ballot only if people in Palm Beach County counted "3, 5, 7, 9, 11, 13, 4, 6, 8, 10." Mebane wondered if people in Florida also taught their children the "ACEs" instead of the "ABCs." Other features of the ballot arguably violated Florida law, but were these features enough to convince a judge that it was defective?

The proposed remedy was even more controversial. All five of the voters' suits, including our own, asked for a revote in Palm Beach County. Yet a revote had never occurred in a presidential election, and there were serious equity problems with a new election. Obviously only those people who had voted on election day should be allowed to vote in the new election, and that could be controlled by voting lists. But what would prevent third-party voters from changing their votes now that they knew their votes could decide the election? In Palm Beach County, about 10,200 people had ostensibly voted for third-party candidates. If we take these votes at face value, then the third-party candidates of the Right obtained 4,481 votes and the third-party candidates of the Left obtained 5,969 votes, most of them for Ralph Nader. If the Right went for Bush and the Left for Gore, then Gore would surely be advantaged in a revote. But this analysis is too simple, because Nader supporters in Florida were, according to exit polls and our own analysis of voting data, more centrist than elsewhere, and a significant minority of them would vote for Bush if they switched from Nader. Maybe Bush had the advantage. Whatever the truth, third-party voters posed a real challenge to a revote.

The facts of the butterfly ballot case proclaimed a significant injustice, but the law appeared blind to the problem and unable to deal with it. After spending hours refining our statistical arguments and becoming sobered by the legal complexities, we went to bed around 3:30 A.M. feeling ready to testify.

Palm Beach and Fort Lauderdale — Wednesday, November 15

By Wednesday, we had been in Florida for several days and were getting anxious to either testify or go home. At the Palm Beach County Courthouse, our lawyer, Gary Farmer, told Judge Labarga that he had expert witnesses who were ready to go, right away. Barry Richard, Bush's lawyer who was participating via a phone link to Tallahassee, objected vigorously and called the request "outrageous" and beyond anything he had experienced in his years of practice. His list of outrages was long and partly justified, although we suspected that his indignation was also part of the Republican stalling strategy. Judge Labarga ended the discussion by saying that he did not want to hear about the facts because he was concerned about the law. He was not sure, he said, that he had the power, constitutionally, to order a revote in a presidential election. The facts might not matter because the law might not be able to solve the problem even if it existed. He told the lawyers, "Here is your homework. Find me a case anywhere in American history where such a revote has been ordered in a presidential election." He wanted briefs by 5:00 P.M. the next day, Thursday. We adjourned. Our lawyers conducted a press conference in front of the courthouse, but, sensitive to the point Richard had raised about publicity seeking, we were kept away from it.

This Wednesday hearing was the bittersweet high point of our trip. The case was going forward, and there might be a chance of success if the lawyers could find some way to argue for a revote. But we would not be testifying anytime soon, and the legal hurdle was very high.

We gathered back at Krathen's office in Fort Lauderdale, and we worked together until early Thursday morning to develop two affidavits, one about the Gore supporters who mistakenly voted for Buchanan and the other about the overvotes that were disproportionately cast by Gore supporters. Brady took the lead on the first and easier task, Mebane on the second, more difficult one. The main points of contention regarding overvotes were how to extrapolate from the 1 percent sample and how much of the overvote in Palm Beach County to attribute to the butterfly ballot design. High proportions of overvotes occurred in other elections that did not use the butterfly ballot. For the purpose of calculating the number of votes that were changed in Palm Beach County as a result of the butterfly ballot it was important to think carefully about how to define the baseline level of error.[16] Through heated discussions, we clarified our thoughts and arguments, and eventually a consensus was achieved. We felt confident about the facts.

Our later work has made us even more confident of our results. Wand and his coworkers show that the difference between the election day Buchanan vote and the absentee Buchanan vote in Palm Beach County is the most anomalous of any county in Florida.[17] Brady and Elms map the election day and absentee ballot precinct-level Buchanan vote for Palm Beach and its surrounding counties.[18] They show that the election day Buchanan vote increases precipitously (typically quadrupling) on reaching the Palm Beach County border from any direction, but there are no abrupt changes for the absentee Buchanan vote. Wand and his coworkers also use precinct-level data to show that Buchanan support is positively associated with support for the Democratic senatorial candidate, which only makes sense if much of Buchanan's support comes from Democrats who mistakenly marked Buchanan's name instead of Al Gore's.[19] Using ballot images that provide a complete record of each voter's choices for all races, Wand and colleagues go on to show that on election day ballots, voting for the Democratic senatorial candidate is positively associated with voting for Buchanan for president. But this is not the case for absentee ballots. Finally, in unpublished work based on overvote data, Brady shows that 83 percent of the 9,971 people who punched two adjacent holes on their ballots included Gore as one of the two punches, but only 16 percent of these 9,971 voters punched Bush as one of their two punches. Brady concludes that the difference, about 6,600, is a plausible lower bound on the net number of votes lost by Gore because of spoiled ballots.[20] Using the various estimates from these papers, the simple fact is that Gore lost a total of at least 9,000 votes because of the butterfly ballot.

RESOLUTION

The facts did not matter. On Friday, November 17, Judge Labarga considered whether there was any legal basis for a revote. "I think," he said at the hearing, "I have as deep an appreciation of the right to vote as anyone else in this county. My parents brought me here so I'd have that right. If I rule the Constitution does not allow for a re-election, it will be the hardest decision I ever make."[21]

On Monday, November 20, he issued his opinion. A revote could not be held because "our forefathers included clear and unambiguous language in the Constitution of the United States which requires that presidential 'electors' be elected on the same day throughout the United States." Moreover, the constitutional prohibition was sensible because "the danger of one candidate benefitting from an undue advantage in a revote or a new election is always a strong possibility. If anything, for this reason alone, Presidential elections must be held on the same day throughout the United States."[22] The plaintiffs' case was denied without any witnesses being presented.

This opinion was immediately appealed and eventually found its way to the Florida Supreme Court. In the appeal, the lawyers for one of the cases that had been consolidated with ours proposed another remedy—statistical readjustment of the vote totals. If accepted, this would mean that the presidency would be determined by statistical imputation, an approach that the Republicans strongly opposed when it was suggested for adjusting the U.S. Census. It seemed unlikely they would find it palatable for adjusting the presidential vote.

The Florida Supreme Court took a different tack than the circuit court judge, but they arrived at the same outcome on Friday, December 1. By a unanimous decision, they found, "[E]ven accepting appellants' allegations, we conclude as a matter of law that the Palm Beach County ballot does not constitute substantial noncompliance with the statutory requirements mandating the voiding of the election."[23] The court's contorted double negative suggested that the ballot had some defects but not enough to trigger a legal challenge. Because the ballot was legal, Judge Labarga's ruling on the remedy was not necessary and was vacated. In the end, the Palm Beach County butterfly ballot case foundered on the unwillingness of the Florida Supreme Court to find the ballot defective, as a matter of law, and not on their likely reluctance to recommend a revote.

Did we accomplish anything? Legally nothing was accomplished. But practically our efforts, along with those of others, were the first step in a national civics lesson about the inadequacies of our voting and vote counting systems. Our work clearly showed that the butterfly ballot cost Al Gore thousands of votes, more than enough for him to have won Florida and the presidency. We made our case through the Internet to academics around the country. Our results were reported widely through the media, and the butterfly ballot itself now serves as a catchphrase for bad design.

WHAT WE LEARNED

The Palm Beach butterfly ballot story reads like a classic case of conservative jurisprudence recoiling from trying to right wrongs that vex the human condition. Anyone can see that the standard for calling a ballot defective must be very high and that revotes should be seldom employed, especially in presidential elections where the Humpty Dumpty of third-party preferences cannot be put back together after the initial vote.

All this would seem more palatable to us if the ultimate outcome of the Florida election follies had not been a 5–4 decision of the U.S. Supreme Court that used the Equal Protection Clause and arcane aspects of the Electoral College to justify the abandonment of a statewide recount. But if equal protection mattered so much for the statewide recount, why did it not matter for the citizens of Palm Beach County? And why did it not matter for those citizens who had to use punch-card systems whose error rates are at least five times greater than optical scanning machines used in other counties?[24]

NOTES

1. Voter confusion may have been increased by the fact that all other races were in the more standard format in which candidates are listed on one side of the ballot. Only in the presidential race were candidates listed on both sides, thus creating the "butterfly."

2. There are two other stories regarding this ballot. David McReynolds, a So-

cialist Party candidate for president was listed just below Buchanan on the right-hand side of the ballot with some overlap with Al Gore on the left-hand side. Mc-Reynolds received 302 votes in the initial Palm Beach County count, almost 50 percent of the 618 votes he received statewide and 268 more than he received in any other county. Howard Phillips of the conservative Constitution Party was listed below McReynolds with some overlap with Ralph Nader. Phillips received 188 votes in Palm Beach County, 78 more than he received in any other Florida county and 14 percent of his statewide total. If the Buchanan, Phillips, and McReynolds votes are taken seriously, then Palm Beach County has the remarkable distinction of being the stronghold among Florida counties both for the right-wing Buchanan and Phillips and for the left-wing McReynolds.

3. We were not the only ones to produce an analysis of the butterfly ballot. Within four days of the election, the following people had posted analyses: Greg Adams at Carnegie Mellon University and Chris Fastnow at Chatham College; Layth Alwan at the University of Wisconsin–Milwaukee; Christopher Carroll at Johns Hopkins University; Burt Monroe at Indiana University; Craig Fox at Duke University; Bruce Hansen at the University of Wisconsin; John Irons at Amherst College; Robert Max Jackson at New York University; Jonathan O'Keefe, Peter Orszag, and Jonathan Orszag at Sebago Associates; Till Rosenband at MIT; Matthew Ruben at the University of California, San Diego; Robert Shimer at Princeton University; and Chris Volinsky at AT&T Labs. We apologize to anyone we have missed, and we note that many others added work later.

4. Considering the limits of the time available, Adams and Fastnow's initial analysis was useful and informative, but methodologists are picky people. It was clear that their work was only a starting point, and they improved on their analysis in subsequent days. See http://madison.hss.cmu.edu/.

5. They also plotted Buchanan vote versus Bush vote and Buchanan vote versus Gore vote.

6. Indeed, skeptics such as Robert Shimer (2000) of Princeton University and Patrick Anderson (2000) of Anderson Consulting soon jumped in to make exactly these points. Shimer argued that "the evidence that Palm Beach voted too much for Buchanan is based on a spurious correlation driven to a large extent by the size of Palm Beach County. The oft-quoted significance of this result is based on an erroneous assumption of normal residuals, which is inapplicable given the low average vote share for Buchanan." Our methods avoid these pitfalls.

7. The authors are listed in reverse alphabetical order.

8. Wand et al. completed their overvote analysis by using a proxy measure, the total number of votes in the Senate election for each precinct as a proxy for the total number of ballots. Subsequent analysis using the actual number of overvotes has led to the same conclusion.

9. In the 1996 presidential election, Tillman, a precinct in Jasper County, cast 288 votes for Clinton, 102 votes for Dole, 19 votes for Perot, and 2 votes for the remaining candidates. Although a revote was ultimately ordered for countywide offices, local officials initially said that "voter error led to the odd results." "Voters Say They Erred in Tillman," *Beauford Gazette* (S.C.), November 10, 2000.

10. Wand et al. (2001).

11. Case No. CL0010992AF in the Circuit Court for Fifteenth Judicial Circuit,

Palm Beach Florida: Beverly Rogers and Ray Kaplan, Plaintiffs v. The Elections Canvassing Commission of the State of Florida; Governor Jeb Bush; Secretary of State Katherine Harris; Clay Roberts, Director of the Division of Elections for the State of Florida; Theresa LePore, Supervisor of Elections for Palm Beach County; The Palm Beach County Elections Canvassing Commission; Al Gore; and George W. Bush, Defendants. The state-level defendants were subsequently dropped, and on November 13 the case was consolidated with other similar citizens' actions by Administrative Order No. 2.061–11/00.

12. *The Stuart News/Port St. Lucie News* (Stuart, Fla.), November 14, 2000, Martin County Section, at A1.

13. The machine recount completed in Palm Beach County on November 11 recorded 19,147 overvotes, whereas the complete manual count completed on November 26 recorded 19,213 overvotes. The Palm Beach County Supervisor of Elections reported these counts in the file http://pbcelections.org/ElectionResults/2000/GEN/00genhc.htm.

14. The Gore campaign selected three of the precincts (162E, 193, and 193E) comprising 4,346 of the 4,694 ballots in the sample. The Elections Commission selected the fourth precinct (6B) to get as near as possible to 1 percent of all the ballots cast in the county.

15. Some of these multiple punches for the same office may have been intended, but the overvote rate for the presidential race in the sixteen Florida counties with state-of-the-art Global Accuvote optical scan machines was less than 0.4 percent, which suggests that intentional overvotes are typically one-tenth the number in Palm Beach County. It is also worth noting that the "failure rate" described in the text does not include the 2 percent undervotes (cases in which there appeared to be no vote for president) that occurred in Palm Beach County.

16. At the time we were unaware of the stories that had broken about the large number of spoiled ballots in Duval County, where the presidential ballot spanned two pages but lacked the two key features of the butterfly ballot. After leaving Florida, we were able to isolate key differences between Duval and Palm Beach Counties, but it would have been very difficult for us to complete such an analysis Wednesday night in the course of preparing affidavits.

17. Wand et al. (2001).

18. Brady and Elms (2001).

19. Wand et al. (2001).

20. This figure was reported in Joel Engelhardt and Scott McCabe, "Election 2000: Over-votes Cost Gore the Election in Florida," *Palm Beach Post,* March 11, 2001, A1A. Brady was a consultant on this article.

21. "GOP Holdups in Palm Beach Upset Dems," Associated Press, November 17, 2000.

22. Fifteenth Judicial Circuit, Palm Beach Florida, "Order on Plaintiff's Complaint for Declaratory, Injunctive, and Other Relief Arising from Plaintiffs' Claims of Massive Voter Confusion Resulting from the Use of a 'Butterfly' Type Ballot During the Election Held on November 7, 2000."

23. Fladell v. Palm Beach County Canvassing Board, 772 So.2d 1240 (Fla. Dec. 1, 2000).

24. The Global Accuvote optical scan devices (used in sixteen Florida counties)

have an undervote rate of about three per thousand and an overvote rate of about three to four per thousand for a total under/overvote rate of 0.7 percent. Punch-card systems (used in twenty-four Florida counties) have an undervote rate of about fifteen per thousand and an overvote rate of about twenty-five per thousand for a total under/overvote rate of 4.0 percent, which is more than five times the rate for the Global Accuvote systems.

REFERENCES

Adams, Greg. D., and Chris Fastnow. 2000. "A Note on Voting Irregularities in Palm Beach, Fl." <http://madison.hss.cmu.edu/>. Manuscript. Accessed: May 1, 2001.

Anderson, Patrick L. 2000. "Statistical Analysis of the Florida Presidential Election Results—Comparison with Michigan." <http://www.andersoneconomicgroup.com/elections/stat_anal_FL.htm>. Manuscript. Accessed: May 1, 2001.

Brady, Henry. 2000. "What Happened in Palm Beach?" <http://ucdata.berkeley.edu>. Manuscript. Accessed: May 1, 2001.

Brady, Henry E., and Laurel Elms. 2001. "Mapping the Buchanan Vote Escarpment in Palm Beach County, Florida." Paper presented at the annual meeting of the Public Choice Society, March 9–11, San Antonio, Texas.

Engelhardt, Joel, and Scott McCabe. 2001. "Election 2000: Over-votes Cost Gore the Election in Florida." *Palm Beach Post,* March 11, A1A.

"GOP Holdups in Palm Beach Upset Dems." 2000. Associated Press. November 17.

Markey, Bob. 2000. "Palm Beach Democrats Confident: Tension Rises as Thousands Join Rev. Jesse Jackson in Downtown March." *Stuart News/Port St. Lucie News.* November 14, Al.

Shimer, Robert. 2000. "Election 2000." <www.princeton.edu/shimer/election.html>. Manuscript. Accessed: May 1, 2001.

"Voters Say They Erred in Tillman." 2000. *Beauford Gazette,* November 10.

Wand, Jonathan N., Kenneth W. Shotts, Jasjeet S. Sekhon, Walter R. Mebane Jr., and Michael C. Herron. 2000. "Voting Irregularities in Palm Beach County." <http://elections.fas.harvard.edu/wssmh/>. Manuscript. Accessed: May 1, 2001.

Wand, Jonathan N., Kenneth W. Shotts, Jasjeet S. Sekhon, Walter R. Mebane Jr., Michael C. Herron, and Henry E. Brady. 2001. "The Butterfly Did It: The Aberrant Vote for Buchanan in Palm Beach County, Florida." <http://elections.fas.harvard.edu/>. Manuscript. Accessed: May 1, 2001.

Part Two

THE MACHINERY
OF DEMOCRACY
IN AMERICA

3

DISPUTING ELECTIONS

Richard H. Pildes

The most incendiary issue any democratic system can confront might well be the selection of its chief executive when election results are disputed, obscure, and sharply divided. If we consider this issue from the perspective of democratic institutional design, we should anticipate that such situations are likely to arise eventually in any long-running democracy. In America, we have had disputed elections to the Senate and House regularly throughout our history and, on occasion, though not in the peculiar form of the 2000 election, for the presidency. From an *ex ante* perspective, then, we might ask what institutional structures and legal frameworks we ought to put in place, in advance of this charged moment, that are most likely to produce the most widely acceptable resolution to this potentially most explosive question. But we also now live in an *ex post* world, for this moment has happened and we are asked to look back and evaluate it: we have watched the American system struggle with this issue and generate a result whose merits—by which I mean whose public acceptance—will be disputed, as the essays in this volume demonstrate, for years to come. In this brief essay, I want to compare an *ex ante* perspective on disputed presidential elections with the actual institutional arrangements and legal structures that were in place and deployed to resolve, at least formally, the disputed 2000 presidential election. My aim is not so much to praise or condemn the Supreme Court's resolution. Instead, I want to provide perspective, and, I hope, illumination, on both the general nature of the issue and the specific institutional and legal reasons so much controversy concerning that resolution was and remains inevitable.

I

We start with a context in which the partisan and national political stakes are at their height. And by definition, the situation is one in which voters are closely divided, perhaps with allegations of fraud, or negligence, or technological error, or changes being made to the rules in the middle of the game swirling in the air. From the perspective of the institutional designer, in my view, the key insight ought to be that, under these circumstances, *any resolution of the disputed election is likely to be viewed as motivated by partisanship by nearly half the electorate*—that half whose candidate ultimately loses. This is a matter of likely public perception, regardless of the "actual facts"—as if we could ever know these, in any event—concerning the actual motivations of the relevant institutional actors. Conceivably, if the rules of resolving such a dispute could be made exceptionally clear in advance and their meaning widely accepted at the moment such rules were being applied, the allegations of partisan motivation could be tempered. But that situation is unlikely: precisely where the stakes are so high, forceful pressure will be brought to bear so powerfully on the preexisting legal structure that any existing ambiguity will be exploited and previously clear rules will be made to seem uncertain. And as we will see shortly, the rules in place before the 2000 presidential election were so uncertain that it would take little pressure at all to displace any sense of consensus, capable of transcending partisan politics, on their proper application.

Virtually any actor who touches an issue bearing on the resolution of a disputed presidential election is, therefore, likely to be scorched by the flames of partisan charges. That is all the more likely if that actor has—or is perceived to have—any discretion at all in the interpretation and application of the previously existing legal rules. Every act of discretion or interpretation now takes place in a context in which the result might determine the outcome of a presidential election; there is simply no way for the actors to blind themselves to the likely political consequences of their judgments. Rather than act behind a veil of ignorance, the relevant actors are irretrievably corrupted with knowledge of who will be advantaged, who will lose, as a result of their rulings. As a result, half of public opinion, at least, will likely view any action as partisan in motivation. This seems to have been true of nearly every player and institution involved in resolving the Florida election dispute, from the trial judges to the secretary of state to the Florida Supreme Court to the United States Supreme Court. At any given moment, nearly half the country appears to have believed that one of these figures acted from partisan motivations. It is no less true of academic commentators: we too are inevitably singed by the partisan charges surrounding such a dispute, for as soon as we take positions on legal issues of such magnitude, we find it hard to convince others of the purity of our reasoning—even to convince fellow academics. And as others have pointed out, there does appear to be an overwhelming correlation between the seeming political preferences of legal academics and their assessments of *Bush v. Gore*.[1]

For the institutional designer, then, the first counsel of wisdom, in my view, is to accept and acknowledge this fact. The task cannot usefully be thought of as eliminating the potential for partisan bias when designing institutions to resolve such disputes. The more clear the rules are in advance, the better, of course, but there will likely be residual areas where closure of this sort is simply unavailable and exercises of judgment and discretion therefore unavoidable. Instead, the task is to embrace the reality that the charge of partisan bias will itself be unavoidable. Whatever the institutional configurations chosen, half the electorate at the end of the day will believe that those who resolved the dispute acted out of partisan politics. The institutions that resolve a dispute of this sort will, therefore, inevitably be contaminated; they will be seen as partisan. The question, then, is not how to avoid this perception but where to allow it to focus itself. Given the inevitability of partisan contagion that will infect those who resolve such a dispute, where is that contagion best located, and given that it cannot be eliminated, how can it be most contained?

II

The Constitution does not provide a mechanism for resolving disputed presidential elections. This has long been considered one of the major gaps in its original design. From the time of the first disputed presidential election, in 1800, Congress recognized the dangers this lacuna posed and attempted to create a legislative solution. But the Constitution does explicitly create an institutional mechanism for resolving disputed elections for the other national offices, the House and the Senate. It is instructive to understand both what those mechanisms are and why the Constitution could not adopt a directly analogous mechanism for resolving disputed presidential elections.

The Constitution turns the power over to political bodies for resolving disputed House and Senate elections. Indeed, the Constitution assigns this power to the very body to which the disputing candidates are seeking election. Thus, Article I, section 5 makes both the U.S. House and the U.S. Senate the ultimate judge "of the elections, returns, and qualifications of its own members."[2] The same is true for many state legislatures.[3] Moreover, this system permits other institutions to play a preliminary role in collecting information relevant to such disputes while still leaving the ultimate power of decision in the hands of the political bodies, the House and the Senate. For example, according to the Supreme Court of the 1970s, in a close Senate election states conduct manual recounts, with the Senate then free to use or reject those recounted figures in forming its own independent judgment[4] (interestingly, the Senate has at times exercised this power by engaging in its own manual recounts—including selective recounts of only that small subset of ballots actually in dispute, as well as recounts that override state law in order to ensure that the "intent of the voter" has been honored).[5]

But the Constitution could not similarly make the Electoral College the judge of disputed elections of *its* members—the presidential electors. For the Electoral College was not designed in any way that it could conceivably be made the judge of its own disputed elections. The Electoral College has no continuous, institutional existence at all. Constructed to be an evanescent body, which comes into being for a single and transitory function and then immediately dissolves, the Electoral College never even meets collectively in one place. Thus the Electoral College simply could not play the same role the House and Senate do in resolving their own disputed elections. We might, then, ask two questions. First, what were the legal structures in place to which the candidates were required to turn instead—and why did those structures have the form they did? Second, if we take the constitutional structure for disputed House and Senate elections as a desirable model, what institutional structures for disputed presidential elections are most nearly analogous, given that the Electoral College itself cannot be used to play this role?

III

From these large institutional questions, to which we will return, let us now shift our focus to the specifics of the Florida election dispute. Much commentary tends to focus on the most dramatic and final moment in this dispute, the Supreme Court's decision in *Bush v. Gore,* but I want to focus on the background legal conditions and structures that created the context in which that decision was rendered. In doing so, I want to highlight four aspects of those specifics that, from my perspective as a voting-rights specialist, reveal why the situation facing the courts, state and federal, was unlikely to produce a legal solution that would find wide acceptance among diverse judges. These aspects might be more visible now than they were in the heat of the litigation. My aim here is to suggest that even before or apart from the perceptions of partisan motivation there were substantial factors that made a clear, internal legal resolution not very likely.

1. The Problem of the Recount as a Surrogate Remedy

The dispute over votes in the 2000 presidential election was not, primarily or initially, a dispute over the kind of issues that came to center on a manual recount of undervotes and overvotes. This fact is easy to forget, but in my view, it is a key to making sense of much of the legal turmoil that eventually followed. The manual recount issues came to dominate the national stage for over a month; the most vivid visual memories of the election no doubt involve individual ballots being held up to the light; and the Supreme Court's ultimate decision rested on the constitutional standards for conducting such a recount. But none of these issues had anything to do with what prompted immediate questions about the vote in the first days after the election. Recall that attention at first centered on the butterfly ballot that had been used in Palm Beach County and that had produced a staggering 19,000 invalid ballots because voters had voted for two presidential candidates and had also generated a difficult to explain 3,407 votes for Patrick Buchanan. At the end of the litigation, the two sides were 537 votes apart and engaged in hand-to-hand combat over individual ballots. The votes that were actually fought over in the recount litigation were dwarfed by the nearly 20,000 invalid ballots in Palm Beach County, ballots that were invalid because, it appeared to many, voters had been confused by the ballot's design into mistakenly voting for two candidates. In the first days after the election, the Gore campaign was able to occupy a kind of moral high ground, with literally tens of thousands of ballots at stake and a badly designed ballot a focal point of blame.

But as the Gore campaign came to discover, the legal system cannot (certainly, it did not) provide any meaningful retrospective remedy in a presidential election for this combination of ballot design and voter confusion. To experienced voting-rights lawyers, the lack of such a remedy came as no surprise: neither the remedy of a new election nor some court-ordered statistical adjustment of votes was plausible, and for good reasons. Courts generally order new elections in only the most egregious circumstances; but in a presidential election, the specter of rerunning the election in one county of the United States would not only likely violate federal law, but it would also raise issues of its own about the integrity of the result. What would the point of a new election be in this context? To try to reproduce the results voters "intended" on the actual day of the election? But how would we know whether we had gotten such a result? In those few cases in which courts order new elections, those elections are not meant to recreate the past but to be fresh acts of decision on their own. But at that point the remedy runs squarely up against the legal and moral requirement that some voters not be able to game the system by voting with full knowledge of how all other voters have voted. Similarly, courts are not keen to decide the outcome of elections by making statistical adjustments for what voters "really" intended when the objective indicia of their intent is a clear vote for a particular candidate—or two clear votes for two candidates. Despite the charges of partisanship leveled at the Florida courts, no court showed the slightest inclination to provide a remedy for the confusion of the butterfly ballot.

There can be a gap between what we "know" as a matter of common understanding and the knowledge the legal system will let us act on. And there can be good reasons for the existence of that gap. Put in other terms, in the law of elections, more than in most areas of the law, "wrongs" can occur—ballots can be badly though unintentionally misdesigned—without corresponding remedies being available to undo the wrong. Courts can order the practice changed for future elections, and often do, but that does not change the result of the election at issue. There may be a moral wrong, in that voters should not be forced to confront unduly confusing ballots, but there is no legal remedy. Faced with that legal reality, the Gore campaign's morally most compelling claim dissolved.

The recount litigation was, in a sense, an effort to find a *surrogate* remedy for the "wrong" of the butterfly ballot confusion that could not itself be remedied. Would the recount litigation even have been initiated had there not first been the sense of outrage and unfairness at the thousands of seemingly miscast votes? Perhaps. But once the issue of the butterfly ballot dropped out, the moral high ground became less certain. And we were now fighting over a statistically minuscule number of ballots—a number likely to be smaller than what statisticians would define as the "margin of error" in a process of counting nearly 6 million ballots. This was the context to which the previously existing institutional and legal apparatus had to be applied.

2. The Problem of Incomplete Law

By now, most of us are aware of the bizarre division of power between state and national institutions even when it comes to the election of the highest national office in the land. I say bizarre because it is difficult to believe, if we were creating our democratic system today, we would allocate this power in precisely the same way. Given that national offices are at stake, we would be more likely to have national standards for regulating that process, including the setting of standards for access to the ballot, the vote counting process, and the like. Democratic institutions turn out to be highly path dependent; their structures are selected at particular moments in time, to serve specific purposes, but those structures often then endure long after their original purposes continue to be compelling ones when circumstances have changed. People become adjusted to the status quo; they fear changes are being sought for nefarious purposes or cannot distinguish when that is the case; and powerful vested interests that benefit from the status quo emerge to preserve it. Thus the state-by-state choice of presidential electors, with the rules for that process decentralized not only to the state level but also in some states, like Florida, down to the county level, put Florida law at the center of the election dispute. Three points about the content of those Florida laws must be stressed that are not often acknowledged. First, as one who has examined election laws in many states, I can attest that Florida's were among the worst I have seen: vastly underspecified and therefore incomplete, with provisions arguably in tension with each other and much that needed to be addressed not addressed at all. Second, it was clear at the time, and has become only more clear since, that when these laws were drafted, the Florida legislators did not give a moment's thought to how the laws ought to be applied to a presidential election. The presidential election process poses myriad unique issues, not the least of which is the presence of federally imposed deadlines that require any vote count and recount to be completed by certain dates. Many state election laws distinguish between processes for contesting state and local elections and the process for contesting a presidential election. Florida law makes no such distinction.[6] Moreover, although Florida has revised its election laws numerous times in recent decades, there is no evidence that the legislators ever thought about the federal election calendar or the relevant federal statutory provisions, or even focused at all on presidential elections; their concern was local and state elections alone.[7] Third, when laws are uncertain, courts and others often look to the actual practices that have developed under those laws; yet here too Florida was a cipher. The last time the state had conducted a recount for a statewide race, in that case the governor's office, was in the early part of the century, long before the current electoral laws had been enacted.

The actors who had to work with these laws, with a presidential election in the balance, thus faced a system of laws not written for the question at issue, so badly drafted in any event as to be incomplete and rife with ambiguities, and with no established, settled state practice to fill in the arguable gaps in the text of the laws. This was a problem that confronted the secretary of state, the state courts, and ultimately the United States Supreme Court. Advocates and partisans, of course, must claim that the rules of the game are utterly clear—and in their favor. Many of us would have liked it had the rules indeed been clear and knowable in advance of the election dispute. But the fact was, the laws were not written with these issues in mind; and they were precisely the kind of poorly drafted legislation that invites controversy.

This then created the worst possible context for resolution of such a charged issue—a context destined to lead to charges of partisan manipulation no matter what the various actors, forced to work with these laws, chose to do. For those actors had to exercise acts of judgment or interpretation in the absence of a legal structure that had specified in advance, with clear rules, precisely how a presidential election dispute was to be resolved. Yet those acts of interpretation were now to take place in the middle of the dispute itself, at moments in which everyone understood which side would be favored by one judgment or the other. Perhaps if there were a legal consensus about how courts ought to act in the face of such incomplete, confusing, and ambiguous legislation, that consensus would be able to ground some widely accepted solution to the problems Florida's election laws posed. But no such consensus exists, thus proliferating the reasons that no widely acceptable moves toward closure would be forthcoming from inside the legal system.

3. The Problem of American Legal Theory

The appropriate role for courts in interpreting statutes is a classic jurisprudential problem to which different legal systems have offered different answers. Put simplistically, two polar positions can be identified: purposive interpretation versus textual interpretation. In the former, courts conceive themselves in a kind of partnership with the legislature; the role of courts is to discover to the extent possible the general purposes for which laws have been passed and then to further those purposes through acts of interpretation in cases in which the statute's reach is otherwise unclear. Courts that emphasize textual interpretation, by contrast, tend to see themselves less as legislative partners and more as faithful agents; such courts view the legislature to have expressed its purpose through the text of the statute itself. The court's role is to apply the text according to its terms. With purposive interpretation, courts take an active role in seeking to harmonize statutory schemes as a whole or to fill in gaps and ambiguities according to judicial judgments about the underlying legislative purpose. With textual interpretation, courts hew as closely as possible to the specific terms of the written text, without further judgments about whether direct textual application appears to further what the courts view as the legislature's underlying objectives.

Which of these views prevails in American law? Neither. The answer varies both over time and between different courts within our radically decentralized system of legal authority. Thus within the United States Supreme Court, it is roughly true that from the 1950s to the 1980s, purposive methods of interpretation were dominant. Since then, a strong push has been made by certain justices for embracing textual interpretation exclusively. That textual approach has gained strength in recent years, though it is probably fair to say that the Court is internally divided right now on these questions. The answer also varies throughout the American legal system; this is not the kind of question on which the Supreme Court can impose a uniform approach on all courts. If state courts, interpreting state statutes, choose to apply purposive interpretation, the United States Supreme Court cannot require those state courts to adopt a different approach, at least as a general matter (if there is a federal interest in the case, the power relationships can change). A consequence of our federal structure is that different courts, state and federal, are able to adopt distinct methods of statutory interpretation. Nor can it be said that the general intellectual culture of law in the United States today generally endorses one of these methods to the exclusion of the other.

Faced with badly drafted election laws, the Florida Supreme Court took a purposive approach and sought to adapt a statutory scheme written only with state and local recounts in mind to the context of a presidential election. This involved the modification of statutory deadlines. Whether or not one agrees with the particular way that court sought to reconcile the various provisions, it was going through the process of purposive interpretation in the way that many courts, including the United States Supreme Court for many years, have approached the task of interpreting confusing, incomplete statutory schemes. On the other hand, several members of the United States Supreme Court fervently believe it is precisely these open-ended methods of purposive interpretation that allow courts to impose their own views of desired outcomes on statutory schemes; for that reason, these justices strongly embrace textual interpretation. It is precisely those justices who focused their constitutional rejection (based technically on Art. II, sec. 1, of the U.S. Constitution) of the Florida court's decision most directly on the latter court's statutory interpretations. So vehement were these textually committed Supreme Court justices—Chief Justice Rehnquist, Justice Scalia, and Justice Thomas—that they excoriated the Florida Supreme Court in the most disparaging rhetoric: the Florida court's readings were "absurd," ones "no reasonable person" would endorse, and "depart[ed] from the legislative scheme."[8] But as far as I can tell, this Florida Supreme Court regularly engages in purposive interpretation of statutes, in elections or other contexts. From a textualist's perspective, purposive interpreters regularly depart from the legislative scheme; it is in the very nature of purposive interpretation to do so. At the same time, these Supreme Court justices regularly demand fidelity to legislative text as text: their textualism also applies across different statutory contexts. To the extent that the Supreme Court majority viewed the Florida Supreme Court as a "runaway court," as many commentators believe the Supreme Court majority did,[9] how much of that belief ultimately stemmed from fundamentally different philosophies of statutory interpretation—philosophies each court majority applies with some consistency yet which differ radically from each other?

Thus, we faced drafted election laws not written in any way for the context of a presidential election dispute. And to the extent the meaning of those laws might have been stabilized in some way to generate consensus, we had no established state practice that might have given determinate content to those laws. Nor does the American legal system have any widely agreed on method of interpreting statutes that would have brought that stability of meaning to these statutes. That the meaning of these statutes remained contested—that any act of interpreting them by any actor was seen by many as a partisan power play—is hardly surprising.

4. The Problem of Expertise in Democracy

One last source might conceivably have brought stability to the practice of interpreting the relevant Florida election laws. That stability could have come from the various administrative officials who implemented those laws during the recount process, ranging from the secretary of state to the individual county canvassing boards. But this is where American institutional structures might suffer from what could be considered an excess of democracy. Or put in other terms, this is where the exceptional distrust of expertise that uniquely characterizes democracy in America—particularly the institutional structures of American democracy created in the nineteenth century—came home to roost. For the administrative officials who were to do the actual counting of the ballots, the county canvassing officials, were themselves officials elected as partisan members of one of the political parties. Certain canvassing boards were known to be dominated by Democrats, others by Republicans.

Even more disturbing, the secretary of state was the state's chair of one of the campaigns; the attorney general, the chair of the other campaign (both should have recused themselves from ruling on the legal issues in dispute). In this democratically saturated context, with partisan elected officials at every juncture playing key roles in the counting process, how likely would it be that outsiders to this process would have confidence in its result? If what was needed was some stability of meaning to the relevant legal rules, it hardly seemed forthcoming from institutional structures set up in this way. The actual results only bear this out: in a series of 2–1 party-line votes, the Broward County Canvassing Board "recovered" Democratic votes from undervoted ballots at a rate three times that of the board for Palm Beach County.[10]

As Shlomo Avineri puts it in his contribution to this volume (chap. 14), this administrative structure "would be unthinkable in any [other] democratic society." Most other systems have a national election commission or equivalent, whose composition varies but that typically includes some mix of judges, candidates, members of public bodies, and the like. Whether these commissions succeed at the fact or appearance of pure impartiality, they may nonetheless achieve, in fact or appearance, *relative* impartiality—certainly, relative to the explicitly partisan-elected figures with this administrative power in the American context. But American political culture tends to disbelieve in the possibility of such independent or detached expertise, at least in most areas outside the management of the money supply through the Federal Reserve System. Moreover, precisely because the U.S. Constitution happens to be so enduring, it goes back to an era before the institutional structures for oversight of democracy were developed in the direction taken in many modern constitutions. Thus the U.S. Constitution does not create intermediary bodies, such as a national election commission. Instead, we vote for more offices than any country in the world: from municipal officials to state judges to treasurers to county election officials. And in America, once an institution has been created as a democratically accountable one, there is very little history of turning such institutions into appointed ones. Yet when partisan-elected officials are asked to make judgments about the distribution of partisan political power, American culture's distrust of expertise can seem pathological. Certainly the on-the-ground administrative institutions in Florida designed to resolve election disputes were not designed in a way likely to inspire confidence in the impartiality of their results—whatever the truth about their actual performance.

IV

Thus we start with a general dispute whose resolution, we ought to recognize in advance, will likely lead half the voters to conclude that partisan preference motivated whatever institution formally resolves the contest. The specific context of Florida added to the mix the further paradox of a considerable moral wrong to thousands of voters, as those voters and their candidate perceived it, yet no apparent legal remedy for that wrong. From that paradox emerged a different formal legal dispute, one involving a relatively small number of ballots and a difference between candidates smaller than the likely statistical margin of accuracy for trying to determine that difference. And the state laws relevant to that dispute were drafted for other purposes and were confusing and incomplete at best. All this in an American legal system that lacks any authoritative consensus for what role courts ought to play with regard to such statutory schemes. Finally, the American electoral administration system is so steeped in democratic modes of organization itself that it lacks the independence from politics that might have given its modes of resolution some authority. With so much at stake, a margin so small, and an absence of clear prior rules or impartial administrative structures, the chances of avoiding an outcome the losing side would find partisan did not seem promising. That is true whether the legal dispute would have ended with the Florida Supreme Court or the United States Supreme Court, or anywhere else.

That returns us to the institutional design question with which I began. What are the institutional possibilities for where to locate final power to resolve a disputed presidential election? To the extent preexisting laws must be interpreted, those laws are likely to be state laws, given the peculiar state role in presidential elections that the Constitution establishes. One possibility, therefore, is to leave the interpretation of those laws in the hands of the state courts. No doubt, that will strike many as bizarre, though it is essentially the positions Justices Stevens and Ginsburg took in dissenting from *Bush v. Gore.* If a presidential election is at stake, how can the outcome be left to turn on the interpretations and judgments of one state court? Once a state court is involved, how can the United States Supreme Court not come to be involved and provide the ultimate resolution of the disputed legal issues? This was indeed the logic the Supreme Court majority invoked: "When contending parties invoke the process of the courts, however, it becomes our unsought responsibility to resolve the [legal issues] the judicial system has been forced to confront."[11]

From the perspective of institutional design that I have emphasized, here is what might be said against that logic. We are speaking of the view that the legal disputes involving presidential elections should start and end in the state courts (apart from whatever else might be said for this view from the more internal legal perspective that Justices Stevens and Ginsburg advanced): if we accept that any institution that resolves the dispute will be infected with the perception of partisan contagion, then we want to limit that contagion. Far better if half the country believes the Florida Supreme Court has construed the law in a partisan fashion than for half the country to believe the United States Supreme Court has done so. If we know institutions will inevitably be damaged by the very fact of their resolution of this dispute, better to isolate and confine that damage to one state judicial system. When the United States Supreme Court acts, it represents the meaning of the rule of law for the entire country. When the Florida courts act, it is easier for those who lose to dismiss those institutions as aberrational, as renegade, but as not symbolizing the rule of law in the same representationally powerful sense as the United States Supreme Court.

If final resolution in the Florida courts seems, nonetheless, troubling, consider a second institutional option, much discussed at the time: resolution in the U.S. Congress. Recall that other disputed political elections are specifically designed by the Constitution to be resolved by the political institutions involved. Resolution in Congress as a whole might be thought the most closely analogous means of resolving disputed presidential elections, given the inability of the Electoral College itself to play this role. Moreover, I noted at the outset that the Constitution fails to specify how such a dispute should be handled. But Congress had attempted to fill precisely this gap over one hundred years ago when, in the aftermath of one of the worst disputed elections in U.S. history, Congress passed the Electoral Count Act of 1887. At that time, Congress deliberated over several years in as nonpartisan a context as could be selected,[12] a decade after the

Hayes-Tilden election and with no disputed election on the horizon, over how to fill this gap in the Constitution's design and create an enduring mechanism for resolving disputed presidential elections. In the Electoral Count Act, Congress specifically chose a national political institution, the Congress itself, for resolving disputed presidential elections. At the same time, Congress specifically considered and rejected the alternative of United States Supreme Court resolution of disputed presidential elections.[13]

It is worth recalling the precise reasons Congress explicitly rejected United States Supreme Court resolution. They reflect recognition of the central theme on which this essay has been premised, which is that any resolution in such contexts is likely to be seen as partisan by nearly half the country. For this very reason, congressional proponents of the Act endorsed congressional rather than judicial resolution. The idea of Supreme Court resolution of such disputes was broached several times over the years in which Congress considered how to resolve disputed presidential elections.[14] Every time it was raised, however, the idea was roundly defeated. Senator Evarts, a key member of the Senate committee considering such legislation in 1886, put the objection powerfully: "I can not look with any complacency upon a reference to the Supreme Court or any judicial tribunal. . . . I must regard, as I do sincerely, the whole transaction from the beginning to the end, and the declaration of the result, a political transaction to be governed by such moderation and duty and faculties as are reposed in those who will the political stations that are to act upon the great transaction."[15] In the House, the soon-to-be Speaker, John Carlisle of Kentucky, similarly agreed: "I have never believed it was wise, or could under any circumstances be entirely safe, to entrust the decision of a great political question like this— because it is a political question—to the courts and to the juries of the country."[16]

Perhaps the most powerful statement of this view, against Supreme Court involvement, came from Senator Sherman, one of the primary speakers in support of the proposed statute. He first asserted that the method of resolving a disputed presidential election was "a question that is more dangerous to the future of this country than probably any other."[17] He went on to argue:

> Another plan which has been proposed in the debates at different times and I think also in the constitutional convention, was to allow questions of this kind to be certified at once to the Supreme Court for its decisions in case of a division between the two Houses. If the House should be one way and the Senate the other, then it was proposed to let the case be referred directly to the prompt and summary decision of the Supreme Court. But there is a feeling in this country that we ought not to mingle our great judicial tribunal with political questions, and therefore this proposition has not met with much

favor. It would be a very grave fault indeed and a very serious objection to refer a political question in which the people of the country were aroused, about which their feelings were excited, to this great tribunal, which after all has to sit upon the life and property of all the people of the United States. It would tend to bring that court into public odium of one or the other of the two great parties. Therefore that plan may probably be rejected as an unwise provision. I believe, however, that it is the provision made in other countries.[18]

The question here is not whether the United States Supreme Court should have felt legally bound by the terms of the Electoral Count Act not to terminate the 2000 election. Instead, from the perspective of the institutional designer, I am asking whether the Court should have been attentive to the collective congressional judgment—should it be called "wisdom?"—expressed in a nonpartisan series of deliberations over several years, a judgment that partisan political elections should be judged in partisan political bodies. The Electoral Count Act of 1887 sought to make that as true for presidential elections as the Constitution expressly did for Senate and House elections.

As with resolution in the Florida courts, the prospect of partisan congressional resolution is also no doubt troubling in some respects (we can only compare the troubles different institutional solutions bring, not free ourselves of those troubles altogether). Of course it would have been partisan. Of course it would have been bitter, brutal, and ugly in many respects. But keep in mind that the Supreme Court has kept out of previous presidential election disputes, much as it has kept out of other disputes viewed as being of such fundamental political import as to require political resolution. At the end of the day, Congress was in fact the ultimate dispute resolver in the 1876 Hayes-Tilden election dispute, as it had been in the disputed presidential election of 1800, and as it had been when the Supreme Court refused to take a stand in the internal civil war that characterized Rhode Island in the 1840s and lay behind *Luther v. Borden*.[19] A deep historical sensibility about elections of 1800 or 1876 is not needed to raise such questions. For we can also ask whether the recent presidential impeachment process would have been improved had the Supreme Court determined for the country what constituted a "high crime and misdemeanor" with the meaning of the Constitution. Impeachment issues have long been treated as purely political questions, despite the presence in the constitutional text of legal terms whose interpretation is central to the ultimate act of impeachment. Similarly, while disputed presidential elections may well involve arguable legal issues, it is possible to consider Congress an acceptable forum for addressing those issues.

If that prospect remains troubling, there is a final institutional mechanism to consider that might have been used to resolve the 2000 election. That would be to combine Supreme Court participation with ultimate resolution in the political processes of Congress. We can imagine the Court playing a role in determining the legal *processes* by which certain aspects of the dispute should be resolved—in particular, the constitutional standards by which a recount would have to be conducted—while leaving the ultimate resolution of that dispute to the congressional process that the Electoral Count Act contemplates. In *Bush v. Gore,* the Supreme Court combined both steps into one: it specified a constitutional recount process as well as the outcome that process required. The Court terminated the constitutionally required process before it began; the Court did so on disputed grounds that the relevant laws allowed no further time. But imagine a recount process, conducted pursuant to Supreme Court–specified standards to assure constitutionality, with the results of *that* process then presented to Congress. How should we imagine what kind of process in Congress would have taken place in those circumstances: with the final Florida vote reflecting consistent, uniform, clearly specified vote-counting standards, under Supreme Court guidelines, including the reexamination of results from earlier county recounts not completed under such constitutionally required rules. Perhaps such a process would have been completed before the day the Electoral College was legally obliged to meet, December 18. Perhaps it would have taken longer (perhaps the Florida Supreme Court, not the United States Supreme Court, would have terminated the process in that event). Would such a process have produced greater acceptance of the final outcome? If Congress chose to accept electoral votes after December 18, would the Supreme Court have stepped back in to declare such action unconstitutional? Should it have? Or should that aspect of such a dispute be treated as a political question, much like impeachment, with Congress to retain the ultimate power to decide on the day it meets to count the electoral votes whether to receive votes cast after December 18?

But the United States Supreme Court chose none of these routes: neither to leave the legal issues exclusively with the Florida Supreme Court, nor to stay its hand and leave final resolution to Congress, nor to play a mixed role with Congress by intervening to establish the constitutional ground rules of a recount process while leaving the ultimate effect of that process to be determined in Congress. Instead, the Court took it upon itself to become the definitive—indeed, close to the exclusive—decision maker in the closing stage of the disputed 2000 election. For the Court's decision not only brought the election litigation to a close, but it also revealed a Court that had been prepared all along to leave little room for the Florida courts to act and little room, likewise, for Congress to act. The Court thus took the most political or democratic issue of all, the disputed choice of a chief executive, and by constitutionalizing the issues involved, it took definitive and nearly complete control of that issue away from the other institutions that might have been deployed to resolve it.

In doing so, *Bush v. Gore* is not the isolated or aberrant example many consider it. Supreme Court resolution of a disputed presidential election is, of course, a singular event in American history. But *Bush v. Gore* is also the culmination of a more enduring, more pervasive judicial tendency. More and more, the Supreme Court is coming to engage in a process of "constitutionalizing democracy." By that I mean the Court is increasingly using constitutional law to make itself the exclusive arbiter—not of conventional individual rights, but of the most basic aspects of democratic politics itself. This is a profound but underappreciated transformation in American constitutional jurisprudence. The resolution of the most political choice of all, the presidential election, is a moment of high drama, but it is best seen as the most visible symbol of a deeper transformation. Whether it comes to the structure of political primaries, or the design of election districts, or the financing of election campaigns, or the role of political parties in the American democratic system, the current Supreme Court increasingly comes to find the Constitution provides answers to these questions. I have documented this emerging jurisprudence elsewhere.[20] As a matter of the underlying design of democratic institutions—whether for resolving disputed presidential elections or other issues of democracy the Court now constitutionalizes almost casually—we ought to wonder where it is wisest to draw the line between constitutional law and democratic politics when it comes to the most fundamental aspects of democracy itself.

NOTES

This essay is based on a presentation on the 2000 Election Dispute given at New York University School of Law on January 17, 2001.

1. Michael C. Dorf and Samuel Issacharoff, "Can Process Theory Constrain Courts?" 72 *U. Col. L. Rev.* 923 (2001).

2. U.S. Const. Art. I, § 5.

3. Florida among them. See 9 Fla. § 102.171 ("The jurisdiction to hear any contest of the election of a member to either house of the Legislature is vested in the applicable house, as each house, pursuant to s. 2, Art. III of the State Constitution, is the sole judge of the qualifications, elections, and returns of its members").

4. Roudebush v. Hartke, 405 U.S. 15 (1972). It should be noted that this full process required nearly two years after election day before Hartke, the Senate's choice, was finally seated officially.

5. *United States Senate: Election, Expulsion and Censure Cases,* 1793–1990, 312–15, 421–25 (Washington, D.C.: GPO, 1995).

6. See Eric Schickler, Terri L. Bimes, and Robert W. Mickey, "Safe at Any Speed: Legislative Intent, the Electoral Count Act of 1887, and *Bush v. Gore,*" *J.L. & Pol.* (forthcoming 2001).

7. *Id.*

8. 121 S. Ct. 525, 537–38.

9. David Strauss, *"Bush v. Gore:* What Were They Thinking?" 68 *U. Chicago L. Rev.* 737 (2001).

10. I take these figures from Michael McConnell, "Two-and-a-Half Cheers for *Bush v. Gore,"* 68 *U. Chicago L. Rev.* 657, 671 (2001).

11. 121 S. Ct. at 533.

12. See, *e.g.,* 17 *Cong. Rec.* 815 (Jan. 21, 1886) (Sen. Sherman) ("[The proposed Electoral Count Act] comes before us again at the beginning of an administration, when no party advantage can be derived from our decision, when the Senate is clearly on one side in party politics and the House clearly is on the other; and now, if ever, this matter ought to be settled upon some basis of principle").

13. 3 U.S.C. § 15 provides the mechanism for a congressional resolution, with ultimate default rules, in the case of a state presenting competing slates of presidential electors.

14. For a full history of these debates, see Schickler, Bimes, and Mickey, "Safe at Any Speed."

15. 17 *Cong. Rec.* 1058 (1886) (Sen. Evarts).

16. 13 *Cong. Rec.* 5148–49 (1882) (Rep. Carlisle).

17. 17 *Cong. Rec.* 815 (1886) (Sen. Sherman).

18. 17 *Cong. Rec.* 817–18 (1886) (Sen. Sherman).

19. 48 U.S. 1 (1849).

20. Richard H. Pildes, "Democracy and Disorder," 68 *U. Chicago L. Rev.* 695 (2001).

Part Three

THE DECISIONS

4

A BADLY FLAWED ELECTION

Ronald Dworkin

The 2000 election has finally ended, but in the worst possible way—not with a national affirmation of democratic principle but by the fiat of the five conservative Supreme Court justices, Chief Justice Rehnquist and Justices Kennedy, O'Connor, Scalia, and Thomas, over the fierce objection of the four more liberal justices, Justices Breyer, Ginsburg, Souter, and Stevens. The conservatives stopped the democratic process in its tracks, with thousands of votes yet uncounted, first by ordering an unjustified stay of the statewide recount of the Florida vote that was already in progress and then by declaring, in one of the least persuasive Supreme Court opinions that I have ever read, that there was no time left for the recount to continue. It is far from certain that Gore would have been elected if the recounts had been completed; some statisticians believe that Bush would have picked up more additional votes than Gore. But the Court did not allow that process to continue, and its decision ensured both a Bush victory and a continuing cloud of suspicion over that victory.

Though it took six opinions for all the justices to state their views, the argument of the five conservatives who voted to end the election was quite simple. The Florida Supreme Court had ordered a recount of undervotes across the state, but instead of adopting detailed rules for determining whether a ballot that the counting machine had declared to have no vote for president was actually a vote for one candidate—rules that might have specified, for example, that if not a single corner of the chad of a punch-card ballot had been detached, the ballot could not count as a vote—it had directed only that counters count a vote if they found, considering the ballot as a whole, a "clear intention" of the voter. The five conservatives noted that this more abstract standard had been applied differently by counters in different counties and might be applied differently by different counters within a single county, and they therefore held that the use of the standard denied voters the equal protection of the law required under the U.S. Constitution's Fourteenth Amendment.

The natural remedy, following such a ruling, would be to remand the case to the Florida court to permit it to substitute a more concrete uniform counting standard. Breyer, in his dissenting opinion, suggested that course. "[The] case should be sent back for recounting all undercounted votes," he said, "in accordance with a single uniform standard." But the conservatives declared that since the Florida legislature intended to take advantage of the "safe harbor" provision of federal law, which provides that election results certified by states to Congress by December 12 are immune from congressional reexamination, any further recount the Florida court ordered would have to be completed by that date—which ended two hours after the Supreme Court handed down its judgment. The conservatives had remanded the case to the Florida court for "proceedings consistent with" their opinion and then told them that no proceedings could possibly be consistent with their opinion. The election was over, and the conservative candidate had won.

The 5–4 decision would hardly have been surprising, or even disturbing, if the constitutional issues were ones about which conservatives and liberals disagree as a matter of constitutional principle—about the proper balance of authority between the federal and state governments, for example, or the criminal process, or race, or the character and extent of individual rights, such as abortion rights or rights of homosexuals, against state and national authorities. But there were no such constitutional issues in this case: the conservatives' decision to reverse a state supreme court's rulings on matters of state law did not reflect any established conservative position on any general constitutional question. On the contrary, conservatives have been at least as zealous as liberals in protecting the right of state courts to interpret state legislation without second-guessing by federal courts, and on the whole they have been less ready than liberals to appeal to the Fourteenth Amendment to reverse state decisions.

It is therefore difficult to find a respectable explanation of why all and only the conservatives voted to end the election in this way, and the troubling question is being asked among scholars and commentators whether the Court's decision would have been different if it was Bush, not Gore, who needed the recount to win—whether, that is, the decision reflected not ideological division, which is inevitable, but professional self-interest. The five conservatives have made this Supreme Court the most activist Court in history. They aim to transform constitutional law not, as the Warren Court did, to strengthen civil liberties and individual rights but rather to expand the power of states against Congress, shrink the rights of accused criminals, and enlarge their own powers of judicial intervention.[1]

For three of them—Rehnquist, Scalia, and Thomas—the agenda presumably includes finally abolishing the abortion rights that were first established in *Roe v. Wade* over a quarter of a century ago, a decision they have never ceased insisting should be overruled. The prospects of future success for the conservatives' radical program crucially depend on the Court appointments that the new president will almost certainly make. Those appointments will determine whether the conservatives' activism will flourish (even adding, perhaps, the two new votes that would be needed to overrule abortion rights so long as O'Connor and Kennedy refuse to take that step) or whether it will be checked or reversed. Bush long ago signaled, in naming Scalia his favorite justice, his intention that it flourish.

We should try to resist this unattractive explanation of why the five conservative justices stopped the recount process and declared Bush the winner. It is, after all, inherently implausible that any—let alone all—of them would stain the Court's reputation for such a sordid reason, and respect for the Court requires that we search for a different and more creditable explanation of their action. Unfortunately, however, the legal case they offered for crucial aspects of their decisions was exceptionally weak. Their first major ruling, on Saturday, December 9 (soon after the recounting began), was to halt the recount even before they heard argument in Bush's appeal of the Florida Supreme Court decision ordering that recount. The ruling was in itself lethal for Gore. Even if the Court had ultimately rejected Bush's appeal and allowed the recount to resume, it could not possibly have been completed by December 12, the date that the conservatives later declared the final deadline.

Scalia argued that this serious injury to Gore was necessary to prevent irreparable harm to Bush: he said that Bush would be harmed if the recounts continued because if the Court later decided that the recount was illegal, the public's knowledge of the results would cast a "cloud" over "the legitimacy of his election." That bizarre claim assumes not only that Bush would have lost in the recount but also that the public is not to be trusted. Public knowledge that Gore would have won, if the recounts had continued and been accepted, would produce doubt about a Bush election only if the public disagreed with the Court's judgment that the recount was illegal; and it is constitutionally improper for the Court to keep truthful information from the public just because the information might lead it to conclude that the election was a mistake or that the Court was wrong.[2]

The conservatives' second major decision was that the Florida court's "clear intention of the voter" standard for manual recounts violated the Equal Protection Clause because different counties and counters would interpret that standard differently. Two of the more liberal justices—Breyer and Souter—agreed,[3] but the other liberal justices, Ginsburg and Stevens, rejected the argument, and they had the better case. The Equal Protection

Clause forbids voting procedures or arrangements that put particular people or groups at an electoral disadvantage. The Court has struck down poll taxes that discriminated against the poor, for example, and, citing a "one-person, one-vote" electoral standard, has prohibited electoral districts of very different size because these give each voter in larger districts less impact on the overall election result than voters in smaller districts have. But a general standard for counting undervotes that may be applied differently in different districts puts no class of voters, in advance, at either an advantage or a disadvantage. If a voter's county uses a more permissive test to determine "clear intent," then he risks having his ballot counted when he did not intend to vote; if it uses a strict standard, he risks having his ballot ignored when he did intend to vote. One cannot say, in advance, that either a permissive or a strict test is more accurate and therefore cannot say that a system that combines both within a single state puts any identifiable group at an automatic disadvantage.[4]

As Gore's counsel, David Boies, pointed out in oral argument, Florida's use of different voting machinery in different counties is much more arguably a violation of equal protection, because some types of machine are well known to be much less accurate than others. Punch-card ballot readers, which are used in counties with a high minority population such as Miami-Dade, ignore more than three times as many ballots as optical-scan ballot readers do and therefore give voters in those counties systematically less chance of having their votes counted.

The Court's equal protection decision is surprising in another way. The one-person, one-vote principle applies not just to presidential elections but also to elections for every federal and state office, major or minor, across the country. I do not know how many states use nothing more concrete than a "clear intent of the voter" standard for manual recounts, but several do, and the Supreme Court has now declared that they have all been acting, no doubt for many decades, unconstitutionally. This ruling alone may require substantial changes in the nation's electoral laws, and the Supreme Court may well regret having made it.

The conservatives' equal protection claim is defensible, however, and, as I said, two of the more liberal justices also accepted it. But the conservatives' third and by far most important major decision is not defensible. The most natural remedy for the supposed equal protection violation, as all the dissenters insisted, would be to remand the case to the Florida court so that it could establish uniform recount standards and attempt to complete a recount by December 18, when the Electoral College votes. But the conservatives held that since the Constitution gives the Florida state legislature authority over its own election law and since that legislature would wish to take advantage of the federal safe harbor law that guarantees a state certification of presidential electors immunity from congressional challenge if the certification is made by December 12, any recounts beyond that date, even those necessary to ensure that all valid votes were counted, would automatically be unconstitutional.

But the safe harbor provision is not mandatory; it does not provide that a state loses its electoral votes if these are not submitted by December 12 but only that its votes, if submitted after that date, might conceivably be challenged in Congress, if reason can be found to challenge them. Certainly the Florida legislature would wish to meet the December 12 deadline if it fairly could, and its legislation should be interpreted, as the Florida Supreme Court said that it did interpret it, with that aim in mind.

But it goes far beyond that safe assumption to declare, as the five U.S. Supreme Court conservatives did, that the Florida legislature meant to insist that the optional deadline be met at all costs, even if it was necessary to ignore the principles of accuracy and fair treatment that underlie the rest of the election code. That would be a bizarre interpretation of any state's election law—what legislature would wish to be understood as purchasing an immunity it would almost certainly never need at the cost of sacrificing its basic commitments of justice?—and there is no evidence that the Florida legislature has ever made that choice.[5] Even if the conservative justices thought this bizarre interpretation plausible, moreover, it would still be wrong for them to impose that interpretation on the Florida Supreme Court, which, according to the most basic principles of constitutional law, has final authority in interpreting its own state's law so long as its interpretation is not absurd. At most, the conservatives should have asked the Florida court to decide for itself whether Florida law, properly understood, declares that the safe harbor must be gained no matter what unfairness to Florida voters is necessary to gain it.

Even the two dissenters who had agreed with the majority that the Florida court's recount scheme violated the Equal Protection Clause thought it absurd to insist on the December 12 deadline, and all of the dissenters feared the impact on the Court itself of so weak an argument for so politically divisive a decision. Justice Stevens said the decision "can only lend confidence to the most cynical appraisal of the work of judges throughout the land." "We do risk a self-inflicted wound," Breyer added, "a wound that may harm not just the court, but the nation," and he also noted, pointedly, that the time pressure the conservatives cited was "in significant part, a problem of the [Supreme Court's] own making."[6] We must try, as I said, not to compound the injury to the Court with reckless accusations against any of its members. But those of us who have been arguing for many years that the Supreme Court makes America a nation of principle have a special reason for sorrow.

The deeply troubling Supreme Court decision in *Bush v. Gore* makes even plainer the urgency of radically changing how we elect our presidents.

Our present system is an eighteenth-century antique: it presupposes a starkly elitist conception of government that was popular then but which no politician would dare endorse today. The Constitution's authors did not trust the people to elect the president directly; they expected the members of the Electoral College to be distinguished and independent citizens who would make up their own minds, after collective deliberation, about who the president and vice president should be. It was not as important as it later became how those electors were chosen, because, in principle, the selecting body would have no control over or even confidence in the opinions of the independent electors they chose. There was nevertheless some initial disagreement at the Constitutional Convention about the selection of electors: some delegates wanted them elected by popular vote, some by Congress, and some by the state legislatures.

The Convention finally decided, by way of compromise, not to establish any electoral method itself but to delegate the choice of methods to the state legislatures. Each state was assigned a number of electors equal to the total number of that state's representatives and senators in Congress (that formula was a concession to smaller states that had fewer representatives but the same number of senators as much larger states), and the state legislatures were directed to decide how their state's electors would be chosen. A majority in the legislature might select the electors themselves or provide for a popular vote within the state to select them (which might be by a statewide vote for all the electors, or by districts, or by proportional representation). Or, presumably, it might direct that electors be selected by lot. Once all the electors were selected in whatever ways the various state legislatures chose, they would meet in their states, deliberate, and vote for a president; if no presidential candidate received a majority of their votes, then the House of Representatives would choose a president, with each state delegation having one vote, so that the smallest state had as much influence as the largest.

America has long since rejected the intellectual premises of this baroque system. Now we embrace the very different principle that the point of elections—particularly the election of a national president, the one office we all elect together—is to determine and reflect the people's will. Electors are no longer expected to exercise their own judgment: it is candidates, not electors, whose names are on the ballot and it would be a scandal if the electors chose someone other than the candidate to whom most of them were pledged. A partisan majority in a state legislature still has the constitutional power, under Article II, to cancel presidential elections in its state and choose the state's electors by themselves. But if any legislature tried to exercise that power, its action would undoubtedly provoke a constitutional amendment ending that power.

We have been lucky not to have been seriously damaged by the Electoral

College system long before this election made its anachronism intolerable. It is dangerous to retain a constitutional structure when its principled base has been so thoroughly repudiated, because the structure then becomes a legal loose cannon. It generates pointless complexities and obstacles, and it is vulnerable to partisan manipulation and bizarre interpretation that cannot be checked by appealing to the structure's purpose, since it now has none. The legal battles in Florida and in the Supreme Court were dominated by a series of deadlines—the Court elected Bush by insisting on the importance of December 12—that are significant only because the eighteenth-century arrangement decreed a stately series of certifications, meetings, and pronouncements that are now only charades. The Republican strategy in Florida of delaying recounts through any means possible, including not only legal challenges but also noisy demonstrations outside counting rooms, was made possible only by those pointless deadlines. It makes no sense to demand that a breathtakingly close election be decided by any magic date in December in order that a new president be chosen by January 20.

The original decision to leave the manner of presidential elections to state legislatures corrupts elections in a different way. The one-person, one-vote principle would suggest, as I said, that we elect presidents through uniform voting methods, with at least roughly equal accuracy, supervised by a national election commission under principles established by Congress. The eighteenth-century compromise guarantees, to the contrary, that different methods of recording votes, which vary dramatically in their accuracy, will be used not only in different states but in different counties within states as well. It also guarantees that inevitable uncertainties and ambiguities in election law will have to be faced anew in each close election, because even if Florida's law is clarified now, the next set of contests will arise in an entirely different state with an entirely different structure of law and ambiguity.

The present system means, moreover, that politics will play an inevitably ugly role in close elections. It is surely unacceptable that the Florida state legislature, dominated by Republicans, should have the power themselves to elect a set of electors pledged to the Republican candidate whenever they deem this to be necessary because the result of the election is uncertain. Many of the most consequential decisions in Florida were made by political officials whose future might depend either on who won the presidential election or on whether powerful Florida politicians, including Bush's brother, who is Florida's governor, would approve what they had done. Katherine Harris, the Florida secretary of state whose several erroneous rulings contributed enormously to the delays that prevented a fair recount, had been co-chair of Bush's campaign in Florida, and the *New York Times* reported that the Democratic mayor of Miami had been subject to a great deal of local pressure just before the Miami-Dade County Canvassing Board reversed itself and decided to halt manual recounts.[7] It would be a mistake to assume wrongdoing or improper motives in any such case, but it would certainly be better to vest critical decisions in nonpartisan federal election officials who would be much less likely to attract suspicion.

We now have the best chance ever to junk the anachronistic and dangerous eighteenth-century system. The public should demand that Congress begin a process of constitutional amendment that would eliminate that system, root and branch, and substitute for it the direct election of the president and vice president by a plurality of the national popular vote. The amendment should direct Congress to establish uniform election procedures and machinery across the nation, and that body might then design and finance computers with screens that clearly display a voter's tentative choices and ask the voter to confirm his votes before they are recorded.[8] (It might be possible to allow people with computers, including absentees, to vote through them at home, although special digital identification and security precautions would have to be developed and care taken to avoid unfairness to voters with no access to computers.)

Congress should further require that voting booths be open for the same twenty-four-hour period across the different time zones of the country, so that voting stops simultaneously everywhere, and that television networks do not report results in one time zone while voting continues in another; and it should establish a national election commission with general supervisory power over national elections. Challenges and disputes would no doubt still arise, but these could be adjudicated by officials of such an agency, who would be appointed to provide nonpartisanship, subject to review by federal judges with life tenure rather than by state political officials and elected state judges.

The nation would benefit in other ways from the change. It does not matter, under the Electoral College system, who won the national popular vote, but that fact is nevertheless widely reported and widely thought significant; a president who has won in the Electoral College but lost the popular vote, even by a relatively slim margin, is thought by many people less legitimate for that reason. Making the popular vote decisive would end the possibility of such a situation. Would we lose anything by the shift? It is said to be a benefit of the Electoral College system that it forces candidates to campaign across the nation rather than only in a few highly populated regions with huge media markets and the largest number of potential votes. But in fact the system does not produce genuinely national campaigns. Candidates wholly ignore states that they are very likely either to win or to lose—few presidential campaign ads appeared in the New York media market in this election, for example—and devote most of their time and money to those relatively few states in which the race appears to be close. If the national popular vote were decisive, they would not campaign just in the major population centers—there are too many votes elsewhere—but wherever they thought they could persuade a substantial number of as yet undecided voters.

It is also said that the Electoral College is necessary to protect regional interest groups that are powerful within certain states, and thus important to those states' electoral votes, but not nationally. But interest groups are now much more dispersed across the nation than they once were: many states that were formerly dominated by agricultural interests, for example, now have a more mixed economy, and farmers might be better protected by voting rules that made their absolute number important even if they were geographically dispersed.

It might appear that the Electoral College system reduces the number of postelection challenges and contests in close presidential races because it gives candidates no incentive to seek to correct mistakes in a state that the other candidate won so heavily that he would take its electoral votes anyway. Under a popular vote system, however, a candidate who lost the popular vote by a very small margin might canvas the entire country looking for a series of challenges that could yield only a few votes in each case but might change the overall result collectively.

But there is no reason to think, in advance, that a change from the Electoral College to a popular vote standard would produce more post-election challenges or contests. If a national election is close, then the election in states whose electoral votes are crucial is also likely to be close, and many fewer vote changes are needed to make a difference in the state than in the nation. Gore needed only to add a few hundred votes in Florida through challenges, but, even in this exceptionally close popular vote contest, Bush would have had to add more than 300,000 votes to his total to win, and there is no indication of irregularities elsewhere in the nation that affected, even cumulatively, that many votes.

The moment seems propitious, as I have said, for pressing for a constitutional amendment: politicians in either party would have great difficulty claiming that the system we have has worked well or supplying any principled rationale for it. But we must recognize that it is extremely difficult and normally takes many years to amend the Constitution. Short of a new constitutional convention, an amendment requires a two-thirds vote of both houses of Congress and then approval by the legislatures of three quarters of the states, and the pressure for an amendment may weaken before that long process has been completed. In any case, no amendment can succeed without the consent of many of the smaller states whose citizens benefit unfairly, in the ways I have described, from the Electoral College system that the amendment would end.

It is therefore important to consider how much of the gain that an amendment would bring could be achieved at once without one or while one is pending. One gain I described—a twenty-four-hour election day ending simultaneously across the country—could be adopted by Congress now, because the Constitution assigns it authority to fix the time of presidential elections. More could be achieved through a model uniform election code that Congress might endorse and propose to the states, agreeing to finance elections for national office, including providing accurate electronic voting machinery, for those states that adopted that code. The model code would no doubt be adopted in somewhat different form in different states, but Congress could identify core provisions that guaranteed uniform voting machinery and mechanisms of challenge and review, for instance, that could not be changed without forfeiting the benefits Congress offered. There could be no objection under Article II to a state legislature adopting the model code; a legislature would of course be free to repeal the code later, but it would presumably face great political pressure not to do so.

These are extraordinary measures, and many people will be understandably timid about altering a constitutional structure that has been, as a whole, dramatically successful. But the Constitution's original design for elections, rooted in an elitism that is no longer tolerable, has proved its most unsuccessful feature. We have had to amend it before—in 1913, when the power to choose senators was taken away from the state legislatures and given to the people—in order to keep faith with our most basic constitutional conviction, which is that the Constitution creates and protects genuine democracy. We have now witnessed new and frightening challenges to that assumption, culminating in a deeply regrettable Supreme Court decision, and we must again change the Constitution in order to sustain our deep respect for it and for the institutions that guard it.

NOTES

1. For a detailed account of this conservative activism, see Larry Kramer, "No Surprise. It's an Activist Court," *New York Times,* December 12, 2000, A33.

2. Scalia also said that since "it is generally agreed" that further handling of the ballots might degrade them, Bush might suffer irreparable harm if that degradation made a further, more accurate recount impossible. But there is no evidence (only Republican allegations) that a recounting of ballots by judges is likely to injure those ballots, no request by the Bush team for any further recounting, and no real prospect of the Supreme Court ordering one.

3. The *New York Times* suggested that they agreed in the hope, which failed, of constructing a compromise decision to send the case back to allow the Florida court to set more concrete counting standards. See Linda Greenhouse, "Bush Prevails," December 13, 2000, A1.

4. The Florida Supreme Court had adopted the "clear voter intent" standard

from the Florida statutes. In his dissenting opinion, Souter said that he could see no rational basis for using such an abstract test for inspecting ballots. But a state might rationally decide that accuracy would be improved overall by using a general standard rather than trying to anticipate in detail all the evidence that a ballot might present: a set of concrete tests might not have allowed, for example, for the Florida voter who wrote "I vote for Al Gore" across his otherwise unmarked and unpunched ballot.

5. This interpretive question asks not whether the present Florida legislature, dominated by Republicans who seemed anxious to deliver their state to Bush in any way possible, would make that choice but whether it would be justified by sound legal interpretation of existing Florida law, which cannot appeal to partisan political motives of that character.

6. When on December 4 the Court vacated the Florida Supreme Court's initial decision extending the time for manual recounts and asked for clarification of the grounds of that decision, several commentators praised the Court for a minimally interventionist decision, noting that the liberal justices could join in that minimal opinion to achieve unanimity. But it was not a minimally interventionist decision: it laid the ground for a dubious understanding of the constraints on state judges interpreting their state's election law that might well have accounted, as Breyer noted in his dissent, for the Florida Supreme Court's reluctance to stipulate more concrete counting standards, for fear that the Supreme Court would declare that it was making new law.

7. See Don van Natta Jr. and Dexter Filkins, "Contesting the Vote: Miami-Dade County," *New York Times,* December 1, 2000, A1.

8. Advanced electronic voting devices might malfunction, of course, though it seems unlikely that they would be subject to as many of the failings that have now been documented in machines and ballots now used, and software could be designed to detect a malfunction immediately.

5

EXCHANGE BETWEEN RONALD DWORKIN
AND CHARLES FRIED

RESPONSE TO RONALD DWORKIN, *A BADLY FLAWED ELECTION*

CHARLES FRIED

I cannot claim to be a disinterested observer of the events Ronald Dworkin comments on in his essay "A Badly Flawed Election." I was counsel of record to the Florida legislature in the two Supreme Court cases spawned by the tabulation of the vote in Florida. In our second brief my Harvard colleague, Einer Elhauge, and I presented arguments that closely paralleled the Court's opinion as well as the concurring opinion of the Chief Justice. In spite of that involvement—maybe because of it—I readily concede that this was a difficult case with two sides. Quite unjustified, however, is Dworkin's high dudgeon and barely concealed innuendo that the Court had acted injudiciously out of a partisan zeal to protect its own agenda against future unsympathetic appointments. On the contrary, I see the Court as having reluctantly done the job its commission required of it.

In its first opinion of December 5 the Court reminded the Florida Supreme Court that its work in this matter was not solely a matter of state law (as Dworkin repeatedly suggests) but that it was the Constitution (in Art. II, sec. 1, cl. 2, dealing with the choice of the president) that committed the matter to the state legislature and a federal statute (3 U.S.C. § 5) that assumed that disputes regarding presidential electors were to be resolved by rules established prior to the election in question. So it was a premise of that first opinion that the faithfulness of the Florida Supreme Court to the directions of the state legislature and to preexisting rules was a question of federal law and thus ultimately a proper subject for review by the United States Supreme Court. That opinion was unanimous. I say the Court showed a proper reluctance about becoming involved because it was at

pains to achieve unanimity and because having issued its reminder, it remanded the case to the Florida Supreme Court.

The second opinion, which Dworkin writes about, came a week later,
when the Florida court, to which the Supreme Court had shown traditional
deference, had—so it seemed to many, including three of the seven justices
of the Florida court—refused to take the hint and come down with a decision that merits at least as much criticism as Dworkin directs at the United
States Supreme Court. It is true that the second time around the Court
showed a good deal less deference to the Florida court, but that is often
the case when a lower court appears to the justices to be taking its direction
in less than a wholehearted spirit.[1] Thus Dworkin's repeated characterization of this as an unprecedented and unwarranted interference in a matter
of state law is misleading and incorrect. He writes that it is "difficult to find
a respectable explanation of why all and only the conservatives voted to
end the election in this way" and, becomingly, that "we should try to resist
this unattractive explanation"—that the Court majority was acting only to
protect its own radical "conservative" agenda. Dworkin does not try hard
enough. Instead he relentlessly casts the disagreement as one between the
five "conservative" and the four "liberal" justices, with only the former
moved by partisan motives. Even if the divide were as neat as he says, one
wonders why exactly the same charge of partisanship could not be leveled
against the four dissenters. But in fact the divide is not at all neat. For
instance, on the most bitterly contested issue dividing the Court for several
decades now, the right to choose established in *Roe v. Wade,* two members
of the majority are committed to a version of the same position Dworkin
espouses and the dissenters favor. Indeed, there are ideas and whole
phrases in the O'Connor, Kennedy, Souter joint opinion in the *Casey* case
that might have come straight out of Dworkin's writings. The same might
be said about Justice O'Connor's opinion in the "right-to-die" cases. Surely
neither she nor Justice Kennedy can fairly be readily relegated to some
caricaturial conservative pigeonhole. And for that matter, Justices Scalia
and Thomas are a good bit more "liberal" (if one must use these degraded
and inaccurate labels) than Justices O'Connor and Breyer on a number of
issues, such as free speech. Many commentators who share Dworkin's outrage cite, as if it proved something, Justice Stevens's dissent saying that the
Court's decision will endanger public respect for the judiciary. But this is
just the kind of thing he and Justice Scalia are sometimes inclined to say
when they lose (e.g., Scalia in *Evans v. Romer,* the Colorado anti–gay rights
initiative). Vehemence in dissent is traditional, but fouling your own nest
always seems desperate.

Dworkin disagrees with the Court's judgment that the kind of recount
ordered by the Florida Supreme Court was a denial of equal protection
because it "puts no class of voters, in advance, at either an advantage or a

disadvantage." But the Supreme Court has made clear—as recently as last year in a unanimous opinion in a jejune case involving one family's sewer connection[2]—that disparate treatment may violate the Constitution's guarantee of equal protection even if no identifiable class of persons is the target of the intentional disparity. The Florida court had explicitly ordered a procedure to take place that treated persons' votes in a senselessly variable manner.[3] Dworkin argues that in fact there was one, general uniform standard: whether each ballot, taken as a whole, showed a clear intent to vote for one or another of the candidates for president. Discerning intent from a will or contract, a statute, or even the Constitution, taken as a whole, is a familiar and appropriate task for legal interpretation. Like Dworkin, I too am a fan of hermeneutics applied to such texts. Applied by many scores of variously trained, instructed, and supervised ballot counters to punched pieces of cardboard, such a concept is manifestly out of place, to say the least.[4] In such stylized settings only a stylized system will do, and that system can and therefore should be uniform. But this is, for some of the reasons Dworkin gives, a question with two sides. In the end only two justices agreed with Dworkin, so this is hardly a cause for fulmination, dire warnings of the sort issued by Justice Stevens, or imputations of dishonestly partisan motives.

Although Dworkin finds the equal protection argument "defensible," agreeing with Justices Souter and Breyer, he argues that the Court's decree shutting down the election was not. The Court based its conclusion on what it discerned as the intent of the Florida law on no account to miss the December 12 safe harbor deadline, a deadline that evidently would not allow a second try by the Florida Supreme Court on that very day. This was the least convincing portion of the Court's opinion, but it too does not justify the depth of Dworkin's or the dissenters' scorn. They would have had the Court remand the case to the Florida Supreme Court to fashion a remedy that met the equal protection objection. But Dworkin and the two justices who dissented from the Court's remedy take it as a given that a recount on those terms would in any event have to have been completed by December 18, the day on which by federal law the electoral votes must be reported. But such a recount could not be completed in six days any more than in twenty-four hours. That is because that recount would go forward under the contest provisions of Florida law, and those envisage not a simple tally but a full-blown legal process, complete with briefing, oral argument, and a full recourse to appellate process. Such contests in Florida have been known to require sixteen months. So imagine what would have happened if Dworkin's and Breyer's solution had been adopted. There would have been further arguments in the Florida Supreme Court on remand, followed by an opinion from that court—which may have occasioned further review in the U.S. Supreme Court. Then the recount would have taken place and there would have to have been still more process about that. If miraculously all this had been compressed into six days that fact itself would have occasioned a complaint to the Supreme Court that the Florida court had once again failed to comply with the preexisting standards of Florida law.[5] Would such a continuation of the legal proceedings, inevitably leading to an indeterminate outcome, really have been a more satisfactory course? Surely if that was the alternative, the Court did well to shut the thing down then and there.

Finally, I think that the three concurring justices, whose views Dworkin does not discuss, were on sounder ground than the seven who found an equal protection violation. They argued that the Florida Supreme Court had not just interpreted some ambiguous language in the Florida statutes in a questionable way—a disagreement that perhaps the Supreme Court would have been well advised to let lie—but had turned that scheme completely on its head. Since fidelity to preexisting Florida law is a requirement of federal law—both statutory and constitutional—such a radical departure called for correction. The argument about Florida law is intricate, but its crux—as Elhauge shows in the portion of our brief for which he was principally responsible—is the Florida Supreme Court's premise that an interpretive manual recount is always preferable to a mechanical one and that in a close election an interpretive recount must always be had even if there was no evidence of fraud or mechanical breakdown. To argue that Florida law requires such a recount whenever the outcome might be affected (i.e., every close election) is to beg the question. Florida law insists that all legally cast ballots be counted, and it was the contention of the secretary of state that all such votes had been counted, while the famous undercounts with imperfectly perforated chads were by hypothesis not legal votes.

But in the end all this high dudgeon is unjustified for a deeper reason. This election, as any statistician will tell you, was in effect a tie. A difference of 0.5 percent in an election in which a hundred million votes were cast—at various times, under diverse circumstances, by a wide variety of means—exceeds our present capacity for accurate tabulation. The mantra of the Gore people, that we should keep counting until we can be sure that every vote has been registered, would have brought us more and more laborious recounts, with different results from each but no greater accuracy.[6] So I agree with Dworkin's proposals that for the next presidential election we standardize and modernize the machinery, schedule, and procedures. (Such improved machinery might have seen Richard Nixon and not John F. Kennedy president in 1960, but we rarely hear that the latter's presidency was illegitimate.) As for this election, what we saw was a range of institutions—from local canvassing boards to the U.S. Supreme Court—struggling with a freakish situation beyond the capacity of any to resolve to everybody's satisfaction.

REPLY TO CHARLES FRIED

RONALD DWORKIN

In the article to which Charles Fried responds, I recommended a constitutional amendment abolishing the Electoral College and providing for the direct election of the president. Many readers warned, as I had suggested, that the smaller states, which have more electoral votes per citizen than the larger ones, would block that amendment because it would eliminate that advantage. But small states would not have that reason for rejecting the Model Uniform Election Code I also recommended, which would be offered for adoption to states one by one in return for federal financing of advanced voting machinery.

The model code would provide that each state's present number of electoral votes be split among presidential candidates as near as possible in proportion to the popular vote for each candidate in that state. If most states adopted that provision, the national electoral vote would match the national popular vote much more closely than it does now, and the risk that the winner in the popular vote would lose in the Electoral College would be much reduced. If Florida had enacted a code with that provision, then even without a recount Gore would have won twelve of the state's twenty-five electoral votes and would therefore have won the presidency.

Other readers expressed disappointment that I was not more critical of the five Supreme Court justices who made Bush president; it is disingenuous, they said, to try to find creditable explanations for what was so obviously a crude political decision. But the sense of legitimacy that the Supreme Court enjoys—demonstrated, once again in this case, by the fact that no one hesitated to accept its verdict even though a great many thought that verdict plainly wrong—is very important to the rule of law and principle in America, and we should not jeopardize that legitimacy out of anger at one apparently indefensible decision. It may well be, as one reader suggested, that whatever the five justices do in the rest of their careers they will be remembered, by the public and in the academic literature, mainly for their part in this decision. But that makes it all the more important to find what I said I could not yet find: at least an ideological rationale rather than one of mere self-interest for what they did.

I therefore looked forward to the comments of Fried, who was Reagan's solicitor general and later a judge on the eminent Supreme Judicial Court of Massachusetts before he returned to Harvard Law School. Fried was a coauthor of one of the many "friend of the court" briefs that urged the Supreme Court to overturn the Florida Supreme Court's recount order. Unfortunately, his essay does not provide the defense I had hoped for, and his failure will only deepen suspicion that no decent defense can be found.

The conservative majority made two claims: first, that the Florida Supreme Court's recount order, which specified only that ballots were to be inspected to determine the "clear intention" of the voter, violated the Fourteenth Amendment's requirement of equal protection of the laws for everyone, because different vote counters would interpret that abstract standard differently; and second, that any new recount, conducted in accordance with more concrete standards, would have to be completed by December 12, which was the very day on which, late in the evening, the Supreme Court issued its opinion.[7] Fried attempts to defend both of these holdings, at least in substance, and then argues that because the election was so close anyway, it does not really matter whether the Court was right in either of them.

The Equal Protection Clause, as I pointed out, was designed to protect people against discrimination: it condemns, not any difference in the way a state's law treats different citizens, but only certain distinctions that put some citizens, in advance, at a disadvantage against others.[8] The Florida court's "clear intention" standard (taken from Florida statutory law) puts no one at a disadvantage even if it is interpreted differently in different counties. Voters who indent a chad without punching it clean through run a risk that a vote they did not mean to make will be counted if they live in a county that uses a generous interpretation of the "clear intention" statute; or they run a risk that a vote they meant to make will be discarded if they live in a county that uses a less generous interpretation. But since neither of these risks is worse than the other—both threaten a citizen's power to make his or her vote count—the abstract standard discriminates against no one, and no question of equal protection is raised.[9]

It was a striking embarrassment for the conservative majority's equal protection ruling that it cited not a single case in which a nondiscriminatory law had been held to violate the Equal Protection Clause.[10] In his response, Fried cites *Willowbrook v. Olech*, in which the Court held that a town had denied a home owner equal protection when it demanded a thirty-three-foot easement over her property, as a condition for connecting a water supply to the house, although it demanded only a fifteen-foot easement in the case of other houses.[11] But this citation shows that he has misunderstood the problem. The town had certainly discriminated against the home owner in that case—Justice Breyer, in his concurring opinion, noted, as important, the fact that the home owner had alleged that the town wanted deliberately to injure her because she had sued it in another case.

Many people have said that even if it was not unconstitutional for the Florida court to have used the abstract "clear intention" standard, rather than a more precise set of instructions about chads and indentations, using such an abstract standard was nevertheless unnecessary and unwise.[12] They believe that even though the law often instructs judges and juries to determine a person's intention with no more precise directions—to determine the intention of a deceased testator in writing the will he did, for example— such an abstract standard is out of place, as Fried puts it, "applied by many scores of variously trained, instructed, and supervised ballot counters to punched pieces of cardboard."

But judges and juries are also variously trained and supervised, and the difference between a ballot and a will is at best a matter of degree. Indeed, it might well be harder to set out in advance sensible criteria for interpreting the visual clues on a "punched piece of paper" than for interpreting the words of a will: it might be reasonably obvious from comparing a slight depression next to the name of a presidential candidate with the much more forceful indentations elsewhere on the ballot that a voter did not mean to vote for president, for example, though very hard to formulate, in a mechanical rule, a test for the comparative force of indentations. Legislatures must often choose between the imprecision of an abstract standard, like "clear voter intent," which risks differing interpretations, and the opposite dangers of a mechanical test that is almost certain to produce mistakes in particular cases. The claim that it is irrational to make either of these choices whenever the evidence in question is visual rather than verbal is surely wrong. Many states besides Florida, we must remember, have chosen the same abstract standard for manual recounts.

In any case, the question for the Supreme Court was not whether the Florida court's choice of standard was wise but whether it violated the Equal Protection Clause, and Fried has done nothing to support the majority's holding that it did or to cast doubt on his own earlier decision, while a Massachusetts judge, upholding and applying the very standard that he now believes to violate the Constitution.[13] His failure, indeed, persuades me that the majority's decision was not even defensible, as I said it was. He next discusses the Court's even more plainly indefensible decision that any new recount under a single standard would have had to be completed by the end of December 12 so that any new recount was therefore made impossible. Fried concedes that this critical holding "was the least convincing portion of the Court's opinion" and does not try to defend it. But he insists that the Court's error made no difference, because, he says, a new recount could not even have been concluded by December 18, six days later, when the Electoral College was scheduled to vote.

His judgment about the feasibility of a recount in six days is speculative: the Florida Supreme Court might well have heard arguments and declared new standards within a day or two, and it could then have ordered that new recounts proceed as expeditiously as possible and that these recounts continue while any party who objected to the new standards appealed to the Supreme Court yet again. In any case, however, it would have been wrong for the Court to prejudge the question of whether a December 18 deadline could have been met. Florida already had a slate of electors pledged to vote for Bush, and they would have voted for him on that date if the recount had not been completed. If it were completed after that date and showed that Gore had actually won, then a rival set of electors might have sent their votes to Congress, and that body would then have decided whose electoral votes to accept. That is the procedure the Constitution specifies, and the Court had no right to subvert it.

Fried next suggests that the strongest argument for what the Court did was one that in fact appealed only to the three most conservative justices, Rehnquist, Scalia, and Thomas. They said, and he agrees, that the Florida Supreme Court did not simply attempt to interpret Florida law, as it had a responsibility to do, but instead radically revised it. The Florida statute provides, as one ground for contesting an election, that the certified count has rejected a "number of legal votes sufficient to . . . place in doubt the result of the election." The key question is whether that provision permits a court to order a manual recount to determine how many of the ballots the vote-counting machines had rejected because of imperfect perforation actually demonstrated a clear intention to vote for one candidate or the other. Fried's brief argued (relying mainly on a debatable interpretation of provisions governing not the challenge stage of a postelection proceeding but the earlier protest stage) that the Florida statute assumed "by hypothesis" that imperfectly perforated ballots were not legal votes, so that the Florida court "begged the question" by assuming that a manual recount of such ballots was permissible even in a challenge proceeding.

But the Florida court's contrary interpretation is surely, at a minimum, defensible. That court attributed a perfectly sensible purpose to the challenge provisions of the statute: those provisions aimed, it supposed, to ensure that machine limitations should not change the result of a very close election by rejecting ballots that were legally cast and showed a clear intention to vote. That interpretation is attractive in itself and fits comfortably into the contest part of the Florida scheme, where success requires showing that the alleged error would have changed the overall result. Bush's own witness in the contest trial, John Ahmann, admitted that the machines used to tabulate punch-card ballots, which he had helped to design, often make mistakes, so that manual recounts are desirable in close elections.[14] If we accept that understanding of the statute's purpose, such ballots are indeed "legal votes," and it is Fried, not that court, who begs the question. He and his colleague, Elhauge, may think their own interpretation better. But they have no basis for the extraordinary conclusion that the Florida court's interpretation was so demonstrably wrong as not to count as an interpretation at all.[15]

Fried's closing observations are unfortunate. He says that it does not really matter whether the Supreme Court's decision was defensible because the election was so close anyway that it might as well have been Bush. He treats the fact that five of the nine Supreme Court justices are political conservatives as, in effect, a tie-breaker like a coin flip. But it will make a very great difference to people everywhere that it is Bush rather than Gore who is America's president. Bush's cabinet appointments (which include, as attorney general, John Ashcroft, the candidate of the religious right) have already refuted the optimistic assumption that he will try to govern from the middle, and there is ample reason to worry that his future Supreme Court appointments will be equally aimed at pleasing the extreme right of his party.

When a presidential election is close, particularly when so much turns on the outcome, it is more and not less important that the rules in place be followed punctiliously in deciding who actually won. If Gore has won not only the national popular vote but also the popular vote in Florida, and hence the Electoral College as well, then it is not only unfortunate that we will be governed by Bush's policies and constituencies but unfair. Florida's vote-counting machines, many of which are conceded to be inaccurate, particularly in counties with a high proportion of minority and poor voters, declared 3 percent of the state's ballots nonvotes. (The average in the rest of the country was 2 percent.) Fried insists that it is beyond "our present capacity" to achieve a more accurate tabulation. But the careful unofficial recounts now being conducted separately by the *Miami Herald* and by a group of other prestigious newspapers, which Fried declares a foolish exercise, will presumably show that his surprising pessimism is unfounded.

NOTES

Fried's Response to Dworkin

1. I offer only one example, but there are many: in 1992 in the Harris case, the Supreme Court in one night set aside three stays issued in a death case by the Court of Appeals for the Ninth Circuit and finally ordered that court to issue no more stays without permission of the justices.

2. Village of Willowbrook v. Olech, 120 S. Ct. 1023 (2000).

3. That this variable method was sanctioned after the election had taken place, and when it was reasonably thought by the Bush forces to favor their opponent, makes the Florida court decree more, not less, offensive.

4. Thus, for instance, some counters would decide whether an indentation was meant as a vote from whether it appeared next to the name of the presidential candidate of the same party as candidates for other offices for whom that voter had unambiguously voted. This is not an absurd inference in a forensic exercise or if doing history. I suggest that as a way to determine an election it is absurd, although as a justice of the Supreme Judicial Court of Massachusetts I participated in just such a process in the Delahunt case.

5. I am glad Dworkin does not make anything of two frequently heard specious arguments. It is said that not even December 18 was a true deadline and that Florida might have delivered its vote right up to the January date when the electoral votes are counted in Congress. Support for this is drawn from Hawaii's having once reported its votes well after the December deadline, but that was in an election where nothing turned on the Hawaii votes. Others have also complained that by stopping the recounts that were then in progress the Court created the very impossibility that they urged to justify their conclusion. This is nonsense. Assuming, as this complaint does, the equal protection violation, the recounting halted by the Court was invalid and would have had to be repeated in any event.

6. The tabulation now under way by various news media, assisted by national accounting firms, is for this reason a particularly foolish enterprise.

Dworkin's Reply to Fried

7. Fried objects to my description of all five of the justices in the majority of the Court's decision as "conservative" and the four dissenters as "more liberal." I agree that the opinions of Justices Kennedy and O'Connor are less predictable than those of Justices Rehnquist, Scalia, and Thomas, and I have praised decisions of the former justices about, for example, abortion and homosexual rights in previous articles. See chapter 4 of my book *Freedom's Law* (Cambridge, Mass.: Harvard University Press, 1996) and chapter 14 of my *Sovereign Virtue* (Cambridge, Mass.: Harvard University Press, 2000). But the large and growing number of 5–4 Supreme Court decisions, in which the five justices I called conservatives have united, justifies my informal description.

8. I describe the contemporary debate among judges and scholars about the correct interpretation of the Equal Protection Clause in chapter 14 of my book *Sovereign Virtue*. All sides to that debate have agreed that the clause only condemns differences that discriminate against someone.

9. It is, I think, arguable that Florida's use of markedly more inaccurate vote-counting machines in some counties than others denies equal protection to those in the former counties, particularly since those are counties with a higher proportion of minority and poor voters. But that holding would have benefited, if either candidate, Gore rather than Bush.

10. It was also a striking embarrassment that the conservatives found it necessary to declare that their bizarre interpretation of the Equal Protection Clause "is limited to the present circumstances, for the problem of equal protection in election processes generally presents many complexities." It is of the essence of the legal process that decisions be based on generally applicable principles, and the remarkable statement that this decision would be precedent for no future ones seems almost a confession that the majority's equal protection argument was a bad one.

11. The Court properly held, in that case, that the Equal Protection Clause protects single individuals as well as groups from discrimination.

12. As many commentators have noted, and as Fried's comments about the impermissibility of courts setting electoral standards not already in the state statutes

suggest, the Florida court had reason to fear that if it did specify more precise standards for a recount than the Florida statute stipulated a Supreme Court majority would have overruled it on that ground.

13. See Delahunt v. Johnston, 423 Mass. 731 (1996). In that case, which Fried mentions in his response, he agreed, as a member of the court, that "if the intent of the voter can be determined with reasonable certainty from an inspection of the ballot . . . effect must be given to that intent." He and the other judges understood that different inspectors would interpret that standard differently—they themselves arrived at a vote count different from the total the lower court judge had reached— but gave no suggestion that any of them detected the slightest equal protection problem in endorsing that standard for all Massachusetts elections.

14. Ahmann had written in a patent application that "incompletely punched cards can cause serious errors to occur in data-processing operations using such cards." See David Barstow and Dexter Filkins, "For the Gore Team, a Moment of High Drama," *New York Times,* December 4, 2000, p. A1.

15. Robert Lochner, who also commented on my essay, suggested that the three-judge concurring opinion, which he agrees was based on unacceptable premises about the Florida statute, can only be understood as manifesting a lack of trust by those justices in the Florida judicial system. He may be right—as he points out, Justice Stevens in his dissent made the same suggestion—but that distrust does not provide even an ideological defense of that opinion, because the deference that those three justices have consistently argued is owed to state decisions supposedly extends to state judicial as well as to legislative and executive officials.

6

BUSH V. GORE:
THREE STRIKES FOR THE CONSTITUTION,
THE COURT, AND DEMOCRACY,
BUT THERE IS ALWAYS NEXT SEASON

Michel Rosenfeld

I

In the often quoted words of Justice Stevens's strong dissent in *Bush v. Gore*,[1] "Although we may never know with complete certainty the identity of the winner of this year's Presidential Election, the identity of the loser is perfectly clear. It is the Nation's confidence in the judge as an impartial guardian of the rule of law."[2]

Actually things were much worse on that fateful day, December 12, 2000, when, in a 5–4 decision, a deeply divided Supreme Court put an end to the election and anointed George W. Bush president. Indeed, not only was the Supreme Court's majority decision patently unprincipled, but it also revealed a troubling flaw in the Constitution and potentially severe cracks in American democracy. As the Court noted, the Constitution does not give American citizens any right to vote for president.[3] Currently, all fifty states provide their citizens with the right to vote for the state electors who become part of the Electoral College charged with the election of the president and vice president. But nothing in the American Constitution prevents any or all of them from taking that right away from their citizens and choosing electors as their respective legislatures may in their sole discretion direct.[4] And, in fact, the Republican majority in the Florida legislature was well on its way to naming its own slate of electors regardless of the final tally of votes and could have thus single-handedly sealed the fate of the 2000 election, had the U.S. Supreme Court not done so beforehand.[5]

America's original 1787 Constitution did not provide a right to vote either for senators or for the president. The Constitution was amended in 1913, however, to afford citizens a right to vote directly for their senators.[6] Nothing of the sort has occurred regarding presidential elections, thus leaving the citizenry without a constitutional right to a voice in the election of the country's only truly national representatives. Whatever virtues this constitutional scheme may have had in 1787, it is certainly hard to justify in 2000 that citizens of the most powerful democracy have no secure right to participate in the selection of the person who is to occupy the most important political office in the world.

One may debate whether reliance on the Electoral College—which gives disproportionate power to smaller states—should be currently considered constitutionally undesirable. It is clear, however, as vividly illustrated by the 2000 election, that the prevailing constitutional scheme does not necessarily go hand in hand with the promotion of democracy. Although periodically discussed as an odd but improbable possibility, for the first time in more than one hundred years, the winner of the Electoral College majority (assuming for the sake of argument that Bush was the clear winner of Florida's twenty-five electoral votes) was the loser of the popular vote nationwide. Overall, Gore obtained in excess of half a million votes more than Bush.[7] Ironically, had it not been for the Florida debacle, this undoubtedly would have been the principal focus of public discussion in the aftermath of the 2000 election. America has changed dramatically since the late nineteenth century, the last time that the winner of the popular vote lost the presidential election. Today, the president's political legitimacy for wielding the vast powers that come with the office is primarily derived from having won the support of a majority (or at least a plurality) of the citizens who cast ballots on election day. Thus, even with an incontestable Bush win in Florida, the 2000 election still would have resulted in a significant setback for American democracy.

At a minimum, democracy requires that elections be won by the candidate who garners the greatest number of cast votes and that each vote that is cast be given equal weight. Recourse to the Electoral College may on occasion run counter to the first of these requirements, but it always runs afoul of the second one. The vote of a citizen of Montana or Wyoming weighs more than that of a citizen of California or New York.[8] Particularly when the winner of the popular vote also wins a majority of the Electoral College, the constitutionally sanctioned departures from the grant of equal weight to all voters may result in a tolerable constraint on democracy for the sake of federalism—although this argument sounds much less persuasive if one remembers that one of the principal reasons for settling on the Electoral College in the first place was to boost the relative electoral power of the slave-owning states vis-à-vis the rest of the Union.[9] Accepting deviations from the grant of an equal weight to each vote *within the same state,* however, lacks any plausible justification and merely weakens democracy. Yet that is exactly what happened in Florida (and many other states that were not subjected to the same intense scrutiny) as a consequence of reliance on countywide rather than statewide control of presidential elections.

Florida's sixty-seven counties were divided, for purposes of the 2000 election, among those using optical scanning voting systems and those using punch-card ballots. Of the approximately 6 million votes cast in Florida, 3.7 million were cast under the punch-card system while 2.3 million were cast under the optical scanning system.[10] The rate of "undercounts" under the former system was three times as high as the rate under the latter, with the consequence that for every 10,000 votes cast under the punch-card systems there were 250 more nonvotes than under the optical scanning system.[11] Accordingly, because of this discrepancy the relative weight of a vote cast in a punch-card county was measurably lower than that cast in an optical-scan county. Furthermore, to the extent that punch-card counties tended to be those with greater proportions of African-American voters and that allegations of intimidation and exclusion of African Americans from the voting process were accurate, the discrepancies in the weight of votes cast in Florida were not merely random. Instead—and this is even more troubling—the weight of the vote in Florida varied to some significant degree depending on the race of the voter.[12]

II

Democracy, equality, and federalism all play important roles in American presidential elections but do not always pull in the same direction. Furthermore, the Constitution provides a framework for conducting and settling elections, but that framework is far from perfect or complete. Because of these factors, the U.S. Supreme Court was faced with a limited set of options when it was confronted with the conflicts that arose from the Florida election. A fair evaluation of the Court's handling of *Bush v. Gore* should properly account for the limitations in question. In the end, however, in spite of these limitations, the Court still deserves full blame for abruptly putting an end to the election. Indeed, under existing constraints, the Court had but one viable option that would have fully vindicated its institutional integrity: declining to intervene. Had that occurred and had the counting of contested Florida ballots been completed, then any remaining issues could have been settled by the U.S. Congress as specifically prescribed by the Constitution.[13]

To better appreciate the full magnitude of Court's ill-advised intervention, let us briefly imagine what reasonable advice Americans might have had for another country having experienced something akin to what happened in Florida. Suppose that in a foreign country with a fragile democracy and with a history of discrimination in voting against certain ethnic minorities, there were a close election under the same circumstances as those that existed in Florida during the 2000 presidential election. Suppose specifically that a large number of members of an ethnic minority having suffered widespread voting discrimination in the past were turned away from the polls, intimidated, falsely accused of having a criminal record that would disqualify them as voters, or given ballots that were so confusing that many cast them incorrectly, leading to an inordinately high number of invalid votes. Imagine further that on top of all that our fragile democracy, located somewhere in the Balkans, had an experience similar to that of Palm Beach County with the butterfly ballots. Because of that ballot's confusing design, more than three thousand Gore supporters who went to the polls to vote for him unwittingly registered a vote for Buchanan, a fact corroborated in many postelection interviews and acknowledged by Buchanan himself.[14] To compound matters, a very large percentage of those 3,000 votes were cast by Jewish voters for whom Buchanan was a most improbable choice given widely held perceptions of him as having anti-Semitic leanings. The 3,000 votes at stake would have been sufficient to hand the presidential election to Gore as the official Bush lead in Florida had been set at 537 votes. Given that and the particular circumstances surrounding the butterfly ballot fiasco, its practical and symbolic place in the Florida election loom large. Moreover, it is easy to imagine that Americans committed to freedom and democracy would be quite upset if a similar set of circumstances had proved decisive in our frail and potentially explosive putative Balkan democracy.

The incidents described above and their likely impact on the 2000 election should certainly be considered an embarrassment for a country that regards itself as an example to be emulated everywhere. Bad as they are, however, these incidents were by no means the only ones that marred the presidential election in Florida. Indeed, partisan politics further damaged the integrity of the Florida vote, in relation to both the conduct of the election and the determination of its outcome.

In view of the closeness of the votes and of the problems already mentioned, it was far from ideal that the person in charge of supervising and certifying the vote count in Florida was that state's secretary of state, Katherine Harris, a partisan Republican who served as co-chair of the Bush Florida campaign committee. Even worse, her boss, the state's chief executive, Governor Jeb Bush, was not only the presidential candidate's younger brother, but he had also publicly given assurances before the election that the state would go to his brother, George, notwithstanding that polls taken as election day neared indicated that Gore might well win Florida. Although no impropriety has been associated with Jeb Bush's preelection statements and although he officially recused himself from the postelection vote counting and certification, behind the scenes he played an active and intense role on behalf of his brother after November 7. Among other things, Jeb Bush mobilized his political associates in Florida to work assiduously and relentlessly against Gore and mustered his vast resources and contacts within the state systematically to assist his brother's efforts to secure Florida's twenty-five electoral votes.[15]

For her part, Harris, who had promised to carry out her duties in a neutral fashion, made a series of crucial decisions, all of which helped Bush and hurt Gore. Moreover, in her zeal to help her political cause, she did not shy away from acting inconsistently. Thus, for example, Harris contradicted her own strict vote counting standards, which had thoroughly frustrated Gore, and shifted to a much more liberal standard when it came to counting absentee ballots, which predictably allowed Bush to pick up a significant number of crucial votes.[16]

Another partisan action that cast a shadow on 25,000 absentee ballots occurred before the election when Republican Party workers improperly took it upon themselves to fix several thousand absentee ballot requests filed by Republican voters in Seminole and Martin Counties. Had these ballot requests not been illegally fixed, the corresponding ballots would not have been issued, costing Bush potentially 4,000 votes. After the election, Democrats brought suit to invalidate all ballots that might have been tainted by the "fixed" applications. Although these lawsuits failed because the Florida courts reasoned that the improprieties involved related to the ballot application rather than to the ballots themselves, the Florida Supreme Court chastised the Republican officials involved for having clearly violated Florida's Election Code.[17] Had these officials not acted illegally Gore might have won the election. In any event, this incident further undermined vindication of the principle that all voters are entitled to equal treatment and to an equal right to vote.

After the election, both political parties mobilized on a national as well as statewide basis to influence the postelection proceedings in Florida. The Republicans were far more effective than the Democrats, which would not have mattered in and of itself. The Republicans, however, controlled both the executive and the legislative branches in Florida, and some of their most reprehensible actions may well have had a decisive impact on the ultimate outcome of the Florida election. The most glaring example of Republican misconduct concerns the suspension of the manual recount of 650,000 ballots in heavily Democratic Miami-Dade County in the aftermath of an intense and briefly violent demonstration by Republican partisans on November 22, four days before the recount deadline set by the Florida Supreme Court. The Republican demonstrators had set to pressure the canvassers proceeding with the recounts, and at one point, they physically assaulted the chairman of the Miami-Dade Democratic Party who had to be escorted to safety by police. Shortly thereafter, the recount was halted to the delight of the protesters. A nonpartisan supervisor of elections stated in an interview that the demonstrators had indeed influenced his decision to suspend the recount. Democrats accused Republicans of deliberately using intimidation and violence to procure a cessation of the recount. Republicans countered that the protest had been nothing but the spontaneous expression by Republican sympathizers of frustration at the seemingly endless recounts.[18] Contrary to this claim of spontaneity, however, the protesters had been led by staff workers sent from the offices of U.S. Senate Majority Leader Trent Lott and U.S. House Majority Whip Tom DeLay. Again, if we transport this sequence of events to our putative Balkan democracy, most Americans would find the organized partisan intimidation reprehensible if not downright unacceptable.

Taking into account the cumulative effect of what has been discussed thus far, only one solution to the Florida election mess would have been truly fair: to conduct a new election under uniform standards throughout the state and to entrust the subsequent vote count and certification to nonpartisan institutions and officials. Unfortunately, that solution was not available for various reasons, chief among them that federal law prescribes that presidential elections must be held simultaneously throughout the United States.

In the face of limited options and a need to minimize the evils of excessive localism and excessive partisanship, the ultimate resolution of the 2000 election was left to the courts. Although courts are supposed to remain above politics, the two courts that played the most important role in the controversy, the Florida Supreme Court and the U.S. Supreme Court, were both branded as partisan. The Florida Supreme Court judges were accused of acting as partisan Democrats and the U.S. Supreme Court majority that in effect put an end to the election as partisan Republicans. As we shall see below, there are ample grounds to conclude that the U.S. Supreme Court majority was excessively partisan. The same, however, cannot be fairly said of the judges on the Florida Supreme Court.

III

To appreciate why the five U.S. Supreme Court justices who handed the election to Bush were excessively partisan and why the Florida Supreme Court judges were not, it is necessary to consider briefly certain basic issues concerning judges and justice. Ideally, justice should be perfect and complete, and judges should be impartial and above all politics. In reality, however, this is rarely, if ever, possible. In a complex modern legal system like that of the United States, dispensing justice depends on interpreting and applying laws, and laws are by no means always good, clear, or complete.

The Florida electoral law that figured so prominently in *Bush v. Gore* is a good case in point. As we will see more fully below, this law was fragmentary and contradictory and fell far short of providing the necessary means to secure justice—justice in this case being fair and equal voting for all eligible Florida voters and accurate, uniform, and complete counting of the votes after the election. If we add to this the imperfections and lacunae of the relevant constitutional provisions and applicable federal laws, full justice in *Bush v. Gore* would have been impossible even if all judges involved had been superhuman.

Human judges, moreover, cannot achieve complete impartiality or remain above all politics. After all, judges are human beings with particular histories, beliefs, identities, prejudices, and political leanings—at least in the sense of leanings concerning what is best for society as opposed to preferences in partisan politics. For example, a judge who had been a civil rights lawyer may have a different outlook on race relations or gender issues and be more sensitive to certain discrimination claims than a judge with no comparable experience.

Judges may not be able to achieve absolute impartiality or to ascend above all politics, but that does not mean that all kinds or degrees of partiality or of politicization of the judiciary should be regarded as being equivalent. It is obvious that the kind of partiality at stake when a judge has a personal financial interest in a case or a close family relationship to one of the litigants is altogether different from the kind of partiality attributable to being generally more or less sympathetic to feminist claims. Accordingly, whereas it is impermissible for a judge to decide a case in which he or she has a personal financial stake or in which a relative is a litigant, no one would seriously suggest that a judge should be forbidden to decide a women's rights case because that judge has views about feminism. Similarly, it is not the same for a judge to decide cases based on partisan politics as it would be to decide based on broader or more general political commitments, such as the pursuit of greater freedom, equality, or solidarity in society.

Judges should be impartial as regards the litigants before them even if they cannot be completely neutral in their approach to the issues raised by the litigants' claims. In a case such as *Bush v. Gore,* however, it is particularly difficult to achieve or maintain the requisite impartiality inasmuch as judges like their fellow citizens have a stake and presumably some level of preference in presidential elections—and even if they were indifferent, it would be difficult to avoid the appearance of having preferences. Moreover, in such a case resolution of the legal claims seems inextricably linked to partisan politics, thus exacerbating the possibility of a decision based on such politics. Accordingly, it is hardly surprising that Bush and his supporters accused the Florida Supreme Court of having caved to partisan politics or that Gore supporters criticized the U.S. Supreme Court for having sacrificed principle to partisan politics.

Because of all this, it would be best if courts could refrain from intervening in presidential elections. That is not always possible, however, and in the absence of a more suitable forum for resolving legal issues bearing on the integrity of an election, not always desirable. Thus the Florida courts properly intervened to address the legal claims arising out of the state's 2000 election as no other suitable state forum was available for that purpose. In contrast, the U.S. Supreme Court's intervention was unnecessary and ill advised and even arguably constitutionally unwarranted as the U.S. Congress is given the ultimate authority to settle disputed presidential elections.[19] Moreover, if courts intervene in elections, because of the danger of becoming engaged in partisan politics, they would do well to avoid settling the election outright. Instead, if possible, courts ought to limit their intervention to minimizing injustices and establishing procedures, leaving it to others to determine the winner. That is what the Florida Supreme Court did, for notwithstanding all the accusations of partisanship, no one was in a position to predict the ultimate outcome of the vote counts it ordered and it was entirely possible that at the end of the process Bush would emerge as the incontestable winner.

In sharp contrast, the U.S. Supreme Court squarely put an end to all vote counting and in effect handed the election to Bush. Even worse, before its final decision on December 12, in granting the stay that ordered halting all vote counting in Florida on December 9, the Court for all practical purposes ensured the election of Bush. The Court did so by running out the clock on the vote recounts that had been proceeding throughout Florida *before* hearing oral argument on, or giving full consideration to, the merits of Bush's claims. This reeks of political partisanship as made plain by Justice Scalia's own words in support of the stay for which he and four of his fellow justices voted: "The counting of votes that are of questionable legality does in my view threaten irreparable harm to [Bush], and to the country, by casting a cloud upon what *he claims* to be the legitimacy of his election."[20] As Justice Stevens observed in his dissent from the grant of the stay, "Counting every legally cast vote cannot constitute irreparable harm," but the stay itself indeed can as it may be "tantamount to a decision on the merits in favor of [Bush]."[21]

Courts are generally reluctant to grant legal relief prior to considering a case on the merits and only do so on a showing of "great likelihood of irreparable injury" absent such interventions. For instance, if I have a legal dispute with my neighbor over ownership of the house I live in, and he shows up one morning with bulldozers, announcing that he is ready to demolish the house to build a bigger and better one, then I should be able to persuade a court that I would suffer irreparable harm if my neighbor were allowed to proceed prior to resolution of our legal dispute. Indeed, if the house is destroyed and I eventually win the lawsuit on the merits, I will have suffered irreparable harm as money compensation that would allow me to purchase a comparable house could never make up for the emotional loss of no longer living in the house I grew up in, and so on. It seems, however, entirely ludicrous to claim that Bush would have suffered a comparable loss had the vote counting been allowed to proceed until the U.S. Supreme Court decided the case on the merits. What Bush wanted was to be declared the winner of the election and to have his election considered legitimate. Not only would a win on the merits before the U.S. Supreme Court have granted him that, but the very contests and controversies in Florida, of which the ongoing vote recount was but a part, had already cast strong doubts on the legitimacy of the slim official lead he held on December 9, the day the stay was granted. Accordingly, Justice Scalia's reason for granting the stay not only seems purely partisan, it is virtually inexplicable given what the controversy before the Court was all about. On the other hand, if one allows for the supposition that the Court's majority had not already decided the case on the merits prior to receiving written briefs and to hearing oral argument and consider it possible for one of the five justices leaning toward Bush to have changed his or her mind on full consideration of the case on the merits, then the five precious days lost between the grant of the stay and the decision on the merits may have made it impossible to complete the vote counting process to which Gore would have been entitled, thus in fact clearly causing him and the American people irreparable harm.

While there may be a difference between partisan politics and less pointedly focused politics, if judges cannot rise above politics, does it really matter all that much that five justices came down on the side of Bush? If judicial outcomes relating to issues of great public interest cannot avoid being either more liberal or more conservative, for example, then the loser will always feel that justice was not well served while the winner will be satisfied that it has been rightly vindicated. If this is true, then the controversy over *Bush v. Gore* ultimately should not be considered different from those that tend to arise when the Court decides cases on such divisive issues as abortion, affirmative action, or flag burning. Whatever the decision, a significant portion of citizenry is bound to feel that the case was wrongly decided because of what they perceive as the Court's liberal or conservative bias, as the case may be.

Some people, chief among them Justice Scalia, on the other hand, altogether deny that judgments have to be in any way political, provided that judges stick to the "plain meaning" of the laws they are charged with interpreting.[22] Ironically—in view of how political the majority's decision in

Bush v. Gore would turn out to be—candidate Bush announced during the presidential campaign that if elected he would name judges in the mold of Justice Scalia and Justice Thomas to the Supreme Court because he was committed to having judges that "interpret the law rather than making the law." Although, as we shall see, this is but a vacuous slogan, it sounds attractive because it suggests that no matter how political a law may be, a judge interpreting it consistent with its "plain meaning" would not resort to any politics, as he or she would be exclusively guided by what the law in question clearly commands. Were this true, moreover, while the relevant constitutional provisions and legal rules in *Bush v. Gore* may have been somewhat defective, the Court's majority decision should be viewed as a faithful application of the pertinent legal norms to the controversy at hand, thus lifting the majority justices above the political fray. And if any lingering doubts remain, it must be because of an erroneous projection of the laws' inherent bias onto the judges.

On careful consideration, this last argument is but a smoke screen. A judge confronting the controverted constitutional issues raised in *Bush v. Gore* could not genuinely expect that the case could be resolved through any kind of reference to the "plain meaning" of the legal texts involved. It does not follow from that, however, that because any plausible resolution of the case would in some sense be political, all political outcomes would be equivalent, or that the use of certain traditional constraints on the politics of judging, most notably those imposed by the requirements of consistency and integrity, could or should not be used.

The constitutional provision that played the pivotal role in *Bush v. Gore* is the Equal Protection Clause of the Fourteenth Amendment, which provides that no state shall "deny to any person within its jurisdiction the equal protection of the laws." What that clause means has been highly contested since its adoption in 1868 after the conclusion of the Civil War. In the sole context of racial equality, the U.S. Supreme Court's interpretation of equal protection has fluctuated from sanctioning officially mandated racial segregation as acceptable to finding it unconstitutional and even in some cases, but not others, to accepting affirmative action programs involving preferential treatment based on race as constitutionally permissible.[23]

It does not take a legal norm whose meaning is as contested as that of the Equal Protection Clause to realize that reliance on any "plain meaning" is bound to be illusory in most if not all cases. Take, for instance, the seemingly simple legal command "No vehicles shall be allowed in this park" posted at the entry of an urban park used for recreation. Suppose further that you are dispatched to the entry of this park with the duty of securing compliance with the prohibition in question. Should you deny entry to the park to a person in a wheelchair? Or in a motor-powered wheelchair? Should you prohibit a three-year-old from riding her tricycle? What answer should you give to someone who asks you whether he can use his roller skates in the park? Suppose further that the park has a pond with rowboats, which had traditionally been rented out by the hour for recreation. In view of the new law, should you order that the use of these boats be terminated? Or imagine that a park visitor has just suffered a heart attack two hundred yards from the park entrance. Should an ambulance be allowed to enter the park to assist the victim? What about a taxicab hailed by the victim's friend to speed up transportation to the nearest hospital?

Even these few questions in this relatively simple situation indicate that it is illusory to expect most laws to have a "plain meaning." Moreover, even assuming that such "plain meaning" were possible—for example, all would automatically agree without the slightest hesitation on the precise meaning of "vehicle"—it would still be undesirable to apply the law "literally." If "no vehicles" means "no vehicles ever regardless of the circumstances," then the ambulance should not be allowed into the park even if that would result in the death of the heart attack victim. But is that what the legislator would have wanted had she considered this possibility? Or, if we do not know or consider relevant the intent of the legislator, is that the best or most desirable interpretation of the law? Suppose the most logical assumption about the purpose of the law is that it was meant to promote enjoyment of the park by those who use it while at the same time ensuring their safety. Would it then not squarely be against the purpose of the law to refuse entry into the park to the ambulance?

Although there may be no "plain meaning" of "vehicle," it does not follow that any meaning will do, or that some meanings are not much more plausible than others. Meanings depend on context in terms of both the situation in question—for example, enjoyment of a park—and the relevant sociocultural setting. Indeed, in any given community at any given time certain meanings are fairly settled and others contested. For example, today it is well settled in the United States that equal protection is incompatible with state-mandated racial segregation, but this was not the case at the turn of the twentieth century. Consistent with this, moreover, whereas there may not be fixed or plain meanings, judges face constraints inasmuch as certain meanings are virtually unanimously shared throughout the polity while others are contested, allowing for a range of plausible interpretations. But even in the latter case, a judge would not be justified in straying far beyond the existing range.

Even interpretation of the law prohibiting vehicles in the park cannot avoid politics—albeit such politics may be minor and uncontroversial. For example, in deciding a case on the legality of an ambulance entering the park in a medical emergency, the judge must take a position concerning the best or most rational policy considering the issues of enjoyment, safety, emergency, and recreation raised by the law and the facts before her. In addition, before reaching her decision, the judge must weigh whether a "literal" application of the law or one better suited to further its most probable purpose over which there is broad-based consensus ought to be adopted. This last issue, moreover, is one of judicial politics. Should judges have greater or lesser latitude when confronting issues not directly foreseen by the legislator?

Whatever the answers to the above questions, the judge will nonetheless have to adhere to certain constraints in order to fulfill her duties legitimately. For example, the political decision as to whether opening the park to motorcycle races would ultimately constitute a better use for it would clearly be an inappropriate one for the judge to consider under the existing law. In short, just as certain meanings are excluded because of the prevailing sociocultural consensus, certain political choices would be inappropriate to the extent that they are implicitly or explicitly incompatible with the purpose of the applicable law or its implementation.

To the extent that the law leaves open *certain* political choices, however, judges are not precluded from following their convictions in deciding cases, and hence under those conditions both liberal and conservative solutions would be equally legitimate. But even then, judges ought to be further constrained by requirements of consistency and integrity. Even where liberal or conservative leanings may be entirely proper, a judge should not jump from one to the other solely to achieve particular results in individual cases. Finally, consistency is not an ultimate value inasmuch as there ought to be room for a judge to recognize past mistakes or changes due to evolving circumstances or a bona fide shift in convictions. Breaks in consistency, however, should be assessed in terms of a standard of integrity. While frequent lack of consistency to further a partisan agenda would lack integrity, rare breaches of consistency because of principled reconsiderations would clearly comport with preservation of integrity.

IV

Consistent with the above standards and constraints, the Florida Supreme Court decisions meet with judicial consistency and integrity in crucial ways that the U.S. Supreme Court's decision in *Bush v. Gore* does not. The Florida Supreme Court had to deal with a state law that was unsatisfactory, incomplete, and contradictory as well as inconsistent with federal law. Nevertheless, the Florida court managed to draw consistent and defensible conclusions, even if they were not the only plausible ones. In other words, the applicable legal norms were sufficiently open-ended to allow judges with different judicial philosophies to reach different results while remaining equally faithful to the requirement of judicial integrity and to widely accepted canons of judicial interpretation.

In the broadest terms, the controversy before the Florida courts revolved at first around two issues concerning the "protest" phase (as opposed to the "contest" phase). The protest phase is that which precedes the official certification of election results by the secretary of state. The contest phase begins after certification. The two issues in question were: (1) the extent to which extensive manual vote recounts were proper; and (2) the requisite deadline for certification in the face of such recounts and the extent of the secretary of state's discretion in fixing that deadline before completion of ongoing vote recounts.

The Florida Election Code, which applies to all state elections including the presidential one, provides both that election results shall be certified seven days after election day and that full manual recounts are appropriate if errors in vote tabulation could affect the outcome of the election. The code, however, does not set any deadline for filing additional or corrected vote totals resulting from such a recount.[24] Moreover, two provisions, one dealing with the state officials in charge of counting the votes and the other dealing with deadlines for submitting vote counts to the secretary of state, were inconsistent. The first *mandated* ignoring counts submitted after the deadline; the second, in contrast, *permitted* but did not require ignoring such counts. Furthermore, the first provision had been enacted in 1951 and the second in 1989.

The code also provided for submission of counts of absentee ballots just like all other votes by the end of the seventh day after the election. Federal law, however, requires that in elections for federal office absentee ballots from overseas must be counted so long as they were signed no later than election day and were received in the state within ten days after the election. This federal requirement, moreover, allowed for an anomalous situation in an election as close as that for president in 2000. If the results were certified within seven days and the overseas absentee ballots received three days later tipped the election to the certified loser, then the latter was entitled to be declared the winner. But if properly ordered manual recounts completed between the seventh and the tenth day after the election would when added together with absentee overseas ballots tip the election in favor of the candidate who was trailing the seventh day after the election, then the secretary of state could in effect choose the election's winner by using her discretion to accept or reject the state votes tallied after the seventh day following the election.

The Florida Supreme Court dealt with the above-mentioned inconsistency in the Florida Election Code through reliance on traditional and well-settled rules of legal interpretation. When a state law is inconsistent, a more specific provision has priority over a more general one, and a more recently adopted provision supersedes a conflicting older provision. In this case, the more permissive provision, which allowed inclusion of vote recounts concluded after the seventh day following the election, was both the most recent and the most specific of the two.

In concluding that the secretary of state had exceeded her discretion in rejecting amended returns that would result from manual recounts completed more than seven days afer the date of the election, the Florida Supreme Court also remained within the bounds of legitimate judicial interpretation. The secretary had rejected the recounts on the grounds that there had been no election fraud and that the mere *possibility* that the recount *could* affect the outcome of the election was insufficient to warrant extending the deadline. Stressing that the Florida Constitution reserves a prominent place to the right of suffrage, the Florida Supreme Court construed the secretary's realm of discretion more narrowly than she had. Given that neither the Florida voters' nor the state's interest in participating to the fullest possible extent in the election of the president would be harmed by extending the certification beyond seven days, the added gain of allowing for a more accurate count in a close election outweighed whatever loss would result from somewhat narrowing the scope of the secretary's discretion. Or at least that was as plausible an interpretation of Florida's electoral and constitutional scheme as one that put greater stress on executive discretion and lesser weight on the democratic principle of making every vote count.

Subsequent to the Florida Supreme Court's decision regarding the protest phase, Bush was certified the winner by 537 votes on November 26. On November 27, Gore set in motion the contest process, which culminated with the December 8 Florida Supreme Court 4–3 decision in *Gore v. Harris*.[25] Florida law allows a candidate to contest an election by bringing a lawsuit in circuit court. Gore did so and lost, but the Florida Supreme Court reversed the trial judge's decision as "clearly erroneous." Relying on a 1982 precedent and refusing to investigate the factual evidence introduced by Gore—which included 9,000 so-called undervotes (i.e., punched ballots that registered no vote for president while registering votes for other offices during the machine count) never subjected to a manual count from heavily Democratic Miami-Dade County—the trial judge, N. Sanders Sauls, flatly rejected Gore's challenge.

What made Judge Sauls's decisions "clearly erroneous" according to the majority on the Florida Supreme Court was that in relying on the 1982 precedent, he had failed properly to account for crucial changes in Florida law that had been adopted by the state legislature in 1999. Chief among these was the addition of the following ground as a basis for contesting an election: "Receipt of a number of illegal votes or rejection of a number of legal votes sufficient to change or place in doubt the result of the election."[26] Clearly, even standing alone the 9,000 Miami-Dade undervotes "placed in doubt" the result of the election as Bush's lead had shrunk to less than 200 votes by that time.

Since machines typically undercount a certain percentage of valid votes and since the Florida legislature had clearly indicated, in laws adopted before the 2000 election, that no vote should be ignored so long as "the clear intent of the voter" could be ascertained, the court ordered a statewide manual count of the undervotes. Gore had requested manual counts only in certain traditionally Democratic counties, and Bush did not ask for any such counts as his strategy was to obtain a judicial order ending all counts while he was still ahead. The court felt, however, that since the overriding legal concern was that all legal votes should be counted, the fairest and likeliest way to accomplish this would be through a statewide count of all the undervotes that bore "a clear indication of the intent of the voter."

This standard comported with the law of Florida as well as that of many other states. Moreover, inclusion of vote counts that had been rejected by the secretary of state for not having been submitted in a timely manner was consistent with recent Florida precedent. In a contest relating to an election to the U.S. House of Representatives, a unanimous Florida Supreme Court rejected the contesting candidate's request to exclude 11,000 ballots that had not been submitted on time.[27] And in so doing, the court decided that failure to abide by time limits similar to those present in the presidential election did not constitute sufficient grounds to disenfranchise thousands of voters. In both cases, the Florida Supreme Court determined that the need for accuracy and the attempt to make every vote count outweighed the need for prompt finality. Whether or not one agrees with this, the Florida Supreme Court certainly acted with consistency and integrity and within accepted bounds of legal interpretation. In short, the Florida law may not have provided a clear and unequivocal road map to the resolution of Gore's contest, but any fair-minded person would have to conclude that the court's decision was comfortably within the bounds of legitimacy.

V

The same cannot be said, however, of the U.S. Supreme Court's majority decision. As already mentioned, the grant of the stay that stopped all vote counts on December 9 is difficult to explain except in purely partisan terms (whether deliberate or not). And so is the same majority's decision on December 12 that no time remained to remedy the equal protection violation found by the Court. Finally, some aspects of the majority opinion, and the main thrust of the concurring opinion by Chief Justice Rehnquist and Justices Scalia and Thomas, contravene fundamental canons of judicial integrity and consistency.

Significantly, the five justices in the majority have been responsible for a veritable judicial revolution reversing a trend going back to the New Deal in order greatly to expand states' rights and powers at the expense of the national government. Indeed, making proof of an activism that easily matches if it does not exceed that embraced by the Warren Court in its protection of fundamental individual rights, the Rehnquist Court's majority has systematically invalidated as impermissibly intrusive on state powers widely supported laws enacted by Congress in numerous different areas, including gun possession in schools,[28] overtime pay for state probation officers,[29] age discrimination,[30] and violence against women.[31] Yet in *Bush v. Gore* this same majority turned against one of the most fundamental tenets of American federalism, namely, that state courts are the authoritative interpreters of state law and that federal courts—including the U.S. Supreme Court—must defer to state court interpretations of state law.[32] Thus not only was the majority on the U.S. Supreme Court acting in a way that was glaringly inconsistent with their active promotion of states' rights, but they did so with respect to a well-settled and deeply entrenched principle of federalism supported alike by both partisans and opponents of expanded states' rights. Under the circumstances, the Rehnquist majority acted not simply in an inconsistent manner but in a way so at odds with the position they had steadfastly embraced before this case, and to which they would return immediately thereafter,[33] as clearly to breach the most elementary requirements of the principle of integrity.

Specifically, the U.S. Supreme Court was confronted with two issues: (1) whether the Florida Supreme Court's interpretation of that state's electoral code amounted to the creation of new legal standards to resolve presidential election contests in violation of Article II, section 1, clause 2, of the federal Constitution; and (2) whether the "clear intent of the voter" standard used to carry out the manual count ordered by the Florida Supreme Court violated the Equal Protection Clause. The first of these issues was addressed only in the concurring opinion, and it tracked the Bush camp's attack against the Florida Supreme Court on the grounds that it had in essence written an entirely new law, thus usurping the role of the legislature instead of faithfully interpreting the law that the latter had previously enacted. On the other hand, the second issue, which was to prove decisive for the five justices who put an end to the election, had been virtually ignored in all the previous judicial proceedings leading to this decisive round. Actually, that was hardly surprising given the potential contradictory and explosive consequences that might follow from a serious and principled application of the Equal Protection Clause to the Florida presidential election.

In a nutshell, the U.S. Supreme Court's decision turned on two legal conclusions: (1) application of the "clear intent of the voter" standard in the manual count of undervotes amounted to an equal protection violation because it failed to give equal weight to every vote to the extent that ballots with equivalent physical features were treated differently by various persons entrusted with the count; and (2) the combination of federal and state legal norms applicable to presidential elections mandated that the Florida electors be finally ascertained by December 12, six days before these electors were required to cast their votes for president. As we shall see, the first of these conclusions is at best barely tenable and clearly unwise. The second, however, is downright indefensible, and as such it seems a mere pretext for purposes of securing a purely partisan result.

In the context of voting, equal protection requires an equal opportunity to vote for all eligible voters and granting an equal weight to all votes cast. As already indicated in the discussion of the problems that plagued the Florida presidential election and its aftermath, neither of these requirements was satisfied. Indeed, the differences between the optical-machine system and the punch-card system when added to the butterfly ballots, to the obstacles encountered by certain African-American would-be voters, and to the inconsistent standards for accepting votes as valid, sanctioned by Katherine Harris, clearly combine into significant departures from equal opportunity to vote and to a vote-counting process bound to result in an unequal weighing of all legally cast votes. Moreover, even if these problems had not occurred, the mere fact that responsibility for organizing, monitoring, and tallying the Florida vote was left to each of the sixty-seven Florida countries made it impossible for the *state* (as the Equal Protection Clause clearly requires) uniformly to guarantee or achieve an equal opportunity to vote or an equal weighing of all cast votes.

In comparison to these major problems, the equal protection concerns actually addressed by the Court seem minor if not downright trivial. Indeed, given the choice of leaving a large number of votes entirely uncounted (Bush partisans insisted that these votes had been counted because they were subjected to machine counts, but inasmuch as these machines did not register some of the votes that had been properly completed, the latter votes can be fairly said to have remained uncounted) or counting all such votes subject to certain inconsistencies, it plainly seems that the second option was by far preferable among the two imperfect alternatives actually available.

It is also important to note that contrary to suggestions in the Court's per curiam opinion to the effect that the Florida manual count was being conducted in the absence of any standard, the Florida Supreme Court had in fact imposed a uniform statewide standard. That standard, which had been adopted by the Florida legislature and which was the standard in a majority of the states—including Texas where it had been signed into law by none other than Bush himself—required counting all ballots that evinced "the clear intent of the voter."[34] The problem, therefore, was not the lack of a standard but rather that the standard was an imperfect means to the end of ascribing an equal weight to all cast votes.

The law often provides imperfect means to clearly defined ends, and in many cases it must do so because there is no plausible alternative. Thus, for example, in the area of criminal trials where the uncontested purpose is to acquit the innocent and convict the guilty, the means employed, namely, "proof beyond a reasonable doubt," are not only imperfect—both because they are skewed in favor of acquitting some of the guilty in order to minimize the chances of convicting anyone who is innocent and because in spite of that they cannot prevent the conviction of a certain number of innocent persons—they are also bound to vary in their implementation from one jury to the next. Because there is no way to quantify what should amount to proof beyond a reasonable doubt, the actual standard for convictions is bound to fluctuate from one jury to the next. Such fluctuations, however, are not deemed to amount to violations of equal protection. So long as the standard is applied honestly, inequities resulting from a different understanding of what that standard requires do not alone give rise to constitutional violations. Even when what is at stake is life imprisonment or the death penalty.

It seems that use of the intent-of-the-voter standard for purposes of granting equal weight to each legally cast vote is analogous from an equal protection standpoint to reliance on the beyond-a-reasonable-doubt standard in the context of criminal trials. Notwithstanding this analogy, one can raise two objections as the two situations under comparison are arguably different in crucial respects. The first objection is that whereas proof beyond a reasonable doubt may be the best we can do in the criminal trial context, the same is not true about the intent-of-the-voter standard in the context of elections. Thus, for example, instead of using the intent-of-the-voter standard, which is bound to lead to certain inconsistencies, one could adopt a physical standard—such as a clear punch through the ballot leaving no hanging chads—which could be applied consistently to all votes subjected to a manual counting. The second objection, which was relied on by the Court's majority to buttress its conclusion that the count ordered by the Florida Supreme Court violated equal protection, is that the analogy between the above-mentioned standards is inappropriate. This is because the fact finder in a criminal trial must deal with testimony by persons and must assess their credibility, whereas the vote counter confronts a "thing" and can therefore ascertain intent through "specific rules designed to ensure uniform treatment."[35]

Neither of these objections is particularly persuasive, however, as the first depends on a policy choice over which reasonable minds may disagree and the second relies on an overly simplistic and hence erroneous conception of interpretation. In dealing with how to handle vote counts, a legislature could choose between a criterion relying exclusively on physical marks on ballots or one focused on intent of the voter. Whereas the first alternative would promote greater certainty, the second would give greater weight to the will of the voter. Accordingly, any legislature that believed that greater fidelity to a voter's intent is a more important objective would be justified in settling for an intent-of-the-voter standard.

As to the second objection, the premise adopted by the Court's majority that specific rules provide better means for ascertaining intent when dealing with an inanimate object, such as a ballot, is plainly wrong. An undervote that is a punch-card ballot bearing certain full perforations, certain partial ones, and perhaps other signs marked by a voter must be viewed as a text conveying a message. Like every other text, the message conveyed by a perforated punch-card ballot may be immediately obvious or it may depend on placing the various signs involved in proper context. For example, should an incomplete perforation relating to the vote for president be treated differently according to whether it is completely unlike any other perforation on the same ballot or whether it bears close resemblance to some of the other perforations? Arguably, the answer is yes, for it is entirely possible that the same physical mark may amount to a clear intent to vote in one context but not in another. And if this is true, then there is no difference in kind between interpreting the testimony of a trial witness and interpreting the intent of a voter from a "reading" of his or her ballot. The main difference between the two is just one of degree.[36]

Although the equal protection ruling handed down by the Court's majority may have been unsupported by precedent and unwise, it does not of itself exceed the bounds of legitimate judicial interpretation. When put in proper context, however, this ruling cannot meet the minimum standards of judicial consistency or integrity. One of the cornerstones of judicial integrity consists in accepting that the rule that determines the results in the case being adjudicated will have precedential value in subsequent cases raising the same or similar issues. Accordingly, in deciding a case, a judge must be mindful that the rule he or she devises for the occasion will be applicable to subsequent cases and determine in whole or in part the winners and losers in those cases in ways that the judge who is now imposing the rule may not be able to anticipate. This requirement encourages judges to think in terms of more general rules suitable for certain classes of cases rather than rules that are so narrow as to appear fit only to lend support to a particular result in the case at hand. For example, a determination that equal protection requires rejection of all requests for manual recounts in presidential elections would certainly have benefited Bush in 2000 but could well work to the advantage of a Democratic candidate in some sub-sequent election. In *Bush v. Gore*, in contrast, the Court's majority carved out a very broad rule linking precise uniform statewide standards to satis-faction of the constitutionally mandated requirement of granting equal weight to all cast votes but expressly limited its application to the unique circumstances of the 2000 Florida election.[37] In thus attempting to avoid the broad precedential implications of their novel decision, the justices in the majority adverted to the "many complexities" relating to application of equal protection to elections. As further refinement of rules to accommo-date unanticipated circumstances is part and parcel of applying precedents, however, the Court's majority efforts to undercut the precedential value of their ruling strongly suggest a breach of integrity for purposes of achieving an expedient result without having to live with its clearly foreseeable con-sequences.

This lack of integrity is exacerbated in the case of the three justices who joined the concurring opinion. Indeed, these justices had a long history of interpreting the Equal Protection Clause in the narrowest possible terms, only invalidating laws that discriminated intentionally on the basis of race, national origin, or religion or that involved affirmative action benefiting racial minorities. Accordingly, the three justices' embrace of a completely inconsistent broad view of equal protection combined with the disavowal of its precedential value only exacerbate the impression that their only concern was to secure Bush's victory.

Of the seven justices who found an equal protection violation, only two, Breyer and Souter, acted with integrity. Indeed, both of them had em-braced a broader conception of equal protection in the past, and both wanted to give the Florida courts an opportunity to tailor an adequate statewide standard that would allow the manual count to proceed. Justices Breyer and Souter were thus prepared to live with the consequences of their decision, and had their position prevailed either Bush or Gore might have won depending on subsequent actions by the Florida courts and on the outcome of the vote count conducted under new standards.

In contrast, the five justices who in effect put an end to the election did not leave themselves open to the slightest possibility that Gore might even-tually prevail. And since there was no basis in law for locking in Bush's victory—as even the expansive view of equal protection that they had em-braced for the occasion did not foreclose concluding the manual recount process—these five justices resorted to a veritable deus ex machina. They invoked a phantom December 12 vote counting deadline required neither by state nor by federal law. Ironically, had they not arbitrarily ordered the vote count halted on December 9, it might well have been completed by December 12 (making the complaints regarding a lack of uniform stan-dards either moot, if Bush prevailed, or amenable to resolution in the

Florida courts, if Gore prevailed, while fully preserving the possibility of an appeal to the U.S. Supreme Court). And had these five justices not imposed the fabricated December 12 deadline making it explicit that any remedy the Florida court might grant to get over the equal protection hurdle would be unconstitutional, the vote count, even under a new standard, might well have been completed by December 18, the first plausible legal deadline.

The arguments offered by the five justices to support their December 12 final deadline can only be characterized as highly disingenuous. These arguments revolve around two relevant sources of law: 3 U.S.C. § 5, the federal law designed to provide a safe harbor shielding states against possible rejection of their selected presidential electors by the U.S. Congress; and the Florida Supreme Court's interpretation of that state's election code. Although the federal law in question is far from clear in all respects, it is rather plain in one respect that is crucial regarding the Florida election dispute. What is clear under 3 U.S.C. § 5 is that if a state acting under a law adopted before the day of the election has settled on a slate of presidential electors six days before the date fixed for the meeting of such electors throughout the nation (in 2000 that latter date was December 18), then that slate must be accepted as legitimate by the U.S. Congress when it meets on January 6 to certify the votes of the Electoral College. Thus, by settling on its electors by December 12, Florida could avail itself of a "safe harbor" and ensure against challenges in the U.S. Congress. What is also clear from consideration of all applicable constitutional and legal provisions is that a state is perfectly entitled to select its electors up to the date set for the convening of electors (December 18 in 2000) and that the vote of such electors would still count in full unless Congress decided to uphold a challenge against them. In short, nothing in federal law prohibited Florida from settling on its slate of electors at least up to December 18. The only thing that would be lost by extending the process beyond December 12 was immunity from possible challenges before the U.S. Congress.

What is not clear about 3 U.S.C. § 5, however, is the scope of the immunity it affords to electors coming within its safe harbor. It is obvious that such a scope cannot be unlimited as the Constitution itself forbids certain persons—for example, a senator or the secretary of defense—from being electors, and if a state had such a person in its slate selected within the safe harbor period, the Congress would not only be *entitled* to reject that person's vote, it would be *compelled* to do so.[38] Therefore, the most plausible interpretation of 3 U.S.C. § 5 would consist in construing the safe harbor provision as immunizing a state's slate of electors against challenges under state law but not against those grounded on the Constitution or federal law.[39]

Federal law thus did not require Florida to wrap up its selection of electors by December 12. The five-justice majority in the U.S. Supreme Court decreed, however, that time had run out under Florida state law as interpreted by the Florida Supreme Court. As the Florida Election Code does not explicitly address this issue, the sole authority on which the five justices could rely were the pronouncements made by the Florida Supreme Court in its December 8 decision ordering the recounts. It is true that the Florida court indicated that consistent with its interpretation of state law, the ordered recount should be concluded by December 12 so as not to lose the benefits of the safe harbor provided by federal law. But that was at a time when the Florida court expected that the manual count could be completed by December 12, before the December 9 stay put a stop to the count and before the December 12 U.S. Supreme Court decision decreed that the count ordered by the Florida court was in violation of the Equal Protection Clause.

Nowhere in the Florida Supreme Court's December 8 decision was there a conclusion that the December 12 deadline imposed an absolute bar to any further remedy under the Florida Election Code. Nor was there any discussion of whether falling within the safe harbor was more important under Florida law than making every vote count, or whether a proper vote count extending to December 18 would not be more consonant with Florida's law than holding fast to an illusory safe harbor as Florida's selection of electors had become vulnerable to equal protection challenges. Indeed, had the U.S. Supreme Court sent back the case to the Florida courts without having determined that the clock had run out on December 12, it is entirely possible that applying the broad equal protection standards articulated for the first time by the U.S. Supreme Court, the Florida courts would have found a whole new host of constitutional violations in the handling of the 2000 election by Florida officials. Consistent with this hypothesis, moreover, the Florida courts could have reasoned that the December 12 deadline was of little use because Congress would be free to overturn Florida's choice on the basis of federal constitutional violations. Or the Florida courts could have simply concluded that in their understanding of Florida law remedying constitutional flaws was more important than seeking safe harbor protection.

The December 12 deadline thus by no means required putting an end to the Florida presidential election aftermath under either federal or state law. Significantly, as one of the judges on the Florida Supreme Court stated in his concurring opinion in the final dismissal of Gore's case in conformity with the U.S. Supreme Court December 12 decision, "December 12 was not a 'drop dead' date under the Florida election scheme. . . .[It] was simply a permissive 'safe harbor' date to which the states could aspire. It certainly was not a mandatory contest deadline under the plain language of the Florida Election Code (i.e., it is not mentioned there) or this Court's prior rulings."[40] As this judge further noted, the U.S. Supreme Court simply misinterpreted Florida law.[41] But even if that had not been the case, the U.S. Supreme Court should still have left it to the state's court to interpret state law and had no basis to usurp that power. In view of all this, there is but one inescapable conclusion: the five justices in the majority threw away all consistency and integrity to ensure that the state courts would not be able to legitimately exercise their exclusive powers in any way that might threaten the certainty or finality of Bush's victory.

Although the concurring opinion of Chief Justice Rehnquist joined by Justices Scalia and Thomas did not directly figure in the disposition of the case, it deserves a brief comment inasmuch as it lacks even the most tenuous links to consistency or integrity and as it clearly betrays these justices' pretense to textualism and "strict constructionism." One can only surmise that one of the principal reasons for writing the concurring opinion was that the three justices felt uncomfortable joining an equal protection opinion standing against what they had consistently and vigorously fought against throughout their tenure on the High Court. It seems that these justices felt compelled to join Justices O'Connor and Kennedy to form the per curiam majority for purely political reasons. Bush still would have won if the three justices refused to join the per curiam opinion, but there would have been no majority support for any legal ground that would justify the outcome of the case—a situation potentially much more politically explosive than that triggered by the actual Court decision. Under this scenario, four justices (O'Connor, Kennedy, Souter, and Breyer) would have agreed that there was an equal protection violation, but five justices (Rehnquist, Stevens, Scalia, Thomas, and Ginsburg) would have disagreed; two justices (O'Connor and Kennedy) would have agreed that the equal protection violation could not be remedied, but seven justices would not have agreed that that was dispositive (the five who would not have agreed there was an equal protection violation plus Souter and Breyer, who did agree but thought it could be remedied); and finally, three justices (Rehnquist, Scalia, and Thomas) would have ordered the end of the Florida election on the extraordinary grounds discussed below, but six justices (Stevens, O'Connor, Kennedy, Souter, Ginsburg, and Breyer) would have disagreed with disposition of the case on those grounds. In sum, Bush still would have won because three justices would have favored him on some grounds and two on other grounds. While this happens in a number of ordinary cases before the Court without much fanfare, imagine the impact of the headline "U.S. Supreme Court Orders End of Florida Recount Making Bush Winner: No Majority on the Court Agrees on the Reasons Why."

At bottom, the concurring opinion echoed Bush's often repeated charge that the Florida Supreme Court had in effect enacted an entirely new election law, thus illegitimately usurping the role of the legislature rather than acting as a court. As we have seen above, this charge is simply false as the

Florida Supreme Court decisions fall well within the range of entirely acceptable judicial interpretations. Moreover, being the staunchest and most steadfast defenders of states' rights on the Court, the justices who joined the concurring opinion could not simply ignore the undisputed constitutional principle that federal courts must defer to their state counterparts when it comes to interpreting state law. Instead, the three justices had to appeal to federal law but had to do so in a bizarre and largely incoherent manner because otherwise they simply could not have come up with any cogent reason for stopping the Florida vote count.

Ordinary recourse to federal law (including constitutional law) in order to invalidate a state law or a state judicial decision involves establishing an irreconcilable conflict between federal law and state law as enacted by the legislature or as interpreted by courts. A clear example of this is the per curiam opinion's invalidation of the court-ordered Florida manual count of undervotes as contrary to what is prescribed by the Equal Protection Clause. The concurring opinion, however, does not follow a similar path but instead invokes federal constitutional law as a means to prevent the Florida court from frustrating the Florida legislature. On the surface, the concurring opinion's rather unusual undertaking may nonetheless seem to lead to a plausible result. Concretely, since Article II of the U.S. Constitution explicitly empowers state legislatures in presidential elections, the legislatures arguably become federal agents for purposes of the presidential election. This would be analogous to—if for the sake of argument we do not assume it to be unconstitutional—a state governor being temporarily appointed by the president as a special envoy to a foreign nation. Clearly, under those circumstances, it would be logical for the governor to be bound by the president's instructions rather than by any laws to the contrary promulgated by his or her state's legislature.

On closer analysis, however, the Constitution does not merely make the state legislatures federal agents, and accordingly the above analogy becomes highly misleading. The relevant constitutional language is: "Each state shall appoint, in such manner as the legislature thereof may *direct,* a number of electors."[42] If the legislature directed that it would itself choose the electors, then the above analogy *may* or *may not* be appropriate, depending on whether "legislature" is merely understood as the sum of all legislators or as an institution within a political framework carved out by a state constitution (in which case, for example, a valid legislative act would require the acquiescence of the governor, or if he or she were to veto the slate of electors approved by a majority of state legislators, a subsequent two-thirds majority vote by such legislators). In the case of Florida, as the legislature enacted an election code and entrusted the selection of presidential electors to the state's eligible voters, questions concerning interpretation and application of the code were bound to arise. Were these questions to be answered by the courts? By the legislature?

The concurring opinion acknowledges that under the Florida election scheme as fashioned by the state legislation there is room for court interpretation of the relevant law. But it also goes on to say that in view of the federal constitutional design, "the text of the election law itself, and not just its interpretation by the courts of the States, takes on independent significance."[43] This last statement, however, amounts to nonsense as no meaning can be derived from a text without interpretation. Indeed, no text speaks for itself as made plain by the fact that a person who does not understand English cannot extract any meaning from the Florida Election Code or any other law written in English.

Once one recognizes that all legal texts require some interpretation before they can become intelligible, then the concurring opinion's position collapses into incoherence. Indeed, the three concurring justices do not recognize an exclusive right of interpretation for the state legislatures or the federal courts, nor do they point to any independent federal norms— such as the Equal Protection Clause—that would rule out certain interpretations of state election law as being in conflict with existing federal law. Accordingly, shorn of all its deceptive accoutrements, the concurring justices' position boils down to the creation out of the blue of a new power for federal judges. As a practical matter, this new power available in the context of presidential elections allows federal judges to set aside state court decisions on state election law whenever federal judges feel like it, as all that is needed is an assertion that the state court interpretation departs from the text of the state law. While this may not, strictly speaking, give federal judges absolute discretion, it nearly does so. That is because only those laws that would be given automatically the exact same interpretation by all those who understood the language in which they were written could remain immune from any deviation between the text and its interpretation.

What is perhaps most remarkable about the concurring opinion is that while it posits texts as having meaning independent of *any* interpretation, it manages to undermine this very hypothesis in its attempt to demonstrate how its premises necessarily lead to its conclusions. Specifically, the concurring justices provide some aberrant readings of the relevant constitutional text and radically depart from their well-established prior (and based on decisions handed down shortly after *Bush v. Gore* soon to become subsequent)[44] commitment to affording broad protection to state prerogatives threatened by congressional legislation—even if such legislation is designed, like the one at stake in the present case, to further prescriptions contained in the Constitution itself.

As I have already emphasized, the Florida Election Code is so full of complexities, inconsistencies, and lacunae that the idea that its text may be given any cogent meaning without elaborate interpretation is preposterous. Moreover, as also already mentioned, the relevant constitutional text mandating selection of presidential electors as the state legislature "shall direct" is far from transparent. Most important, this text does not in and of itself specify whether the term "legislature" should be interpreted as meaning a detached self-contained body acting by and for itself or as part and parcel of an organically linked set of interrelated institutions designed to act in a coordinated fashion within a commonly shared normative framework carved out by the state's constitution. Yet the difference between these two interpretations is crucial for the principal argument on which the concurring opinion relies. Indeed, if the second of the above interpretations is the correct one, then the entire thrust of the concurring opinion is completely absurd. The Florida Constitution and election law make it clear that the Florida courts (including the Florida Supreme Court) are competent to interpret the state's election law and to adjudicate disputes under it. Consequently, since the Florida legislature is a creature of the state's constitution and since that legislature did not exclude Supreme Court review of contests in presidential elections in the election code it adopted, then the only logical conclusion is that the Florida legislature "directed" before the 2000 election that the selection of presidential electors should proceed according to the prescriptions in the election code as interpreted and applied by the Florida courts. And consistent with this, the concurring opinion's stated grounds for protecting the state legislature from the state's judiciary amount to no more than a completely arbitrary unjustifiable departure from the principle of respect for state court interpretations of state law. Furthermore, this departure is utterly inconsistent with the aggressive and highly activist record of the three justices involved regarding zealous protection of state prerogatives in general and state judicial prerogatives in particular in the context of congressional legislation designed to further federal constitutional objectives.[45]

Whereas the preceding remarks should satisfy any fair-minded person that neither Article II of the Constitution nor the Florida Election Code "speak for themselves," it may still be arguably possible to justify the concurring opinion's conclusions based on adoption of the first of the two above-mentioned interpretations of the relevant constitutional language. In other words, the concurring justices may have been utterly inconsistent and may have paid lip service to a theory of interpretation that they themselves were squarely contradicting, but they may have nonetheless reached a conclusion that may have satisfied the requirements of consistency and integrity if it had been articulated by liberal judges with much more restrictive views of the proper scope of states' rights.

On closer examination, however, not even a liberal justice could put forward a credible justification for interpreting Article II as suggesting, much less requiring, that state legislatures ought to be understood as operating completely independently from all other institutions to which they are otherwise intrinsically linked pursuant to the dictates of their state's constitution. Moreover, that no judge could plausibly or consistently justify such a conclusion underscores the following crucial point. It does not follow from the recognition that legal texts do not speak for themselves, that they may be construed as meaning virtually anything, or that all plausible meanings are likely to be equivalent.

There are several reasons why interpretation along the lines suggested immediately above ought to be rejected. First, nothing in Article II suggests that "legislature" should be understood as an entity extracted from its customary context. While this suggests that there is no positive reason for leaning in favor of the interpretation under consideration, it does not provide a negative reason for rejecting such an interpretation outright. Such a negative reason is readily available, however, and it can be established through application of a well-established rule of constitutional interpretation.

The rule in question holds that whenever constitutional text may be plausibly interpreted in more than one way, preference should be given to those interpretations that are more likely to uphold the consistency of the Constitution (or of one of its articles or clauses as the case may be) taken as a whole. In other words, the Constitution should be construed as an internally coherent document. In particular, seemingly small differences in formulation should not be considered as superfluous, as the Constitution's drafters are not to be assumed to have used language gratuitously. For example, in Article I the Constitution authorizes exercise of powers that are characterized as "necessary" in one place and as "absolutely necessary" in another—a difference noted by the U.S. Supreme Court in its interpretation of the scope of the powers that qualify as "necessary."[46] Along similar lines, in contrast to Article II of the Constitution, which provides for appointment of presidential electors as the state legislature *"may direct,"* Article I, section 3, provides that the two senators form each state shall *"be chosen* by the legislature thereof." Although this latter language was superseded in 1913 by the Seventeenth Amendment, which provides for direct elections of senators, while it was in force it endowed state legislatures with a federal power that was completely independent from their powers under the constitution of their own state. Indeed, even if the state constitution were silent on, or worse, against, the power of the legislature to choose senators, such a legislature would still have it as a matter of federal constitutional law. The power to choose senators implied, therefore, that if necessary state legislatures could operate independently from, or in contradiction to, the state constitutional order in which they were otherwise embedded. In contrast, appointment of presidential electors as the state legislature "may direct" under Article II does not require powers outside, or in contradiction to, the state constitution, or at the very least does not require such powers if the legislature, such as Florida's did before the 2000 election, already "directed" a mode of appointment that is consistent with state constitutional constraints. Moreover, this mode of appointment embodied in the Florida Election Code was meant to be carried out like all other legislation within a state constitutional framework that contemplated recourse to the state's judiciary as a matter of course.

In the end, therefore, the concurring justices not only sharply departed from what was—and would shortly become again—their radical devotion to the vindication of seemingly ever-expanding conceptions of state rights, but they also embraced for the occasion a path of constitutional interpretation that even their most liberal colleagues would have had a very difficult time trying to explain.

VI

The 2000 Florida presidential election and the U.S. Supreme Court decision in *Bush v. Gore* reveal serious flaws in the American Constitution, in American democracy, and in the Court's handling of a politically charged case in which the justices did not (and perhaps could not) dispel the perception that they were ultimately acting out of partisan self-interest. Indeed, according to a report in *Newsweek,* Justice O'Connor and her husband expressed annoyance when on the day of the election the television networks initially projected Gore the winner in Florida and thus had him well on his way to the presidency. O'Connor told friends that she was disappointed because she wanted to resign from the Court and go back to her native Arizona but that the expected Gore victory would force her to postpone her plans as she did not want a Democrat to nominate her successor.[47] There had also been much talk about the chief justice wanting to resign but preferring that his successor be nominated by a Republican. It also seems reasonable to surmise that Justices Scalia and Thomas would be interested in consolidating their powers on the Court, a prospect that would be much brighter with Bush as president, particularly in view of his announcement during the campaign that he would nominate to the court persons in these two justices' very image. Finally, it also seemed in the interest of Justice Kennedy, the fifth justice in the series of 5–4 decisions expanding states' rights, to have a Republican president who would be more likely to perpetuate or enlarge the Court's existing majority. In short, on various levels ranging from the personal to the institutional, the five justices who put an end to the election had much to gain from a Bush presidency.

In spite of the problems with the Constitution, democracy, and the Court, it would be possible to institute many worthy improvements by the next presidential election. Unfortunately, six months after the 2000 election, very little has been done (except in Florida and Georgia where significant reforms have been enacted), and many proposals generated shortly after the election debacle are at this writing languishing unattended.[48] Significantly, in his first presidential budget sent to Congress, Bush has not asked for any funds for electoral reforms. Although, as former President Carter has observed, voter registration is far superior in Peru than in the United States, not much is likely to be done about this as *all* reform proposals tend to become hostage to partisan bickering among Democrats and Republicans.[49]

Little is likely to be done, though much could be accomplished through fairly simple and straightforward reform. From the standpoint of the Constitution, the two flaws that ought to be corrected are the lack of a constitutional right to vote for president and the existence and role of the Electoral College. The first of these could be overcome through a constitutional amendment, which, like the Seventeenth Amendment did for elections to the Senate, would grant the right to vote for president and vice president directly to the citizens rather than "in such manner as the [state] Legislature . . . may direct." Since all states already grant their citizens the right to vote for president, this proposed amendment should not be controversial, and it seems fair to assume that if proposed it would ultimately succeed. Although citizens already vote, this amendment would not be superfluous. For one thing, it would enshrine the right to vote for president in the Constitution; for another, it would make it impossible for state legislatures to take matters into their own hands after elections as the Florida legislature began doing before the December 12 U.S. Supreme Court decision.

The elimination of the Electoral College, however, is bound to be much more controversial. Also, because small states would lose power if the Electoral College were abolished and since constitutional amendments must be ratified by the legislatures of (or conventions in) three quarters of the states, there is virtually no chance of abolishing the Electoral College anytime soon. Nevertheless, the arguments for abolishing it are quite compelling. Besides fostering the possibility of electing the loser of the popular vote president—which tends to undermine democratic legitimacy—the electoral vote system produces other pathologies. Thus, for example, the three largest states, California, Texas, and New York, were virtually left out of the 2000 presidential campaign as Bush enjoyed an insurmountable lead in Texas, Gore in the other two states. In contrast, toss-up states got an inordinate amount of attention, prompting an extraordinary focus on local issues affecting but a tiny percentage of the electorate and leading candidates to take inconsistent positions throughout the country as they adjusted their promises to fit the needs of different localities. For example, in Michigan, where the election was considered a toss-up, Bush and Gore concentrated much effort on wooing certain blue-collar workers interested in strong unions and free guns. Gore was vulnerable to the extent that he was perceived as in favor of gun control, Bush to the extent that he was viewed as antiunion. Both, therefore, had an incentive to distort or downplay some of their positions to increase their appeal to this seemingly crucial constituency. But by carrying on a series of local campaigns rather than one national one, the candidates are subjected to great temptations to change their positions as they travel through the country, thus increasing public cynicism about their veracity and integrity.

Some argue that elimination of the Electoral College would level an unacceptable blow against federalism. So long as one agrees that the president should represent all Americans rather than the states that have combined to give him or her a majority of presidential electors, however, this argument is completely unpersuasive. Although Bush lost the popular vote, he has already acted in ways that appear designed to reward the states that voted for him and punish those that did not. For example, he has failed to take steps to alleviate California's energy crisis or to adjust his tax cut proposals to address a problem they would cause primarily in the northeastern states, which almost unanimously voted for Gore. To the extent that states can be punished for having voted for the loser in a presidential election, reliance on the Electoral College can clearly have an adverse effect on the operation of democracy on a national scale.

A truly national election for president would not compromise federalism. The interests of the states in the federal government are most directly represented in the Senate but also to a large extent in the House of Representatives. Indeed, although members of the House are supposed to represent the people rather than the states, every House district is encompassed within a single state, thus allowing voters to concentrate on state issues and concerns. Furthermore, issues of federalism, particularly those dealing with increasing or decreasing state powers vis-à-vis national ones can properly be made part of presidential campaigns. Accordingly, candidates for president could compete on how much power ought to be left to the states without having to pit one state against another.

The two constitutional changes suggested above would improve democracy without threatening federalism. Moreover, if they were adopted, the Twelfth Amendment, which provides for Congress to resolve disputed elections, would have to be replaced with a provision that would be consistent with the suggested changes and that would reinforce Congress's role in settling election disputes to the exclusion of the Court. There are two principal reasons for favoring Congress over the Court: (1) Congress is democratically accountable, so that the electorate can refuse to reelect those representatives whom it feels did not deal with the election dispute fairly; and (2) the Court depends on the president for nominations of new justices, which makes decisions like *Bush v. Gore* inherently undesirable.

Nationalizing presidential elections by developing uniform voting conditions and uniform vote counting procedures throughout the land would also improve democracy, by replacing the current array of local county-level standards by a single uniform standard applicable to all. Because of the improbability of eliminating the Electoral College, however, it may be necessary to set our sights lower and to seek improvements to democracy at the statewide level rather than at the national one. Ironically, in this respect the Court's otherwise ill-advised equal protection holding in *Bush v. Gore* may yet prove quite useful. Indeed, if the majority's efforts at suppressing its precedential value fail, then the equal protection rights first announced in *Bush v. Gore* could usefully be involved to give substance to equal opportunity to vote and to ensure granting an equal weight to all votes on a statewide basis. At least then equality of voting could be guaranteed within states even if not among them.

Finally, because of its blatant inconsistencies, pervasive lack of integrity, and inescapable airs of unmitigated partisanship, the Court's decision in *Bush v. Gore* forces us to rethink whether judicial decisions can ever be held to fair, acceptable, and feasible standards. Paradoxically, because its many vices are so obvious, the Court's decision in *Bush v. Gore* serves to underscore that in spite of inevitable imperfections and of the impossibility to rise above all politics, there are significant differences between principled and unprincipled decisions. Indeed, the above analysis demonstrates that it does not have to follow from the fact that legal texts do not have "plain meanings" or that human beings cannot ascend above politics that all judicial opinions are ultimately arbitrary and subjective. Judicial interpretation may be imperfect, but so long as it can be achieved with consistency and integrity, it may be political or even liberal or conservative without becoming illegitimate. What *Bush v. Gore* demonstrates is that the important line to draw is that between the purely political, the partisan, and the willingness to sacrifice consistency and integrity to secure a particular result, on the one hand, and the politically situated, morally committed, and historically confined judge who labors as a fallible human being with a steadfast resolve to upholding consistency and integrity, on the other. And if this line is clearly kept in mind, then *Bush v. Gore* may eventually be credited for having provided a salutary lesson. Perhaps the best we can expect from our judges is to render decisions that slow down political strife and that blunt its rougher edges. The majority opinion in *Bush v. Gore* did the exact opposite.

NOTES

I wish to thank Robert Bennett, Larry Kramer, and Rick Pildes for helpful comments.

1. 531 U.S. 98; 121 S. Ct. 525 (2000).

2. 121 S. Ct. at 542.

3. 121 S. Ct. at 529.

4. Article II of the Constitution provides in relevant part that "Each state shall appoint, in such Manner as the Legislature thereof may direct, a number of Electors, equal to the whole number of Senators and Representatives to which the state may be entitled in Congress."

5. See New York Times, *36 Days: The Complete Chronicle of the 2000 Presidential Election Crisis* (New York: Times Books, 2001), 300–301. It is not clear, however, that the Florida legislature's unilateral action would have been consistent with federal law.

6. See U.S. Const. amend. XVII (1913).

7. See *36 Days*, at 319.

8. The 435 congressional districts represented in the House of Representatives are supposed to be made up of roughly equal size populations. Moreover, the number of presidential electors assigned to each state is determined by adding two electors (representing the state's two senators) to a number of electors equivalent to the number of congressional districts in that state. In 2000 Montana and Wyoming each had one congressional district and hence 3 presidential electors. California had 52 congressional districts and 54 electors; New York, 31 congressional districts and 33 electors. Consistent with this, from the standpoint of the individual voter, the voter in a small state has a weightier vote than the voter in a large state. When other considerations are factored in, however, the resulting picture becomes much more complex. See Robert W. Bennett, "Popular Election of the President without a Constitutional Amendment," this vol., chap. 22.

9. *Cf.* U.S. Const. art. I, § 2, cl. 1. 3, providing that each slave should be counted as three-fifths of a person, thus boosting the number of congressional districts and presidential electors of slave-owning states without having to extend the franchise to the slave population in the state.

10. See 121 S. Ct. at 541, n4.

11. *Id.*

12. See *36 Days*, at 36–38, 91–92 (describing problems encountered by African Americans during the 2000 presidential election in Florida).

13. See U.S. Const. art. II, § 1; and amend. XII (1804).

14. See *36 Days*, at 32, 34, 36, 152.

15. *Id.*, at 336–37.

16. *Id.*, at 339–40.

17. *Id.*, at 301, 308–9.

18. *Id.*, at 134–35.

19. See U.S. Const. art. II, § 1; and amend. XII (1804).

20. 121 S. Ct. at 512 (emphasis added).

21. 121 S. Ct. at 513.

22. See Antonin Scalia, "Common-Law Courts in a Civil-Law System: The Role

of United States Federal Courts in Interpreting the Constitution and Laws," in *A Matter of Interpretation,* ed. Amy Gutmann (Princeton: Princeton University Press, 1997).

23. For a general discussion of equal protection and affirmative action jurisprudence, see Michel Rosenfeld, *Affirmative Action and Justice: A Philosophical and Constitutional Inquiry* (New Haven: Yale University Press, 1991).

24. See Palm Beach County Canvassing Board v. Harris, 772 So.2d 1220 (2000).

25. 772 So.2d 1243 (2000).

26. Fla. Stat. § 102.168 (3)(c) (1999).

27. See State ex rel. Chappell v. Martinez, 536 So.2d 1007 (1988).

28. See United States v. Lopez, 514 U.S. 549 (1995).

29. See Alden v. Maine, 527 U.S. 706 (1999).

30. See Kimel v. Florida Board of Regents, 528 U.S. 62 (2000).

31. See United States v. Morrison, 529 U.S. 598 (2000).

32. See 121 S. Ct. at 534 (Rehnquist, C. J., concurring) (acknowledging the finality of state court interpretation of state law "in most cases" but not in the case at hand).

33. See, e.g., Solid Waste Agency of Northern Cook County v. United States Army Corp., of Engineers, 531 U.S. 159 (decided January 9, 2001) (5–4 decision striking down federal power to regulate local ponds that form part of the habitat of migratory birds); Board of Trustees of the University of Alabama v. Garrett, 121 S. Ct. 955 (decided February 21, 2001) (5–4 decision denying protection guaranteed by the Federal Americans with Disabilities Act [ADA] in the name of states' rights).

34. See 121 S. Ct. at 541, n2 (Stevens, J., dissenting).

35. 121 S. Ct. at 530 (per curiam opinion).

36. For a more extensive discussion of issues relating to legal interpretation, see Michel Rosenfeld, *Just Interpretations: Law between Ethics and Politics* (Berkeley: University of California Press, 1998).

37. See 121 S. Ct. at 533.

38. See Michael Glennon, "Nine Ways to Avoid a Train Wreck: How Title 3 Should Be Changed" (unpublished manuscript, 2001).

39. See Glennon, "Nine Ways." Professor Glennon advocated amending 3 U.S.C. § 5 to make this clear.

40. Gore v. Harris, 773 So.2d 524, 529–30 (2000) (Shaw, J., concurring).

41. *Id.,* n. 12.

42. U.S. Const. art II, § 1, cl. 2 (emphasis added).

43. 121 S. Ct. at 534.

44. See cases cited in notes 29, 30, 31, and 33, *supra.*

45. See, *e.g.,* New York v. United States, 505 U.S. 144 (1992) (protection of state legislatures); Printz v. United States, 521 U.S. 898 (1997) (protection of state executive officers); Seminole Tribe v. Florida, 517 U.S. 44 (1996) (protection of state judicial through unprecedented expansive interpretation of the Eleventh Amendment).

46. See McCulloch v. Maryland, 17 U.S. 316 (1819).

47. See Evan Thomas and Michael Isikoff, "The Truth behind the Pillars," *Newsweek,* December 25, 2000, at 52.

48. See "Election Reform Stalls," *New York Times,* April 30, 2001, at A18.

49. *Id.*

7

THE UNBEARABLE RIGHTNESS OF
BUSH V. GORE

Nelson Lund

Bush v. Gore was a straightforward and legally correct decision. If one were familiar only with the commentary that ensued in the decision's wake, this claim might sound almost lunatic. This essay explains why the Supreme Court acted properly, indeed admirably, and why the ubiquitous criticisms that have been leveled at the justices from both the Left and the Right are at best misguided.

For almost forty years, the Supreme Court has treated the stuffing of ballot boxes as a paradigmatic violation of the Equal Protection Clause. Much subtler and more indirect forms of vote dilution have also been outlawed. Like some of those practices, the selective and partial recount ordered by the Florida Supreme Court may have been an inadvertent form of vote dilution. But that recount had effects that were virtually indistinguishable from those in the paradigmatic case. There is no meaningful difference between adding illegal votes to the count and *selectively* adding legal votes, which is what the Florida court was doing. The Supreme Court rightly concluded that the vote dilution in this case violated well-established equal protection principles.

Nor did the Supreme Court err in its response to this constitutional violation. Although the Court acted with unprecedented dispatch after the Florida court's December 8, 2000, decision, it was highly improbable that a legally proper recount could be conducted by the December 18 deadline set by federal law. And it was quite impossible for such a recount to meet the December 12 deadline that the Florida court itself had found in Florida law. Contrary to a widespread misconception, the U.S. Supreme Court properly accepted the Florida court's interpretation of state law *and* provided that court with an opportunity to reconsider its own interpretation of state law. When the clock ran out, it was entirely due to mistakes and delays attributable to the Florida court.

The least known passages in *Bush v. Gore* are those in which the dissenters explain why the majority's legal analysis was erroneous. These passages are not well known because they do not exist. The best known passage, which comes from Justice Stevens's dissent, consists of a rhetorical flourish rather than an analysis:

> What must underlie [George W. Bush's and the other defendants'] entire federal assault on the Florida election procedures is an unstated lack of confidence in the impartiality and capacity of the state judges who would make the critical decisions if the vote count were to proceed. Otherwise, their position is wholly without merit. The endorsement of that position by the majority of this Court can only lend credence to the most cynical appraisal of the work of judges throughout the land. It is confidence in the men and women who administer the judicial system that is the true backbone of the rule of law. Time will one day heal the wound to that confidence that will be inflicted by today's decision. One thing, however, is certain. Although we may never know with complete certainty the identity of the winner of this year's Presidential election, the identity of the loser is perfectly clear. It is the Nation's confidence in the judge as an impartial guardian of the rule of law.[1]

This passage became famous because it has been read to mean that Stevens was impugning the integrity of the five justices who joined the majority opinion.[2] But if Stevens was slyly encouraging this interpretation, he was careful not to say or imply any such thing. Indeed, if we take his statement at face value, Stevens's point is almost the opposite: cynical appraisals of the work of judges—any judges—are a threat to the rule of law.

Justice Stevens may well have been correct that the real loser in the 2000 election was "the Nation's confidence in the judge as an impartial guardian of the rule of law." Partisans on both sides accused judges of manipulating the law in order to assist the candidate they favored, and aspersions were cast on the integrity of some judges even before they ruled. For the vast majority of observers who lacked the time or expertise to form an independent judgment, it must have seemed unlikely that *all* the judges involved had behaved impartially. And many Americans may well have quietly concluded that they are all just a bunch of political hacks in robes.

That conclusion would be a mistake, if for no other reason than the impossibility of proving or disproving such charges. Justice Stevens, however, offered a very different reason for worrying about the reputations of the Florida judges: "It is confidence in the men and women who administer the judicial system that is the true backbone of the rule of law." A thoughtful citizen unschooled in legal folkways might regard this as a very odd notion. This citizen might suppose that the true backbone of the rule of law is *actual adherence* to the law by the men and women who administer the judicial system. And the citizen might then suppose that refusals by judges to adhere to the law should be exposed and corrected. In fact, that is all Bush's lawyers asked for, and that is all the Supreme Court gave them.

Odd as Stevens's statement might seem to an ordinary citizen, it is quite consistent with a theory deeply embedded among sophisticated legal elites but seldom advocated in popular discourse. That theory essentially holds that the law is what the judges say it is, so that an aura of impartiality around judges would serve mainly to help them impose better laws on the nation than the people are willing to enact through their legislatures. This theory was rejected by the *Bush v. Gore* majority, which took an approach much more closely aligned with the ordinary citizen's view. That rejection provides the most important reason for defending the Court's decision, and I take up that defense here.

A thoughtful citizen's attitude is a useful tool when thinking about this case, but it will not be enough. Judges are expected to apply the law set out in the Constitution and statutes. For two main reasons, however, that law often cannot be applied with the same certainty offered, say, by the laws of algebra. First, many provisions of the law are ambiguous, which means that judgment has to be used in choosing among a range of possible interpretations. Second, our legal system has adopted a practice in which courts adhere to their previous decisions even when they have reason to believe that those decisions were wrong. This rule of stare decisis, however, is not completely inflexible, and courts must therefore also exercise judgment in applying it.

Although this means that colorable arguments can often be made on both sides of the legal questions with which courts are confronted, it does *not* mean that the distinction between legally right and legally wrong answers is a chimera. Nor does it mean, as the fashionable academic theories would have it, that judicial decisions should be judged on the basis of their political effects rather than their fidelity to the law. If there are some close legal questions, as there are, there are also such things as stronger and weaker legal arguments. And if there are some legal questions with no indubitably clear answers, as there are, there are also some questions that have right and wrong legal answers.

Simply stated, my claim is that *Bush v. Gore* should be evaluated as a *legal* decision and that it stands up very well when judged by appropriate legal standards. Conversely, whatever motivated the Florida judges whose decision was reversed, their ruling was indefensible as a legal decision. The criticisms that can most plausibly be leveled against the Supreme Court majority are essentially *political* criticisms of a kind that might more fittingly be directed against a Senate majority leader or an ambassador to China. Justice Stevens's rhetorical flight, in which the rule of law becomes conflated with confidence in its supposed guardians, is one example. I say that the Florida Supreme Court grossly violated the law and that the U.S. Supreme Court properly acted to stop the travesty. That decision was the legally correct decision, and political criticisms of the Court are based on the corrosively sophisticated assumption that the justices cannot be anything except politicians in robes.

OVERVIEW OF THE FACTUAL SETTING

An extraordinary confluence of events presented the American judicial system with a genuinely difficult challenge in the aftermath of the voting that took place on November 7, 2000. The decisive election in Florida was so excruciatingly close that certainty about the outcome could not have been achieved under the best of conditions. In the final official counts of Florida's ballots, the difference between Bush and Gore was only 537 votes out of some 6 million, which is less than one one-hundredth of 1 percent. Even if there were some unerring and unambiguously correct way to tabulate the ballots, which there probably is not, certainty would still have eluded us because we would not know how many ballots were cast by ineligible or nonexistent voters. In an election this close, with such a large number of ballots cast, only God can know who "really" won.

As a practical and legal matter, this would not have mattered very much if there had been some clear and agreed-upon rules for determining which ballots to count for which candidates and how to tabulate the results. But there were not. The Florida statutes governing election disputes had apparently been drafted with local rather than statewide elections primarily in mind, and without considering the unique time constraints that federal law imposes on the resolution of disputes about the electoral college. This should not be too surprising. Statewide elections in a jurisdiction as populous as Florida have rarely if ever been close enough to have their outcomes turn on an interpretation of the rules for counting ballots. And who would have thought that this unlikely contingency would ever be compounded into freakishness by coming to pass in a state whose electoral votes were going to make the difference in a presidential election? When the freak event did occur, it turned out that the statutes drafted with local elections in mind did not fit a statewide election dispute very easily.

On top of everything else, federal law had its own share of problems and uncertainties. In the wake of the notorious Hayes-Tilden contest in 1876, Congress had enacted a number of provisions aimed at avoiding another such disorderly mess.[3] But the meaning of these provisions, and their relationship to even older statutes, was not entirely clear. On the books for more than a century, they had never been tested in practice or in the courts. Meanwhile, the twentieth century had witnessed the independent development of a complex and evolving body of *constitutional* election law in the federal courts.

Thus when George Bush and Al Gore entered what looked at times like mortal legal combat, there were lots of weapons scattered around the arena. Because Bush had more votes tallied in the initial count and in the automatic recount that Florida law provided for close elections, Gore could win only by attacking the official vote counts. Correlatively, Bush's self-interest dictated that he defend those same counts. Whether from pure self-interest or not, both candidates skillfully and relentlessly deployed all their legal weapons in a fight for victory.

Without blaming either candidate for his litigation strategy, one can note that this created an unusual problem for the courts. A great many novel legal issues were raised in a large number of lawsuits filed by the candidates and their supporters. Furthermore, unlike most other election disputes, those involving the Electoral College must be resolved very quickly. *Bush v. Gore* itself was probably decided faster than any comparably important decision in history,[4] and it came at the end of a series of judgments that had themselves been made in unusual haste. What is perhaps most remarkable about the Supreme Court's opinion is how easily defensible it is.

OVERVIEW OF THE LEGAL SETTING

A full analysis, or even an adequate summary, of the legal disputes that set the stage for the decision in *Bush v. Gore* is beyond the scope of this essay. I therefore offer only the barest essentials here.

The Constitution requires each state to appoint, "in such Manner as the Legislature thereof may direct," a number of presidential electors equal to the size of the state's congressional delegation.[5] The Constitution also requires these electors to meet in their states to cast their ballots and then to send a certified list of the votes to the president of the Senate (who in this case was Al Gore).[6] He is required to open them in the presence of the Senate and House of Representatives, where they are then counted.[7] An absolute majority of the "Electors appointed" is needed to win the election.[8] Absent such a majority, the House of Representatives chooses the president under a rule that gives each state's delegation one vote.[9] If no president is chosen by January 20, an acting president takes office "until a President shall have qualified."[10]

Congress has attempted to fill in some of the details that are left unspecified by the Constitution. Two of those statutes are especially relevant. First, federal law required that presidential electors meet and give their votes on December 18, 2000.[11] Second, federal law provided that if a state had enacted laws for resolving disputes before November 7, 2000, and used those laws to resolve election disputes by December 12, 2000, such resolution would be treated as conclusive when the votes were counted in Congress.[12]

Florida election law is much more complex and detailed. The procedure for dealing with disputes has four main elements. First, an automatic statewide recount is conducted in close elections.[13] Second, a "protest" period occurs, during which certain kinds of challenges can be brought before county canvassing boards (which comprise two local elected officials and one local judge).[14] Third, state officials accept election results from these county officials and "certify" a winner.[15] Fourth, that certification can be challenged in court during the "contest" period.[16]

THE LITIGATION BEGINS

Bush won the initial count by 1,784 votes, and he was still ahead by 327 votes after the automatic statewide machine recount.[17] Gore then filed protests,[18] demanding a hand recount of the ballots in four heavily Democratic counties, only three of which are relevant to the following discussion: Broward, Palm Beach, and Miami-Dade.[19] Gore apparently chose these counties for one or both of two reasons.[20] First, to the extent that errors by the counting machines were randomly distributed, Gore could expect to be a net gainer in these most heavily Democratic jurisdictions.[21] Second, the hand recounts would be supervised by local elected officials, and the chances that such officials would be biased in Gore's favor (or at least not biased in Bush's favor) would be highest in the most heavily Democratic counties.[22]

Gore's strategy was consistent with the letter of Florida law, at least in the sense that it permitted Gore to *request* recounts in selected counties, but it raised serious constitutional questions that had lurked unnoticed so long as the law had been applied only to local elections. If the law actually allowed one candidate to obtain a geographically biased recount in a statewide election, the Florida statute may have unconstitutionally (albeit inadvertently) run afoul of established principles requiring the fair and equal treatment of similarly situated voters. Accordingly, Bush promptly filed a lawsuit in federal court, in which he sought to stop the recounts that Gore had demanded.

The courts never addressed the merits of Bush's arguments, concluding instead that the relief he sought was premature.[23] What proved to be the decisive litigation resulted instead from lawsuits brought by Gore in an attempt to overcome a series of obstacles in state law that threatened to frustrate his chosen strategy.

The first obstacle was a statutory provision requiring that the local officials provide a final tally to the secretary of state within seven days after the election, whereupon the statewide result would be "certified." None of the three counties had finished their hand recounts by that deadline, and Secretary of State Katherine Harris concluded that they had not offered legally sufficient reasons for any further delay. In response to a lawsuit filed by Gore and others, a Florida court rejected Gore's claim that Harris had behaved illegally by refusing to accept tardy recounts. Gore then appealed to the Florida Supreme Court, which took the first of many highly questionable actions. Without being asked to do so by any litigant, the court issued an unexplained order forbidding state officials from "certifying" the results of the election.

This order, to which Gore raised no objection, had the practical effect of artificially extending the protest phase (in which preliminary decisions are made by local elected officials) and therefore necessarily shortening the contest phase of the legal process (in which final decisions are made by courts). As we shall see, the shortening of the contest period had fateful consequences.

BUSH V. PALM BEACH COUNTY CANVASSING BOARD ("BUSH I")

The unprompted decision by the Florida Supreme Court was the first in a series that culminated in the U.S. Supreme Court's decision that the Florida recount was being conducted in an unconstitutional manner. The next step was the Florida Supreme Court's decision, four days later, to reverse the trial court, thereby overturning two decisions made by the secretary of state, who had concluded (1) that manual recounts were legally available only to correct errors made by the voting or counting machines, not errors by voters; and (2) that conducting recounts based on voters' errors did not justify relaxing the statutory deadline for the counties to report their election returns.

The Florida court sought to justify its decision by resolving what it identified as three troublesome or ambiguous features of the state election statute. First, the statute allowed full manual recounts only to correct an "error in the vote tabulation," without specifying whether this would include a failure by the voter to mark or punch a ballot in the manner required to render the ballot machine-readable. Second, one statutory provision says that the secretary of state "shall" ignore late returns from the counties, while another provision says that she "may" ignore late returns. Third, one statute allows a candidate to request a recount at any time before the county returns are certified, while another requires the county officials to certify the returns within seven days; thus, cases might arise in which a candidate requested a recount just before the seventh day, leaving no time to conduct the recount.

The Florida court believed that it should resolve these issues so as to facilitate the right of the voters to express their will, without abiding by "[t]echnical statutory requirements."[24] The court rejected Secretary of State Harris's argument that an "error in vote tabulation" could only refer to malfunctioning machines, concluding instead that the statutory language also referred to cases in which a ballot was punched or marked in such a way that a human, but not a machine, could detect an intent to vote for a particular candidate.

For two reasons, this was the court's most important decision. First, the disputes about the deadline only became relevant on the assumption that there was a legal basis for the recounts in the first place. Second, and most important, it was this interpretation of the statutes that made Gore's cherry-picking strategy feasible, thus raising serious constitutional questions about those statutes.

The decision was also more far-fetched than it may at first appear. According to the court's interpretation, machine tabulations will *always* be erroneous if any voter failed to follow the instructions for marking the ballot, which always happens. Why then would the statutes provide for an automatic *machine* recount in close elections? Such a procedure would almost always be pointless because a hand recount to correct these inherently erroneous machine recounts would always be justified. It should therefore come as no surprise that recounts had never before been conducted to correct *voters'* errors.[25]

The court's conclusions with respect to the other two issues were similarly implausible. The Florida court resolved the apparent conflict between the "shall ignore" and "may ignore" provisions by inventing a new meaning inconsistent with them *both*, namely, that the secretary of state *may not ignore* late returns. The court then went on to give the counties an entirely new deadline of nineteen days after the election. This deadline had no basis anywhere in the statutes, and it was adopted without any explanation except a vague allusion to "the equitable powers of this Court."[26] The justification given for these conclusions was that "the will of the electors supersedes any technical statutory requirements."[27]

Bush sought review in the U.S. Supreme Court, arguing that the Florida court had simply disregarded the statutes, thus violating the Constitution's command in Article II that electors be chosen "in such Manner as the Legislature [of the State] may direct." What the Florida court had done, Bush argued, was not to interpret the statutes but to rewrite them, in contravention of the U.S. Constitution.[28]

Bush's argument presented the U.S. Supreme Court with a genuinely difficult question. The Constitution plainly says that the directions of the state legislature must be followed, and the Florida court was pretty plainly not following the legislature's directions. However, the decisions of state supreme courts are almost always treated as authoritative interpretations of state law, no matter how implausible they may seem. It thus would not have been altogether unthinkable to assume that the Florida legislature had implicitly "directed" that electors be chosen in accordance with Florida law as interpreted by the Florida courts.

A unanimous Supreme Court avoided this difficult Article II question, and rightly so. In resolving what it saw as the troublesome features of the statutory scheme, the Florida court had appeared to rely in part on the notion that statutes should be interpreted so as to render them consistent with its own prior interpretation of the Florida Constitution, according to which "[u]nreasonable or unnecessary restraints on the elective process are prohibited."[29] This would have seemed a normal approach to resolving a state law question because a state constitution has greater authority than state statutes.[30] In this case, however, that seemingly normal approach may have been misplaced. *McPherson v. Blacker,* an 1892 Supreme Court case apparently overlooked by the Florida Supreme Court, had suggested (without deciding) that state constitutions are *not* authorized to constrain state legislatures in the special context of choosing presidential electors.[31]

Thus the Supreme Court was confronted with a double uncertainty. First, it had previously said, but had not actually decided, that a very unusual relationship exists between state constitutions and state statutes in the context of selecting presidential electors. Second, the Florida Supreme Court had not made it clear that its construction of the state statutes was *crucially* dependent on the Florida constitution. If the Florida court were given a chance to construe the state statutes without reference to the state constitution, then the U.S. Supreme Court might not have to decide whether to adopt the suggestion made in *McPherson.* Accordingly, the Supreme Court vacated the decision and remanded the case so that the Florida court could clarify or reconsider its ruling.[32]

In the course of its opinion, the Supreme Court also cautioned the Florida court to give attention to a federal statute that it had previously ignored. That statute, 3 U.S.C. § 5, provided that if a state resolved any election disputes by December 12, 2000, using laws in place before November 7, 2000, such resolution would be treated as conclusive when the votes were counted in Congress. The Supreme Court noted that "a legislative wish to take advantage of the 'safe harbor' [offered by this federal statute] would counsel against any construction of the [Florida] Election Code that Congress might deem to be a change in the law."[33]

It certainly seems reasonable to suppose that Florida's legislature would want to take advantage of this safe harbor. And it might make sense to resolve statutory ambiguities so as to bring the state within the safe harbor, though there is no evidence that anyone in the Florida legislature had ever heard of 3 U.S.C. § 5 before the 2000 election. But what did any of this have to do with the case before the Court? The fact is that it had no relevance at all *unless* the U.S. Constitution *required* the Florida court to give effect to such a "legislative wish." As we have seen, however, the Supreme Court had never decided that the Constitution does impose this requirement, and the Court had taken pains to avoid deciding the question in this case.

Thus the message that the unanimous Court was sending to the Florida judges should have been quite clear: We are not anxious to decide difficult questions of federal constitutional law without giving you an opportunity to address those questions first. But you had better take federal law much more seriously than you did in your first opinion.

THE FLORIDA COURT CAREENS OUT OF CONTROL

Clear as it was, either the Supreme Court's message did not reach a majority of the Florida judges or they decided they could safely ignore it. Whatever the cause, those judges soon embarked on an extraordinary journey outside the bounds of federal law. To appreciate the necessity and the restraint of the Supreme Court's controversial decision in *Bush v. Gore,* one must first understand the sheer outlandishness of the Florida decision that provoked it.

Before coming to that, however, I need to summarize a few more facts. Florida, like many other states, has a decentralized system for conducting elections. Each of Florida's sixty-seven counties conducts elections under the supervision of local officials. These officials are bound by a number of rules established by state law, but many details are left to their discretion. Different counties, for example, have used different kinds of voting machines, and the counties have not been told by state law exactly what rules to use when conducting hand recounts.

As the whole nation learned in 2000, there is room for considerable debate about the proper way to classify punch-card ballots during a manual review. Without reviewing the intricacies of the controversies over matters such as hanging and dimpled chads, it should be enough to note that the three counties chosen by Gore for his protests used different standards of review and that one county actually changed its standard repeatedly during the recount. Although Democratic officials controlled all of the recounts, and despite the extra twelve days that the Florida Supreme Court had created for the recount process, Bush remained ahead when the new deadline arrived.

Accordingly, state officials "certified" Bush as the winner of the election, by a margin of 537 votes. Gore then invoked the contest provisions of state law, filing a lawsuit challenging this certification. To prevail in this suit, the statute required Gore to begin by proving the "receipt of a number of illegal votes or rejection of a number of legal votes sufficient to change or place in doubt the result of the election."[34] Gore claimed that he could do this, primarily on the basis of the following claims: (1) even though Palm Beach County had not completed its recount by the extended deadline and even though Miami-Dade had not completed its recount at all, Gore should be credited with the net gains he had thus far made in those counties (215 and 168 votes, respectively); and (2) more important, some 9,000 Miami-Dade "undervote" ballots—those on which the machine did not detect a choice for any candidate for the office of president—would change the result of the election if reexamined by hand.[35]

After a trial at which Gore had the opportunity to establish his claims, Judge N. Sanders Sauls found that he had failed to do so. The most important element in Sauls's reasoning was that Gore had offered "no credible statistical evidence and no other competent substantial evidence" to establish that the certified result of the statewide election would be changed if further scrutiny of the Miami-Dade ballots were undertaken.[36]

The fundamental difficulty confronting Gore was this: He had demanded a manual recount only in selected counties, and that demand was manifestly calculated to produce a shift in the statewide totals *on the basis of chance alone.* But even after the Florida Supreme Court had created an extra twelve days for Gore to pursue this constitutionally dubious strategy, the result of the election had remained the same. Thus Gore appeared to be locked into a losing game, even assuming that his strategy was permissible under federal law.

On December 8, 2000, however, the Florida Supreme Court created a whole new theory under which Gore might be able to get the outcome of the election changed. Reversing the trial court's decision by a vote of 4–3, the majority ordered the trial court to take the following actions:

- Add a net of 215 votes (or perhaps 176, depending on a factual issue that the judges did not resolve) to Gore's total, based on the Palm Beach recount, whose results were not reported to state officials within the judicially extended protest period.
- Add a net of 168 votes for Gore to the officially certified vote totals, based on the incomplete recount conducted by local election officials in Miami-Dade County.
- Conduct a manual recount of the 9,000 Miami-Dade ballots that Gore claimed might shift the statewide totals in his favor.
- Conduct a statewide recount of some kind, which the Florida Supreme Court strongly suggested should be limited to a recount of the undervote ballots in each county.[37]

This was a truly bizarre ruling. First, it ignored the legal effect of the U.S. Supreme Court's decision in *Bush I.* On December 4 the Supreme Court had vacated the Florida court's November 21 decision in that case, thus rendering it a legal nullity. The Florida court's December 8 decision, however, appeared to assume the validity of the nullified decision because it ordered additions to Gore's vote total that had been made possible only by the November 21 decision's extension of the statutory protest period.[38]

Second, the statutory interpretation underlying the December 8 decision was even more questionable than that on which the November 21 decision rested. Florida's contest statute required Gore to prove the existence of errors sufficient to change or place in doubt the outcome of the election.[39] The only evidence he had was the existence of some 9,000 undervote ballots that the Miami-Dade officials had found it impracticable to examine during the protest period.[40] The court held that the mere existence of these ballots was sufficient to place the outcome of the statewide election in doubt, even though Gore had not proved that a recount of these ballots would even favor him.[41] The assumption here seemed to be that in a very close election, almost *anything* could put the outcome in doubt.[42] That has a certain plausibility, but the court also held, in a bizarre reversal of logic, that the statute did not require a recount of all Miami-Dade ballots (let alone all ballots statewide) because Gore had only put these 9,000 at issue.[43] The absurdity of putting these two conclusions together was apparently obvious to the court itself, for it then spun off in a different direction, concluding without explanation that a recount could *not* be confined to Miami-Dade, though it *could* be confined to undervote ballots.[44] How the court got this conglomeration of conclusions out of the statute is anyone's guess.

Thus the effect of this ruling by the Florida court was to raise exactly the same difficult constitutional question that the U.S. Supreme Court had carefully avoided in the *Bush I* case, namely, whether a state court's interpretation of state statutes can be so clearly untenable that it constitutes an impermissible departure from the legislative directions referenced in Article II of the U.S. Constitution.

Third, the court ordered the addition of 168 votes to Gore's certified totals, based on the *partial* recount in Miami-Dade. This order is worth pausing over because it is truly shocking. Whatever rationale one might use to justify conducting recounts in some jurisdictions but not others, stopping in the *middle* of a recount and *definitively* awarding one candidate the number of new votes he had picked up by that point simply defies explanation in terms of an effort to produce a more accurate count of the votes. What is worse, there was unrebutted evidence at trial that Miami-Dade had begun its recount with the most heavily Democratic precincts, which means that the partial recount was obviously biased in Gore's favor.[45]

Fourth, the statewide remedy of reexamining undervote ballots had not been requested by any of the parties, it had no source in the Florida statutes, and the court provided no meaningful instructions for conducting it.[46] The court's decision, moreover, came only four days before the federal safe harbor deadline that was pointedly discussed in the U.S. Supreme Court's *Bush I* opinion. It was perfectly obvious, as the three Florida Supreme Court dissenters insisted, that the majority was "departing from the essential requirements of the law by providing a remedy which is impossible to achieve and which will ultimately lead to chaos."[47] And, as Chief Justice Wells pointed out in his dissent, the lawlessness was so obvious that it seemed likely to "eventually cause the election results in Florida to be stricken by the federal courts or Congress."[48]

What could have caused the majority to take this reckless action? Leaving cynical hypotheses aside and looking only at the justification offered by the Florida judges themselves, it turns out that their reasoning actually contradicted their actions. The majority purported to adopt what it called a "common sense" approach to the statute, summed up in the notion that the outcome of elections should be determined by "the will of the voters" rather than by "strategies extraneous to the voting process."[49] The actual ruling, however, was based on a very different theory, which was never stated in the opinion and which was essentially the opposite of the stated theory.

The real theory went something like this. Once the ballots have been counted by machine, we will allow the loser to choose which ballots to reexamine by hand. Any changes in the vote totals resulting from this selective and partial recount, such as the 168 votes in Miami-Dade, will be adopted. But because this would so manifestly allow the outcome to turn on "strategies extraneous to the voting process," we will try to create what we regard as a tolerable approximation of evenhandedness by directing the trial court to make an *effort* to perform a *somewhat less* selective and *somewhat less* partial recount than the loser had at first demanded.

If the Florida Supreme Court had actually been seeking to ascertain the "will of the voters" of Florida, it would have designed a statewide recount that could believably be called more accurate or more reliable than the initial machine counts. At an absolute minimum, that would have required reexamining all the overvotes (where the machines detected a vote for more than one candidate and therefore recorded no vote) as well as the undervotes (where the machines detected no vote for any candidate). Once one assumes that the "intent of the voter" should be honored even when the voter failed to comply with the instructions on how to vote, these two categories of ballots become logically indistinguishable.[50]

Furthermore, the need to treat undervotes and overvotes the same way is only the most obvious requirement of a recount aimed at determining the will of the voters. If one were actually serious about designing a recount that was more accurate than the machine counts, one would also have to recount all 6 million "legal votes." Whatever criterion is adopted for changing undervotes to legal votes (the presence of a hanging chad or the presence of a dimpled chad, for example), that same criterion should be applied to ballots containing both a machine-readable hole and a hanging or dimpled chad. That means that some "legal votes" would have to be changed to "overvotes" and thus deducted from the vote totals. This could be quite significant, for ballots containing both a clean hole for one candidate and a dimpled or indented chad for another candidate were quite common.[51] Alternatively, the court might have been justified in restricting a recount to undervote ballots *if* it had employed a standard designed to count the ballots of those voters whose efforts were frustrated by faulty machines, without counting the ballots of voters who failed to follow the instructions. But the Florida court insisted on the proposition that "a legal vote is one in which there is a 'clear indication of the intent of the voter,' " with or without evidence of a faulty machine.[52]

Thus the Florida Supreme Court could not have been seeking to ascertain the will of the voters of Florida. Instead, it was seeking to ascertain the will of a peculiar subset of Florida voters, namely, those who had cast undervote ballots and those other voters who happened to reside in the counties Gore had selected for full recounts. The court gave no explanation for this illogical choice.[53]

Not only did the Florida Supreme Court focus the statewide recount on a manifestly inappropriate subset of the ballots, it did not even indicate that the statewide recount of undervotes would actually have to be *completed* in order for Gore to prevail in his challenge. What the majority apparently contemplated was that it would stop the recount at some point (December 12? December 18? January 6? January 20?) and declare a winner on the basis of whatever new vote totals existed at that time. Although the court did not announce this, it is the logical inference from the majority's decision definitively to award Gore the 168 votes he had already picked up in the uncompleted recount in Miami-Dade. If that uncompleted recount was enough to justify changing the official vote count, why couldn't a similarly uncompleted statewide recount be used to justify changing the outcome of the election? And why wasn't the world told in advance when the recounting would stop?

THE SUPREME COURT'S DECISION IN *BUSH V. GORE*

The day after this amazing decision by the Florida court, the U.S. Supreme Court voted to halt the statewide partial recount that the Florida judges had initiated and to schedule a full hearing two days later.[54] On December 12, only four days after the Florida court's decision, the Supreme Court held that the recount violated the Equal Protection Clause of the Fourteenth Amendment to the U.S. Constitution, with only two justices dissenting from this conclusion.

The majority's equal protection analysis was quite straightforward and firmly grounded in precedent. After a brief summary of the Court's vote-dilution jurisprudence, the majority described several ways in which the Florida recount entailed the uneven treatment of different voters: (1) varying standards for determining a voter's intent had been employed; (2) the statewide recount had been limited to undervotes, while the recounts in the Gore-selected counties had included all ballots; (3) the partial recount in Miami-Dade had been used for certification, and the Florida court evidently contemplated the future use of partial recounts; and (4) the statewide recount was being conducted by untrained personnel, without an opportunity for observers to make contemporaneous objections. Without saying that any one of these features of the recount process would by itself have been legally fatal, the majority concluded that the process as a whole failed to satisfy "the minimum requirement for non-arbitrary treatment of voters necessary to secure the fundamental right" to vote.[55]

Not a single one of the Court's dissenters made any effort to show that the Florida recount satisfied the minimum requirements of equal protection. This should be no surprise, for reasons that will become clear when we take a closer look at the Court's precedents.

Under well-known and long-established case law, the right to vote has been treated as a fundamental right that must be extended equally to all citizens.[56] This means that state governments cannot deny the vote to any citizen without an extremely powerful justification. The Court has also held that "the right of suffrage can be denied by a *debasement* or *dilution* of the weight of a citizen's vote just as effectively as by wholly prohibiting the free exercise of the franchise."[57]

The Court has held, for example, that the seats in state legislatures must be equally apportioned on a population basis;[58] that statewide elections may not be conducted under a "county unit" system resembling the federal Electoral College;[59] and that a state may not require that a nominating petition for presidential elector include the signatures of at least two hundred qualified voters from each of at least fifty counties.[60] Faced with such rules, which effectively gave more "weight" to the votes of those living in rural or sparsely populated areas of a state than to those living in more densely populated areas, the Court declared:

> [T]he weight of a citizen's vote cannot be made to depend on where he lives. Population is, of necessity, the starting point for consideration and the controlling criterion for judgment in legislative apportionment controversies. A citizen, a qualified voter, is no more nor no less so because he lives in the city or on the farm. This is the clear and strong command of our Constitution's Equal Protection Clause. This is an essential part of the concept of a government of laws and not men. This is at the heart of Lincoln's vision of "government of the people, by the people, (and) for the people."[61]

The application of the vote-dilution principle is not confined to any particular class of voting rules: "Weighting the votes of citizens differently, *by any method or means,* merely because of where they happen to reside, hardly seems justifiable. One must be ever aware that the Constitution forbids sophisticated as well as simple-minded modes of discrimination."[62] And "sophisticated" modes of discrimination include those that are *unintentionally* discriminatory.[63]

In this case, the Florida court devised an extremely complex system of weighting, in which certain kinds of ballots were more likely to be counted as legal votes in some places than in others, thus discriminating for and against different groups of voters based on where they happened to reside. Most obviously, voters who cast overvote ballots in Broward, Palm Beach, and Miami-Dade Counties were treated more favorably than those who cast similar ballots elsewhere. Similarly, voters who cast dimpled chad ballots in Broward were treated more favorably than those who cast similar ballots in Palm Beach. Voters living in the unrecounted (and more Republican) precincts of Miami-Dade were disadvantaged in comparison with those living in the recounted (and more Democratic) precincts. The complexity of the vote dilution involved did not convert it into something other than vote dilution.

Before *Bush v. Gore,* geographic vote denial and dilution controversies had arisen primarily in two kinds of cases: (1) where imbalances arose because legislatures had failed to reapportion in response to population shifts;[64] and (2) where discriminatory arrangements had been adopted deliberately in order to serve what legislatures thought were overriding purposes, such as to protect the influence of certain constituencies or to create districts whose boundaries would coincide with preexisting political or geographic borders.[65] In these cases, the Court applied what is often called "strict scrutiny," which requires that any inequality or discrimination be justified by legitimate and compelling government purposes and that the inequality not extend farther than those purposes require.[66]

Bush v. Gore did not involve the application of a *preexisting* rule that systematically discriminated against an identifiable class of voters, such as those residing in more sparsely populated jurisdictions. But nothing in the rationale underlying the vote-dilution cases limits it to such cases. Unconstitutional vote dilution has been found, for example, where there is no systematic discrimination against a class of voters with shared political interests.[67] Furthermore, the rationale of the decisions implies, if anything, that the application of new and discriminatory rules *after* an election has been held should receive an especially skeptical review by the courts because after-the-fact manipulation of voting rules is especially prone to abuse.[68]

Indeed, the Court has frequently used the stuffing of ballot boxes as a paradigmatic example of an obvious constitutional violation.[69] But any distinction between adding *illegal* ballots to the count and *selectively* adding legal ballots in a way that favors one candidate over another would be entirely sophistic. The Court long ago ruled out such sophistry when it declared that the Fourteenth Amendment "nullifies sophisticated as well as simple-minded modes of discrimination."[70]

Vote dilution obviously occurs when illegal ballots are counted along with legal ballots. It also occurs when legal ballots are counted for one candidate but not the other. It occurs when ballots are counted only from precincts with a history of favoring one party over the other. And it occurs when a special effort is made to find previously overlooked legal ballots in arbitrarily chosen subcategories. Nor does it make any difference whether such vote dilution proceeds from partisan motives. Thus, for example, if a vote count were inadvertently inflated with illegal ballots and a court arbitrarily refused to correct the count, it would not matter whether the judge was dishonest or just mistaken about his or her obligations. Similarly, it makes no difference whether the Florida judges were trying to help Gore or were simply the victims of confused thinking.

The discrimination in the Florida recount was novel, complex, and subtle, which helps to explain why it was unprecedented. No legislature would ever adopt a recount process like the one adopted by the Florida court, and no court had ever done so either. Whether this uniquely bizarre procedure resulted from bad faith (which I do not assert) or from a misunderstanding of the law, it should not even survive rational-basis scrutiny, let alone the strict scrutiny that the Supreme Court has previously employed in vote-dilution cases.

To see why this simply was not a close or debatable case, it is important to remember that the recount process designed by the Florida court was a substitute for the standardized, machine counts on which the secretary of state had sought to rely. Although the machine counts were undoubtedly imperfect, there could be no legitimate, let alone compelling, interest in substituting hand recounts unless those recounts could reasonably have been expected to be *more accurate as a whole* than the machine recounts. The Florida Supreme Court never made any attempt to show that its recount procedure would likely be more accurate, and any such effort would have been laughable.

The only justification the Florida Supreme Court ever offered for its orders was that *some* new "legal votes" (i.e., ballots containing evidence of an "intent to vote" undetected by the counting machines) would turn up in the various partial manual recounts. The underlying theory was apparently that any "legal votes" that happened to turn up in any of these selective recounts should be added to the totals generated by the machine counts.

But this completely misses the point of the equal protection cases—that substantially the same rules, whatever those rules are, must be applied to all voters and all ballots. Suppose, for example, that undervote ballots containing evidence of an intent to vote for Gore were changed to legal votes, but similar ballots showing an intent to vote for Bush were not changed to legal votes. Such a recount would be "better" than the machine counts under the criterion employed by the Florida court because it would result in more legal votes being tabulated. But it would not be better in any constitutionally relevant sense,[71] or indeed under any sane criterion. The difference between this hypothetical and the actual order of the Florida court is only one of degree, and a very slight degree at that.

It is true, as the U.S. Supreme Court has always recognized, that the law cannot and does not require *perfect* equality in the treatment of all voters. Every law has different effects on different people, but that does not mean that all laws are unconstitutional. Similarly, voting procedures do not have identical effects on everyone, but that does not make them unconstitutional.

Rural voters, for example, must on average travel farther to their polling places than urban voters, but the Court has not required that election officials somehow correct this inequality. Nor would the Court permit a "correction" that entailed a more pronouncedly unequal effect, such as the creation of malapportioned districts that gave greater weight to the ballots of rural voters. Similarly, there may be latent forms of inequality associated with particular kinds of voting machines, or in the use of different kinds of machines in different counties. But it does not follow that such relatively minor and speculative inequality can permissibly be "corrected" with the kind of gross and palpable inequality that pervaded the Florida court's recount process.

It should therefore come as no surprise that *not a single member* of the U.S. Supreme Court actually defended the Florida court's recount process against the equal protection critique articulated by the majority. Two of the dissenters (Souter and Breyer) acknowledged that the recount process could not be defended against equal protection objections.[72] Justice Stevens, who refused to find the Florida recount unconstitutional, offered nothing more than an utterly anodyne allusion to the need for "a little play in the joints" of the machinery of government.[73] That maxim could be used to defend any vote-dilution scheme, including all of those that have been invalidated by the Supreme Court in the past. Justice Ginsburg, for her part, merely offered an unsupported and unreasoned refusal to recognize the constitutional violation.[74]

There is a good reason for the failure of the *Bush v. Gore* dissenters to offer any legal defense of what the Florida court did. It was simply indefensible under the principles established in the Supreme Court's equal protection jurisprudence.

WERE THERE LEGALLY PREFERABLE ALTERNATIVES
TO THE COURT'S APPLICATION
OF EQUAL PROTECTION ANALYSIS?

Although the dissenters did not provide any legal criticism of the majority's equal protection analysis, they did dissent. It is therefore worth considering whether their dissenting opinions contained or suggested any legally appropriate objections to the majority's disposition of the case.

Refusing to Review the Case

The most plausible legal objection offered by any of the *Bush v. Gore* dissenters was Justice Breyer's suggestion that the Twelfth Amendment assigns to Congress, not to the federal courts, the responsibility for correcting constitutional violations like those the Florida Supreme Court committed. The Twelfth Amendment does assign to Congress the authority and responsibility for counting electoral votes. And it seems undeniable that Congress must also have the authority to make decisions about the legal validity of votes that are submitted to Congress, most obviously in cases where more than one slate of votes is received from the same state.[75] And it may well be that Congress is authorized to ignore judicial decisions that conflict with its own judgments about the legality of the electoral votes it receives.

For Justice Breyer's suggestion to have any merit in the context of this case, however, one would have to go even further and argue that the Constitution gives Congress the *exclusive* authority to rule on the legality of electoral votes, thereby depriving federal courts of the jurisdiction they would otherwise have to adjudicate claims arising under federal law. The constitutional text, however, does not by its terms provide such exclusive jurisdiction to Congress. An argument supporting such exclusivity would therefore have to rely on inferences from the structure and history of the Constitution and/or on the judicially developed "nonjusticiability" doctrine.[76]

Breyer made no attempt to develop an argument along these lines in his *Bush v. Gore* dissent, probably because of one simple and powerful legal fact: the Supreme Court had previously held, in *McPherson v. Blacker,* that Congress does *not* have such exclusive authority.[77] Breyer was obviously aware of this holding, since the Court had unanimously relied on dicta in the same case just a few days earlier in *Bush I.* It would have been quite a challenge to explain why the Court should overrule the holding in a case on whose dicta the justices had so recently and unanimously relied.

Accordingly, Breyer never quite asserted that the Court was legally forbidden to review the Florida court's judgment. Instead, he merely contended that the Twelfth Amendment, as well as various federal statutes that had been enacted to guide the counting of electoral votes, somehow conveyed a counsel of "judicial restraint."[78] In the end, Breyer did not and could not contend that the majority committed a legal error in agreeing to review the Florida court's decision. Instead, he offered a nakedly political critique of the majority: "*[A]bove all,* in this highly politicized matter, the appearance of a split decision runs the risk of undermining the public's confidence in the Court itself."[79]

This political approach to the exercise of jurisdiction deserves some attention, for it goes to the core of the most commonly articulated criticism of the *Bush v. Gore* majority. The justices, we are often told, have a duty to preserve the institutional capital of the Court by avoiding entanglements in the "political thicket," where their reputation for impartiality might be sullied, fairly or not. As Breyer so eloquently put it:

> [T]he public's confidence in the Court itself . . . is a public treasure. It has been built slowly over many years, some of which were marked by a Civil War and the tragedy of segregation. It is a vitally necessary ingredient of any successful effort to protect basic liberty and, indeed, the rule of law itself. We run no risk of returning to the days when a President (responding to this Court's efforts to protect the Cherokee Indians) might have said, "John Marshall has made his decision; now let him enforce it!" Loth, *Chief Justice John Marshall and The Growth of the American Republic* 365 (1948). But we do risk a self-inflicted wound—a wound that may harm not just the Court, but the Nation.[80]

Breyer forgot to mention that this argument about avoiding the "political thicket" was one that the Court had *rejected* in the vote-dilution cases on which the majority relied.[81] Moreover, the notion of a general duty to avoid decisions that might undermine the public's confidence in the Court is not one that anybody actually believes. In fact, many of the Court's most intensely admired decisions are exactly those that were *most* controversial when decided: *Brown v. Board of Education,* which forbade racially segregated schools; *Engel v. Vitale,* which forbade prayer in the schools; *Miranda v. Arizona,* which forbade the use of voluntary confessions at trial unless preceded by a series of judicially created warnings; *Reynolds v. Sims,* which required equality of population in state legislative districts; *Roe v. Wade,* which established a right to abortion; *Texas v. Johnson,* which protected a right to desecrate the American flag.

Notwithstanding the sound of Breyer's rhetoric, the theory underlying his call for judicial restraint is actually not one that would preclude any of the decisions in the above list. On the contrary, it is a theory meant to *foster* just such controversial decisions, along with their frequently profound political effects, even or perhaps especially when those effects are so profound as to shake the public's confidence in the Court. The real theory, well known to sophisticated students of law and political science, is that the Supreme Court should refuse to decide *certain* politically sensitive cases, especially those involving the constitutional allocation of power between the federal and state governments, in order to conserve the Court's political resources for more important tasks, especially those involving the protection of "individual liberties."[82] In practice, what this means is that the Court should sometimes allow the Constitution to be violated when Congress infringes on the rights of the states while protecting judicially selected "individual liberties" that often have no basis in the Constitution.

This calculated, asymmetrical, and ultimately lawless concern with the maintenance and deployment of judicial political capital has been a hallmark of modern liberal jurisprudence. It is, in fact, a corollary of the political theory reflected in Justice Stevens's dissent, where the rule of law and the rule of judges become conflated. And it is very plainly the basis for Breyer's dissent. Even though he acknowledged that the Florida court's recount process was inconsistent with constitutional standards, Breyer contended that "the Court is not acting to vindicate a fundamental constitutional principle, such as the need to protect a basic human liberty."[83]

Breyer attempted to justify his position by arguing that the Court could have waited to see whether the unconstitutional recount process would actually alter the election's outcome, thus giving the Florida courts an opportunity to address the constitutional issue "if and when it was discovered to have mattered."[84] For reasons explored below, Breyer was wrong to assume that there was time left for the state court to correct the problem it had created. Even apart from that mistake, however, it is simply not the case that Justice Breyer believes that the Supreme Court should generally stay its hand until the very last moment before a constitutional violation becomes unquestionably irremediable.

Just a few months before *Bush v. Gore,* for example, Breyer himself had written the majority opinion in a case that had the following interesting features: (1) the Court was reviewing a state statute that had been deliberately drafted to be consistent with the Supreme Court's case law; (2) the Court rejected an interpretation of the statute that would have made it consistent with that case law, instead adopting a far-fetched interpretation that allowed the Court to invalidate the statute; (3) the state itself had argued before the Supreme Court in favor of the interpretation that the Court rejected; (4) the state courts had never been allowed to review the statute at all because the Supreme Court struck it down before it was ever applied to anyone; and (5) the Court's 5–4 decision exposed divisions within the Court whose bitterness easily exceeded what was expressed in *Bush v. Gore.*[85]

And what was the "fundamental constitutional principle" at stake in this case, the likes of which were supposedly absent in *Bush v. Gore*? The right to so-called partial birth abortion, a procedure that is deeply repugnant to many millions of American citizens, that had been outlawed by at least thirty states, and that Congress had twice voted by wide margins to forbid. Compared with preserving this truly important right, what is a little matter like conducting a presidential election in a constitutional manner and protecting the constitutional rights of those who voted in it? According to Justice Breyer, not much.

Perhaps it should come as no surprise that the left wing of the current Court would object to deciding a controversial, high-profile case involving partisan politics that would contribute nothing to the protection of the Left's favored individual liberties. Somewhat more surprisingly, however, the theory of judicial politics underlying Breyer's dissent in *Bush v. Gore* is one to which more conservative members of the Court have sometimes been attracted.

In 1992, for example, the Court reaffirmed the judicially created right to abortion, even while strongly hinting that some justices who voted to do so had serious misgivings about the decision's consistency with the Constitution.[86] And just last year, the Court reaffirmed a constitutional right to so-called *Miranda* warnings,[87] notwithstanding the fact that some members of the majority had previously said that such warnings are *not* required by the Constitution.[88] In both cases, stare decisis was offered as the principal rationale for the decision, but neither decision can be explained on that ground, for they both reaffirmed some precedents while overruling other and more recent precedents.[89]

Far more important in both cases than any supposed respect for precedent was an easily discernible concern with the Court's own public image and a fear of diminishing its own political capital. In the abortion case, for example, a majority of the justices issued one of the most grandiose expressions of the judicial self-importance on record:

> Like the character of an individual, the legitimacy of the Court must be earned over time. So, indeed, must be the character of a Nation of people who aspire to live according to the rule of law. Their belief in themselves as such a people is not readily separable from their understanding of the Court invested with the authority to decide their constitutional cases and speak before all others for their constitutional ideals. If the Court's legitimacy should be undermined, then, so would the country be in its very ability to see itself through its constitutional ideals.[90]

The *Miranda*-warning opinion, which was mercifully free of such rhetoric, confined itself to observing that *Miranda* "has become embedded in routine police practice to the point where the warnings have become part of our national culture."[91] But the implications of this bland statement are no less troubling. Indeed, I would translate the Court's remark to mean something like this: We would look pretty silly if the one rule of constitutional law that every American is familiar with, from watching untold numbers of cops-and-robbers shows on television, were suddenly declared by the Supreme Court to be a figment of the Court's own imagination. The masses might even start to wonder where all the other rules of constitutional law are coming from. And who knows what would happen to our national culture then?

Three members of the *Bush v. Gore* majority had joined one or both of these opinions.[92] It is therefore striking that all three rejected the temptation to conserve the Court's political capital by avoiding any involvement in *Bush v. Gore*. They could easily have avoided such involvement, simply by voting not to review any of the Florida election cases. Such refusals require no explanation and are without precedential effect. Indeed, it had been widely anticipated that this is exactly what would happen before the Court surprised the world by granting review in *Bush I*.

The *Bush v. Gore* majority had to know that a decision in Bush's favor would trigger an avalanche of scurrilous accusations and politically motivated attacks and endless insinuations about their personal integrity. They were thus faced with a very unpleasant choice: if they enforced the law, they ran the risk of acquiring a reputation for having done the opposite, but if they refused to enforce the law, they would preserve their reputation for judiciousness. In deciding to hear the case and then resolving it in accordance with the law, the majority demonstrated genuine integrity and impartiality in exactly those circumstances in which it is most difficult to practice.

In contrast to Justice Stevens's remarkable assault on George W. Bush for having had the temerity to defend himself against Vice President Gore's lawsuit, and in contrast to Stevens's emotional attack on his colleagues for agreeing to hear Bush's appeal, the majority treated this as a legal case that deserved to be treated as such by judges, even if others chose to use it as a political football:

> None are more conscious of the vital limits on judicial authority than are the members of this Court, and none stand more in admiration of the Constitution's design to leave the selection of the President to the people, through their legislatures, and to the political sphere. When contending parties invoke the process of the courts, however, it becomes our unsought responsibility to resolve the federal and constitutional issues the judicial system has been forced to confront.[93]

One might think that fulfilling their unsought responsibilities is just about the minimum that we ought to expect from Supreme Court justices, who are given life tenure for just this purpose. But when one reflects on the concept of judicial integrity that infuses the dissenting opinions in *Bush v.*

Gore, a simple willingness to enforce the law begins to look like a kind of heroism.

The Article II Argument

The majority's decision in *Bush v. Gore* relied entirely on an equal protection analysis. One line of criticism, particularly appealing to the conservative legal mind, is that the decision should have rested instead on the analysis set forth in Chief Justice Rehnquist's concurring opinion. That opinion resolved the question that the Court had avoided in *Bush I.*

Article II of the Constitution provides: "Each State shall appoint, *in such manner as the Legislature thereof may direct,* a Number of [presidential] Electors."[94] Along with Justices Scalia and Thomas, Rehnquist argued that the Florida Supreme Court had violated the Constitution by discarding the election statutes written by Florida's legislature and writing a new election code that was inconsistent with the legislature's directions.

One can make a powerful argument for this conclusion. Even apart from its many strange "interpretations" of statutory language, the Florida court's crucial decisions—especially the order for a partial and selective statewide recount—were simply disconnected from anything in the statutes. Taken as a whole, moreover, the court's exposition of Florida law had results that were so absurd and inequitable that they could not possibly have been intended by the legislature. Whatever authority there might be for a state court to ignore the legislature's directions in other contexts, Article II of the Constitution appears on its face to forbid such judicial reshaping of the law in connection with the appointment of presidential electors. This straightforward textual argument has a kind of intellectual power that no equal protection analysis can match. A more detailed comparison of the majority's equal protection approach with the Article II approach, however, will show that the one is not so clearly preferable to the other as may first appear.

Consider first the weaknesses of the majority's analysis. The Supreme Court's entire equal protection jurisprudence is notoriously ill rooted in either the text of the Fourteenth Amendment or in the expectations of those who enacted it. The voting rights branch of equal protection law, moreover, is particularly vulnerable to criticism based on the text and history of the Constitution, as Justice Harlan demonstrated in his devastating and unanswered dissent in *Reynolds v. Sims.*[95] The evolution of the law of equal protection, moreover, has been something less than a model of logical consistency. New doctrinal pathways have sometimes been opened up with scarcely a legal reason offered,[96] while equally plausible lines of development have been foreclosed or suddenly stopped in their tracks without much more than a wave of the hand.[97]

Over the decades, the Court has developed a complex scheme under which it requires varying degrees of justification for the inequalities associated with different kinds of laws. Both critics and proponents of the aggressive use of equal protection analysis have contended that this scheme does not constitute a set of preexisting rules that are applied to new factual situations as they arise but rather reflects a series of judgments made independently of the theoretical apparatus that is used to explain the results.[98] Notwithstanding the very real difficulty of identifying a coherent set of principles that are applied in a principled manner throughout the Court's equal protection cases, however, it does not follow that every equal protection decision is an unprincipled exercise of political judgment.

For example, given that the Court has required states to apportion their legislatures on the basis of equal population in order to avoid diluting the votes of some citizens, consistency requires that this rule be applied to all states. Creating an arbitrary exception—such as one for states with two Republican senators, or one for states through which the Mississippi River passes—would clearly be unacceptable. Conversely, refusing to create such exceptions is appropriately principled. At the other extreme, the creation of some exceptions is clearly proper and therefore does not manifest an arbitrary or unprincipled approach to the law. The Court, for example, has recognized that perfect equality of population in state legislative districts would create enormous and possibly insurmountable practical difficulties and has therefore never demanded it.

Between these two extremes is a middle range, where more or less reasonable differences of opinion might arise. As the failure of the *Bush v. Gore* dissenters to mount any meaningful criticism of the majority's equal protection analysis suggests, this case is much closer to one extreme than the other. The Florida court's recount procedure was rife with differences in the treatment of various categories of ballots that were at best arbitrary, and there was no compelling or even legitimate reason to create an equal protection exception that would permit such capricious forms of inequality. Indeed, the truly unprincipled course of action would have been to create an exception on the basis of the legally flimsy or irrelevant grounds advanced by the *Bush v. Gore* dissenters.

Thus the application of equal protection analysis by the *Bush v. Gore* majority did not exhibit the sort of unprincipled, essentially political judgments that have rightly made legal conservatives uncomfortable with some of the Court's equal protection decisions.

A related but slightly different objection to the majority's analysis is that it will lead to a flood of socially undesirable litigation challenging a vast number of traditional election practices.[99] Must every voter now use exactly the same kind of ballot, which will be counted by exactly the same kind of machine? If some ballots are counted or recounted by hand, must the same treatment be given to all ballots in that election? Must voters who ask questions of officials at their local polling place receive exactly the same answer in precisely the same words? Must those who count the ballots and tabulate the results receive exactly the same training and conduct themselves according to exactly the same procedures? Is it even permissible for election officials to be chosen in partisan elections, as Florida's secretary of state and many of its local canvassing officials were?

These and a host of similar questions are now thought to be the inevitable subject of litigation in the wake of future elections, where they will inevitably produce new suspicions about judicial bias. That danger certainly does exist, even though the Court expressly limited its holding to cases involving a court-ordered statewide recount lacking even the rudimentary requirements of equal treatment and fundamental fairness.[100] Defendants in future cases will cite the narrow statement of the Court's holding in order to show that *Bush v. Gore* does not compel radical and unwarranted changes in traditional election practices. But plaintiffs will nonetheless be able to argue that a great many of those practices have in one way or another crossed an ill-defined boundary between what is fundamentally unfair and what is permissibly or tolerably unfair.

It is too soon to know how many benefits will come at what cost as future courts wrestle with the questions that are certainly going to arise in an area that the majority freely acknowledged is fraught with "many complexities."[101] But it is not too soon to recognize that this is nothing new in the jurisprudence of equal protection. Indeed, virtually every major equal protection decision has created the potential for similar consequences. When the Court held that segregated public schools are unconstitutional, it inevitably opened up a host of questions about the permissibility of other forms of official segregation and discrimination. Some of those questions continue to be litigated almost a half century later.[102] Similarly, when the Court ruled that legislative districts must be apportioned equally on the basis of population, it opened the way for a great deal of ensuing litigation about the exact degree of equality that is required, about the possibility of special circumstances in which there might be good reason to relax the general rule, and about the application of the underlying principle of equal weighting for all votes to arguably analogous situations like that presented by gerrymandered districts.

If *Bush v. Gore* does lead to litigation that results in significant alterations of American election practices, that might merely indicate there is a real problem that needs to be addressed, as was clearly the case with *Brown v. Board of Education*. But that hardly seems the most likely outcome. For all their impressive industry and creativity, Vice President Gore's lawyers utterly failed to produce examples of the existence of election practices that even approached the level of arbitrary and unnecessary unfairness that pervaded the court-ordered recount in Florida. There may be some existing practices that will come into serious question as a result of *Bush v. Gore,* such as the availability of recounts in selectively chosen jurisdictions under Florida's protest mechanism.[103] But there is little reason to believe and nothing in the Court's opinion to suggest that any massive or inappropriate reconsideration of America's traditional, decentralized electoral system is about to be undertaken by the federal courts.

Thus, the majority's equal protection analysis is not quite so problematic as legal conservatives may be inclined to suppose, either with respect to its roots in prior case law or with respect to its implications for future case law. On the other side of the scale, Chief Justice Rehnquist's Article II analysis is not without significant difficulties of its own.

First, although Rehnquist's analysis is anchored in the text of the Constitution, that textual anchor is an ambiguous one. It is certainly quite plausible to read Article II to outlaw election procedures that are devised by courts in contravention of a state legislature's directions. But it is not inconceivable that the Constitution's reference to the legislature's directions could refer to state statutes *as interpreted* by state courts. The framers were well aware that statutes often do require judicial interpretation in order to be applied, and federal courts ordinarily assume that state statutes mean what state courts say they mean. It would not be outlandish to interpret Article II as incorporating the same background assumption.

Second, using Rehnquist's Article II theory would have been unprecedented. In one sense, that is unproblematic. An Article II objection to a state election had apparently never come before the Court, and every issue has to be a new issue once. In another sense, however, using the Article II argument would have created some tension with existing precedent. Let us assume that the Florida Supreme Court's application of the Florida election statutes was so far-fetched and untenable that it constituted an act of legislating rather than an interpretation of existing law. The same can be said of a significant number of decisions by the U.S. Supreme Court itself.[104] Indeed, the dissenters in some of these cases have plausibly suggested that the Court was violating the Constitution by legislating from the bench.[105] Although some of us would have been well pleased if *Bush v. Gore* had signaled the beginning of a new era of judicial respect for the text of the statutes that the Supreme Court is charged with interpreting, a decision relying on Article II would have exposed the Court to a colorable objection that it was holding the Florida court to standards of fidelity in statutory interpretation that it has not imposed on itself.

Third, an opinion based solely on Article II grounds might have suggested that the Florida statutes themselves were constitutionally unproblematic. In fact, however, substantial equal protection objections can be raised against a statutory scheme under which the losing candidate can demand recounts in counties selectively chosen so as to tilt the incidence of random errors in his own favor. Although the majority did not need to reach this issue, its application of equal protection analysis suggests, more strongly than an Article II analysis would have, that such objections should be taken quite seriously.

Thus, the equal protection and Article II rationales for reversing the Florida Supreme Court have somewhat different legal strengths and corresponding weaknesses. In important ways, the equal protection rationale is less bold—and in that respect perhaps more judicious. Even if one is inclined to prefer an argument based on Article II, as I am, it is not preferable across all the relevant dimensions.[106] And it is not on the whole so clearly preferable as to provide a good reason for criticizing the majority's use of equal protection. It should therefore come as no surprise that those members of the Court who joined Chief Justice Rehnquist's opinion also joined the majority opinion.

The Suspiciously Narrow Holding

Courts, especially appellate courts, are supposed to apply general rules and standards to particular cases. When an appellate court cannot or will not articulate its reasons at an appropriate level of generality, one is entitled to wonder whether it is being driven by something other than principle. For that reason, there is something immediately troubling about the *Bush v. Gore* majority's narrow statement of its holding:

> The recount process, in its features here described, is inconsistent with the minimum procedures necessary to protect the fundamental right of each voter in the special instance of a statewide recount under the authority of a single state judicial officer. Our consideration is limited to the present circumstances, for the problem of equal protection in election processes generally presents many complexities.
>
> The question before the Court is not whether local entities, in the exercise of their expertise, may develop different systems for implementing elections. Instead, we are presented with a situation where a state court with the power to assure uniformity has ordered a statewide recount with minimal procedural safeguards. When a court orders a statewide remedy, there must be at least some assurance that the rudimentary requirements of equal treatment and fundamental fairness are satisfied.[107]

At least at first, this could sound rather like the statement of people who know what result they want but cannot quite say what their reasons are. Before jumping to that conclusion, it is important to remember that overly broad holdings can be worse than those that are too narrow. Broad holdings may effectively decide future cases that are factually dissimilar in ways that should be legally distinguished. That danger is particularly acute in an area of the law, like equal protection, in which the Court is necessarily drawing lines between "too much" and "not enough" without the benefit of guidance from the Constitution itself.

Closer consideration of the *Bush v. Gore* holding reveals good reasons for a narrow holding. First, it was appropriate to limit the decision to *recounts*. Procedures employed after the decision makers know they are dealing with a close election, in which one candidate is provisionally the loser, present opportunities for abuse that are at the very least much less pronounced in other circumstances. This case provides an example, for nobody would have dreamed of proposing that an initial count of the ballots be conducted in the way that the court-ordered recount was proceeding in Florida. Without accusing or exonerating anyone in Florida of misconduct, it is obvious that the incentives to adopt inappropriately discriminatory procedures increases dramatically once the responsible officials know which candidate is more likely to be adversely affected by them.

Second, it was also appropriate to limit the decision to cases involving *judicial* recounts because these enjoy a finality that is not present when executive officials make decisions that are subject to judicial review. Similarly, it was probably appropriate to limit the decision to cases involving a recount by a *single* judge because (a) those are the cases in which there is least likely to be any good practical reason for tolerating significant differences in the way similar ballots are treated; and (b) those are the cases in which there is the least chance that arbitrary differences in the treatment of ballots will cancel each other out and thus leave the result of the election unaffected.

That leaves one limitation on the holding for which I cannot see a plausible justification: the restriction to *statewide* recounts. Although the inclusion of this limitation seems mistaken to me, it is a relatively small point that cannot justify the conclusion that the majority was result oriented or unprincipled. If this is the only error in the majority opinion, it is almost miraculous that an opinion written under such enormous time pressures would be so slightly blemished.

Third, it is worth emphasizing that the Court did not *preclude* the application of vote-dilution principles to other election procedures, such as statewide recounts or counts conducted by executive officials. The majority decided only that they lacked sufficient time and information to evaluate such procedures responsibly in the context of this case. If there is one thing about this extraordinary case that should be undeniable, this would seem to be it.

Fidelity to Federalism

Another common criticism of the *Bush v. Gore* majority is that they behaved hypocritically by interfering in Florida's resolution of its own state election. These are the same five justices who have been moving in what many consider an aggressive fashion to protect the states from federal interference in a variety of other contexts. What happened to their solicitude for states' rights in this case?[108]

One might simply turn the question around and ask: What happened to the dissenters' solicitude for federal authority and the fundamental equal protection rights of voters? This kind of "so's your Mother" response, however, is both inadequate and inappropriate. It is inadequate because it is perfectly possible for everyone on the Court to be guilty of hypocrisy. It is not much of a defense to a charge of hypocrisy to show that someone else is hypocritical as well. And it is inappropriate because it distracts attention from the real question, which is whether the case was correctly decided.

The hypocrisy objection is never framed in precise legal terms, nor could it be, for there is no legal tension between the holding in *Bush v. Gore* and the holdings in any of the Court's other recent decisions. In legal terms, moreover, a "federalism objection" to *Bush v. Gore* would be ludicrous.[109] States are required to conform their conduct with the U.S. Constitution, and the Supreme Court has jurisdiction to correct state court judgments that are inconsistent with the Constitution. No member of the *Bush v. Gore* majority has ever questioned these propositions, and none has ever suggested that the Supreme Court should stop enforcing either the Fourteenth Amendment or the Court's vote-dilution precedents.

The federalism objection thus turns out to be yet another criticism based on the premise that the *Bush v. Gore* majority were politically rather than legally misguided. But unless one can show that the majority were politically rather than legally motivated, which I think has not and cannot be done, this objection is simply another regrettable manifestation of the fashionably decadent view that judges cannot and should not be anything except robed politicians.

The Controversial Remedy

Among the more interesting criticisms of the *Bush v. Gore* majority is that they erred by declining to remand the case to the state court with instructions to conduct a recount under constitutionally permissible procedures. Justices Souter and Breyer, who thought the Court should have refused to hear the case at all, advocated this approach as the best way of dealing with the constitutional violation whose existence they could not deny.

To understand this criticism, it is important to recall that *Bush v. Gore* was decided on December 12, the deadline for Florida to take advantage of the safe harbor offered by federal law.[110] Whether this nonbinding deadline was met or not, however, federal law required that all presidential electors meet and cast their votes on December 18.[111] As a practical matter, it is almost inconceivable that the Florida courts could have established constitutionally adequate procedures and then used them to conduct a statewide, hand recount during this six-day period. And even if one supposes that this could somehow have been done, how could the loser have been given any meaningful right of appellate review?

These difficulties are exactly what made the Souter-Breyer approach look so politically attractive. Writing immediately after the Court's decision, Michael W. McConnell put it this way:

> Such a disposition would have maintained the 7–2 majority for the entire holding, which the American public would find vastly more reassuring. To be sure, it is probably impossible to conduct a proper recount by [the statutory deadline of December 18], but by cutting off the possibility, the court encouraged critics to blame the court majority—rather than the passage of time—for the outcome.[112]

I agree with McConnell that this disposition would have spared the Supreme Court *some* of the criticism it has received and that the institutional political interests of the Court *might* have been served by a nearly unanimous ruling that encouraged the Florida court to make yet another effort to find a "better" way to count the ballots than the initial machine counts had provided. It would then have become more clear to more people that the Florida court's project had been frustrated by simple reality, as well as by its own mistake in extending the protest period beyond the statutory deadline.

Although it is easy to see how this approach might have prevented some of the political criticism that the Court has received, it is also easy to see how such a stratagem could have blown up in the Court's face. First, the Florida court had already proved highly aggressive and irresponsible in dealing with federal law and with the U.S. Supreme Court. It is therefore quite possible that the next stab at a statewide recount would have been infected with new constitutional problems, which the U.S. Supreme Court would then have had to deal with under time pressures even greater than those it faced in *Bush v. Gore*.

Second, the passing of the December 12 safe harbor deadline would virtually have assured intervention by the Florida legislature. With the election results themselves still tied up in litigation and the absolute legal deadline of December 18 fast approaching, Florida would have been in real danger of having made no clear choice of electors in time for the Electoral College to meet. Accordingly, the legislature was already gearing up to appoint a slate of electors directly. Given the makeup of the Florida legislature and the fact that Bush was the certified winner of the election, it is safe to predict that a slate of electors pledged to Bush would have been selected. That would have created a whole new swarm of legal and political controversies.

Good arguments can be made, on the basis of both the Constitution and a specific federal statute, that the legislature had a right, or even a constitutional duty, to step in and appoint electors.[113] But this had never happened before, and the legal basis for it was anything but crystal clear. More litigation, probably beginning in the Florida courts, would therefore have ensued, and it is entirely possible that the U.S. Supreme Court would have been faced with a new set of difficult legal questions, which would have been posed in an atmosphere even more politically charged than before. And if the ongoing recount of Florida ballots had at some point tipped just once in Gore's favor, the political histrionics on both sides would probably have reached levels well beyond the very impressive exchanges of venom that we had already observed. Intervention by the Florida legislature also would have heightened the chances that Congress would have received votes from multiple slates of putative electors, as had happened in 1876. This would have generated yet more litigation, with all the added potential for the U.S. Supreme Court to be accused of politically motivated decisions, no matter how it ruled.

We have no way of knowing whether the *Bush v. Gore* majority had considerations like these in mind when they decided the case, let alone whether it would have been shrewder to accept the Souter-Breyer invitation.[114] And there is no reason to criticize the majority for rejecting the Souter-Breyer approach. Apart from the questionable propriety of employing such calculations, they were entirely unnecessary.

My reason for offering this conclusion is quite simple: the Souter-Breyer approach was *legally untenable*, for exactly the reasons given by the majority. On December 11, just one day before the decision in *Bush v. Gore*, the Florida Supreme Court had finally issued its decision in response to the remand in *Bush I*. In that opinion, the Florida court had interpreted state law to allow the late filing of amended election returns by county officials in only two circumstances: when a late filing would preclude someone from exercising his rights under the statutory "contest" provisions and when the late filing would "result in Florida voters not participating fully in the federal electoral process, as provided in 3 U.S.C. § 5 [the safe harbor provision of federal law]."[115] Perhaps even more emphatically, the Florida Court said in the same opinion: "Although the [Florida Election] Code sets no specific deadline by which a manual recount must be completed, the time required to complete a manual recount must be reasonable,"[116] to which it added the following footnote:

> What is a reasonable time required for completion will, in part, depend on whether the election is for a statewide office, for a federal office, or for presidential electors. In the case of the presidential election, the determination of reasonableness must be circumscribed by the provisions of 3 U.S.C. § 5, which sets December 12, 2000, as the date for final determination of any state's dispute concerning its electors in order for that determination to be given conclusive effect in Congress.[117]

And again, in the same opinion:

> As always, it is necessary to read all provisions of the elections code in pari materia. In this case, that comprehensive reading required that there be time for an elections contest pursuant to section 102.168, which all parties had agreed was a necessary component of the statutory scheme and to accommodate the outside deadline set forth in 3 U.S.C. § 5 of December 12, 2000.[118]

Thus, the Florida Supreme Court had already concluded, *as a matter of state law,* that recounts had to be concluded by December 12.[119] If the U.S. Supreme Court had remanded the case on December 12 with instructions or encouragement to conduct a recount under constitutionally adequate procedures, it would have been ordering or inviting the Florida court to violate Florida law *as construed by the Florida Supreme Court.* The U.S. Supreme Court simply had no grounds for doing that because the ensuing violation of state law would not have been dictated by any requirement of federal law.

One might argue that the Florida court's discussion of the binding nature of the December 12 deadline came in the context of a discussion of the protest provisions of the Florida Election Code, whereas the issues in *Bush v. Gore* arose under the contest provisions. Nothing in the Florida court's December 11 opinion, however, suggested that this should make any difference at all. The Florida court's decision in the contest case, moreover, referenced the federal safe harbor statute, without mentioning any alternative possible deadlines.[120] The U.S. Supreme Court simply had no basis at all for imagining that some deadline other than December 12 would be applicable under state law to the "contest" at issue in this case.

Still, one might say, the Supreme Court should at least have remanded the case to the Florida court so that it could reexamine the state law question itself. Perhaps that court would have concluded that state law ultimately subordinated the December 12 deadline to the goal of obtaining a constitutionally acceptable hand recount.

Fair enough. *But that is exactly what the Supreme Court did.* Contrary to a widespread misperception, the Supreme Court did *not* forbid the Florida court from attempting to conduct a statewide recount under constitutionally permissible standards.[121] That would have been the effect of a judgment that reversed the Florida court and remanded with instructions to dismiss the case.[122] But the Court did *not* order the case dismissed. Instead, it reversed and remanded with instructions "for further proceedings not inconsistent with this opinion." The only statement in the Supreme Court's opinion that could conceivably be considered "inconsistent" with a new recount is the following:

> Because the Florida Supreme Court has said that the Florida Legislature intended to obtain the safe-harbor benefits of 3 U.S.C. § 5, Justice BREYER's proposed remedy—remanding to the Florida Supreme Court for its ordering of a constitutionally proper contest until December 18—contemplates action in violation of the Florida election code, and hence could not be part of an "appropriate" order authorized by Fla. Stat. § 102.168(8) (2000).[123]

It is true that this statement assumes that Florida law had not changed between December 11 and December 12, and it assumes that the December 11 opinion meant what it appeared to say. But this statement does not purport to *forbid* the Florida court from concluding on remand that the U.S. Supreme Court had misinterpreted the statements it made on December 11. The Supreme Court's statement, for that matter, does not purport to forbid the Florida court from overruling its own December 11 interpretation of Florida law. Thus, as a legal matter, the Florida court was indeed left free to order the sort of recount that Justices Souter and Breyer suggested.

Gore's lawyers reportedly recognized that the Florida Supreme Court had been left free to order a new recount but decided on political grounds not to request one.[124] There is not much to be gained by speculating about what the Florida court might have done in response to such a request,[125] but it is important to recognize that the U.S. Supreme Court did *not* prevent Gore from continuing to litigate his case and that the U.S. Supreme Court did *not* dictate the interpretation of Florida law to the Florida courts.

Here again, as in every other aspect of this case, the majority simply applied the law. If that turned out to be bad politics, which is a pretty dubious proposition anyway, it at least had the merit of being the right thing for judges to do.

CONCLUSION

For several decades, constitutional law has held that states may not weight the votes of people according to where they reside without a legitimate and compelling public purpose. Such vote dilution permeated the recount process designed by the Florida Supreme Court, and that court offered no coherent, let alone compelling, justification for the discrimination it was imposing on the election process. Nor was any justification offered by either of the two dissenting U.S. Supreme Court justices who claimed that they could not perceive the completely obvious constitutional problem identified by the other seven.

The *Bush v. Gore* majority opinion has been harshly criticized—by the dissenters and by a wide range of commentators—for a variety of supposed sins. The Court should have refused to hear the case for fear of creating an "appearance" of political partiality. The Court should have refused to apply its Fourteenth Amendment precedents for fear of having them taken seriously in future cases. The Court should have ignored the Florida court's one-day-old decision about the meaning of Florida law, thereby inviting that court to commit further violations of federal law. The Court should have refused to apply well-established federal law in this case because of a supposed commitment by the Court's conservatives to some notion of federalism imputed to them by people who have apparently never read their opinions.

None of these criticisms has the slightest legal merit. All of them are political criticisms, offered by people who have forgotten the distinction between law and politics, or who do not want the distinction to exist, or who do not want to be snickered at for defending the distinction. Once one surrenders that distinction, however, all of law becomes at best a decadent exercise in sophistry.

Faced with a gross violation of law by a subordinate court, the *Bush v. Gore* majority did exactly what an appellate court is supposed to do. It reversed the erroneous decision and upheld the law. That this action has provoked so much outrage and so little reasoned approval suggests that the history of our contemporary legal culture may have to be written by a Tacitus, or perhaps a Juvenal.

NOTES

Thanks to Peter Berkowitz, Douglas R. Cox, C. Boyden Gray, Mara S. Lund, John O. McGinnis, and Richard A. Posner for helpful comments, and to the Law & Economics Center at George Mason Law School for generous financial support. I am especially grateful to Stephen G. Gilles for his relentlessly skeptical and constructive criticisms of several preliminary drafts. A more detailed and fully annotated version of this chapter will appear in the *Cardozo Law Review* as part of its "Votes and Voices" symposium.

1. 121 S. Ct. at 542.

2. The per curiam majority opinion was joined by Chief Justice Rehnquist and Justices O'Connor, Scalia, Kennedy, and Thomas.

3. Electoral Count Act, 24 Stat. 373 (1887) (codified as amended at 3 U.S.C. §§ 5–18).

4. Only four days elapsed between the Florida Supreme Court's decision on December 8, 2000, and the U.S. Supreme Court's reversal of that decision on December 12.

5. U.S. Const. Art. II, § 1, cl. 2.

6. *Id.* amend. XII.

7. *Id.*

8. *Id.*

9. *Id.*

10. *Id.* amend. XX, § 3.

11. 3 U.S.C. § 7.

12. 3 U.S.C. § 5.

13. Fla. Stat. § 102.141(4). Such a recount need not be conducted if the losing candidate concedes the election. *Id.*

14. *Id.* §§ 102.141, 102.166.

15. *Id.* § 102.111.

16. *Id.* § 102.168.

17. These figures were tentative because all the absentee ballots had not yet been counted. In retrospect, we know that the remaining absentee ballots were going to widen Bush's lead.

18. Gore acted through the Democratic Party, as he was permitted to do under Florida law. For simplicity of exposition, my discussion will refer to Gore as the initiator of the protests.

19. One of the four counties (Volusia) apparently had real tabulation problems, caused by malfunctioning machines and the like, which almost everyone agreed is a legitimate reason for performing a manual recount. See Siegel v. LePore, 234 F.3d 1163, 1194 n.2 (11th Cir. 2000) (Carnes, J., dissenting).

20. The notion that these counties were chosen because they were the ones in which voters were most likely to have cast a vote that was missed by the machines is untenable. Gore never made such a claim in court, and there were at least seven counties using punch cards that had a higher percentage of "no vote" ballots than Palm Beach, none of which was selected for a manual recount. See *id.* at 1203.

21. The counties chosen by Gore were the three most populous in Florida, and they were counties where Gore won by the widest margins. (Jefferson County gave Gore a slightly higher margin of victory than Miami-Dade, but Jefferson is a small county in which very few ballots were cast, thus making it a poor prospect for Gore's recount strategy.) See *id.* at 1213–14 (Chart A).

22. Two of the three members of each canvassing board are elected in local, partisan elections. See Fla. Stat. §§ 102.141; 124.01(2); Fla. Const. art. 8, § 1(d).

23. See Touchston v. McDermott, 234 F.3d 1133 (11th Cir. 2000) (upholding the district court's denial of a preliminary injunction requested by Bush), *cert. denied,* 121 S. Ct. 749 (2001). See also Bush v. Palm Beach County Canvassing Board, 121 S. Ct. 501 (2000) (declining to grant certiorari on equal protection and due process claims). Assuming that Florida law allowed Gore to obtain a geographically biased recount premised on voter error, rather than machine error, the arguments in

Bush's favor on the merits were very strong. See, *e.g.*, Siegel v. LePore, 234 F.3d at 1194–1213 (Carnes, J., dissenting).

24. Palm Beach County. Canvassing Board v. Harris, 772 So.2d 1220, 1237 (2000).

25. At oral argument before the U.S. Supreme Court in *Bush I,* the lawyer for Florida's attorney general (who was aligned with Gore) conceded that he was unaware of any previous election "in which recounts were conducted, manual recounts, because of an allegation that some voters did not punch the cards the way they should have through their fault."

The Florida court attempted to support its counterintuitive conclusion by citing a statutory provision that said: "No vote shall be declared invalid or void if there is a clear indication of the intent of the voter as determined by the canvassing board." See 772 So.2d at 1229 (citing Fla. Stat. § 101.5614[5]). But that provision applies only to cases in which the ballot *itself* is damaged or defective, which simply reinforces the conclusion that the Florida laws did not contemplate manual recounts designed to correct errors by *voters.* The court also pointed to the next subsection, Fla. Stat. § 101.5614(6), which provides: "If an elector marks more names than there are persons to be elected to an office or if it is impossible to determine the elector's choice, the elector's ballot shall not be counted for that office, but the ballot shall not be invalidated as to those names which are properly marked." 772 So.2d at 1229. This rule does not support the court because it says only that (1) improperly marked overvote ballots shall *not* be counted; (2) ballots shall *not* be counted when the elector's choice is (for whatever reason) impossible to determine; and (3) a ballot *properly* marked for one candidate shall not be invalidated *as to that candidate* because of improper marks elsewhere on the ballot. This three-part rule covers a number of situations, but it does not purport to cover all situations. And it emphatically does not say or imply that ballots must always be counted when a reviewer believes he or she can discern the intent of the voter.

26. 772 So.2d at 1240. In a later opinion, issued after the U.S. Supreme Court reviewed the case, the Florida court contended that the recounts had been "thwarted" by an advisory opinion from the Florida Division of Elections that interpreted the law differently than the Florida court interpreted it. The court then explained that it had tried to create as much time for the recounts as would have existed had the counties not complied with this advisory opinion. Palm Beach County Canvassing Board v. Harris, 772 So.2d 1273, 1290 (2000). This makes no sense. The advisory opinion from the Division of Elections did not prevent the county canvassing boards from continuing the recounts. Indeed, Florida's attorney general had immediately responded to the Division by issuing his own advisory opinion, which directly repudiated the conclusions reached by the Division of Elections. See Fla. Att. Gen. Advisory Opinion No. AGO 2000–65 (Nov. 14, 2000). Furthermore, those boards were well aware that the Division of Elections might be overruled by the courts, for a lawsuit challenging the opinion of the Division of Elections had been filed the very day that opinion was issued. See 772 So.2d at 1226. The division's advisory opinion "thwarted" nothing.

27. 772 So.2d at 1239 (relying on language in State *ex rel.* Chappell v. Martinez, 536 So.2d 1007, 1008–9 [Fla.1988]).

28. Throughout this essay, I focus on the arguments and parties that in retro-

spect turned out to be most significant. Here, for example, Secretary of State Harris presented somewhat different arguments from Bush's, and Bush himself presented some arguments that I have not summarized.

29. See Palm Beach County Canvassing Board v. Harris, 772 So.2d 1220, 1236–37 (Fla. 2000) (quoting Treiman v. Malmquist, 342 So.2d 972, 975 [Fla. 1977], which was in turn construing the Florida Constitution's statement that "[a]ll political power is inherent in the people").

30. The U.S. Supreme Court frequently follows the closely analogous practice of resolving statutory ambiguities in a manner that avoids raising serious constitutional questions. See, *e.g.*, Cheek v. United States, 498 U.S. 192, 203 (1991); Edward J. De Bartolo Corp. v. Florida Gulf Coast Bldg. & Constr. Trades Council, 485 U.S. 568, 575 (1988); Hooper v. California, 155 U.S. 648, 657 (1895).

31. 146 U.S. 1, 25 (1892); *id.* at 35 (quoting Senate Rep. No. 395, 1st Sess., 43d Cong. [1874]).

32. Bush v. Palm Beach County Canvassing Board, 121 S. Ct. 471 (2000).

33. *Id.* at 474.

34. Fla. Stat. § 102.168(3)(c).

35. Gore made a number of other claims as well, all of which were rejected both by the trial court and by the Florida Supreme Court.

36. Transcript of oral ruling, Dec. 3, 2000, at 9, *available at* http://election 2000.stanford.edu/.

37. Technically, the Florida Supreme Court only required the trial court to *consider* conducting a statewide recount, perhaps because of doubts about the supreme court's jurisdiction to order the recount. Because the trial court did order the recount, this technical distinction had no subsequent significance.

38. It might be possible to devise some legal theory under which recounts conducted pursuant to a subsequently nullified judicial decision should be treated as valid, but no such theory was articulated by the Florida court.

39. Fla. Stat. § 102.168(3).

40. Gore's attempt to construct a statistical argument for calling the election results into doubt foundered when his expert witness, Yale professor Nicolas Hengartner, was demolished under cross-examination. Those who missed seeing this embarrassing spectacle when the trial was televised can consult the transcript, *available at* http://election2000.stanford.edu/.

41. 772 So.2d at 1256. Gore had picked up 168 votes in the partial recount in Miami-Dade, but that recount had been limited to a set of disproportionately Democratic precincts.

42. This assumption is the apparent explanation for the court's claim that the statute did not place the burden of proof on the plaintiff, as is universally done in civil litigation, but rather imposed on the *trial judge* the burden of *disproving* the plaintiff's allegations. See Gore v. Harris, 772 So.2d 1243, 1259 (Fla. 2000).

43. 772 So.2d at 1253.

44. *Id.*

45. See Trial Transcript, *Gore v. Harris*, No. 00–2808 (Leon Cty. Jud. Cir. Dec. 2, 2000), at 461–83 (testimony of Thomas Spencer), *available at* http://election 2000.stanford.edu/.

46. For a brief discussion of the problems created by the majority's standardless

remand, see Gore v. Harris, 772 So.2d 1243, 1269 (Fla. 2000) (Wells, C.J., dissenting).

47. *Id.* at 1273 (Harding, J., dissenting).

48. *Id.* at 1267 (Wells, C.J., dissenting). Justice Harding's dissent made a similar point. *Id.* at 1272.

49. 772 So.2d at 1249, 1253.

50. The majority was certainly aware of this completely obvious point because Chief Justice Wells insisted on it in his dissent. See 772 So.2d at 1264 n.26.

51. See Trial Transcript, *Gore v. Harris,* No. 00–2808 (Leon Cty. Jud. Cir. Dec. 2, 2000), at 262–64 (testimony of Judge Charles Burton), *available at* http:// election2000.stanford.edu/.

52. 772 So.2d at 1257 (apparently quoting Fla. Stat. § 101.5614[5], which applies only to damaged or defective ballots, but clearly adopting the quoted standard as a general principle applicable to all ballots subject to manual recounts).

53. Justice Breyer later tried to supply an explanation by pointing out that Bush and the other defendants in the case "presented no evidence, to this Court or to any Florida court, that a manual recount of overvotes would identify additional legal votes." 121 S. Ct. at 551. This is patently untenable. First, the only "evidence" cited by the Florida Supreme Court for the proposition that the undervote ballots included some additional "legal votes" was the mere existence of the 9,000 undervote ballots from Miami-Dade. See 772 So.2d at 1256. Second, there was not even that much "evidence" of undervotes in counties other than those selected by Gore for his "protests," yet the Florida courts were conducting a manual recount of undervotes in *all* Florida counties. Third, the *defendants* in the lawsuit had no occasion to present "evidence" to support a legal theory that they were not advancing, and in fact they had no reason even to think of such a theory until after the Florida Supreme Court ordered, quite out of the blue, a statewide recount of undervote ballots. Fourth, Gore's own lawyer acknowledged to the U.S. Supreme Court that there were approximately 110,000 overvote ballots in Florida. Transcript of oral argument in *Bush v. Gore,* 2000 WL 1804429, at 62.

54. Contrary to a lot of heated commentary, this order had no adverse effects on Gore's legal rights. Seven members of the Supreme Court subsequently agreed that the suspended recount was inconsistent with constitutional standards, and nobody can have a right to something that is itself illegal. The counting that would have been done after the stay order and before the Court's decision on the merits would have been legally void, and Gore could have had no legal right to the results of an illegal recount.

55. 121 S. Ct. at 530.

56. *E.g.,* Harper v. Virginia Board of Elections, 383 U.S. 663 (1966).

57. Reynolds v. Sims, 377 U.S. 533, 555 (1964) (emphasis added).

58. *Id.*

59. Gray v. Sanders, 372 U.S. 368 (1963).

60. Moore v. Olgivie, 394 U.S. 814 (1969).

61. Reynolds, 377 U.S. at 567–68 (footnote omitted).

62. *Id.* at 563 (citations and internal quotation marks omitted) (emphasis added).

63. See, *e.g.,* O'Brien v. Skinner, 414 U.S. 524 (1974). In this case, state law permitted absentee voting only by those who were absent from their county of residence on election day. When applied to persons in jail, it had the odd and unforeseen effect of discriminating between those who were jailed in their county of residence and those who were jailed elsewhere. Without even suggesting that the legislature's intent was relevant, the Court held that this application of the statute violated equal protection. More generally, the Court has never suggested that discriminatory intent is a necessary element of an equal protection claim in vote-dilution cases or that the absence of discriminatory intent is any defense.

64. *E.g.,* Reynolds v. Sims, 377 U.S. at 569–70.

65. *E.g.,* Carrington v. Rash, 380 U.S. 89 (1965); Board of Estimate v. Morris, 489 U.S. 688 (1989).

66. The Court has declined to apply strict scrutiny to cases involving elections to certain offices that do not exercise general governmental powers. See Ball v. James, 451 U.S. 355 (1981); Salyer Land Co. v. Tulare Lake Basin Water Storage Dist., 410 U.S. 719 (1973). These precedents are manifestly inapplicable to an election for president of the United States.

67. See, *e.g.,* Karcher v. Daggett, 462 U.S. 725 (1983).

68. See, *e.g.,* Roe v. Alabama, 43 F.3d 574 (11th Cir. 1995).

69. See, *e.g.,* Anderson v. United States, 417 U.S. 211, 227 (1974); Reynolds v. Sims, 377 U.S. at 554–55; Wesberry v. Sanders, 376 U.S. 1, 17 (1964); Baker v. Carr, 369 U.S. 186, 208 (1962). Because the stuffing of ballot boxes has been prohibited by statute for a very long time, the Court has apparently not had the opportunity formally to decide that this practice would violate the Constitution even in the absence of a statutory prohibition.

70. Lane v. Wilson, 307 U.S. 268, 275 (1939).

71. *Cf.* Gray v. Sanders, 372 U.S. 368, 379 (1963).

72. See 121 S. Ct. at 533 (per curiam) ("Seven Justices of the Court agree that there are constitutional problems with the recount ordered by the Florida Supreme Court that demand a remedy"); *id.* at 545 (Souter, J., joined by Breyer, J., dissenting) (reviewing several examples of disparate treatment of ballots in the Florida recount, and concluding: "I can conceive of no legitimate state interest served by these differing treatments of the expressions of voters' fundamental rights. The differences appear wholly arbitrary"); *id.* at 551 (Breyer, J., joined by Souter, J., dissenting) ("absence of a uniform, specific standard to guide the recounts . . . does implicate principles of fundamental fairness").

73. 121 S. Ct. at 541 (footnote omitted):

Admittedly, the use of differing substandards for determining voter intent in different counties employing similar voting systems may raise serious concerns. Those concerns are alleviated—if not eliminated—by the fact that a single impartial magistrate will ultimately adjudicate all objections arising from the recount process. Of course, as a general matter, "[t]he interpretation of constitutional principles must not be too literal. We must remember that the machinery of government would not work if it were not allowed a little play in its joints." *Bain Peanut Co. of Tex. v. Pinson,* 282 U.S. 499, 501 (1931) (Holmes, J.). If it were otherwise, Florida's decision to leave to each county the determination of what balloting system to employ—despite enormous differences in accuracy—might run afoul of equal protection. So, too, might the similar decisions of the vast majority of state legislatures to delegate to local authorities certain decisions with respect to voting systems and ballot design.

This reasoning has no natural limit: one might, for example, use it to say that local officials should be allowed to stuff the ballot boxes because forbidding them to do so might create constitutional doubts about the common practice of delegating determinations of voter eligibility to local authorities. But the truism about allowing some play in the joints obviously cannot mean that the states are free to do anything they want. Stevens offered no reason whatsoever for treating the kind of discrimination dictated by the Florida court as constitutionally distinguishable from the kinds of discrimination that had previously been struck down by the Supreme Court.

74. 121 S. Ct. at 550:

I cannot agree that the recount adopted by the Florida court, flawed as it may be, would yield a result any less fair or precise than the certification that preceded that recount. See, *e.g.*, *McDonald v. Board of Election Comm'rs of Chicago*, 394 U.S. 802, 807 (1969) (even in the context of the right to vote, the state is permitted to reform " 'one step at a time' ") (quoting *Williamson v. Lee Optical of Oklahoma, Inc.*, 348 U.S. 483, 489 [1955]).

Justice Ginsburg's citation to *McDonald* is almost comically inapposite. *McDonald* was a vote-*denial* case in which the Court declined to apply strict scrutiny because the plaintiffs had failed to prove that they were actually prohibited from voting. See Goosby v. Osser, 409 U.S. 512, 520–21 (1973). It therefore has nothing at all to do with a vote-*dilution* case like *Bush v. Gore*. If it did, the apparent implication would be that all vote-dilution cases should be judged by the *Lee Optical* rational-basis test, which means that Court's controlling precedents in this area would have to be overruled.

75. The most notorious examples of this occurred in connection with the disputed election of 1876, but it has happened as recently as the 1960 election.

76. The "nonjusticiability" or "political question" doctrine has a somewhat complicated history, and its contours are not perfectly clear. The standard formulation is in Baker v. Carr, 369 U.S. 186, 217 (1962), which held that vote-dilution claims are indeed justiciable. The Florida legislature made a nonjusticiability argument to the U.S. Supreme Court in *Bush I*. The Court ignored the argument.

77. 146 U.S. 1, 23–24 (1892).

78. 121 S. Ct. at 555–57 (Breyer, J., dissenting).

79. *Id.* at 557 (emphasis added).

80. *Id.*

81. See, *e.g.*, Baker v. Carr, 369 U.S. 186, 267 (1962) (Frankfurter, J., dissenting); Reynolds v. Sims, 377 U.S. 533, 566 (1964); Karcher v. Daggett, 462 U.S. 725, 751 (1983) (Stevens, J., concurring).

82. The classic statement is presented in Jesse H. Choper, *Judicial Review and the National Political Process: A Functional Reconsideration of the Role of the Supreme Court* (Chicago: University of Chicago Press, 1980).

83. Bush v. Gore, 121 S. Ct. 525, 557 (Breyer, J., dissenting).

84. Bush v. Gore, 121 S. Ct. at 555 (Breyer, J., dissenting). There is no legal

basis for this "wait and see" idea, notwithstanding Breyer's effort to insinuate that some kind of ripeness problem existed. The Court has decided many vote-denial and vote-dilution cases without suggesting that it made the slightest difference whether the outcome of an election actually had been or would be affected by the constitutional violation.

85. Stenberg v. Carhart, 120 S. Ct. 2597 (2000).

86. Planned Parenthood of Southeastern Pa. v. Casey, 505 U.S. 833, 853 (1992).

87. Dickerson v. United States, 120 S. Ct. 2326 (2000).

88. As Justice Scalia pointed out, these statements include the following: Davis v. United States, 512 U.S. 452, 457–58 (1994) (opinion of the Court, in which Kennedy, J., joined); Duckworth v. Eagan, 492 U.S. 195, 203 (1989) (opinion of the Court, in which Kennedy, J., joined); Oregon v. Elstad, 470 U.S. 298 (1985) (opinion of the Court by O'Connor, J.); New York v. Quarles, 467 U.S. 649 (1984) (opinion of the Court by Rehnquist, J.).

89. Throughout its opinion in *Casey,* the Court refers to its decision to reaffirm the "essential holding" or the "central holding" in *Roe v. Wade,* thereby conceding that it was overruling that decision in part. See also Casey, 505 U.S. at 870 (plurality opinion) ("we must overrule those parts of *Thornburgh* and *Akron I* which, in our view, are inconsistent with *Roe*'s statement that the State has a legitimate interest in promoting the life or potential life of the unborn").

In *Dickerson,* the Court reaffirmed *Miranda.* But, as Justice Scalia pointed out in his dissent, the proposition that failure to comply with *Miranda*'s rules does *not* establish a constitutional violation was central to the holdings in at least four post-*Miranda* cases. 120 S. Ct. at 2342.

90. Casey, 505 U.S. at 868.

91. Dickerson, 120 S. Ct. at 2336.

92. Justices O'Connor and Kennedy were coauthors (with Justice Souter) of the Court's opinion in *Casey.* They both joined Chief Justice Rehnquist's majority opinion in *Dickerson.*

93. 121 S. Ct. at 533.

94. U.S. Const. Art. I, § 1, cl. 2 (emphasis added).

95. 377 U.S. at 616–32.

96. See, *e.g.,* U.S. Dept. of Agriculture v. Moreno, 413 U.S. 528 (1973) (holding that it is "irrational" for a legislature to take action solely to harm a politically unpopular group); Romer v. Evans, 116 S. Ct. 1620 (1996) (apparently concluding that a state may not forbid its subordinate governmental units to grant special legal protections to certain politically unpopular groups).

97. See, *e.g.,* Massachusetts Board of Retirement v. Murgia, 427 U.S. 307 (1976) (refusing to apply heightened scrutiny to age-based classifications); San Antonio Ind. Sch. Dist. v. Rodriguez, 411 U.S. 1 (1973) (refusing to examine wealth-based classifications under heightened scrutiny or under fundamental-interests analysis).

98. See, *e.g.,* San Antonio Ind. Sch. Dist. v. Rodriguez, 411 U.S. 1, 98–110 (1973) (Marshall, J., dissenting); Craig v. Boren, 429 U.S. 190, 220–21 (1976) (Rehnquist, J., dissenting); United States Railroad Retirement Board v. Fritz, 449 U.S. 166, 176–77 n. 10 (1980) (opinion for the Court by Rehnquist, J.); Cleburne v. Cleburne Living Ctr., Inc., 473 U.S. 432, 451–54 (1985) (Stevens, J., concurring).

99. Justice Stevens expressed concern about this supposedly slippery slope. 121 S. Ct. at 541. Commentators, including some conservatives, have criticized the Court's decision for the same reason. *E.g.,* Robert H. Bork, "Sanctimony Serving Politics: The Florida Fiasco," *New Criterion,* Mar. 2001, at 4; Robert F. Nagel, "From *U.S. v. Nixon* to *Bush v. Gore,"* *Weekly Standard,* Dec. 25, 2000, at 20.

100. 121 S. Ct. at 532.

101. *Id.*

102. *E.g.,* Adarand Constructors, Inc. v. Slater, 228 F.3d 1147 (10th Cir. 2000), *cert. granted,* 2001 WL 369474.

103. See, *e.g.,* Siegel v. LePore, 234. F.3d 1163, 1194–1218 (Carnes, J., dissenting).

104. *E.g.,* Public Citizen v. U.S. Dept. of Justice, 491 U.S. 440 (1989); NLRB v. Catholic Bishop of Chicago, 440 U.S. 490 (1987); United Steelworkers v. Weber, 443 U.S. 193 (1979); Griggs v. Duke Power Co., 401 U.S. 424 (1971); Rector of Holy Trinity Church v. United States, 143 U.S. 457 (1892).

105. Catholic Bishop of Chicago, 440 U.S. at 508–18 (Brennan, J., dissenting); Weber, 443 U.S. at 219–55 (Rehnquist, J., dissenting).

106. I believe both that the analysis developed in Chief Justice Rehnquist's concurrence has some significant problems and that the conclusion he reaches can be defended. Space precludes my presenting an alternative to his argument here, but my doubts about aspects of his argument reinforce my disinclination to criticize Justices O'Connor and Kennedy for declining to embrace it.

107. 121 S. Ct. at 532.

108. See, *e.g.,* E. J. Dionne Jr., "So Much for States' Rights," *Washington Post,* Dec. 14, 2000, at A35; John J. DiIulio, "Equal Protection Run Amok: Conservatives Will Come to Regret the Court's Rationale in *Bush v. Gore,"* *Weekly Standard,* Dec. 25, 2000, at 25.

109. Accordingly, the dissenters made no objections based on federalism and did not suggest that the majority opinion was in any sense out of line with the Court's recent federalism decisions. Justice Ginsburg did raise federalism objections to Chief Justice Rehnquist's concurrence but not to the majority opinion.

110. This statute, 3 U.S.C. § 5, purports to bind Congress in exercising its constitutional duty to count electoral votes. I doubt that this can constitutionally be accomplished by a statute. Each house of Congress has the authority to determine its own rules of proceeding, U.S. Const. Art. I, § 5, cl. 2, and it is far from clear that a statute can override that authority. But even if 3 U.S.C. § 5 is unconstitutional in this sense, that has no bearing on the legal issues that arose in *Bush v. Gore.*

111. 3 U.S.C. § 7. Unlike 3 U.S.C. § 5, this statute is clearly binding because it is directed at the states and the presidential electors rather than at Congress.

112. Michael W. McConnell, "A Muddled Ruling," *Wall Street Journal,* Dec. 14, 2000, at A26.

113. Article II of the Constitution specifies that each state "shall" appoint electors. In addition, a statute first enacted in 1845 provides: "Whenever any State has held an election for the purpose of choosing electors, and has failed to make a choice on the day prescribed by law, the electors may be appointed on a subsequent

day in such a manner as the legislature of such State may direct." 3 U.S.C. § 2. Among the most obvious examples of an election that failed to result in a choice of electors would seem to be one that remained tied up in litigation after the safe harbor period designated in 3 U.S.C. § 5 had expired.

114. Judging from the opinions that actually issued, it is doubtful that McConnell is right to suppose that there could have been seven votes for a remand along the lines that Souter and Breyer suggested. Breyer and Souter clearly thought that it was constitutionally permissible to confine a recount to undervote ballots, 121 S. Ct. at 551 (Breyer, J., joined by Souter, J., dissenting), while the five justices who joined the majority opinion treated this aspect of the Florida court's decision as a serious problem, *id.* at 531 (per curiam). A remand order that submerged this disagreement would have been irresponsible because it would have left the Florida court without clear instructions as to how they could ensure that any further recount they attempted would comply with constitutional standards.

115. Palm Beach County Canvassing Board v. Harris, 772 So.2d 1273, 1289 (2000). (This statement was cited by the *Bush v. Gore* majority in the Court's slip opinion. Some confusion has been created by West Publishing's insertion of an incorrect citation in their *Supreme Court Reporter.*) The Florida court had repeatedly made the same point in its initial opinion in the case. See 772 So.2d 1220, 1237,1239, 1239–40 (2000).

116. 772 So.2d at 1285–86.

117. *Id.* at 1286n17.

118. *Id.* at 1290n22. In the concluding section of the opinion, the court reiterated the point yet again. *Id.* at 1291.

119. Whether or not 3 U.S.C. § 5 is legally binding on Congress, Florida law could safely presume that Congress would be virtually certain to comply with it, for political reasons if for no other.

120. See 772 So.2d at 1248.

121. The myth that the Supreme Court forbade the Florida court from conducting a recount under constitutionally permissible standards began with statements in the dissenting opinions. See 121 S. Ct. at 541 (Stevens, J., dissenting) ("the majority nonetheless orders the termination of the contest proceeding"); *id.* at 551 (Breyer, J., dissenting) ("there is no justification for the majority's remedy, which is simply to reverse the lower court and halt the recount entirely"). Stevens's claim is simply wrong. Breyer's statement is not so clearly wrong as a technical matter, but it is misleading. The majority did halt the particular (unconstitutional) recount ordered by the Florida court, but that is all it did.

122. When the Court decides to order a case dismissed, it knows how to say so. See, *e.g.,* Calderon v. Ashmus, 523 U.S. 740 (1998); Growe v. Emison, 507 U.S. 25 (1993); Mississippi v. Louisiana, 506 U.S. 73 (1992).

123. 121 S. Ct. at 533.

124. *Washington Post* political staff, *Deadlock: The Inside Story of America's Closest Election,* 234–35 (New York: Public Affairs, 2001).

125. Gore's lawsuit was dismissed by the Florida Supreme Court two days after the U.S. Supreme Court's decision. On December 22, after the Electoral College had met, the Florida court issued an opinion in which it mistakenly though con-

veniently interpreted the U.S. Supreme Court's opinion as having "mandated that any manual recount be concluded by December 12, 2000." Gore v. Harris, 773 So.2d 524, 526 (2000). But the court added:

> Moreover, upon reflection, we conclude that the development of a specific, uniform standard necessary to ensure equal application and to secure the fundamental right to vote throughout the State of Florida should be left to the body we believe best equipped to study and address it, the Legislature.

Id. If taken at face value, this suggests that the Florida court might not have been willing to torture the state's election laws any further in order to provide Gore with a few more days of recounting, even if he had asked the court to do so.

8

THE GHOSTWRITERS

Arthur J. Jacobson

One feature of the majority's opinion in *Bush v. Gore*[1] struck a sophisticated observer of the Court immediately. "[T]he opinion," wrote Linda Greenhouse in the *New York Times,* "was labeled 'per curiam,' meaning 'by the court,' a label used by courts almost exclusively for unanimous opinions so uncontroversial as to not be worth the trouble of a formal opinion-writing process."[2] The per curiam in *Bush v. Gore* was far from unanimous, hardly uncontroversial, and certainly the subject of a "formal opinion-writing process." If Greenhouse is right and the majority in *Bush v. Gore* not wrong, theirs must fall within the category of opinions suggested by "almost." Greenhouse does not speak directly about the Court, only courts, and does not go into any detail about the occasions on which the Court, or, more precisely, a majority on the Court, labels an opinion "per curiam." Without knowing this, a reader may be forgiven the impression that recourse to the per curiam device in *Bush v. Gore* was unusual if not aberrant and that only sinister motives explain it. So I decided to investigate the Court's per curiam practice in order to right any rhetorical injustice the press inadvertently may have inflicted on the majority by testing their use of the per curiam against such norms as may be implicit in the practice.

My review of the Court's use of per curiams does suggest norms justifying the majority in *Bush v. Gore*. But more than that, the norms put the shoe on the other foot. For it is the motives of the minority—specifically, Justices Breyer and Souter—not the majority, that the norms put in question. Had Justices Breyer and Souter complied with them, then seven justices would have joined the per curiam, not just five, and the result in *Bush v. Gore* would have been 7–2, not 5–4. The rhetorical, hence political, effect of the opinion would have been very different, depriving critics of the decision of a host of denunciations tied to a one-vote victory by the conservative wing of the Court.

FROM ORIGINS . . .

The history of the Court's use of per curiams effectively begins in 1883. Before then the Court had designated opinions "per curiam" only twice, in 1839 and 1862. *West v. Brashear*[3] and *Mesa v. U.S.*[4] dealt with minor (albeit interesting) matters of Supreme Court procedure on which the Court's decisions were indeed unanimous. In the five years from January 1883 to November 1888, the Court labeled two more opinions "per curiam," both unanimous.[5] Both dealt with the actual disputes between the parties and not with Supreme Court procedure. Over the next twelve years, until the end of the century, the practice accelerated, with the Court labeling thirty-four opinions "per curiam," all unanimous. It has continued to accelerate since. Why the sudden increase after 1883?

Two forces converged in the 1880s and 1890s to account for it. One is obvious, the other more subtle. The obvious force is simply the dramatic increase in the Supreme Court's business during the course of the nineteenth century but especially in the 1880s, after Congress significantly enlarged the Court's jurisdiction in 1875. The pressure to dispose of cases quickly without dissents requiring elaborate reasoned responses by the majority was enormous. Unanimity invites brevity. Yet brevity and unanimity do not by themselves commend attribution of authorship to the Court. They make it feasible. Other mechanisms were at work that explain the Court's particular response to the press of business.

First was expansion of the category of procedure. The per curiams in 1839 and 1862 dealt with minor matters concerning the Court's own rules. To be sure, ten of the thirty-six per curiams between 1883 and 1900 did involve just such matters.[6] But seven were dismissals for want of jurisdiction, where what was at stake was the power of the Court to hear the case—neither a minor matter nor about the Court's own rules.[7] Nevertheless, lawyers routinely classify jurisdiction under the rubric of procedure and would have considered labeling opinions that dispose of jurisdictional defects "per curiam" a natural extension of the Court's pre-1883 practice.

The second extension was more synthetic. Fourteen per curiams in the period 1883–1900, including the two mentioned above, addressed questions that were not obviously procedural. The cases were a version of what lawyers today would call "companion cases," raising questions similar to or identical with ones the Court had just answered in a previous case, often that very day.[8] Yet these are procedural in a sense and thus natural extensions of the per curiam practice as well. After all, it was only an accident of procedure that led cases involving the same set of facts or questions of law to the Court separately. Today, separate cases presenting common questions of law and fact can be pulled together for trial and come up together as one case on appeal. The second extension prefigures this idea. Also, the label fit. When the Court had several cases before it, all presenting the same question, it would have been silly for it to repeat the majority and dissenting opinions in each case, inserting different names. Certainly the dissenting justices were not conceding agreement with the majority by not dissenting in the companion cases. Nevertheless, they could (and did) agree with the majority that if the case chosen as showcase for the opinions came out one way, the others should as well. The per curiams were not really decisions on substance but concessions to procedural justice.

Obviously, the second extension of the idea of procedure is extremely elastic. What counts as a "similar" question or a sufficiently recent answer can be stretched (and was stretched starting in the 1930s).[9] So the second extension ultimately led to unanimous summary dispositions of clearly nonmeritorious appeals—where the loser below had the right, not the wisdom, to demand review—in excruciatingly short per curiam opinions. "Clearly nonmeritorious" here means just that the Court had answered a question sufficiently similar to the question raised on appeal and done so sufficiently recently that the Court could adequately and efficiently explain its decision by a citation, and nothing more.

The third extension plunged even deeper into the territory of substance. In four cases between 1883 and 1900 the Court labeled its opinion "per curiam" when, for one reason or another, the case came back to it after it had already made a decision.[10] For example, in the first, *Hunt v. Blackburn,* the appellee died after the Court had entered judgment against him two years before. So the appellant returned to the Court asking that its decree "be made absolute against the heirs and representatives of Sallie S. Blackburn, deceased," which it did, per curiam. Once again, the only reason the case was presented separately to the Court was procedural accident; the Court had to fix a decree entered previously. Once again, it made perfect sense for the justices to be unanimous, even if some of them had dissented in the first round, and it was not unreasonable for the Court to speak per curiam.

Thus the category of procedure together with these three extensions of it account for thirty-five of the thirty-six per curiams between 1883 and 1900. The odd case out presented what was clearly *not* a question of Supreme Court procedure, however capacious the category, and clearly did not fit the practice the Court had been following consistently since 1839. In *Smith v. United States*[11] the Court was asked to review a conviction in the U.S. circuit court in Maryland for a murder committed on Navassa, a guano island in the Carribean (more about circuit courts soon). (Guano islands were immensely valuable in those days for the digging and exportation of

guano, "a natural manure found in great abundance on some sea-coasts
. . . consisting of the excrement of sea-fowl.")[12] In the Guano Islands Act of
1856 Congress had extended the criminal jurisdiction of the circuit courts
to any guano island whose discoverer proved to the satisfaction of the State
Department and ultimately the president that he was indeed the discoverer
and had peaceably occupied the island. The act provided that an indictment may be tried in the district into which the offender was first brought.
Smith's indictment was tried in the district of Maryland. The problem was
that Haiti was contesting American control over Navassa and in 1858 dispatched two warships to disturb the discoverer's peaceable possession. President Buchanan stated that he considered Haiti's claim unfounded and
ordered a force to the island to protect citizens of the United States from
Haitian interference. These events led Smith to question whether the circuit court had jurisdiction over his crime. The circuit court decided that it
did, and in an almost wordless per curiam "opinion" the Supreme Court
affirmed.[13]

Like the seven jurisdictional per curiams before it, *Smith* concerns judicial power, but it would be a mistake to put it in the same category. For the
power at issue in *Smith* is not the power of the Supreme Court within a
system of courts already exercising jurisdiction over a dispute but rather
the power of the system of courts altogether. It is also not strictly or solely
about the power of courts but about the power of the United States to
extend the criminal jurisdiction of courts to territories discovered and
occupied by its citizens. In that sense *Smith* is the first undeniably nonprocedural per curiam.[14] While a natural extension of the jurisdictional per
curiams, *Smith* steps over the line into substance.

Smith was decided on November 24, 1890. The timing of the decision
suggests a subtler but nonetheless powerful force leading to the flowering
of per curiams in this era and the sudden appearance of a nonprocedural
per curiam sharply departing from the Court's previous practice. November 24 was a scant three months before the enactment (and smack in the
middle of the crafting) of legislation that would profoundly alter the Supreme Court's relationship to the other courts in the federal system. It was
this alteration, I submit, that transformed the Court's per curiam practice
from unanimous opinions about minor questions of procedure to include
major and ultimately controversial questions of substance, like the per
curiam in *Bush v. Gore*.

On March 3, 1891, the Evarts Act[15] became law, a key step in dismantling
a structure that had persisted since the founding of the Republic. Throughout the nineteenth century Supreme Court justices "rode circuit," just as
high court judges in England had done in the Middle Ages. In England
circuit riding was meant to bring central control over judicial matters to
the provinces. In the United States its purpose was to put the justices in

touch with the people, to lessen the distance between Washington and the states. Here is how the system worked. Instead of having an intermediate appellate court between the Supreme Court in Washington and the local district (trial) courts, Congress established regional circuit courts. Rather than have judges of its own, each circuit court was composed, at first, of two Supreme Court justices together with the local district court judge. These three would decide cases "appealed" (actually brought by "writs of error") from the district court and would also conduct trials in certain cases, as in *Smith*. Cases could then be brought from the circuit court to the Supreme Court. The circuit court held two sessions a year in each district. Though the system effectively brought them to the people, the justices hated it, and as judicial business increased over the course of the nineteenth century the system threatened to collapse.[16] Congress tinkered with changes, such as reducing the number of justices riding circuit from two to one and increasing the number of circuits (hence the number of justices). But in 1869 it bit the bullet. The Act of 1869[17] created special judgeships for the circuit courts, authorizing the appointment of one circuit judge for each circuit, and reduced the frequency of the circuits from two every year to one every two years.

The Act of 1869 had two significant effects, which the Evarts Act and the campaign for its passage would later enhance: it estranged the justices from other federal judges, and it sharpened the institutional distinction and hierarchical supremacy of the Supreme Court. Withdrawing the justices from riding circuit withdrew them from mingling with the people but also with the judges on the lower courts. Riding circuit muted the distinctions between the district courts and the Supreme Court. Curtailing it heightened those distinctions. On the old circuit court both district judges and Supreme Court justices often heard cases together—some on appeal and some in trial—and cases reaching the Supreme Court usually bore a justice's personal imprimatur. After 1869, with the appointment of specialized circuit court judges and the reduction of circuit riding, Supreme Court justices became less coworkers and more supervisors of judicial business on the appellate level. More decisions reached the Court that lacked a justice's imprimatur. The Supreme Court thus developed opinions, but also interests, unattached to collegial relations with lower court judges. The justices now faced not one but two cadres of lower court judges whose professional and personal affiliations were far more intense than their ties to the justices. In such an atmosphere it became ever more plausible for the justices to divorce their opinions from the relationship of signature, to speak impersonally, per curiam, for the Court.

That, coupled with the enlargement of the Court's jurisdiction in 1875, accounts for the rise in per curiams and the broadening of their scope from 1883 through 1889. It does not, though, by itself account for the appearance of a nonprocedural per curiam in 1890, in *Smith v. United States*. The key to *Smith* lies in its appearance on the eve of passage of the Evarts Act, which further heightened the estrangement and distinction of the Court. The Evarts Act created genuine regional intermediate appellate courts alongside the circuit courts. These were the circuit courts of appeal, each staffed with three judges of its own. The act also introduced the key concept of discretionary review by "writ of certiorari" in a large number of cases, in contrast to the old "writ of error," which provided for review as a matter of right. It did not abolish the circuit courts, since Congress was still wedded to the vision of justices mingling with the people, but took away their appellate jurisdiction over the district courts instead. Congress was not to eliminate circuit riding and the circuit courts completely until the Judicial Code of 1911. But in 1891 the modern system of local district courts, regional intermediate appellate courts, and a Supreme Court with activities confined to Washington was effectively in place. The evolution of the Court as a distinct and supreme institution in American life had largely been accomplished.

Smith reflects this evolution. Why did the Court speak per curiam while saying virtually nothing except "affirmed"? Because the controversy in *Smith* engaged a profound interest of the United States as a government, its power to extend criminal jurisdiction (if not sovereignty) over contested and economically valuable territory. In particular, it engaged an interest of the judiciary as an institution and the Court as the pinnacle of the judiciary. A judgment asserting that interest ought not to be signed by a single justice, even unanimously joined by the others. It ought to be a judgment of the Court as a distinct and supreme institution of the government. And the Court was ready to act as a distinct and supreme institution because of the articulation, isolation, and elevation of its position in the judicial hierarchy in the Acts of 1869 and 1891.

The voice of the per curiam in *Smith* was, in a way, the same as the voice of the procedural per curiams preceding it, the voice of a decision implicating the interests of the Court as an institution distinct from the judicial and political visions and interests of any one justice or aggregation of justices. In the case of the procedural per curiams, the decisions were minor and peculiar to the Court by nature of their subject matter. In *Smith* the decision was limited but in no sense minor, and it was not at all peculiar to the Court but a general interest of the government as a whole. Thus the voice of the per curiam in *Smith* was also new. It was not a per curiam by default, not a concession to the requirement of authorship in a case otherwise unworthy of its claim. It was a per curiam asserting the distinctive contribution of the Court as an institution to the interests of the Republic in a political arena where no assertion succeeds by default and every contribution must be earned. Such a per curiam is not the voice of an under-study but of a star. It does not speak for or instead of the justices. Rather, the justices speak for the per curiam, as ghostwriters. It is the voice of this per curiam, by lineal descent and accomplishment, for which the majority ghostwrote the per curiam in *Bush v. Gore.*

The distinctiveness of the Court's voice in *Smith* is underscored by a second innovation in the same era—the Court speaking without attribution of authorship, either to the Court or to an individual justice. In the wake of the Evarts Act's creation of discretionary jurisdiction the Court began to craft methods of handling petitions for writs of certiorari. (The leader of these innovations was Chief Justice Melville W. Fuller, whose term, significantly, began two years before *Smith*.)[18] One was to record denials of these petitions in the Court's official reporter in one brief sentence—"Petition for writ of certiorari denied"—without explanation. (The first of these was in 1896, in *American Sugar Refining Co. v. Steamship G. R. Booth*.)[19] Often the explanation was that the issues raised were without merit; often they had merit, but a sufficient number of justices felt that addressing them was inopportune. The important point is that the majority did not, in general, attach the label "per curiam" to summary denials of petitions for writs of certiorari. One reason was that some denials were not unanimous, not truly "by the court" as a whole. But many were unanimous, and still the Court did not label them "per curiam."

The absence of signature in certiorari denials contrasts with the practice, amplified in the years following *Smith*, of attaching the "per curiam" label to unanimous summary dispositions of clearly nonmeritorious appeals. Why the difference? Summary dispositions of appeals are decisions on the merits constrained by the Court's understanding of the law. Summary dispositions of petitions for writs of certiorari are not decisions on the merits but rather decisions whether to hear a case at all. They are discretionary decisions, unconstrained by law. By granting a petition and deciding to hear a case, the Court is not saying that the position of the petitioner necessarily has merit; exactly the opposite might well be true. Nor by denying a petition and deciding not to hear a case is the Court saying that the petition necessarily lacks merit, only that the Court is declining to make a decision for reasons that may have little to do with the merits of the petition. Decisions whether to grant or deny petitions for writs of certiorari express an institutional interest in making a decision rather than judgments of law. Of course, the Court's interest is often informed by legal judgment but only as refracted through broader considerations of interest—whether the Court wishes to develop legal doctrine in a certain area, whether it is politically expedient for the Court to intervene, whether the Court can tolerate the addition to its workload, and a host of other factors. From the perspective of strict legality, therefore, decisions about petitions for writs of certiorari are grounded in what can only be characterized as whim. And one does not sign whim.

Both innovations of the 1890s—giving voice to the Court as an institution in substantive per curiams while taking it away in decisions about petitions for writs of certiorari—express the same thought: the Court has a distinct interest as an institution of government apart from its obvious role as a supreme arbiter of legal doctrine. They tell us that the Court's interest extends from minor issues peculiar to the Court as an institution—Court procedure, Court jurisdiction, companion cases, returning cases—to great issues of state implicating the Court's role in articulating and defending an entire system of governance and in the case of per curiams, to nothing in between.[20]

. . . TO NORMS . . .

All was well until 1909. Then a curious and fateful event, launched by none other than Justice Oliver Wendell Holmes Jr., began to bend the per curiam opinion from a device necessarily expressing unanimity about uncontroversial cases to a very different aim: Holmes, joined by Justices William H. Moody and Edward D. White, dissented from a per curiam. The case came to the Court by a procedure that while different from appeal, had the same demanding character. In *Chicago, Burlington, & Quincy Railway Company v. Williams*,[21] the Eighth Circuit Court of Appeals had "certified a question" to the Supreme Court. The certification procedure allows a circuit court of appeals to ask the Supreme Court to answer a "pure question of law," a question that does not require the Court to consider any factual disputes. The purpose of the procedure is to allow the lower court to dispose of a case on the basis of one issue and thus avoid deciding others it wishes to avoid. Over a dissent without opinion by Justice David J. Brewer, the Supreme Court, in an opinion written by the elder Justice John Marshall Harlan, had decided that the Eighth Circuit's question was not a pure question of law, which was grounds for dismissing the certificate. The Eighth Circuit tried again, this time refining the question into three. The Supreme Court, per curiam, dismissed all three, saying that "this certificate is essentially the same as that disposed of" previously.[22] Holmes dissented:

> When this case was here before I felt doubts, but deferred to the judgment of the majority, as I think one should when it does not seem that an important principle is involved or that there is some public advantage to be gained from a statement of the other side. But it seems to me that the present order is a mistake upon an important matter, and I am unwilling that it should seem to be made by unanimous consent.[23]

Note that the per curiam itself was appropriate: the Supreme Court had decided the question previously and six of the justices undoubtedly felt that the Eighth Circuit was fiddling with them. The dismissal of the questions was not unlike the per curiams for returning cases or for summary dismissal of clearly nonmeritorious appeals. Holmes could not bring himself to support unanimity. The ranks of per curiam had been broken.

Over the next thirty-five years, through 1944, one or more justices dissented from eight per curiams. That is still not a deluge, but *Williams* had established that per curiam and dissent—the rhetorical assertion that the Court's opinion is unanimous accompanied by a clear statement that it is not—could coexist in the same decision. The deluge came after. From 1945 through 1959, dissents accompanied per curiams in 156 cases, or an average of 10.4 cases per year (compared to an average of 0.26 per year in the period 1909–44). From 1960 to the present, the reports show approximately 1,000 per curiam dissents, two and one-half times the rate in the previous period. What Holmes began in 1909 has obviously become accepted practice.

A practice laced with irony. When a majority labels an opinion "per curiam," it is saying, "We, though a mere majority and not unanimous, speak for the *entire* court," and when a minority dissents in the face of that, it answers, "No you don't!" The majority is avowing an opinion unanimous that manifestly is not. By persisting in labeling the opinion "per curiam," it is, in effect, taking the position that the decision ought to be unanimous. By persisting in dissent, the minority takes the position that it need not. Dissent here plays an unusual, dual role: it registers the minority's disagreement with the underlying decision but also its objection to the majority's implicit invocation of a norm of unanimity. This *rhetorical* struggle between the minority and the majority—a struggle without *legal* consequence[24]— shifts our focus from the ordinary dispute over the rightness of the decision to the propriety of the per curiam and the legitimacy of dissent. Accompanied by dissents, per curiams suddenly must be justified.

The divergent behavior of the justices in the next two per curiams after *Williams* burdened by a dissent—*Murphy v. Sardell*[25] and *Donham v. West-Nelson Manufacturing Co.*[26]—inchoately expresses the normative struggle. Both were cases decided within four years of *Adkins v. Children's Hospital,*[27] in which the Court had held that a District of Columbia law prescribing minimum wages for women violated due process. Eight of the nine justices thought them indistinguishable from *Adkins* and joined a brief per curiam, in each affirming the judgment of the court below. Once again, the per curiams fell comfortably within the Court's practice, specifically, the use of per curiams to dispose of cases sufficiently similar to a case previously decided. But Holmes, along with Chief Justice William Howard Taft and Justice Edward T. Sanford, had dissented in *Adkins*. What were they to do? If they could not get a majority of their colleagues to vote to reverse *Adkins*— and the norm of stare decisis suggests that they should not even try—*Adkins* was the law, and it would be useless protest to dissent in *Murphy* and *Don-ham*. Indeed they did not. Taft and Sanford simply joined the per curiams. But Holmes did something interesting. In *Murphy,* decided two years after *Adkins,* he "request[ed] that it be stated that his concurrence is solely upon the ground that he regards himself bound by the decision in *Adkins v. Children's Hospital.*"[28] He did not even file a formal concurrence. In the second, two years later, he silently joined the majority.

Justice Louis D. Brandeis behaved quite differently. He dissented in both *Murphy* and *Donham*. Brandeis was one of the justices to whom one can trace what Robert Post has described as a decline in "institutional norms of unanimous decision-making" on the Court during the course of the twentieth century.[29] Though he was on the Court, Brandeis had not partic-ipated in the decision in *Adkins,* and it would have been reasonable for him to express his disagreement in the two subsequent cases in order to underscore how he would have voted. Brandeis's dissents need not have been implicit criticisms of the majority's claim to unanimity. Moreover, the norm of unanimity still had considerable heft in those days. The acquies-cence of Holmes, Taft, and Sanford was undoubtedly motivated by that norm, which would have governed whether or not the majority used the per curiam designation. It was not necessarily a response to the call for unanimity implicit in the designation.

All but one of the six remaining per curiam dissents in the series are similarly inconclusive.[30] In *United States v. Swift & Co.,*[31] however, Justice Robert H. Jackson dissented from a jurisdictional per curiam even more articulately than Holmes did in *Williams*. The case came to the Court as a direct appeal under the Criminal Appeals Act,[32] which provided for direct appeal to the Court of a decision or judgment based on the invalidity or construction of the statute on which the indictment was founded. The rea-son for direct appeals to the Court—skipping intermediate review by a circuit court of appeals—is to expedite resolution of a dispute challenging a component of the frame of governance, exactly the spur to signing per curiam.[33] The trial court had dismissed an indictment under the Sherman Antitrust Act, and the United States appealed to the Supreme Court, saying that the dismissal was based on a construction of the Sherman Act. That was not necessarily clear from the trial judge's rather sibylline account of his decision. Nevertheless, a bare majority of the Court decided, per cur-iam, to remand the case to the circuit court of appeals for regular treat-ment, on the ground that the trial court's dismissal of the indictment did not involve construction of the Sherman Act. Without even labeling their disagreement with the Court's disposition a "dissent," Justices Hugo L.

Black, William O. Douglas, and Frank Murphy asked the reporter to record that they "think that the ruling of the district court was based on a 'construction' of the Sherman Act and that this Court therefore has jurisdiction to review the judgment."[34] Jackson agreed with them but nonetheless filed a concurring opinion. "I agree," he said,

> with the dissenting Justices that the decision of the District Court is "based" upon the construction of the Sherman Act. . . .
>
> If the Court is to dispatch its business as an institution, some accommodation of views is necessary and, where no principle of importance is at stake, there are times when an insistence upon a division is not in the interests of the best administration of justice.
>
> Such a case I consider this to be. To persist in my dissent would result either in affirmance of the judgment by an equally divided Court [Justice Wiley B. Rutledge did not participate in the decision, so a 4–4 vote would have resulted in affirmance] or in a reargument. . . .
>
> However the case may be disposed of, reargument seems to be in order, and I believe that the practical advantages favor rearguing it before the Circuit Court of Appeals, where there is no doubt that all of the questions can be decided.
>
> Under these circumstances, to persist in my dissent would seem a captious insistence upon my reading of a District Court's informal opinion as to which there is reasonable ground for difference.
>
> I should not desire to appear committed to this case as a precedent. I concur in the result only because it seems the most sensible way out of our impasse in the immediate case.[35]

Jackson's statement in *Swift* helps to illuminate Holmes's explanation of his dissent in *Williams*. Recall that Holmes began by avowing his allegiance to the general norm of unanimity: "When this case was here before I felt doubts, but deferred to the judgment of the majority, as I think one should when it does not seem that an important principle is involved or that there is some public advantage to be gained from a statement of the other side." He then justified departure from the norm: "But it seems to me that the present order is a mistake upon an important matter, and I am unwilling that it should seem to be made by unanimous consent." "Consent" is curious. One does not ordinarily think of Supreme Court justices voting in favor of a position as "consenting" to it. They join it, they support it, they believe in it—anything but consent. Yet that effectively is also Jackson's characterization of his position in *Swift*: "I should not desire to appear committed to this case as a precedent. I concur in the result only because it seems the most sensible way out of our impasse in the immediate case." By voting for the majority position, he is not "supporting" it (if he were, the case could be used as precedent), just "consenting." Why did he, as Holmes would not, "consent" to the per curiam? "To persist in my dissent would result either in affirmance of the judgment by an equally divided Court or in a reargument." He certainly did not wish to affirm the trial judge's dismissal of the indictment. To that extent he agreed with the per curiam. He disagreed only about the appropriate venue for *initial* reargument—Supreme Court or circuit court of appeals—not a momentous matter. So he relented and concurred. He voted for the per curiam position, not because he agreed with it, but "because it seems the most sensible way out of our impasse."

Jackson's account of his behavior in *Swift* puts some meat on the bones of Holmes's "consent." A justice consents to a position with which he does not agree when some interest of the Court as an institution demands it. The interest in *Swift* was to grant reargument to the government when a trial judge, possibly erroneously, dismissed an indictment under the Sherman Act without clearly saying why. Had Jackson not consented to the per curiam the government's interest in enforcing the act and the judiciary's interest in supervising enforcement would have been sacrificed. The reason for consenting to the per curiam was the same reason the majority had used the designation in the first place.

The forces at work at the end of the nineteenth century only became more intense in the twentieth. In the 1950s the Court began to use per curiams to announce *major* decisions on matters of substance, far exceeding in notoriety and importance the earliest substantive per curiam or any of those that followed in its wake. At the same time, the practice of dissent made it plausible for the Court to use per curiams even in contentious cases. The concurrence of these two lines of force produced a remarkable handful of cases in the second half of the century that weave some further normative threads into the per curiam fabric.

The modern history of the major substantive per curiam begins, I believe, with *Cooper v. Aaron*[36] in 1958. The story is well known. In *Brown v. Board of Education*[37] four years earlier the Supreme Court had rejected the "separate but equal" doctrine of *Plessy v. Ferguson*[38] as it applied to public schools, beginning the long and as yet unfinished task of ending school segregation. A few days after *Brown* the school board of Little Rock, Arkansas, announced that it was studying the establishment of an integrated school system and eventually came up with a plan to desegregate gradually, starting with the high schools in the 1957–58 school year. The plan was approved by a federal district court in 1956[39] but met massive popular resistance and obstruction at all levels of state government. Governor Faubus famously called out the National Guard in September 1957 to stop nine African-American students from entering Central High School in Little Rock. The students were eventually escorted into school under the protection of combat troops of the regular U.S. Army, but public unrest and incidents in the school required the continuing presence of federal troops and eventually the federalized National Guard. In February 1958 the school board asked the federal district court for permission to suspend implementation of the plan. The trial court granted the request on June 20,[40] but the Court of Appeals for the Eighth Circuit reversed on August 18.[41] In a special August term, the Supreme Court granted the board members' petition for certiorari, heard argument on August 28 and September 11, and affirmed the Eighth Circuit's refusal to stay implementation of the plan on September 12 in a unanimous half-page per curiam opinion. The Court explained the rush and lack of a full opinion:

> In view of the imminent commencement of the new school year at the Central High School of Little Rock, Arkansas, we deem it important to make prompt announcement of our judgment affirming the Court of Appeals. The expression of the views supporting our judgment will be prepared and announced in due course.[42]

The full opinion followed on September 29.[43] It was not per curiam. Rather, it was written by Chief Justice Earl Warren and signed by every member of the Court (including Justice Felix Frankfurter, who filed a concurring opinion on October 6).

Not only did the justices drop the voice of the per curiam, but the report of the case in the official *United States Reports* virtually suppresses its existence. Instead of printing the per curiam as a freestanding opinion, the reporter prints it as a footnote to the full opinion (five pages into the report). (West Publishing Company handled the two opinions differently in its unofficial *Supreme Court Reporter,* printing the per curiam starting on page 1399 of volume 78 and the full opinion starting on page 1401; thus when Chief Justice Warren cited the per curiam in his footnote, only the West citation was available, not the official one!) By this time the Supreme Court per curiam had a long and honorable history. It had been used in numerous decisions on matters of substance, and major ones at that. So sweeping it under the rug this way seems odd. Yet it is one thing to make a deliberate decision, as I did, to look back at the history of Supreme Court per curiams and quite another to experience what was effectively only an oral tradition about their appropriate use handed down over the generations of justices since the 1890s. Tradition undoubtedly took the procedural fictions of the early per curiams at face value, though procedure had long strayed into substance, and no justice could possibly have found it useful or convenient to track the fiction into the obscure cases that expose its underlying reality and that computerized legal research has recently made accessible. It is also likely that the justices in *Cooper* felt that signature by each and every one of them was a more emphatic way of meeting Arkansas's challenge to the authority of the federal government. The members of the Court undoubtedly justified use of the per curiam in their initial affirmance as a procedural necessity, well within the tradition of the fiction. Yet listen to Warren's account of what was at stake in the first sentences of his full opinion:

> As this case reaches us it raises questions of the highest importance to the maintenance of our federal system of government. It necessarily involves a claim by the Governor and Legislature of a State that there is no duty on state officials to obey federal court orders resting on this Court's considered interpretation of the United States Constitution.[44]

It is only in retrospect, on scrutiny of the actual history of per curiams, that it becomes possible to assure the justices that a per curiam would have been appropriate in the full opinion as well and that the per curiam they did use need not have been swept under the rug.

Once *Cooper* was decided, however, per curiam was lifted from obscurity, and oral tradition was supplemented by the prominence of a decision on a major matter engaging the interests of the Court as an institution, a decision rendered per curiam and subject to efficient recollection. That was the state of affairs when the Court confronted the effort of the United States to enjoin the *New York Times* and the *Washington Post* from publishing the Pentagon Papers in 1971.

New York Times Co. v. United States (the *Pentagon Papers* case)[45] shared three characteristics with *Cooper v. Aaron:* it was decided in a rush, the Court extended its term to accommodate the decision, and the majorities labeled their opinions, which were exceedingly short, "per curiam." But it was very different in one significant respect: where both the per curiam and the full opinion were unanimous in *Cooper,* the per curiam in the *Pentagon Papers* case was burdened with no less than six concurring opinions and one dissent, written by the younger Justice John Marshall Harlan and joined by Chief Justice Warren E. Burger and Justice Harry A. Blackmun. David Rudenstine has speculated that "the reason for a per curiam opinion seems to have been that the justices lacked the time before the summer recess to hammer out a majority opinion they could endorse."[46] But in *Cooper* the Court delayed going to press with the full opinion, first publishing the per curiam disposition of the judgment below. It could have done likewise in the *Pentagon Papers* case. That it did not had a supremely important consequence for the modern history of Supreme Court per curiams: in *Cooper* the justices could justify the per curiam as a procedural necessity, while the *Pentagon Papers* case was clearly a decision on substance without any procedural justification. All six justices who joined the per curiam could have signed it as nine justices did in *Cooper.* The per curiam in the *Pentagon Papers* case thus presents an unabashedly substantive per curiam without a shred of procedural justification and without the consolation of unanimity. None of this was now concealed by an oral tradition; all of it had entered self-conscious history.

The stage was set for *Buckley v. Valeo*,[47] a scant four years after the *Pentagon Papers* case, in which the Court held unconstitutional several provisions of the Federal Election Campaign Act of 1971,[48] notably those limiting soft money and self-financing by candidates. Like *Cooper* and the *Pentagon Papers* case, *Buckley* was decided under tremendous (and, the dissenters insisted, gratuitous) time pressure.[49] Unlike those cases, however, the per curiam in *Buckley* was not short: it occupies 136 pages in the official reports. It was also not without dissent: five justices—Chief Justice Burger and Justices Byron R. White, Thurgood Marshall, Blackmun, and William H. Rehnquist—separately concurred in parts of the per curiam opinion and dissented from other parts.

In contrast to the *Pentagon Papers* case, no justice dissented outright. Whatever disagreements each of the dissenters had with the per curiam—and there were many—all but Chief Justice Burger agreed with the Court's *disposition* of the lower court's judgment—"affirmed in part and reversed in part." Under the shred that is left of the norm of unanimity, each of the justices who agreed with the disposition was compelled to concur in part with the per curiam, no matter how thoroughly they may have disagreed with its reasoning. Interestingly, Chief Justice Burger also concurred in part, even though he disagreed with the partial affirmance (he thought the act had created a comprehensive and interlinked scheme of regulation, the invalidation of parts of which should render the entire scheme void). Nevertheless, he overcame his objections rather than dissent, one supposes, from the Court's invalidation of parts of the act. In the *Pentagon Papers* case the three dissenting justices did *not* agree with the Court's disposition, however much they ultimately might have come to agree with its reasoning had the case been tried below in the ordinary manner and a record created, as they urged.

The trio of major modern per curiams—*Cooper v. Aaron*, the *Pentagon Papers* case, and *Buckley v. Valeo*—provide a model of judicial behavior in response to a majority's decision to designate an opinion per curiam. A justice who agrees with the per curiam's disposition of the lower court's judgment ought to join or concur with the per curiam to the extent that he agrees with it and dissent to whatever extent he does not. That is true as well for ordinary signed opinions, but even more true for a per curiam. Despite the disintegration in our age of the norm of unanimity, a per curiam designation, in one of its modes, is at least a rhetorical call for unanimity where a decision implicates the interests of the Court as an institution in a major issue affecting the frame of governance. In *Cooper* the issue was the contumacy of a state toward the authority of the federal government; in the *Pentagon Papers* case it was the overreaching of the executive; and in *Buckley* it was the constitutionality of an act of Congress threatening the integrity of the process by which the people chooses its government. That each of the trio was decided in an atmosphere of urgency or even crisis only underscores the need for as much unanimity as possible. The reason the Court ought to strive for unanimity is exactly the reason for a per curiam: events demand that the Court speak with one voice and that the voice it speaks with be its own.

. . . TO *BUSH V. GORE* . . .

The Supreme Court issued not one but two per curiams in the course of the battle over the Florida recounts. Only the second was in *Bush v. Gore*, on December 12. The first was in *Bush v. Palm Beach County Canvassing Board*,[50] a related case that the Supreme Court decided eight days before, on December 4.

As other essays in this volume have described in detail, the *Palm Beach County* case arose out of the protest phase of the Florida struggle, before certification of the election results by the Florida secretary of state, Katherine Harris. Gore and the Florida Democratic Party had challenged Harris's refusal to include late amended returns from several counties in her statewide certification. Wrestling with a rather jumbled Florida Election Code, the Supreme Court of Florida had ordered Harris to accept late returns through Sunday, November 26. Bush filed a petition for certiorari to review the Florida decision. The U.S. Supreme Court granted certiorari to decide whether the Florida Supreme Court had violated the U.S. Constitution or a federal statute providing that a state's resolution of any dispute over the choice of electors by December 12, using laws in place before November 7, would be treated as conclusive when the votes for the Electoral College were counted in Congress. After reviewing the opinion of the Florida Supreme Court, the U.S. Supreme Court found that there was considerable uncertainty as to the precise grounds for the Florida court's decision, vacated its judgment, and remanded the case to the Florida Supreme Court to clear up the uncertainty. The per curiam opinion was unanimous.

The Court's use of the per curiam in *Palm Beach County* was completely appropriate according to the norms implicit in the line of cases beginning with *Cooper v. Aaron*. Not only was the decision unanimous, but it was also a response to a great occasion of state engaging the interests of the Court as an institution. The Court's decision would affect the choice of a president; it would chasten and if necessary correct the role that the highest court of a state had chosen to play in the process. If *Buckley v. Valeo* was per curiam, then certainly *Palm Beach County* could be as well.

Four days later the Florida Supreme Court handed down its decision in *Gore v. Harris*.[51] The case arose from the contest phase of the struggle, after Secretary Harris's certification of the statewide results. Gore and Lieberman had sued Harris in Leon County Circuit Court, asserting that Harris and the State Elections Canvassing Commission had erroneously included illegal votes and failed to include legal votes in their November 26 certification. Circuit Judge N. Sanders Sauls rejected the claim. Gore and Lieberman appealed. In a 4–3 decision, per curiam(!), the Florida Supreme Court agreed with Gore and Lieberman that they were entitled to completion of a manual count of the undervotes in one county, Miami-Dade, but agreed with Harris that ultimate relief would require counting undervotes in *all* the counties where the undervote had not been subject to manual tabulation.

This was the state of the play when Bush and Cheney asked the U.S. Supreme Court to stay the mandate of the Florida Supreme Court in *Gore v. Harris*. On December 9 the Court stayed the mandate but also granted certiorari, and on December 12 it rendered its decision. With five justices joining, the Court held, per curiam, that the Florida Supreme Court's remedy violated the Equal Protection Clause (and possibly the Due Process Clause) of the U.S. Constitution two ways—by ordering the inclusion of votes counted according to variant standards in different counties and by ordering a statewide recount with minimal procedural safeguards. That conclusion certainly warranted reversal of the Florida court's judgment, which is precisely what the per curiam did. But it would also warrant instructions to the Florida court to conduct a statewide recount according to uniform standards with adequate procedural safeguards. That the per curiam did not do, because the five justices joining it gleaned from the Florida Supreme Court's opinion in *Gore v. Harris* that under Florida law any count or contest designed to lead to a conclusive selection of electors must be completed by December 12—the very day of the U.S. Supreme Court decision. Hence, the U.S. Supreme Court reversed the judgment of the Florida Supreme Court and remanded the case, in the time-honored formula of respect for the courts of another sovereign, "for further proceedings not inconsistent with this opinion."

The per curiam in *Bush v. Gore* was well within the tradition established by the trio of per curiams beginning with *Cooper v. Aaron,* for the same reason as the per curiam in *Palm Beach County*. But it was appropriate for an additional reason: *Bush v. Gore* was a case returning to the Court for further action, not technically, to be sure, but in reality. If *Palm Beach County* was per curiam, it made sense for *Bush v. Gore* to be per curiam as well. Furthermore, the presence of dissents in *Bush v. Gore* does not at all detract from the propriety. Nor does the majority's use of the per curiam detract from the propriety of the dissents. Minorities on the Court have long seen fit to disagree with the voice of the Court, and the voice of the Court to disagree with minorities, ever since Holmes in 1909.

What they have not done, however, is dissent when they agree,[52] exactly what Souter and Breyer did in *Bush v. Gore*. Souter, whom Breyer joined, agreed with the per curiam that the Florida Supreme Court's remedy violated the Equal Protection Clause. He disagreed only with the majority's conclusion that Florida law required closure by December 12. He believed that the real deadline was December 18, the date set for the meeting of electors. Thus neither Souter nor Breyer disagreed with the Court's *disposition* of the Florida court's judgment, which was "reversed and remanded," only with the palaver accompanying it.

And palaver it was! The sole impact the majority's understanding or misunderstanding of Florida law had on their opinion was that it dissuaded them from instructing the Florida court to conduct a recount consistent with equal protection. As Nelson Lund points out in this volume (chap. 7), the Florida Supreme Court was free to chide the U.S. Supreme Court for getting wrong what they said in *Gore v. Harris*, or, if they felt that the U.S. Supreme Court got it right, to change their minds about Florida law. The U.S. Supreme Court is completely powerless to dictate Florida law to the Florida Supreme Court, and they did not do so in *Bush v. Gore*. They did not order the Florida court *not* to conduct a recount; they simply declined to instruct it to conduct one, as a consequence of their understanding, drawn from the Florida Supreme Court, of Florida law.

There was simply nothing in the per curiam's disposition of the Florida judgment inconsistent with Souter's and Breyer's wish for a recount consistent with equal protection. There was nothing in the disposition to prevent them from concurring in part with it and dissenting in part, exactly as a majority of the Court did in *Buckley v. Valeo*. It is what they should have done.

. . . AND FINALLY PRAISE

I want to say one final word—a discordant note of praise for *all* the justices. They performed under astonishing pressure as a result of the gravity of the events in which they were participating and the stark calendar dictated by the United States Constitution. *All* their opinions, agree with them or not, are cogently argued and tightly written. If I criticize Justices Souter and Breyer for not concurring in part with the per curiam and dissenting in part, it is on the basis of much reflection and intense discussion with extraordinarily able colleagues, reflection and discussion that circumstances did not permit the justices. I do believe that Souter and Breyer were the only justices on the Court who plainly stayed true to their jurisprudential colors. I do not, however, fault any of the others, especially those who spoke through a voice not their own but the voice of the Court. Had Justices Souter and Breyer had the model of *Buckley v. Valeo* in mind, they might well have decided to join that voice, concurring in part and dissenting in part. No one can say. But on the basis of the history of the Court's use of per curiams, one can say that the majority's use of a per curiam was abundantly appropriate, indeed the right way.

NOTES

I would like to thank Rich Friedman, Nelson Lund, John McGinnis, Robert Post, and Michel Rosenfeld for their invaluable help and encouragement.

1. 521 U.S. 98 (2000).

2. Linda Greenhouse, "The 43rd President: News Analysis; Another Kind of Bitter Split," *New York Times,* December 14, 2000, A1, col. 6.

3. 76 L.Ed. 1341 (1839).

4. 67 U.S. 721 (Mem) (1862).

5. Chicago & A. R. Co. v. Wiggins Ferry Co., 154 U.S. 678 (Mem) (1883); Willis v. Belleville Nail Co., 111 U.S. 62 (Mem) (1884).

6. Means v. Dowd, 128 U.S. 583 (1888); Nichols, Shepard & Co. v. Marsh, 131 U.S. 401 (1889); Dent v. Ferguson, 131 U.S. 397 (1889); Inland & Sea-Board Coasting Co., 136 U.S. 572 (1890); Mason v. U.S., 136 U.S. 581 (1890); Washington Market Co. v. District of Columbia, 137 U.S. 62 (1890); Tuskaloosa N. Ry. Co. v. Gude, 141 U.S. 244 (1891); State of California v. Southern Pac. Co., 153 U.S. 239 (1894); Central Nat. Bank v. Stevens, 171 U.S. 108 (Mem) (1898); Rio Grande Irrigation & Colonization Co. v. Gildersleeve, 174 U.S. 610 (Mem) (1899).

7. Radford v. Folsom, 131 U.S. 392 (1888); Pacific Exp. Co. v. Malin, 131 U.S. 394 (1888); List v. State of Pennsylvania, 131 U.S. 396 (Mem) (1888); Chicago, B. & Q. Ry. Co. v. Gray, 131 U.S. 396 (1889); Menken v. City of Atlanta, 131 U.S. 405 (Mem) (1889); Ex Parte Huntington, 137 U.S. 63 (1890); Texas Land & Cattle Co. v. Scott, 137 U.S. 436 (1890).

8. Chicago & A.R. Co. v. Wiggins Ferry Co., 154 U.S. 678 (Mem) (1883); Willis v. Belleville Nail Co., 11 U.S. 62 (Mem) (1884); Liverpool & G.W. Steam Co. v. Insurance Co. of North America, 129 U.S. 464 (Mem) (1889); Spalding v. City of Watertown, 130 U.S. 327 (Mem) (1889); Knowlton v. City of Watertown, 130 U.S. 334 (Mem) (1889); Sherman v. Robinson, 136 U.S. 570 (1889); Irwin v. San Francisco Sav. Union, 136 U.S. 578 (1890); Davenport v. Town of Paris, 136 U.S. 580 (Mem) (1890); Cluett v. McNeany, 140 U.S. 183 (Mem) (1891); Porter v. Banks, 144 U.S. 407 (Mem) (1892); Stellwagen v. Tucker, 144 U.S. 548 (Mem) (1892); U.S. v. Fitch, 163 U.S. 631 (Mem) (1896); Wilson v. State, 169 U.S. 600 (Mem) (1898); Pierce v. Ayer, 171 U.S. 650 (Mem) (1898).

9. See, *e.g.,* Alaska Steamship Company v. Petterson, 347 U.S. 396 (1954) (Burton, Frankfurter and Jackson, J. J., dissenting).

10. Hunt v. Blackburn, 131 U.S. 403 (1889); City of Brenham v. German American Bank, 144 U.S. 549 (1892); State of Missouri v. State of Iowa, 160 U.S. 688 (1896); New York Indians v. U.S., 170 U.S. 614 (1898).

11. 137 U.S. 224 (1890).

12. *The Oxford English Dictionary*, vol. 6, 2d ed. (Oxford: Clarendon Press, 1989), 911 ("guano").

13. In Smith's case along with two others—an unusual and aggressive home-made joinder of companion cases at the appellate level.

14. The second was not until 1907, when in Galban & Co. v. U.S., 207 U.S. 579 (Mem) (1907), the Court summarily affirmed a judgment on appeal from the Court of Claims.

15. 26 Stat. 826.

16. Charles Warren, *The Supreme Court in United States History*, vol. 1 (Boston and Toronto: Little, Brown, 1922), 86–88.

17. 16 Stat. 44.

18. Modern scholarship undervalues Fuller for providing administrative rather than "intellectual" leadership for the Court. See, *e.g.*, Owen M. Fiss, *History of the Supreme Court of the United States, VIII, Troubled Beginnings of the Modern State 1888–1910* (New York: Macmillan, 1993), 25–28.

19. 164 U.S. 707 (Mem) (1896). The second varied the formula a bit—"No opinion. Petition for writ of certiorari denied"—to emphasize the absence of an opinion. Columbus Construction Co. v. Crane Co., 174 U.S. 803 (Mem) (1898).

20. We can test the interest hypothesis against two standard categories of per curiams that have appeared since the 1890s.

The first is in direct appeals from three-judge courts, a device Congress created (first in 1903) to fast-track disputes about a variety of matters, most prominently suits where the constitutionality of a state or federal statute was in question. Congress has recently restricted the use of three-judge courts to redistricting disputes and other matters it specifically mandates. An example of the latter is suits by members of Congress challenging the constitutionality of the Gramm-Rudman budget act. An example of the former is a dispute that reached the Court in the same year as *Bush v. Gore*. In Sinkfield v. Kelley, 531 U.S. 28 (2000), the Court unanimously affirmed the judgment of the three-judge court, per curiam. The suits committed to three-judge courts challenge one way or another some fundamental component of the overall system of governance. That is why Congress thought it necessary to fast-track them to the Court and why the Court uses per curiams for them with some frequency.

The second is in judgments "affirmed by an equally divided Court," when one justice does not participate for some reason (conflict of interest, absence). One such affirmance was Free v. Abbott Laboratories, Inc., 529 U.S. 333 (2000). The entire report reads: "Judgment affirmed by an equally divided Court. Opinion per curiam announced by THE CHIEF JUSTICE. Justice O'Connor took no part in the consideration or decision of this case." An affirmance under these circumstances has no precedential value—no one knows how Justice O'Connor would have voted—and a full-dress opinion (actually two!) would be worthless. Nonetheless, the affirmance is on the merits, and the per curiam designation expresses that. The per curiam in this instance responds to a procedural need of the Court: to have a decision.

21. 205 U.S. 444 (1907).

22. Chicago, Burlington, & Quincy Railway Company v. Williams, 214 U.S. 492 (1909).

23. 214 U.S. at 495.

24. At least one state supreme court has explored the question whether per curiam decisions have a different legal consequence than signed decisions. See Commonwealth v. Tilghman, 543 Pa. 578, 673 A.2d 898 (1996) (sometimes). Nevertheless, it is clear that per curiams in the Supreme Court of the United States have the same legal effect as any other decision.

25. 269 U.S. 530 (1925).

26. 273 U.S. 657 (1927).

27. 261 U.S. 525 (1923).

28. 269 U.S. at 530.

29. Robert Post, "The Supreme Court Opinion as Institutional Practice: Dissent, Legal Scholarship and Decisionmaking in the Taft Court," 85 *Minnnesota Law Review* 1267, 1351, 1355 (2001). The decline is not universal; at least one other court has found it useful to maintain the norm. See David A. Skeel Jr., "The Unanimity Norm in Delaware Corporate Law," 83 *Virginia Law Review* 127 (1997).

Post traces the decline in the norm of unanimity to a transformation in our understanding of the nature and purposes of the law, from a set of immutable principles (which, if they are not immutable by nature, must be made to seem so in practice) to an act of statesmanship—exactly the theory I have proposed for the rise in the number of per curiams. The difference is that I trace the shift to the 1890s and the change in the Court's institutional position within the scheme of governance and Post traces it to the 1920s and American Legal Realism. I would also cite the beginnings of the Progressive Era as the origin of the jurisprudential component of the Court's transformation.

30. Three involved direct appeals to the Supreme Court from three-judge courts. Mortenson v. Security Insurance Co., 289 U.S. 702 (1933) (Brandeis, J., dissenting); Valentine v. Great Atlantic & Pacific Tea Co., 299 U.S. 32 (1936) (Brandeis and Cardozo, J. J., dissenting); Nevin v. Martin, 307 U.S. 615 (1939) (Butler, J., dissenting). Another case involved an attack on the constitutionality of a state tax. Stewart v. Commonwealth of Pennsylvania, 312 U.S. 649 (1941). The Supreme Court of Pennsylvania had upheld the tax, and the Supreme Court of the United States affirmed, per curiam, citing a recently decided case, Curry v. McCanless, 307 U.S. 357 (1939). *Stewart* was thus a companion case per curiam. Chief Justice Charles Evans Hughes and Justices James C. McReynolds and Owen J. Roberts dissented without comment. Along with Justice Pierce Butler, who was no longer on the Court, they also dissented in *Curry*. They were thus following Brandeis's lead in *Murphy* and *Donham* but without the meliorating factor of not having participated in the prior decision. The dissents in *Stewart* can thus be understood as one interpretation of Brandeis's per curiam dissents. But the other interpretation also gets an airing. In Morgan v. United States, 304 U.S. 1 (1938), Justice Hugo L. Black dissented from a rather lengthy per curiam denying a request by the solicitor general for a rehearing. Solicitor General Robert H. Jackson, who would soon join the Court, accused it of reversing a stance it had taken in a prior appeal in the same case, an accusation the Court rejected. *Morgan* was a classic per curiam for two

reasons: it was a returning case, and the Court was defending an institutional interest in fair procedures. Black was the lone dissenter the first time around, and just as dissent must have seemed reasonable to Brandeis in *Murphy* and *Donham,* Black was simply sticking to his guns, not clearly challenging the propriety of eight justices speaking as if the Court were unanimous.

31. 318 U.S. 442 (1943) (Black, Douglas, and Murphy, J. J., dissenting).

32. 18 U.S.C. § 682, as amended by the Act of May 9, 1942, 56 Stat. 271.

33. Hence, one expects to find and does find a prevalence of per curiams in decisions on direct appeal from three-judge courts. See note 29, *supra.*

34. 318 U.S. at 446.

35. *Id.* at 446–47.

36. 358 U.S. 1 (1958) (No. 1 Misc. 1).

37. 347 U.S. 483 (1954). Chief Justice Warren wrote the opinion in *Brown* (the official report says nothing about the other justices, but everyone understands that they joined the decision). But there was a procedural per curiam, Brown v. Board of Education of Topeka, Shawnee County, Kansas, 344 U.S. 1 (1952). *Brown* itself came to the Court as cases from three different three-judge courts. In the per curiam, the Court took notice of a fourth case pending in the Court of Appeals for the District of Columbia challenging the segregation of African-American and white students as a violation of the Fifth Amendment (the others were proceeding under the Fourteenth Amendment, which did not apply to the District of Columbia). Over a dissent by Justice Douglas, the Court decided to continue the other cases on its docket so that arguments in all four cases could be heard together—a classic procedural per curiam.

38. 163 U.S. 537 (1896).

39. Aaron v. Cooper, 143 F.Supp. 855 (D.Ark. 1956), affirmed 243 F.2d 361 (8th Cir. 1957).

40. Aaron v. Cooper, 163 F.Supp. 13 (D.Ark. 1958).

41. Aaron v. Cooper, 257 F.2d 33 (8th Cir. 1958).

42. 358 U.S. at 3.

43. Cooper v. Aaron, 358 U.S. 1 (1958) (No. 1).

44. *Id.* at 4.

45. 403 U.S. 713 (1971).

46. David Rudenstine, *The Day the Presses Stopped: A History of the Pentagon Papers Case* (Berkeley: University of California Press, 1996), 301.

47. 424 U.S. 1 (1976).

48. 86 Stat. 3, as amended by the Federal Election Campaign Act Amendments of 1974, 88 Stat. 1263.

49. In defense of the majority, who sped the case along without benefit of a record created by the trial courts, Congress had mandated speed in section 315(b) of the act, 2 U.S.C. § 437h(a), a special jurisdictional section providing for expedited review of the constitutionality of the act. In particular, section 315(b) provided: "It shall be the duty of the court of appeals and of the Supreme Court of the United States to advance on the docket and to expedite to the greatest possible extent the disposition of any matter certified under subsection (a) of this section." Subsection (a) provided: "The district court immediately shall certify all questions of constitutionality of this Act . . . to the United States court of appeals for the circuit

involved, which shall hear the matter sitting en banc." The statutory language arguably justifies the Court yanking the case from the Second Circuit by certiorari before the trial court had time to create a record.

50. 121 S.Ct. 471 (2000).

51. 772 So.2d 1243 (Fla. 2000).

52. I've found only one exception, National Association for the Advancement of Colored People, Inc. v. Bennett, 360 U.S. 471 (1959), in which Justice Douglas, joined by Chief Justice Warren and Justice Brennan, dissented from a disposition even though they agreed with it. They did so because the per curiam directed a three-judge district court considering the constitutionality of a state statute to consider whether to ask Arkansas courts to construe the statute before declaring it unconstitutional. The dissenters thought that the federal court should proceed without a reference in order to save time. Thus they disagreed only with the direction. But that was the *entirety* of the direction, unlike *Bush v. Gore,* so dissent was clearly appropriate.

9

NOTES FOR THE UNPUBLISHED
SUPPLEMENTAL SEPARATE OPINIONS
IN *BUSH V. GORE*

Burt Neuborne

These opinions were prepared for discussion in a constitutional law class. They are, of course, wholly fictitious; I have attempted to capture the voice of an opinion, without the use of the usual legal citations and technical arguments. They are designed to explore the legal issues raised in the actual opinion and to provoke discussion on judicial role. They are also designed to rebut the notion that the decisions of the various judges can only be explained by efforts to advance a favored presidential candidate.

O'Connor and Kennedy, J.J.:

We write separately to explain why we believe that the Florida legislature adopted the federal December 12 "safe harbor" provision for certifying presidential electors as a firm, nonextendable deadline for completing the count of ballots for presidential electors and why it was permissible, indeed necessary, for us to have decided that very important question of Florida law. We take the extraordinary step of issuing this supplemental opinion in response to suggestions that our decision to join the Court's stay of the Florida hand recount and our decision to join the Court's per curiam opinion were unprincipled exercises of raw power designed to assure the election of a favored presidential candidate. Ordinarily, we would not respond to such criticism. In the unique circumstance of this case, however, we believe that respect for the integrity of the judiciary warrants a more complete explanation of our reasoning than was possible in the difficult circumstances surrounding the release of the Court's per curiam opinion.

We understand the intense disappointment felt by persons who argue that Vice President Gore not only won the national popular vote by almost 400,000 votes, but was denied the opportunity to demonstrate that a hand recount of the so-called undercounted Florida ballots would have shown him to be the winner of Florida's crucial 25 electoral votes. We also understand that reasonable persons may harbor different opinions concerning the legal issues raised by *Bush v. Gore,* including the crucial questions of (1) whether the December 12 safe harbor date had been adopted by the Florida legislature as a firm deadline; (2) whether we were authorized to decide that question of Florida law; and (3) whether it was permissible for us to have stayed the manual recount ordered by the Supreme Court of Florida. We write to make clear that we engaged in the same process of statutory interpretation as did the Florida Supreme Court in its effort to resolve ambiguities in the Florida statutory scheme and that we—and every other judge who sought to perform his or her judicial duty in these cases— acted in accordance with our views of the law and not as politicians wearing black robes.

We begin with the relatively uncontroversial but crucial proposition that any hand recount of the so-called undercounted ballots in Florida that tallied "dimpled" ballots in one county but rejected them in the neighboring county or that tallied ballots with partially punched holes in one county but required a complete punch in another county would apply such divergent ground rules in measuring a valid vote as to deny Florida voters the equal protection of the laws within the meaning of the Fourteenth Amendment. Seven members of this Court appear to have endorsed that proposition. Requiring minimal standards of clarity and uniformity in connection with counting the ballots in a single election not only assures that all votes weigh equally but also provides an important prophylaxis against efforts by local officials to manipulate the application of an unduly discretionary standard for or against a particular candidate. In analogous areas of the law, we have often invalidated government programs that vest an impermissible level of discretion in local officials to make politically charged judgments in the areas of the First and Fourteenth Amendments.

If, as we believed, the standards governing the statewide court-ordered hand recount mandated by the Florida Supreme Court were fatally vague and nonuniform, the difficult decision to stay the recount was certainly defensible. A statewide recount carried out pursuant to unconstitutionally vague and nonuniform tabulation standards simply could not have resulted in a legally valid outcome. Unless stayed, the vote count as ordered by the Florida Supreme Court could only have culminated in a legally meaningless result fraught with confusion and misunderstanding.

Once we determined that it was impossible to reach a legally acceptable result using the vague and nonuniform vote-counting standards announced by the Florida courts, we were faced with the choice of whether to remand to the Florida Supreme Court, once again, with instructions to attempt to fashion an appropriate uniform standard under Florida law, or to enforce the December 12 safe harbor deadline on the choice of presidential electors that we understood to have been imposed by the Florida legislature. Ordinarily, we would have followed the course urged by Justices Souter and

Breyer, as well as by Justices Stevens and Ginsburg, and remanded to the Florida Supreme Court in order to permit the highest court of that state to make the decision as a matter of Florida law. Given the unique time constraints of this case, however, it would have been impossible for the Florida Supreme Court to have acted in time to place Florida's electors within the federal safe harbor. Thus, if we believed that the Florida legislature wished to impose a December 12 deadline as a matter of Florida law in order to ensure that Florida's electors would not be subject to congressional challenge, we had no choice but to act immediately.

In fact, the issue before us was quite similar to the issue that confronted the Florida Supreme Court in its initial decision on whether to extend the deadline for certification in order to permit hand recounts in four Florida counties at the request of Vice President Gore. The Florida court weighed the text and policies underlying the statutory seven-day deadline against the text and policies underlying the statute authorizing hand recounts and found that the Florida legislature probably intended the deadline to give way to the recount, as long as the ultimate safe harbor certification of electors was not imperiled. Our refusal to join in the separate opinion of Justices Scalia and Thomas and Chief Justice Rehnquist is premised on our belief that in making that judgment the Florida Supreme Court was acting within the parameters of legitimate judicial behavior in interpreting ambiguous or conflicting statutory provisions. We need not agree with the interpretation of Florida law advanced by the Florida Supreme Court to recognize that, under our federal system, the choice of interpretive philosophies adopted by a state's judicial organs is none of our business. We therefore reject the notion implicit in Justice Scalia's opinion that state courts in interpreting state statutes governing the selection of presidential electors are obliged to adopt a strict constructionist philosophy under Article II, section 1, of the U.S. Constitution. While Article II, section 1, grants power to state "legislatures" to control the selection of presidential electors, we read the clause as meaning the state "legislature" as it operates in the sovereign political and legal matrix chosen by each state. Any other reading would federalize both the state legislature and the state courts in cases involving the selection of presidential electors in ways that are deeply inconsistent with the Constitution's fundamental decision to treat the states as sovereign political entities.

Our decision required us to weigh the text and policies underlying a firm adherence to the December 12 safe harbor deadline against the text and the undeniably important policies underlying a continuation of the effort to count every vote. Thus we too were forced to make an educated guess about whether the Florida legislature intended the December 12 deadline to give way to additional efforts to complete the recount. This time, however, the significant concern with imperiling the selection of Florida electors identified by the Florida Supreme Court as the outside limit for judicially extending the certification deadline was in play. If the certification of Florida electors had not been definitively settled by December 12 and if a hand recount had resulted in a judicial determination that Vice President Gore was the winner of the Florida election, it appears that two rival slates of Florida electors—one certified by the state legislature and governor and one certified by the Florida courts—would have been presented to the Electoral College. The first tie-breaking mechanism designed to choose between the rival slates, selection by both houses of Congress, probably would have failed, as the newly elected Senate likely would have voted 51–50 for the slate pledged to Vice President Gore, and the newly elected House of Representatives likely would have voted narrowly for the slate pledged to Governor Bush. The next tie-breaking mechanism, gubernatorial certification, probably also would have failed, since the imprimatur of the governor of Florida would have been of questionable validity because it would have been affixed in violation of the order of the Florida Supreme Court. If both tie-breaking mechanisms failed, the Electoral College would have met without electors from Florida, raising the question of whether an absolute majority of 270 electors is required to elect the president or whether a majority of the electors actually appointed is sufficient. If 270 is required, the presidential election would be thrown into the House of Representatives, where the delegations would ballot by state, with the probable winner being Governor Bush, since the Republican Party is in the majority in twenty-eight states. If a majority of the appointed electors is required, Vice President Gore would be the winner with 267 electors. Suffice it to say that there is no clear answer to the issue, since the text of the Twelfth Amendment may be read either way. Thus, if the December 12 safe harbor deadline had been breached, the nation would have been swept into the wholly uncharted waters of a genuine constitutional crisis. After considering the ambiguous Florida text and the observations of the Florida Supreme Court and the participants in the litigation, we believed that the Florida legislature wished to make such a divisive potential constitutional crisis impossible by imposing a firm December 12 deadline on the certification of Florida electors that would make it impossible to challenge the certified electors in Congress. After reviewing the same material, Justices Souter and Breyer appear to believe that Florida would have risked a congressional challenge in order to assure that every vote was counted. That is a plausible reading of Florida law. We believe, however, that it is even more plausible to believe that Florida's legislature wished to establish a firm deadline of more than five weeks after the election in order to cut off the possibility of the nightmare constitutional scenario described above. Ideally, of course, we would have left the question to the courts of Florida. December 12 was upon us, however, making it necessary for us to decide the issue immediately in order to prevent the de facto breaching of the safe harbor deadline. Finally, although we acknowledge that contrary practical pressures were hydraulic, our remand to the Florida Supreme Court gave that court an opportunity to challenge our reading of Florida law in the event we misunderstood the importance of the December 12 deadline. Neither Vice President Gore nor the Florida Supreme Court acting sua sponte questioned the accuracy of our effort to apply Florida law.

In short, we believe that reasonable persons can disagree with the initial judgment of the Florida Supreme Court that Florida law authorized an extension of the initial certification beyond the statutory deadline. We also believe that reasonable persons can differ with our judgment that Florida law forbids a further extension beyond the December 12 safe harbor deadline. Indeed, the essence of judging in both cases involved good faith efforts to resolve questions concerning the meaning of statutory and constitutional text about which highly competent and well-meaning people can reasonably differ. In reaching decisions in both cases, the participating judges in both Florida and Washington were required to balance the mandate of adherence to textual command against the difficulty of knowing precisely what the command is, using appropriate methods to break ties when good faith doubt about the content of a textual command exists. We are confident that arguments of principle dictated the outcomes of both courts.

Souter and Breyer, J.J.:

We join in recognizing that principle, not political expediency, was the motivating force behind the decisions of the Supreme Court of Florida and the decisions of the justices of this Court. Irresponsible criticism of judges by persons who assert that outcomes are dictated by partisan loyalty misunderstands the complexity of the judicial process and badly disserves the rule of law. But acknowledging the good faith of the majority's per curiam opinion should not immunize the opinion from the scathing criticism it deserves.

To begin with, the per curiam badly mishandled the crucial equal protection issue. As the separate opinion of Justices O'Connor and Kennedy makes clear, a finding that the hand recount was proceeding under conditions that violated the Fourteenth Amendment was critical both to the grant of the stay and to the ultimate judgment to vacate the opinion of the Florida Supreme Court mandating a statewide hand recount of potentially uncounted presidential ballots. It was, however, both inaccurate and misleading to have viewed the court-supervised hand recount as though it were the genesis of the equal protection problem. In fact, Florida had violated the Equal Protection Clause by deploying voting machines of widely disparate accuracy throughout the state. In some counties, optical scanning machines were used with an undercount error rate of one in three hundred. In many other counties, voting machines based on older punch-card technology were used with an undercount error rate of 1.5 percent and higher, to say nothing of an exponentially higher potential for confusion and double voting. Thus, voters in counties with outdated technology were five times more likely to have had their votes undercounted and far more likely to have their votes inaccurately recorded than voters in counties with newer machines. Moreover, if, as has been alleged, the outdated voting machines were concentrated in counties with low per capita income and high rates of racial minority voters, the disparity takes on an even greater significance under the Fourteenth and Fifteenth Amendments and section 2 of the Voting Rights Act.

Whether or not use of the older machines, standing alone, would have raised questions of electoral fairness, surely such mechanically induced electoral inequality cannot be squared with the per curiam's intense concern with Fourteenth Amendment voting equality. Thus, when Florida courts intervened in an effort to cure the unconstitutional outcome of the unequal vote counting machinery, it was clearly improper for this Court to have blocked the judicial remedy in the name of equality while allowing the underlying Fourteenth Amendment violation to have gone unremarked. The Court was obliged to either mandate a federal remedy for the ongoing equal protection violation that would have superseded any state imposed deadline on counting votes or leave the less-than-perfect state remedy in place as the lesser of two constitutional evils. The one indefensible result was to have blocked the Florida courts from seeking to remedy the blatant federal violation of electoral equality caused by the unequal propensity of differing voting machines to undercount presidential ballots. The result is particularly indefensible because the failure of the Florida courts to have imposed a uniform standard for evaluating undercounted ballots was, in large part, caused by this Court's expression of concern in our initial unanimous per curiam opinion that Florida courts were not exhibiting sufficient deference to the will of the Florida legislature. If, in the teeth of the first per curiam, the Florida courts had adopted a uniform standard, they would have been accused of judicial legislation. Having refrained from judicial activism by adhering to the Florida legislature's textual standard in deference to the apparent wishes of this Court, it is an extraordinary whipsaw to be told that greater judicial activism was necessary to avoid violating the Fourteenth Amendment. Imposing statewide uniform standards risked invalidation under Article II, section 1, and Title 3 U.S.C. § 5. Not imposing uniform standards risked invalidation under the Fourteenth Amendment. An observer might conclude that the Florida Supreme Court's effort to secure a hand recount was doomed no matter what the court did. Finally, the suggestion that the per curiam decision to terminate a judicially supervised statewide hand recount of undercounted ballots was consistent with decisions invalidating the grant of standardless discretion to local police officials in the First Amendment area ignores the fact that the recount was being conducted, not by local canvassing boards subject to political influence, but by the Florida judiciary operating in two-judge teams, reporting to a single judge for the resolution of contested ballots. While the void-for-vagueness doctrine places some limits on a delegation of standardless discretion to judges, the Florida statutory standard falls well within the bounds of our traditional view of judicial power.

Nor does the separate opinion justify the per curiam's insistence on deciding that the Florida legislature had imposed a firm deadline of December 12 for the counting of ballots. All agree that issues of state law must, ordinarily, be finally determined by state courts. At most, this Court would have been authorized to remand the matter to the Florida Supreme Court to resolve the state law issue. The suggestion that by remanding the matter to the Florida Supreme Court at 11:00 P.M. on December 12, this Court provided the Florida court with a meaningful opportunity to disagree with this Court's reading of Florida law is wholly unpersuasive. If such an option was intended, the language of the per curiam rendered it terminally opaque.

Moreover, the effort to posit a necessity-based exception to our inability to resolve state law issues fails to persuade for two reasons. First, it was this Court's improper issuance of a stay that brought the case to the brink of December 12 without the completion of the statewide hand recount; and, second, the existence of a federal Fourteenth Amendment issue justified, if it did not mandate, the lifting of the December 12 deadline in order to complete the ballot count in accordance with Fourteenth Amendment standards.

Thus, while the separate opinion reveals a principled explanation for the action of the swing justices, it fails to provide a persuasive refutation of the charge that the opinion is extremely bad law, however well intentioned it may have been. This Court may have elected a president by one vote, but it has not written a defensible opinion.

Stevens and Ginsburg, J.J.:

The failure of the separate opinion of Justices O'Connor and Kennedy to provide a wholly persuasive legal justification for the action of the per curiam in terminating the hand recount of undercounted presidential ballots in Florida poses a profound question about the role of this Court. As the separate opinion of Justices Souter and Breyer demonstrates, the separate opinion of Justices O'Connor and Kennedy, while making it clear that arguments of principle can be deployed in support of the majority's position, fails to persuade on the issues of voting equality, standardless discretion, and respect for the power of Florida courts to interpret Florida law. In fact, the real basis for the decision of the swing justices to join the per curiam opinion does not appear to have been the persuasive power of its legal reasoning but consequentialist concerns over the lack of an orderly process to determine which, if either, of two rival slates of electors would speak for Florida in the Electoral College if the statewide hand recount, using uniform standards, had been permitted to proceed to a conclusion favoring Vice President Gore. Faced with the prospect of dueling slates of electors and lacking a clear mechanism for choosing between the rival slates, the swing justices appear to have subscribed to a weakly reasoned opinion in order to hasten the emergence of a clear, formal winner of the 2000 presidential election. In effect, the swing justices appear to have projected their concerns over the risks inherent in a potential constitutional crisis onto the Florida legislature and found that the Florida legislature had mandated a firm deadline of December 12, the federal safe harbor date, in order to prevent the emergence of rival slates. To make the December 12 deadline stick, the swing justices were obliged to subscribe to a view of the Equal Protection Clause that invalidated an imperfect judicial cure for Florida's unequal mechanical ballot counting, leaving the underlying disease untreated, and to a view of federalism that preempted Florida's power to decide for itself whether to continue the counting after December 12.

The legitimacy of such judicial behavior turns on whether the legal arguments for or against the recount were in rough equipoise. If a judge finds herself confronted with powerful legal positions pulling in different directions, there is nothing wrong with using consequentialist reasoning to help break the legal tie. If, however, legal reasoning is used merely to provide a veneer of legitimacy for a judicial decision that is wholly based on consequentialist reasoning, the judicial process impermissibly merges into the political process. We believe that, in this case, the traditional legal arguments tilt so strongly against the per curiam's equality position, and so strongly against its federalism position, that it cannot be defended as an effort to break legal ties in favor of avoiding potentially disastrous consequences. Rather, it appears to be an example of well-meaning justices so concerned with potentially disastrous consequences that they are prepared to deploy weakly reasoned law to avoid those consequences.

Although we believe that it is inappropriate to bend the law in such a way even to avoid serious potential harms, it must be noted that such an effort to shield the nation from the risks inherent in dueling slates of electors and an indefinite prolongation of uncertainty over the winner of the 2000 presidential election is a far cry from the charges of narrow partisan decision making that have been leveled by many observers. At worst, the decision of the swing justices to join the Court's per curiam opinion is a misguided attempt to prevent the nation from sailing onto uncharted constitutional seas, not an exercise in personal self-indulgence.

In the particular circumstances of this case, we believe that the effort by the swing justices to turn the Court into a deus ex machina to spare the nation the agony of a protracted fight over the Florida electors was particularly unjustified. First, the per curiam sacrificed the value of democratic legitimacy to the value of stability and predictability. Preventing the completion of a count of the ballots that might well have determined the presidency is an enormous intrusion by judges into the democratic process. The swing justices apparently believed that the risk to democracy caused by instability and unpredictability outweighed the cost to democracy of failing to count all the votes in Florida. While such a belief was doubtless honestly held, it is uncomfortably close to arguing that it is acceptable to burn down a village in order to save it.

Second, the per curiam appears to have badly overestimated the likelihood of a constitutional crisis. It is true that the Florida legislature was poised to select a post–December 12 slate of electors pledged to Governor Bush that would have been presented to the Electoral College as an alternative to any slate pledged to Vice President Gore that might have emerged from the statewide judicial recount. But democratic mechanisms designed to choose between the rival slates were in place. Both slates would have been presented to Congress. If the Gore slate had received more votes in Florida pursuant to a fair recount procedure using uniform standards pursuant to a process that enjoyed the imprimatur of this Court, it is quite unlikely that either house of Congress would have insisted on recognizing the nondemocratic slate. Thus, by short-circuiting the operation of the democratic process, the swing justices prevented the mechanisms of democracy from defending themselves. With friends who exalt stability and predictability over democratic legitimacy even in settings where democracy can defend itself, democracy does not need enemies.

Third, in purely consequentialist terms, the per curiam actually weakened crucial American institutions. The presidency of George W. Bush was denied the democratic legitimacy that would have flowed from a victory in the statewide recount. He takes office by the grace of a single vote in the Supreme Court, having lost the nationwide popular vote by almost 450,000 votes and having possibly lost the Florida popular vote as well. In addition, the Supreme Court weakened its capacity to act as a forum of principle in unpopular cases. At best, the per curiam will be perceived as bad law; at worst, it will be perceived as bad faith. Even the rule of law was weakened. While the willingness of the nation to abide by the razor-thin vote of the Supreme Court is testimony to the enduring power of our respect for the rule of law, when, as here, formal law departs from the underlying principles that give it moral strength, respect for law is inevitably weakened. In this case, by using law to prevent the operation of the democratic process in a highly public display of power, the per curiam has forced the nation to accept the formal rule of law but only at the expense of divorcing the law in this case from its moral underpinnings as the defender of democracy.

Scalia and Thomas, J.J., and Rehnquist, C.J.:

The struggle by our colleagues to decide whether particular exercises of judicial power are, or are not, legitimate highlights the fundamental weakness in the analytic approach of all three separate opinions. Each separate opinion explores the limits of judicial power in going beyond or ignoring the plain meaning of textual commands. The separate opinion of Justices O'Connor and Kennedy argues that the decisional processes of both the Florida Supreme Court and this Court were essentially identical, with each court involved in a free-floating decision whether to abide by a statutory deadline or to continue the vote count. According to the O'Connor-Kennedy opinion, the Supreme Court of Florida elected not to be bound by the statutory deadline, finding the judicial power to continue the recounts beyond the seven-day certification deadline in the values of the Florida constitution and in the alleged collision with other statutes authorizing a hand recount. Conversely, argue Justices O'Connor and Kennedy, this Court in its per curiam opinion elected to be bound by the December 12 statutory deadline at the expense of continuing the hand recount of undercounted ballots. According to Justices O'Connor and Kennedy, both exercises in reading text are within the range of legitimate judging, even though they come out 180 degrees apart. But, as described by Justices O'Connor and Kennedy, neither exercise of judicial power is legitimate. It is currently fashionable to describe exercises in reading text judicially as exercises in discretion, with most cases providing a court with a choice between cleaving closely to text or departing from text in search of a more perfect justice. In settings where text is so ambiguous as to provide no real guide to a court, such an exercise may well be necessary. But where, as here, the text is clear, courts simply have no power to depart from it, even in defense of important values such as democracy and fairness. The widely disparate views of the six justices who have declined to join this opinion demonstrate that once judges are embarked on the kind of open-ended search for justice that licenses them to disregard controlling text, the judicial process becomes hopelessly subjective. It is an irony that Justices O'Connor and Kennedy have chosen to defend an opinion designed to curb overly broad discretion in the counting of ballots by ascribing overly broad discretion to judges in the reading of text.

We concede that such a narrow conception of the role of a court confronted with a textual command is not widely held. Several generations of vigorous exercise of judicial power to operate as a full partner in the shaping of statutes have made it commonplace for courts to assume a duty to "perfect" statutory schemes. Ordinarily, it would be up to the Florida courts to choose an interpretive philosophy. Were this a garden variety case, we might believe that the Florida courts, in ignoring statutory deadlines and inventing judge-made remedies, were acting beyond the scope of legitimate judicial activity, but that question would be for the people of Florida to determine. Cases involving the selection of presidential electors are not, however, garden variety cases. They are governed by a specific provision in the federal constitution, Article II, section 1, that grants power to the state "legislature" to control the selection of presidential electors. If we are to be true to that textual command, we must insist that state courts respect the primacy of state legislatures in selecting presidential electors. In one sense, the separate opinion of Justices O'Connor and Kennedy does just that by enforcing the Florida state legislature's wish that ballot counting stop on December 12. But the road to that result took them through a series of discretionary choices that are beyond the limited scope of judicial power.

The separate opinion of Justices Souter and Breyer takes the per curiam to task for ignoring the alleged equal protection violation caused by the use of voting machines with widely disparate error rates in tabulating ballots. Whatever the validity of such a Fourteenth Amendment claim, it is foreclosed in this case because no one raised it at any level. No claim of denial of federal equal protection was raised by Vice President Gore, either in the Florida courts, in the lower federal courts, or in this Court. If the parties choose to forgo raising federal claims as a matter of strategy in an effort to deprive this Court of jurisdiction, this Court can hardly be taxed with a failure to decide them.

Finally, the separate opinion of Justices Stevens and Ginsburg demonstrates the risks of going beyond the text in the search for justice. If, as they allege, consequentialist reasoning dictated the actions of the swing justices, it is difficult to separate the Court's thought processes from that of a legislature. If judging is merely a judicial policy preference dressed up as law, it does not deserve to be called adjudication. Thus, of the varying approaches presented by the separate opinions, only an approach that reads Article II, section 1, as commanding respect for state legislative policy preferences and denying state or federal judges an active role in the selection of presidential electors can be applied in a principled manner. The moment one goes beyond that strict legislative tether, judges assume a subjective and unjustified role in the selection of the president that cannot be squared with constitutional text.

Stevens, O'Connor, Kennedy, Souter, Ginsburg, and Breyer, J.J.:

We cannot allow these separate opinions to end without responding to Justice Scalia's insistence that Article II, section 1, imposes a single philosophy of judging on state courts confronted with a case involving the selection of presidential electors. Justice Scalia argues that words in a statute often have a single meaning and that while judges *ought* not to depart from that meaning in any case involving text, they *may* not depart from textual plain meaning in any statutory case involving the selection of presidential electors. His separate opinion breaks down, however, at precisely the two points that his theory of judging often breaks down. First, words used in legal texts are notoriously ambiguous, making it almost impossible to insist that they carry an objectively knowable single meaning. Second, efforts to construe complex statutory schemes often reveal lacunae and disharmony that cannot be resolved by resort to literal readings. This case illustrates both problems.

Justice Scalia argues that the word "legislature" in Article II, section 1, plainly delegates plenary power to state legislatures to control the selection of presidential electors free from state judicial interference based on activist theories of statutory construction, or interpretations of the state constitution. While such a reading of "legislature" is plausible, it is far from the only possible reading. It is equally plausible to read "legislature" as that term is used in Article II, section 1, as a description of a political institution operating within a matrix of statutory and constitutional provisions that cause it to interact with other organs of state government. Why would the Founders, having just invented the idea of a legislature acting subject to judicially enforceable constitutional constraints, mandate that state legislatures be freed from state constitutional constraints when selecting electors? Moreover, how could such a deracinated reading of the term be squared with conceptions of state sovereignty that shield state institutions from being "commandeered" by the federal government? Forcing state courts to adopt a controversial judicial philosophy in cases involving presidential electors and untethering legislatures from their state constitutional moorings cannot be harmonized with a vision of the states as true sovereigns. Not surprisingly, despite Justice Scalia's confident insistence that the word "legislature" as used in Article II, section 1, must mean only what he says it means, six members of the Court declined to accept such a reading.

Similarly, Justice Scalia argues that the effort of the Florida Supreme Court to interpret Florida's election laws to determine whether the original certification deadline could be extended so as to permit precertification hand counts of the ballots, or whether power existed to order a postcertification statewide hand count of all undercounted ballots, violated Article II, section 1, and 5 U.S.C. § 3 because it constituted postelection judicial lawmaking in derogation of the power of the legislature to set preelection rules governing the selection of presidential electors. Under Justice Scalia's personal judicial philosophy, we have no doubt that the Florida court's aggressive efforts to construe the Florida Election Code against the background of an intense commitment to having each vote counted might appear unduly activist. But nothing in Article II or the federal code entitles the members of the Supreme Court to impose a personal view about how statutes should be read by a state supreme court merely because presidential electors are involved. In fact, the Florida court acted well within the parameters of generally accepted norms of statutory construction in seeking to discern the meaning of the Florida election laws. In deciding the precertification issue, the Florida court was confronted with two statutory provisions that appeared to point in different directions—a seven-day deadline and an authorization of hand counts that, often, could not be completed in seven days. Justice Scalia insists that only one right answer existed—respecting the deadline. But, whatever one's views about what the right answer was, it is clear that the Florida Supreme Court was following a well-trodden path when it sought to harmonize two conflicting provisions of the Florida code.

Similarly, in deciding the postcertification issue, the Florida court was confronted with a general grant of remedial power with little guidance as to how the power should be used in specific situations. Once again, while Justice Scalia's narrow view of the judicial role would undoubtedly cause him to pause before imposing an innovative statewide remedy, it is clear that many courts would have done exactly what the Florida court did in seeking to forge a specific remedy armed only with general statutory authorization.

Thus, to make Justice Scalia's model work, we must be prepared to accept an arbitrary, highly undesirable reading of the term "legislature" in Article II, section 1, and to impose a single, narrow philosophy of statutory construction on all state courts in cases involving presidential electors. That we decline to do. Judging in hard cases is not reducible to a single objective formula. The best that we can do is to provide honest explanations for why we believe that text and precedent should be read in a particular way, provide a principled defense of that reading, and rely on the give-and-take of the adversary process, judicial debate, and public criticism to help us reach the best set of answers. We have widely different views concerning the best answers to the difficult legal issues raised in these cases. Those disagreements flow, however, not from efforts to advance a favored presidential candidate but from honest differences over judicial role, the relative weight of conflicting values, and divergent philosophies of reading text. There simply is no other way.

Part Four

AMERICAN PERSPECTIVES

10

ANATOMY OF A CONSTITUTIONAL COUP

Bruce Ackerman

It was a curious time for a crisis. An extraordinary boom had provided the rich with fabulous wealth and America with full employment. The disappearance of the Red menace gave the nation an effortless cultural primacy. The air force had even established that wars could be won without casualties. What was there to worry about? Certainly Al Gore and George W. Bush weren't calling on Americans to ask any large questions. Both pushed their ideologues of the Left and the Right off the airwaves (at least during prime time). After one of the most boring campaigns in history, Americans were sleepwalking their way to the ballot box. Crisis hit after it was supposed to be all over.

Call it a crisis of the written Constitution, caused by the enormous historical gap that has opened up between the Constitution of 1787 and the living Constitution of the twenty-first century. During the thirty-five days following the election, the written and living Constitutions interacted in unpredictable and awkward ways that challenged America's commitments to democracy and the rule of law.

The challenge proved too great for the country's political and legal elite. Succumbing to the crudest partisan temptations, the Republicans managed to get their man into the White House but at grave cost to the nation's ideals and institutions. It will take a decade or more to measure the long-term damage of this electoral crisis to the presidency and the Supreme Court—but especially in the case of the Court, *Bush v. Gore* will cast a very long shadow.

According to the living Constitution, the American president is the leading symbol of the nation, the bearer of a democratic mandate, the engine of domestic change and international commitment. This commanding office is largely a creation of the twentieth century, the work of leaders such as Wilson, Roosevelt, and Reagan. But it bears no resemblance to the presidency that the Founders wrote into the Constitution. Those eighteenth-century gentlemen lived in a world without political parties or universal suffrage. They feared that direct election to the presidency would enable demagogues like Caesar or Cromwell to destroy the Republic. They sought to reassure the folks back home that the president was not going to become another tyrant like King George III. He would instead be a dignified notable presiding over a federation with sharply limited powers.

The Electoral College expresses this federalist vision. Each state counts, not each voter. Populous Pennsylvania and tiny Delaware got two electoral votes apiece to reflect that, as equal states, each is represented by two senators. Pennsylvania wields more votes in the College only because it also obtains an elector for each of its seats in the House of Representatives, and these are awarded on the basis of population. Thus a small state like Delaware has three electoral votes (two senators, one representative) and big states like Pennsylvania many more (two senators, many representatives): this formula expresses a substantial bias toward states' rights.

The Philadelphia Convention expressed the same federalist tendency when deciding who should vote for president. Suffrage requirements were then highly controversial, and so the Convention chose to sidestep the matter by delegating the franchise question to each state's legislature. Indeed, the legislatures were even free to name their state's electors without referring the matter to the larger voting public, and many legislatures availed themselves of this privilege during the early decades. The prevailing ideology regarded political parties as dangerous, and it seemed risky to allow them to engage in demagogic campaigns in support of their presidential favorites. Why not trust the legislature to select men of probity who might wisely cast the state's electoral votes without populist pandering?

These eighteenth-century ideas have been swept away by history, but the text has remained basically intact. In 2000, as in 1787, the Constitution penalizes states with large populations; and each state selects individual electors to cast ballots as if they were making independent judgments. To emphasize the federalist nature of the choice yet further, the electors do not even travel to Washington, D.C. They vote in their states and send their ballots to Congress to be counted.

This stately ritual has long since been reduced to shadow play. The rise of universal suffrage forced state legislatures to cede the selection of electors to the voters, and the rise of political parties eliminated the electors' claim to independence. As early as the 1830s, each party nominated a partisan slate of electors, who pledged their ballots to rival national candidates. The living Constitution had created a system in which Americans think and act as if they choose their president directly. Over the last sixty years, public opinion polls have shown that 60 percent of Americans consistently supported the abolition of the Electoral College.

The written Constitution is notoriously difficult to amend—requiring two-thirds majorities in Congress and the assent of three-fourths of the state legislatures. The resulting gap between the living and written Constitutions frames the problems posed by the Bush presidency. Most obviously, Bush's victory is entirely a product of the federalist bias inherited from 1787. Al Gore won the popular vote by more than 500,000, carrying California, Illinois, New York, and Pennsylvania. But he won only twenty states (plus the District of Columbia, which votes like a state for this purpose). In contrast, Bush won thirty states, even though he managed to carry only Florida and Texas among the major prizes. Bush's sweep of the small states netted him 18 extra votes in the Electoral College—rather a lot, considering that he beat Gore by only 4.

This will inevitably make him a weak president but not an illegitimate one—at least not if we assume that his win in Florida was legitimate. In turning to this question, keep one basic point in mind: the U.S. Constitution imposes few constraints on the way each state structures its own form of government. This means that the practical operation of the Electoral College depended on how Florida chose to organize its own voting process.

Florida's constitution shares three characteristics with many other states. The first is decentralization. Local—not state—government wields vast decision-making power on a broad front. In only eight states, for example, do all citizens use the same election machines. Elsewhere, the selection of equipment is delegated to local election boards. Although the minority party is represented on these boards, the local majority typically calls the tune.

Not that these boards can act arbitrarily. They are constrained by authorities operating at state level. This leads us to a second similarity between Florida's constitution and that of other states: its populist cast. Voters not only choose the governor. They also insist on electing important cabinet officers. The appointment of the secretary of state, who supervises elections, is not always considered important enough to require popular choice. Florida's secretary, for example, will be appointed, not elected, as of 2003. But when the crisis hit, the incumbent was a minor politician aspiring to better things, Katherine Harris.

The state judiciary is the third element of the living Constitution. After each election, disappointed candidates seek judicial relief from arbitrary decisions by local and state administrative bodies. Broadly, state supreme courts are concerned not only with blatant electoral fraud but also with many subtler forms of arbitrariness. And their judgments have typically pushed the electoral process toward tolerable—if not admirable—results.

To be sure, radical decentralization means that the poorest counties choose the cheapest, most error-prone methods of counting the vote. And the dangers of partisan appointment to election boards are also real. Nevertheless, local boards often consist of county judges and other notables who are generally unwilling to throw away hard-earned reputations for civic probity to steal an election for a single crony. The same is true of the secretary of state. Getting hauled into court on charges of voting fraud is very bad for a budding politician's career. Voters will take notice as newspaper headlines drag the secretary's name through the mud.

Alas, the normal caution was swept aside by the Electoral College. Despite Gore's national lead of half a million votes, Florida's twenty-five Electoral College votes turned on a few hundred ballots. Suddenly, it made sense for both sides to go for broke. This point was made most explosively in Miami, where more than ten thousand ballots had been rejected by the city's pathetically inadequate voting technology. As the election board prepared for a manual recount, a Republican mob successfully intimidated them into calling it quits. These unforgettable scenes, beamed across the world, will darken the image of American democracy for a long time to come.

There is more to these television pictures than meets the eye. Who funded and organized the Republican mob? Newspaper speculation is rife, pointing to one or another national leader of the Hard Right. No less tantalizing: why was Gore so ineffective in stiffening the election board's resolve? Miami is a Democratic city, and its leading politicians could have exerted great influence. Newspaper accounts suggest that the Elian Gonzalez affair was to blame. When the Clinton administration seized Elian, it so alienated local politicians that they were unwilling to help Gore in his hour of need.

The Republicans were more fortunate in their choice of party warriors. Secretary of State Harris repeatedly fell on her sword for the Republican cause before a worldwide television audience. As co-chair of Bush's campaign in the state, she was suffering from an obvious conflict of interest. Without question, she should have disqualified herself, leaving legal rulings to career officials in the Department of State. But the brazen Harris swept such inhibitions aside and single-mindedly proceeded to block, delay, or nullify any manual recount that threatened Bush's diminishing lead.

It is a mistake to linger on the role of the well-placed mob or the well-dressed flunky. Florida's final choice would be determined by powers much higher up the totem poll. Following standard procedures, the Florida Supreme Court was the ultimate decision maker. Throughout the crisis, it had one overriding aim—to ensure that all challenged votes were counted. Nothing remarkable here: Florida's constitution emphasizes the sanctity of the vote, and its laws expressly allow for manual recounts.

At the same time, its election code is the work of many decades and contains ambiguities and inconsistencies when read as a whole. This is typical in the law, and the Florida Supreme Court was on firm ground in harmonizing different provisions by reference to the fundamental purpose of an election law in a democracy. If its decisions had not involved the presidency but some lesser office, the court would have won a minor place of honor in the annals of American law. All serious scholars recognize that the ramshackle American election system would collapse if state courts failed to demonstrate an ongoing commitment to basic democratic principles.

Once again, however, the forces unleashed by the Electoral College proved overwhelming. The court's political complexion provided an excuse to discredit its decisions. All seven members were Democrats appointed by previous Democratic governors (with the partial exception of one appointment in which Governor Jeb Bush participated). This allowed Republicans to denounce the judges as partisans who were trying to steal the election. This was to be expected, but then there was a real surprise. During the early stages of the controversy, Jeb Bush had retired from public view, allowing the egregious Harris to take the political heat. As Florida's courts began to threaten his brother's victory, he reemerged from the shadows to endorse a breathtaking proposal: if the judges insisted on counting the votes rejected by machines, why not take the presidential decision out of the hands of the voters?

Bush's weapon was the written Constitution. The 1787 text does not guarantee the right to vote in presidential elections: it simply authorizes each state legislature to determine how its electors should be chosen. Bush called on his fellow Republicans to act "courageously" and return to the early days of the Republic when legislatures ignored the voters and appointed electors on their own initiative. Under Bush's plan, these legislatively appointed electors could then vote for his brother even if the courts found that the popular vote had gone to Gore. The Republican leaders of the Florida legislature called a special session to do their governor's bidding, and the Florida House had already named a Bush slate when the crisis reached its climax. With the Bush family at its head, the Republican Party was making a brazen effort to seize the presidency by assaulting the state courts and wresting power from the voters—all in the name of the written Constitution.

The only thing that stopped this constitutional coup was the United States Supreme Court. Just as the Florida Senate was preparing to endorse the Bush slate, the Court intervened to stop the Florida recount and establish George Bush as the next president. With its mission accomplished by higher powers, Florida's Senate quickly adjourned in the hope that the attempted Bush coup would be quickly forgotten.

This would be a mistake, however, not only because of what it tells us about the Bushes, but also for what it tells us about the American Constitution. Suppose that the United States Supreme Court had stayed on the sidelines and allowed Florida to determine its own electoral destiny. In this scenario, the state could well have sent sets of votes from two different groups of electors to Washington, D.C.—one slate certifying the judicial conclusion that Al Gore had won the election of November 7, the other certifying the legislative decision in favor of Bush on December 13. How would Congress have resolved the conflict when it convened on January 5 to count the electoral votes?

With difficulty, but not without precedent. In 1876 the country was still experiencing the aftershocks of civil war, and elections in three Southern states, including Florida, were so chaotic that rival governments in each of these states submitted rival electoral slates to Congress. In response, Congress appointed a special bipartisan commission—consisting of five congressmen, five senators, and five justices of the Supreme Court. After considering the rival slates, this commission awarded the presidency to the Republican candidate, Rutherford B. Hayes. Then, in 1887, Congress passed a statute ensuring that things would be easier the next time. This statute would have guided Congress as it chose between the Gore slate picked by Florida's voters and the Bush slate picked by its legislature. But there would have been a problem, for the statute requires the two houses to agree on a single slate, and Republicans controlled the House of Representatives, while Democrats controlled the Senate.

This split might not have entailed a deadlock. Both houses were controlled by very narrow margins, and the Bush coup in Florida would have provoked a great argument across the nation. The ensuing debate might have forced a few Republican moderates to vote for Gore. After all, it was not going to be easy to explain to outraged constituents why they had insisted on Bush after he had lost both the popular vote by 500,000 and the Florida vote by a hair—merely because his brother managed to ram a piece of paper through the Florida legislature.

Suppose, however, that the Republican majority in the House had stood firm. The 1887 statute is drafted too imprecisely to tell us what should have happened at this point, and some form of creative compromise would have been required. My best guess is that Congress would have followed precedent and created an electoral commission with five senators, five representatives, and five Supreme Court justices. The five justices might well have cast the deciding votes, but they would have been acting in a plainly political rather than judicial capacity, and their decision would not have tainted the future operation of the Court.

This is, of course, precisely what did not happen. Rather than stand on the sidelines, the Supreme Court flung itself into the political vortex. Curiously, the Court denies that it had any choice in the matter, asserting that it is "our unsought responsibility" to resolve the case. Every American lawyer knows otherwise. Like thousands of cases each year, *Bush v. Gore* appeared on the Court's discretionary docket. Since the Court accepts only eighty of these requests for a hearing, it was aggressively displacing Congress in its zeal to decide the election.

Judicial activism is not necessarily a vice in America—so long as it is thoughtfully conceived and carefully executed. In the Court's famous interventions in the past, the justices have made heroic efforts to achieve unanimity, or something close to it, before rushing to the center of the political stage. *Brown v. Board of Education,* as well as *Marbury v. Madison,* was unanimous, and even *Roe v. Wade* was initially decided by a vote of 7–2. But the Court awarded the presidency to Bush by a 5–4 vote, with the dissenters filing bitter public protests. Nor was there much time for deliberation. The Court typically labors many months before handing down a significant judgment: *Bush v. Gore* was issued thirty-four hours after oral argument. This is not a recipe for clear legal thinking.

There is only one serious defense for the Court's precipitous leap into presidential politics. In my hypothetical sketch the House and Senate come to a commonsense solution, either picking the Gore slate or following the precedent of a bipartisan electoral commission. But pessimists might foresee hordes of right- and left-wing extremists marching on Washington, congressional elites deadlocked, and the situation spinning out of control. (Had the impasse continued beyond the end of Clinton's term, existing law would have authorized the Speaker of the House, Dennis Hastert, to serve as acting president until Bush or Gore was finally selected.) If one is haunted by the specter of acute crisis, one can view the justices' intervention more charitably. However much the Court may have hurt itself, did it not save the larger constitutional structure from greater damage?

Perhaps. But even pessimists should question the way the Court chose to intervene. The more democratic solution would have been not to stop the Florida courts from counting the votes but to stop the Bush brothers from creating constitutional chaos by submitting a second slate of legislatively selected electors. The Court could have taken care of all the serious difficulties by enjoining Jeb Bush not to send this slate to Congress. With the legislative slate eliminated by judicial decree, the legal situation would have been dramatically clarified. Like every other state, Florida would then have submitted a single slate of electors—pledged to Bush or Gore, depending on the outcome of the final vote count. Under the statute of 1887, this slate must be accepted by Congress unless both houses vote to reject it. But while Republicans in the House might have been tempted to reject a Gore victory, the Democrats in the Senate would never go along with it; and vice versa. In short, if judicial intervention was justified at all, the Supreme Court chose the wrong target. The root of the problem was the Bush constitutional coup, not the judicial demand that every vote be counted.

There would have been another advantage to this solution. The Court could have written an opinion that made legal sense. The constitutional text gives state legislatures the power to determine "the manner" in which electors are selected, but a second provision gives Congress the power to establish a uniform day for choosing electors throughout the United States. Florida's legislature violated this when it sought to choose its own slate of electors in December, a month after election day. It is one thing for a legislature to determine the "manner" of election, quite another for it to authorize popular election by the voters of Florida on November 7 and then try to change the result by legislative fiat after the fact. In short, Supreme Court action against the Bush coup was commended not only by democratic principle, but also by the constitutional text.

The actual opinion of the Court in *Bush v. Gore* is a shabby affair. The majority's conclusion does not follow from its premises. Most important, the majority does not challenge the Florida court's demand for a manual recount. It simply questions the standard under which the recount was proceeding. The Florida court had instructed officials to inspect each ballot to determine each voter's intention. In the Supreme Court's view, this allowed for too much arbitrariness in the evaluation of individual ballots. To pass muster under the Equal Protection Clause, the Court held that more concrete criteria for ballot evaluation must be judicially elaborated before the recount could proceed.

I do not challenge this doctrinal conclusion. But it does not remotely justify the next—and crucial—move in the Court's argument. Having emphasized the need for concrete standards, the next obvious step was to send the case back to Florida to allow the state courts to satisfy federal requirements and move on with the recount. This is precisely what the Supreme Court refused to do. Instead, it took upon itself the task of interpreting Florida law and found that Florida no longer wished to proceed with the recount. According to the majority, Florida law required that all disputes be resolved by December 12 and not a moment later. Since the Court handed down its decision in Washington at 10:00 P.M. on December 12, there was—alas—no time left to do anything but declare George Bush the winner!

Nothing in Florida law remotely justified this remarkable act of interpretation. No state statute says anything whatsoever about December 12. Nor did the Florida Supreme Court make a fetish of this date. In a brief discussion, it did take passing notice of a federal law that gives states a special privilege if they manage to file an undisputed slate of electors by December 12. Under this provision, Congress guarantees that it will treat such uncontested filings as absolutely binding when it counts electoral votes.

This statute does not, however, disqualify late returns. This year, for example, at least four states—California, Iowa, Maryland, and Pennsylvania—submitted their slates of electors after the Supreme Court's magical deadline. Their casual attitude is readily explained. As we have seen, late filings cannot be rejected unless both houses agree, and this is unimaginable when the House is controlled by Republicans and the Senate by Democrats. Moreover, Congress has been especially liberal when manual recounts have revealed that an earlier return was erroneous. In 1960, for example, Congress accepted a change made by Hawaii, based on a recount, as late as January 4.

The Florida courts, in short, had more than three weeks to complete their recount when the Supreme Court cut them off. And the Florida court's entire conduct suggests that it was eager to continue. In asserting otherwise, the majority of the Supreme Court was engaging in an act of "interpretation" without any basis in law—as the four dissenters took pains to note.

Suppose I had been reporting on the recent election of Vicente Fox as president of Mexico. I would have described how a mob of Fox's partisans stopped the vote count in Mexico City, how Fox's campaign chair used her authority as chief elections officer to prevent the count from continuing, how Fox's brother exercised his position as governor to take the presidential election out of the hands of the voters, how the Supreme Court intervened to crush, without any legal ground, the last hope for a complete count. Would we be celebrating the election of President Fox as the dawn of a new democratic day in Mexico?

11

THE MANY FACES OF *BUSH V. GORE*

George P. Fletcher

It was a cold night, December 12, 2000, as the journalists gathered in front of the Supreme Court building in Washington, D.C. They were awaiting word on the third intervention taken by the Supreme Court in the election controversy of the century—the unresolved presidential race between George W. Bush and Al Gore. The Supreme Court had never decided a presidential election. The ubiquitous television pundits were surprised that the Court took the case at all. No one had figured out how the Court could establish its jurisdiction over a question that appeared to be a matter exclusively of Florida law. The Florida Supreme Court had just ordered the counting of uncounted ballots in certain counties, and therefore it appeared that although the Florida secretary of state had already certified Bush winner of the state, Gore could win enough votes on the recount to gain the lead.

December 12 carried an ominous ring. Many people thought that this was the deadline for recounting the votes in Florida and declaring the winner. Whoever carried the state would gain a majority in the Electoral College. December 12 was the date implied in the structure of a federal statute, enacted in 1877, designed to regulate disputed elections.[1] If a state could determine its slate of electors by "at least six days before the time fixed for the meeting of the electors," the slate would be guaranteed legitimacy when the House of Representatives counted the electoral votes.[2] As the electors were required to meet on December 18, by implication, December 12 became a desirable cutoff day to settle the dispute over Florida's electors. There were no penalties provided for states that designated their slate of electors after December 12, but if for some reason two conflicting slates of electors were sent to Congress, as had happened in 1876, Congress would have to make a choice between them.

Finally, as the hour approached midnight, the clerks brought out sheaves of bound opinions and passed them out to the eager journalists. The clerks said nothing about who won. With cameras holding the world's attention, the journalists leafed rapidly through the bulky opinions, looking for the gist—the word favoring Bush or Gore. But the opinions were far too complicated to understand at a glance. There were four of them, two for the five-vote majority, and two for the four-vote dissent.[3] If the journalists were lucky they hit upon a paragraph at the end of the concurring opinion:

> The scope and nature of the remedy ordered by the Florida Supreme Court jeopardizes the "legislative wish" to take advantage of the safe harbor provided by 3 U.S.C. Sec. 5. December 12, 2000, is the last date for a final determination of the Florida electors that will satisfy Sec. 5. . . . Surely when the Florida Legislature empowered the courts of the State to grant "appropriate" relief, it must have meant relief that would have become final by the cut-off date of 3 U.S.C. § 5.[4]

This argument about what the state of Florida must have meant was all that really mattered. December 12 was the cutoff day, and this was late in the evening, December 12. There was nothing else to discuss. Thus the Supreme Court showed a new face to the public. They were prepared to rule and did rule, directly and firmly, that a state could not count the votes to determine who won the election.

Gore supporters alluded darkly to a stolen election. Academic lawyers could not completely believe that the Court would use its power so openly and blatantly. But the critical act of power turned solely on a disagreement about the interpretation of Florida law. Admittedly, the Florida law was not clear. The Florida Supreme Court was ambivalent on the matter. On December 11 they had written that the state must finish the manual recount within a reasonable time and that in the case of a presidential election the federal statute (the now famous section 5 with the December 12 deadline) should "circumscribe the determination of reasonableness."[5] Yet after the U.S. Supreme Court decision, on December 22, the same Florida Supreme Court judges refused to confirm that the U.S. Supreme Court had interpreted their election law correctly.[6] But this ambivalence means that there was a real disagreement about what Florida law required. The majority of the Supreme Court said one thing, the four votes in dissent said another, and no one will ever know who was right about the true meaning of Florida law.

This, then, is the *first face* of *Bush v. Gore:* a historical judgment about Florida's desire to terminate the election on December 12. But this date could become relevant only if a *second face* bared its teeth, and that was the aggressive assumption that federal courts should regulate state-run elections for the American presidency. For the Court to undertake this task it would have to appear to abandon its recent decisions emphasizing federalism and the autonomy of the states. The question was whether the five justices in the majority had a solid legal foundation for undertaking this new assertion of judicial power.

In considering the arguments the Court offered for its intervention in the election, I want to distinguish the motivation of the majority and the principled defense of their decision. Even if they intervened solely to enable Bush to win the election, if they wanted Bush to win in order to increase the likelihood that those replacing the older conservative Republican justices would also be conservative Republicans, they still might have good reasons to support their decision.

There are many who think that a decision can be legitimate only if the legal rules and principles themselves generated the decision in the case. But we are all children of the legal realists. We know, as Justice Holmes said, that "general principles do not decide concrete cases."[7] And in constitutional law, with few exceptions, the only law we have consists of "general principles." We cannot expect the Constitution itself to generate results in concrete disputes. There will always be some personal element in judging. Sometimes this personal element is expressed as moral commitments, sometimes, unfortunately, as political commitments. To despair about this personal element in judging is to long for the illusion that the law itself generates judicial decisions. And we all know that this is an illusion that mature people are willing to give up.

The end of illusion—that the god of legal determinism is dead—does not mean that we should abandon the assessment and evaluation of Supreme Court decisions. Beginning with the materials of the law—the Constitution, statutes, and precedents—the Court crafts an argument to justify its decision. The argument takes the form of general principles. These principles live into the future, for if the original opinion is well crafted, it will be one of the precedents that the Court will invoke to ground its future decisions. This, then, is the second face of *Bush v. Gore:* the principled argument for intervening in the way a state conducts a presidential election.

The majority of five relied on two distinct arguments. Of course, these arguments make reference to the specific facts that occurred in Florida, and in some sense this decision, like every decision, is limited to its facts. But the arguments about these facts represent more abstract arguments of justice, which obviously carry implications for the future of American jurisprudence.

The Court's first argument was that the variable standards for counting ballots in Florida represented a violation of the Equal Protection Clause of the Fourteenth Amendment.[8] The problem centered on "chads"—the pieces of white paper that are supposed to be dislodged when the voters stick a pin in the desired hole. If the chad dislodges, then a machine-driven light can pass through the hole and register the vote. If the chad does not come off, if it is merely "dimpled" or "pregnant" or merely hangs there, the light beam will not tally the vote. The only way to count these votes is by hand. There are two problems with this procedure. It takes time, and there are different standards of interpretation.

Everyone agreed that the relevant standard was the intent of the voter as expressed in physical marks on the ballot. But in formulating criteria for assessing that intent, some counties went one way, others went the other way. This created a situation of apparent chaos. Too much depended on the judgment of the local canvassing board. The machines were predictable but incomplete. The human ballot counters were potentially complete but unpredictable. The nation was caught between the Scylla of apparent arbitrariness and the Charybdis of ignoring thousands of actual votes. The situation was complicated by the partisan interpretation of the uncounted votes. Though Gore supporters had little evidence for their view, most of them thought that the ballots rejected by the machines would have counted for their candidate and thus enabled him to carry the state and the election.

Seven justices on the Court seized on the idea of equality to express their dissatisfaction with this situation.[9] The majority thought that the counting procedures violated equal protection of the law, as guaranteed by the Fourteenth Amendment adopted in 1868.[10] Two dissenting justices thought there was a problem under the Equal Protection Clause.[11] A little reflection makes it clear, however, that the problem was not equality under law. The analysis of an equal protection problem requires, first and foremost, the identification of a group that suffers unfavorable treatment under the application of the law. This is the group that has standing to sue on the ground of state-sponsored discrimination. Who is that group in *Bush v. Gore?* One of the questions before the Court was whether Miami-Dade County should count the nine thousand "undervotes" that did not register in the machine recount. Does the petitioner George Bush suffer as the result of this recount? How do we know whether he would have gained or lost votes as a result of this procedure?

The victims of the recount would arguably be all voters whose ballots would have been counted by the application of less accurate criteria. But why would ballots so counted constitute a wrong to the voters? They would suffer an injustice only if the criteria applied in their case failed to gauge their true intentions. And there is no way of knowing which standard would be best suited to getting the voters' intentions right in the greatest number of cases. Suppose there are three possibilities: standard A (disregard ballots with dimpled chads), standard B (search for the voter's intent in the case of a dimpled chad), and the random application of sometimes A and sometimes B. Because we do not know whether A is always better than B, there is no way of knowing whether the random application of A and B would be a worse way of getting at the truth than either A or B standing alone.

An additional argument shaped the opinion of the three so-called conservative justices—Chief Justice Rehnquist, who wrote the concurring opinion, and Justices Scalia and Thomas. Their claim that there was a federal question in the dispute was based on an interpretation of the provision in the 1789 Constitution that established the Electoral College.[12] Article II, section 1, clause 2, provides, in part: "Each State shall appoint, in such Manner as the Legislature thereof may direct, a Number of Electors, equal to the whole Number of Senators and Representatives to which the State may be entitled in the Congress." I shall refer to this as the Electoral College provision.

The remarkable reading of this provision by the conservative justices holds that when a state legislature directs that the people shall elect slates of electors for president and vice president, the legislature acts by virtue of a direct grant of authority under the Electoral College provision of the 1789 Constitution.[13] There is some truth to this view, but the phrase "grant of authority" obscures a fundamental conceptual distinction.

The traditional view of a state legislature is that its legitimacy depends on the authority conferred on it by its state constitution. Its decisions are *recognized* as carrying weight at the federal level. Under the new reading, the federal "grant of authority" to the state legislature means that the U.S. Constitution creates the authority in state legislatures to act in the way necessary to select electors in a presidential race.

To see the difference very clearly, think about the language in Article V that requires amendments proposed by Congress to be "ratified by the Legislatures of three fourths of the several States, or by Convention in three fourths thereof." This provision *recognizes* the authority of legislatures to say yes or no to an amendment, but it does not *confer* authority on the legislature to take a stand on the proposed amendment. There would be something disturbingly circular about a system in which the agency charged with amending the Constitution acquired all its authority from the Constitution itself. If there is anything fundamental in our constitutional structure, both before the Civil War and after, it is that the source of all authority is "We the People" or, in the postbellum phrase, the "American nation."

There are many references in the Constitution to matters prohibited to the states, but nowhere does the Constitution *grant* authority to the states. The very idea that the states or a state legislature would acquire authority from the Constitution violates the structure of constitutional authority that flows from the people to the states and finally to the federal government, including the Supreme Court. And yet the Supreme Court now proposes to turn this structure on its head and treat the federal Constitution as the source legitimating the states' appointing presidential electors.

Yet in December 2000 the Supreme Court actually seemed to endorse the view that when a state legislature defines a manner of presidential election, the legislature's authority derives not from the people of the state but from the federal Constitution itself. In other words, their authority flows not from the bottom up but from the top down. This is probably the most radical reinterpretation of states' rights ever proposed, more radical than anything accomplished in the Civil War. And note that the idea is formulated by the so-called conservative justices who are known for favoring a decentralized system of government with greater authority left to the states.

How are we to understand the willingness of five Supreme Court justices to subscribe to arguments that are so radical, so innovative, that they must be considered revolutionary changes in the principles that guide the Court's thinking? First, seven justices endorse a theory of equality that dispenses with the traditional requirement of an identifiable victim of inequality. Second, the so-called conservatives reinterpret the relationship between the states and the Constitution in a way that undermines the traditional view that the authority of the states derives not from the federal government but from the people.

Whatever the political motivation for these two arguments—equality and the assertion of federal authority in presidential elections—they must have had an intrinsic rhetorical appeal. Even if their purpose was merely to camouflage a judicial determination that Bush would win the presidency, they must be arguments that have merit on their own.

How are we to explain the rhetorical appeal of these two arguments? The answer is the past—the evolution of American constitutional thinking since the Civil War. The *third face* of *Bush v. Gore*, therefore, is the impact of history. The decisions of December 2000 reflect the heavy hand of Abraham Lincoln, the Civil War, and Reconstruction.

To understand the third face of *Bush v. Gore,* we have to turn our attention to the great transformation that occurred in the American Constitution in the throes of the war between the North and the South. As I read American history, the Civil War, 1861–65, represents the end of one constitutional order and the beginning of another. The differences between these constitutional orders are so profound that if we were forthright about our history we would recognize that in fact we have experienced two republics. The first republic was founded on the Constitution that came into force in 1789. The second republic began in the fire of battle, was declared in Lincoln's Gettysburg Address in November 1863, and found formal embodiment in the Reconstruction amendments adopted after the war, between 1865 and 1870.

The first Constitution was based on the principles of peoplehood as a voluntary association, individual freedom, and republican elitism. The guiding premises of the second Constitution were, in contrast, organic nationhood, equality of all persons, and popular democracy. These are principles radically opposed to each other. That we may appreciate the sharp contrast between these two visions of America, let us rehearse the points of difference, with a modest explanation of each set of opposites.

FREEDOM VERSUS EQUALITY

The Constitution of 1787 stands for a maximum expression of individual freedom, at least against the federal government. Not only does the Bill of Rights safeguard the basic freedoms of speech, religion, and assembly, but the charter of the first republic stood as well for the right of white people to assert themselves freely to seize and control the lives of certain other people known as Negroes. The Civil War Constitution is dedicated to the proposition that all men are created equal. The individual rights sanctified in the Bill of Rights carved out a space for each person to stand alone, free of governmental interference. The postbellum Constitution emphasized not freedom from government but equality under law. The state would have to do more than leave us alone. It would have to ensure the equal protection of the laws for all.

CHOICE VERSUS SELF-REALIZATION

The Preamble to the 1787 national charter begins with the words "We the People." The people come together, at least as imagined by their self-appointed representatives in Philadelphia, to form "a more perfect Union." The emphasis is on voluntary association. We the people *choose* our form of government. The keyword that defines Americans in the fraternal war of the 1860s is not their voluntary association in a *people* but the bond that defines them as a single *nation*. Choice marks the People. History breeds the Nation. In the face of dissolution, Abraham Lincoln and his generation realized the ties—"the bonds of affection" of Lincoln's First Inaugural Address[14]—that led men to fight for the Union. The 1787 Constitution stands therefore for the choice of the people. The Civil War Constitution builds on a recognition of organic nationhood as the legacy of the American experience.

ELITISM VERSUS POPULAR DEMOCRACY

The Constitution of 1787 entrenched elitist government. The model was the New England Town Meeting. The virtuous few, basically the white propertied males of the community, would concern themselves about the issues of public life. If this was self-government, the "self" was very limited indeed. The notion of "government by the people" takes on different contours in the second American Republic. Virtue gives way to preferences and politics. Rule by the few surrenders, slowly and progressively, to the rough-and-tumble of universal adult suffrage.

Besides these striking dualities, other differences between the first and second American Constitutions present themselves. The first Constitution is an expression of secular will: We the People convene to "establish a more perfect Union." The Founders think of the future—not of their debt to the past. The second Constitution rests on the recognition that "four score and seven years" of history had created an organic bond among Americans, a bond that was expressed by thinking of the nation as having a distinct mission in history. Lincoln expressed this distinct mission by referring, in the Gettysburg Address, to the "nation under God." Thus the movement from peoplehood to nationhood also represented a shift from a purely secular will to create a better government toward a philosophy of submission to historical obligation and the recognition of a divine mission in history.

All of these themes are signaled in the Gettysburg Address, particularly in the opening sentence: "Four score and seven years ago our fathers brought forth on this continent a new nation, conceived in liberty and dedicated to the proposition that all men are created equal." Lincoln delivered his now-famous two-minute speech on November 19, 1863, in the apparent belief that "the world will little note nor long remember what we say here." In fact, the nation did remember and cherish these words at Gettysburg as the articulation of a new vision for American society. The themes expressed at Gettysburg captured the American yearning for a post-bellum order based on principles radically different from the ideas that founded the Republic in the Constitution that took force in 1789. These 268 words,[15] repeated regularly in school assemblies and preserved in stone at the Lincoln Memorial in Washington, became the secular prayer of the postbellum American Republic. Every time they are intoned, they remind us of our collective commitment to consciousness of equality, nationhood, and democracy.

The bold plan for Reconstruction based on the principles of equality and nationhood encountered resistance from entrenched attitudes that had taken root before the agony of the Civil War. The Supreme Court invalidated the first major civil rights[16] bill designed to eliminate discrimination in the public sphere and the justices tried to cabin the "equal protection" provision of the Fourteenth Amendment so that it applied, at most, to state-sponsored racial apartheid laws.[17] Even official segregation eventually won approval in the temporary defeat of Lincoln's vision of a nation "conceived in liberty and dedicated to the proposition that all men are created equal."[18]

Judicial decisions can suppress principles of higher law, but they cannot destroy them. Even after the judges turned their backs on the new order, the Civil War Constitution, sanctified by the six hundred thousand who died in its gestation, remained a firm but minimally visible commitment of American political culture. The Civil War Constitution became our alternative charter, our Secret Constitution, waiting in the wings for a more propitious time to step out on the stage of open judicial debate.

The principles of equality, nationhood, and democracy began to express themselves in arenas other than the courts. The most significant traces are found in the variety of amendments to the Constitution enacted since the Civil War. The Fourteenth Amendment, adopted in 1868, is the centerpiece of the new constitutional order. It established the principle that no state may deprive any individual of equal protection of the law. It expresses the theme of nationhood by defining, for the first time, a constitutional concept of citizenship in the United States. The fourteen official amendments adopted between 1865 and 1993[19] reveal a little-noticed pattern, a systematic effort to remake the United States in the image originally cast at Gettysburg. These amendments spread the franchise to blacks,[20] to women,[21] to those between the ages of eighteen and twenty-one,[22] and to the residents of the District of Columbia.[23] They also reform our elitist institutions by guaranteeing the popular election of senators.[24] They serve the implicit purposes of Lincoln's constitutional vision. They all have been designed to further the causes of equality, nationhood, and popular democracy.

The themes of equality and nationhood help us to understand the historical roots of *Bush v. Gore*. Both the commitment to and the rhetoric of equality have been ascendant since Lincoln rediscovered the basic proposition of the Declaration of Independence and reaffirmed that "all men are created equal." In the first few decades after the Civil War, the claim of equal treatment extended beyond blacks to include Chinese and other races and ethnic groups that might suffer discrimination by the government. There was admittedly a relapse of sixty years in which the Court officially approved of segregated schools. Since 1954, however, we have witnessed an incessant push toward expanding the circles of inclusion and equal treatment. The blanket of equality has come to cover women, children born out of wedlock, the children of illegal immigrants, and, in some situations, noncitizens. The contexts vary from jury service to social security benefits. Equality is a theme whose time has definitely come.

The rhetoric of equality has come to play a major role in academic disputes about the limits of free speech. Germans refer to the dignity of victims in order to justify their prohibition of hate speech.[25] Americans—without a constitutional concept of human dignity—must make do with the principle of equality.[26] Thus in the work of academics who favor limitations on free speech, equality is the argument of first resort. Also, in the field of religion the principle of equality has acquired considerable rhetorical power. The First Amendment contains seemingly conflicting clauses on religious liberty. One clause guarantees the free exercise of religion, which arguably leads to exceptional treatment of religious groups whose practices violate the law. Another clause prohibits the establishment of religion. It appears as though every exception for a religious minority indirectly privileges that religion and therefore arguably violates the establishment clause. One popular technique for reconciling these conflicting clauses is to insist that they be read to stand for a principle of equality toward all faiths, religious and secular.[27]

In light of the growing rhetorical influence of equality, both in the law and in the academic literature, it is not surprising that seven justices of the Supreme Court would grasp for the principle of equality to explain their intuition that there was something wrong with the variable and seemingly haphazard standards used in counting the Florida votes. Although the case does not fit the conventional paradigm of an equal protection violation (there was no identifiable victim or class of victims), the rhetoric of equality was very appealing. History shined through. The second constitutional order expressed itself loud and clear.

Equality, nationhood, and democracy. These are foundations of the second constitutional charter. The principle of nationhood also made itself felt in *Bush v. Gore,* and in a remarkably strong manner. The sense of nationhood was stronger in 2000 than it had been in the course of the 1980s and 1990s. The country showed that despite the casual acceptance of multiculturalism, we were one nation after all. To be sure, there were divisions evident in the popular vote. Men inclined toward Bush (53 percent) and women toward Gore (54 percent). Blacks and Hispanics voted overwhelmingly for Gore (90 and 62 percent, respectively) and whites favored Bush (54 percent). The larger cities came out for Gore, the smaller towns for Bush. And yet no one claimed that their advantage in a subdivision of the electorate gave them an edge in legitimacy.

No one ever claimed that Bush deserved to win because he was the candidate of the whites, or of the men, or of the small towns that make up the "real" America. The America that expressed itself in the popular majority of half a million votes for Al Gore included everyone. And no one dared suggest otherwise.

Popular democracy cannot work simply as a random collection of blocs. The idea requires a strong sense of nationhood. France, Germany, and England can vote on a nationwide basis and treat the outcome as the voice of the nation as a whole. But the countries of the European Union have not yet reached the point in the evolution of consciousness where they can contemplate a popular vote for the officers of the Union. Joschka Fischer, foreign minister of Germany, dreams of a single European president on the American model. But national loyalties are still too strong. An over-whelming majority in one large country such as Germany or France would determine the outcome, thus drowning out the voices of the smaller nations. Because the Europeans are not yet a single nation, they cannot accord to a fraction of the German or Italian vote the same weight as the entire voting population in Ireland or Denmark.

Those who support the Electoral College might think the same way about the United States. We are supposedly still a collection of states or, at best, a union of regions. We see these regions in the electoral map of 2000. The South and the Midwest voted solidly for Bush. The Northeast, the Great Lakes region, and the Far West voted for Gore. If we had a nationwide popular election, we would take the risk that an overwhelming majority in New York or California could determine the outcome whenever the candidate could poll a respectable percentage in the rest of the country. In our present system, a super-majority in one state is for naught. This forces the candidates out of their home states and home regions and requires them to engage the undecided electorate all across the country.

The downside of the Electoral College is that it runs afoul of the principle of one person, one vote. A vote by someone in the Gore majority in California or New York did not carry as much weight in the election as the average vote in Florida or Oregon or New Mexico—all closely divided states. In fact, under the winner-take-all system, all votes in excess of the one necessary to create a majority are superfluous.[28]

Also, because each state starts with a base of three electoral votes, regardless of its population, the allocation of electoral votes is skewed toward the smaller states. The Electoral College incorporates the principle of representation in the Senate, which treats each state as though it were a separate nation entitled to an equal voice with all others. Although regionalism remains alive in the United States, it is hard to take seriously the idea that each state stands for a distinctive culture entitled to representation in its own right. At one time we tolerated a similar representation of counties in the upper houses of state legislatures, but the Supreme Court declared this mode of representation unconstitutional in violation of the principle "one person, one vote."[29] The Court dismissed the idea that geographic units per se were entitled to representation. Yet the text of the Constitution itself prevents the logical extension of this critique to the Senate and the Electoral College.

The power that the Senate and the Electoral College give to the smaller states ensures that they will both survive.[30] Three-fourths of the states would have to ratify a constitutional amendment, and the smaller states are unlikely to vote to surrender their relative influence.

The continuing control of the states over the electoral process is one of the remarkable features of our system that became painfully apparent to observers of the deadlock in Florida in November 2000. It is hard to believe that the election of the president of the United States would be governed by a series of fifty-one independent state (and District of Columbia) laws. One could understand how and why state elections would proceed according to the preferences and the law of the local electorate. But why should a national office—the one spokesperson for the nation as a whole—follow the same rules? The only answer is history.

In the original conception of the Constitution, the public—the nation— had no independent existence. All power was reserved to the states and the people. The nation as an organic entity comes to consciousness in the Civil War; it finds its first full expression in Lincoln's Gettysburg Address.

The realization of nationhood has altered our sense of legitimacy about who deserves to be president. There are many who thought Gore deserved to be president simply because he won the national popular vote by over half a million votes. Yet the system of election—the winner is the person who receives the majority of electoral votes—harks back to a time when there was no sense of nationhood, no appreciation for the values of popular democracy.

The best defense of the decision in *Bush v. Gore* is that it sought, by radical surgery, to adapt the system of electing the president to the reality of the presidency as a national office. A president who represents the nation requires a procedure of election that is grounded in the unity of the nation. This is the simple historical truth that motivated the normally pro–states' rights justices to make the extraordinary claim that for purposes of the national election, the Constitution grants power to the states to select electors for the Electoral College. The Electoral College thus ceased being an expression of fifty-one sovereign states and became an expression of the nation with the task of electing officers representing the nation.

This, then, is an apology for *Bush v. Gore* that draws on the third face of the decision—its roots in the historical evolution of the Constitution since the Civil War. The apology makes sense, but it also bears a serious flaw. The opinions realize the values of equality and of nationhood, but the majority turns its back on the value of popular democracy.

The most disturbing line in the majority opinion expresses contempt for the citizens' democratic right to vote:

> The individual citizen has no federal constitutional right to vote for electors for the President of the United States unless and until the state legislature chooses a statewide election as the means to implement its power to appoint members of the Electoral College.[31]

This seems true, if we just look at the words in the document of 1787.[32] But the Constitution has evolved, and the second Constitution born of the Civil War is clearly committed, as Lincoln said at Gettysburg, to "government of the people, by the people, and for the people." The vast array of constitutional amendments prohibiting discrimination in the franchise would make no sense if the states could simply abolish the right to vote across the board. The federal government is obligated to guarantee a "republican" form of government to the states, and in our time this would surely imply a recognition of the democratic franchise. The idea that the popular vote is a contingent matter, dependent on a choice by state legislatures, is hardly faithful to the legacy of Lincoln at Gettysburg.

Perhaps we should settle for a decision of the Supreme Court that affirms two principles born of the Civil War and rejects the third. But the American people and all peoples should take their democratic sovereignty seriously. The court and citizens of Florida care about whether Floridians should have been allowed to complete their electoral process without being told what their legislature "must have meant." The election may have been settled, remarkably, without even a thought of taking up arms, but the nation will not forget.

The values of equality, nationhood, and democracy have become embedded in the American psyche. We now share these values with the numerous newly created democracies in the world that find inspiration in the American experience. The duty of Americans now is to make good on the example we have set for the world.

NOTES

1. 3 U.S.C. § 5.

2. *Id.*

3. Bush v. Gore, 531 U.S. 98 (2000).

4. Bush, 121 S. Ct. at 538 (Rehnquist, J., joined by Scalia, J., and Thomas, J., concurring).

5. Palm Beach Canvassing Board v. Harris, 772 So.2d 1273, 1286 n.17 (Fla. 2000).

6. Gore v. Harris, 773 So.2d 524 (Fla. 2000).

7. Lochner v. New York, 198 U.S. 45, 76 (1905) (Holmes, J., dissenting).

8. Bush, 121 S. Ct. at 533.

9. *Id.* ("Seven Justices of the Court agree that there are constitutional problems [on equal protection grounds] with the recount ordered by the Florida Supreme Court that demand a remedy").

10. *Id.*

11. *Id.* at 545 (Souter, J., dissenting); *id.* at 551, 557–58 (Breyer, J., dissenting).

12. *Id.* at 534 ("A significant departure from the legislative scheme for appointing Presidential electors presents a federal constitutional question").

13. *Id.* at 535.

14. First Inaugural Address, March 4, 1861.

15. According to the standard version and the usual counting there are 268 words. See Garry Wills, *Lincoln at Gettysburg: The Words That Remade America* (New York: Simon & Schuster, 1992). The word count differs, however, depending on the draft used and the way of counting such words as "battle-field." Ken Burns claims 269 words. Ken Burns, *The Civil War* (Episode 5).

16. The Civil Rights bill was originally passed on April 9, 1866, ch. 31, 14 Stat. 27, and reenacted with some modifications in sections 16, 17, and 18 of the Enforcement Act, passed May 31, 1870, ch. 114, 16 Stat. 140.

17. Civil Rights Cases, 109 U.S. 3 (1883).

18. Plessy v. Ferguson, 163 U.S. 537 (1896).

19. U.S. Const. amend. XIII–XXVII.

20. U.S. Const. amend. XV.

21. U.S. Const. amend. XIX.

22. U.S. Const. amend. XVI.

23. U.S. Const. amend. XXIII.

24. U.S. Const. amend. XVII.

25. Article I of the German Basic Law of 1949.

26. See Susanne Baer, *Würde oder Gleichheit?* (Baden-Baden: Nomos, 1995) (on the interaction between the dignity and equality arguments).

27. See Philip Kurland, "Of Church and State and the Supreme Court," 29 *University of Chicago Law Review* 1 (1961).

28. In light of our recent election controversy, however, additional votes beyond a slim majority might be useful in dissuading election challenges and voter recounts.

29. Baker v. Carr, 369 U.S. 186 (1962).

30. See Daniel Lazare, *The Frozen Republic: How the Constitution Is Paralyzing Democracy* (New York: Harcourt Brace, 1996).

31. Bush, 121 S. Ct. at 529.

32. U.S. Const. Art. II, § 1.

12

SPRINGTIME FOR ROUSSEAU

Richard Brookhiser

Late in November 2000, three weeks into the postelection election, Representative Jerrold Nadler, a liberal Democrat representing the West Side of Manhattan—one of the bluest of what political America would soon be calling the blue counties—sniffed the atmosphere and made a noteworthy charge. "I don't think I've ever called anything else like this before, but I will now," Nadler said. "The whiff of fascism is in the air."

Why would he say such a thing? The trappings of traditional fascism, in or out of power—riots, book burnings, death squads, monster rallies—were nowhere to be seen. If Nadler looked at the desultory marching and yelling that both Democrats and Republicans were sponsoring in Florida and Washington, D.C., and saw Brownshirts, then his sensibilities were arguably too tender for the ordinary rough-and-tumble of political life. The Founding Fathers were made of tougher stuff. In summer 1795, six thousand New Yorkers (out of a total population of about forty-five thousand) gathered at the intersection of Wall and Broad Streets to denounce a treaty that the Washington administration had negotiated with Great Britain. Former Treasury Secretary Alexander Hamilton and Senator Rufus King, who supported the treaty, tried to address the crowd; they were stoned, and one rock hit Hamilton in the head. (Imagine Robert Rubin and Senator Charles Schumer confronting a mob, or a mob bothering to stone them.) Later that day, in small-scale arguments with treaty opponents, Hamilton was challenged to two duels. The aggrieved parties managed to resolve their differences short of pistol fire; it would be nine years before Hamilton was shot and killed by a political adversary, the vice president of the United States.

But if one looked beyond the merely raucous and made-for-television crowds in Florida and elsewhere and instead listened to what they and their leaders were saying, Nadler was right. There was a whiff of something un-American in the air, and it arguably smelled of fascism, or what may be the next best thing, Rousseau.

The first protestors to hit the ground, on November 9, two days after the election, were pro-Gore groups of local voters led by the Reverend Jesse Jackson. As with all subsequent demonstrations on both sides, these were padded with ringers: political operatives flown in from the Beltway. I remember one evening news clip of these earliest demonstrators that showed, in the small crowd, a middle-aged white man in a suit waving a sign that read, "Ollie North Shredded My Vote!" Pseudo-locals should be better camouflaged: who, apart from professional political junkies, even remembers who Oliver North was? More important than the numbers or the signage was what the first crowds were saying.

One thousand pro-Gore protesters who gathered outside the Palm Beach County Courthouse chanted "Re-vote! Re-vote!" The message was taken up during the next few days by sympathetic demonstrators across the country: hundreds of Gore supporters rallying outside the Westwood Federal Building in Los Angeles held signs that said, "Re-vote or Revolt," and dozens of protestors in Providence, Rhode Island, waved signs that said, "Revote Florida." (Crowd estimates are from news stories in the *Chicago Tribune* and *USA Today*.)

Americans have held revotes since colonial times: they are called the next election. Why hold a new election so soon? William M. Daley, Gore's campaign manager, did not join in any demonstrations and did not call for a revote, but in a press conference on November 9 he gave the rationale for corrective action. "Here in Florida it . . . seems very likely that more voters went to the polls believing that they were voting for Al Gore than for George Bush. If the will of the people is to prevail, Al Gore should be awarded a victory in Florida and be our next president."

If more Florida voters believed they were voting for Gore, why hadn't Gore gotten more votes in Florida? No one, in the press conference or on the street, alleged fraud—altering Gore votes or throwing them away. Daley would be particularly sensitive to such a charge, given his family's expertise. The Gore voters, Daley explained, had instead been "victims" of "ballot confusion," their intentions frustrated by the complexity of the ballot. Again, no one claimed that the ballots in Florida had been deliberately opaque, in the manner of literacy tests in the segregated South that were designed to target blacks. The ballots for the 2000 election in Florida had been approved by both parties and published in the newspapers ahead of time. Daley acknowledged as much: the Bush campaign, he said scornfully, "cite[s] legal provisions about published ballots and technical notice."

But these technicalities were irrelevant in the face of Daley's rationale. "All we are seeking is this: that the candidate who the voters preferred become our president. . . .[L]et the true and accurate will of the people prevail." Daley did not specify how that should happen, but according to his argument, a revote was certainly an option: if one vote had not accurately transcribed the will of the voters, why not hold another?

Over the next weeks, the Gore campaign, following a long tradition of American politics, hedged and obscured its rationale. The call for a revote dropped from view, while the standard of the people's will was defined or modified. On November 10, Daley spoke of "a careful, lawful effort to ensure that the will of the people is done." The next day, Warren Christopher, another top Gore spokesman, appealed to the "will of the people, expressed in accordance with our Constitution." Al Gore himself said it was "time to respect every voter and every vote" and "time to honor the true will of the people." According to these formulations, the people's will was an expression of their preferences, but it was also something more tangible and precise: it took the form of a vote, which had to follow the Constitution and the law. In practice, that meant it had to have the imprimatur of the relevant officeholders, though the Gore campaign preferred some officeholders to others. The Florida Supreme Court, said Gore at one point, "allow[s] us to honor that simple constitutional principle . . . that the will of the people should prevail"; but Gore's lawyers said at another point that "the will of the voters cannot be frustrated by the whim of local officials"— in this case, county canvassing boards.

The contest passed almost immediately into the hands of those modern American gladiators, the lawyers, and the arguments of the Bush and Gore legal teams and the decisions of the judges before whom they performed consumed all attention. But after the last court made its last judgment, and George W. Bush was declared the winner in Florida and in the Electoral College, a prominent Gore supporter returned to the rhetoric of the streets two months earlier. "[T]he only way [Bush] could win," joked outgoing President Bill Clinton in January 2001, "was to stop the voting in Florida." Stop the counting, or stop the voting? "The only way I can really get any big headlines is to say what I really think," President Clinton said later, of this and other witticisms about the postelection struggle. He still had many ways of getting big headlines, as his pardons would prove, but he really seemed to think that people in Florida should have kept voting until they expressed their will.

The American government is based on the people. The Declaration of Independence speaks for "one people" who are altering or abolishing their form of government, and the Constitution invokes "We the People," who are to form "a more perfect Union." At the Constitutional Convention, Alexander Hamilton defined republican government as one in which "all magistrates are appointed and vacancies are filled by the people, or a process of election originating with the people." But how is republican government based on the people? Is it based on their will?

The will of the people is multiform, and it is expressed in numerous ways, many times a day. People register their will when they drink Budweiser or Heineken; when they buy a Ford or a Toyota; when they join a church or a synagogue or nothing. They express their will when they answer a telemarketer or a pollster or slam down the phone; when they write letters to the editor or change channels. Even the past is a source of will: G. K. Chesterton called tradition "the democracy of the dead." The marketplace is a scrum of wills, on which trillions of dollars ride. The marketplace of ideas is another huge forum, containing the latest Britney Spears song and the correspondence of Leo Strauss and Carl Schmitt. Politics is yet another focus of wills, from David Gergen's to Timothy McVeigh's to the average voter's.

Voting in an election, as William Daley argued, is an expression of will. But there are so many other important expressions of will, even in the arena of politics itself, that voting might better be called a choice. Voting occurs at specific places, at specific times (even absentee ballots, or the mail ballots adopted by Oregon, have to be sent to certain addresses by certain dates). Votes are irrevocable; you can dither in the voting booth for a long time, but you cannot come back an hour later and change your mind. Voting in this country is unitary: one vote for one candidate (some countries, such as Ireland, allow multiple votes). Voting is a right, but it is restricted. We have expanded the franchise over 225 years—though not, perhaps, as much as we imagine: some blacks and women voted even in the late eighteenth century—yet we still deny the right to minors, resident aliens, felons, and lunatics. Because the United States is, and was, even in 1789, a large and diverse country, votes for officeholders at the national level are regionally distributed: representatives and presidential electors represent the electorates of states or even smaller units.

The rules of voting in the United States have changed over the years and will continue to do so. But the fact that there are rules makes voting a choice. One element of the voter's choice is his or her will or preference (sometimes the preference is oblique, as when one votes for the lesser evil). But there are so many other factors that to equate voting with expressing a preference is to distort the meaning of the act.

Voting is designed to be a choice rather than a preference so that voters will be encouraged (nothing can be guaranteed) to take the act seriously. Children and lunatics are excluded because they are irresponsible; aliens, because they have no stake in the country; felons, because they have forfeited theirs. We usually explain—and dismiss—property qualifications, which lasted into the nineteenth century, by the "stake in the country" argument, as if early Americans thought of the United States as a joint stock company, in which poor people could not quite scrape up a share. But another reason for property qualifications, expressed by the Founding Fathers, was the fear that the votes of the poor could be too easily bought. Rich landowners in the early Republic were quite conscious of this power. Robert Livingston, one of Hamilton's contemporaries, blandly admitted that the tenants who farmed his family's Hudson Valley estates voted "in some measure under the influence of their landlords"; James Kent said the Livingston tenants were driven to the polls like "sheep." The crusade for campaign finance reform expresses a similar anxiety. We now say we want to limit the power of the rich, but what we are really concerned to avoid is the malleability of voters bombarded by ads. Since votes pick our rulers, we want them to be soberly cast.

If the voting booth had misread the preferences of the people of Florida, what new measure of their will did the Gore campaign propose in the postelection contest? Their first move was to put crowds in the streets, to create a prime-time image of outrage. But given the turbulent history of American politics, the effort they made was trivial. Reflecting perhaps the power of the legal class in America, the Gore campaign made its big push in court; the Bush campaign immediately did the same. In the end, the votes of three Florida counties, which decided the vote of the state, which decided the vote of the nation, were themselves decided by a 4–3 decision of the Florida Supreme Court, which was overruled by a 5–4 decision of the United States Supreme Court. That was a restriction of the franchise that would have made the eighteenth century blush.

The dispute could have been left in the hands of elected officials: county canvassers, the secretary of state of Florida, the state legislature, and finally, Congress. That would have had the virtue of leaving the problem to decision makers who, if they misbehaved grossly, risked being punished, not in a revote demanded by demonstrators or by Bill Clinton, but at their next regularly scheduled election. Instead, Democrats and Republicans reached for their lawsuits and hid behind judges' robes. Politics ain't bean bag, said Mr. Dooley; in the postelection of 2000 it wasn't even politics.

The anticlimax in the courts should not blind us, however, to the seriousness of the argument from will and its consequences. If will is measured by volume, liberal Democrats may regret that they invoked it. Philip Weiss, an idiosyncratic author—he might be called a liberal Clinton-hater—covered, in the *New York Observer*, the pro- and anti-Gore demonstrators that dueled in front of the vice president's residence in December. The energy, he found, was on the Republican side of the street. "The energy was ragtag and ferocious, something wild and ungovernable in the rib cage, something hating government and big media, something romantic and fearful, born in Impeachment or born in 1890." "The Democrats," one Republican told Weiss, "got to hope we don't end up liking this."

If will is to be our political standard, then, since will is ever changing, people and politicians will be encouraged to be fickle. It is no accident that Bill Clinton, who thought Bush could win only by stopping the voting, was the most poll-driven president of recent times. In office he shaped his policies by constantly taking new votes, brought to him by Dick Morris or other breeze-testers.

Fickleness can coexist with injustice and even brutality. Will has had a grim history as an organizing principle of politics in the modern world. Rousseau invoked what he called "the general will" in *The Social Contract*. Poor Rousseau has been held responsible for everyone and everything, from Tocqueville to totalitarianism. I will not try to unreel the gleaming spools of his thought. Maybe there is nothing to unreel and the critic George Saintsbury was right when he called him "a literary man pure and simple[,] . . . a describer of the passions of the human heart, and of the beauties of nature." But it is obvious what politicians on the make can do with a notion like the "general will" and with the claim that they speak for it. The Jacobins made such a claim; both Napoleon I and Napoleon III "proved" their claim to rule by calling and winning plebiscites. The last century was marked by popular despots.

Although my title alludes to him, I will not mention the most charismatic of them, since his mere name ends all thought. There is no need to do so here, as Al Gore and George W. Bush were very far from even Louis Napoleon, much less anyone worse. "[T]o say that 'a whiff of fascism' was in the air," Representative Nadler explained defensively after his original remark, ". . . didn't mean to imply that anyone was a fascist." Surely he was right. There was no danger that the end-game of the election of 2000 would change our political system. But the rhetoric of will might, if indulged, lead us into misunderstanding. We will plod along with the same system we have had for so many years. But we will not know why, and our ignorance will make us unhappy.

MACHIAVELLI IN ROBES?
THE COURT IN THE ELECTION

Frank I. Michelman

I

"The republic's debates cannot be half secret and half free." Thus not Lincoln but Linde—Oregon Supreme Court Justice and noted legal scholar Hans Linde, lecturing in 1988 under the title, "A Republic . . . If You Can Keep It."[1] Events such as Iran-Contra, in which dissimulation or secrecy itself becomes a component of government policy, were making Linde wonder whether we had kept our Republic, or could.

"To whom," Linde demanded to know, "is a government accountable for acts that are meant to be disowned?"[2] He asked his audience to consider which of our constitutional institutions finally must carry the burden of "safeguard[ing] the republic" against subversion by officials taking hidden liberties with the laws.[3] Linde himself thought the "chief burden" must rest with Congress.[4] He also granted the courts an important role, on the ground, among others, that a court has the reputation of always "explain[ing] its conclusions publicly, not advis[ing] in secret."[5] Courts also supposedly are well positioned to provide the "objectivity," the "calm," and the "long-range view" that the country is said most urgently to need in "periods of . . . emergency."[6] Justice Linde, reading the record, expressed his doubt that the courts in fact always had lived up to their theoretical capability of rising above the pressures of the moment, or always would.[7] He did not suggest, as Machiavelli might, that perhaps a saintly judicial detachment from worldly pressures would not always be in the country's interest.

I raise again Linde's question: How far, if at all, may a country's rulers take liberties with that country's laws without undermining the country's republican character? Now let me begin to define my terms. I suppose I need not specify that I mean lowercase republican.[8] I will in due course explain what I mean by "taking liberties." By "the country's laws," I mean what Socrates would have meant: the basic laws, the constitutive laws, the laws that would *make* a country a republic, assuming it were one. Call them "the laws of the republic."

"Ruler" is a bit more complex. In a narrow sense, it means one who claims and is conceded the sovereign power (as I shall call it) to make law—to impose a lawful social ordering by declaring it so regardless of the ordering's rightness or fitness by any external standard and indeed of anyone's opinion of its rightness or fitness. In a more extended but still quite normal sense, the term includes all to whom a country's people look for top-rank political leadership, such as an American president. As the example shows, *leader* rulers need not be *sovereign* rulers. Lincoln claimed a presidential duty to make his own responsible interpretations of the laws of the Republic. He laid no claim as president to any power to make the laws—the highest laws—anything but what in fact they were.[9]

II

If the idea of republican government means anything to us in our own times, it means government under law, government constituted by laws. Not that that is *all* it means. Not that republicanism is coextensive with constitutionalism. No more must all legally constituted governments be republican governments than all basic or constitutive laws need be republican laws—as opposed, for example, to monarchical ones. The point remains that a government cannot be republican *unless* it is a government constituted by laws. Republican politics flow, in republican theory can only flow, from having in place the right kind of basic or constitutive legal order, one that is conducive—and here I speak specifically of a democratic republic—to the kinds of equality, independence, and freedom among citizens that can render them into a body politic that is capable of true, collective self-government under the authorship of all and in the interest of all.[10] Thus the laws of a democratic republic will establish norms of the kind that today we find in constitutional bills of rights, demanding respect for individual rights of speech, association, property, privacy, and civic equality even in the face of the expected, recurrent, popular desires to the contrary.[11] And indeed more than that may be required of democratic-republican laws. To constitute an ongoing process of debate and decision that is both fully and fairly receptive to everyone's view and reliably considerate of everyone's interest, democratic republics arguably must attend to *all* the laws shaping civil society, including those regarding civil associations, families, the economy, trades and professions, work and workplaces, schools, and so on.[12]

All this falls well within the bounds of traditional republican debate. And yet Machiavelli was a republican, and from a Machiavellian standpoint this also must be said: It is when their state is lost that people suffer "the cruelest and most terrifying things"[13]—the state and its order being all that stand between us and domination, between us and chaos, between us and ruin. So when the state that we have is a republican state and what hangs in the balance is the very survival of the laws of the republic—when what is at stake is the very continuation of the practical legal order by which republican politics, government, and statehood are established, conducted, and maintained—then republican leaders may and faithful leaders must, in emergency, take such liberties with righteousness and with the laws as may be necessary and sufficient to secure the survival of the order of the state.[14]

Taking liberties, then, is the Machiavellian expectation at least for certain leaders, the ones he denominates *principi*, princes, and most especially the ones he calls *principi nuovi*, new princes. You might ask what princes can possibly have to do with republics. Machiavelli's answer would be "everything." Princely leaders are those on whom the burdens rest of taking emergency liberties with righteousness and with the laws. You cannot exclude leadership of that category from the history of any enduring republic, or so Machiavelli would have insisted, because no republic persists through time without emergency.[15] That is exactly why the category seems rather comfortably to include at least one revered American republican leader, the one whose name I keep bringing up. Lincoln, a skilled lawyer, took what many contemporaries considered, and many lawyers since have considered, substantial liberties with the laws of the republic. True, his posture was of construing them, not making them. But do you imagine the overriding claims of *salus populi* (or shall we say *salus unionis*) by any chance ever entering consciously into his constructions, possibly bending them? Do you suppose him meticulously declaring, officially and publicly, the extent to which they did? How greatly should we blame him if they did, and he did not?[16]

Lincoln, however, although a lawyer, was not a judge in the courts of law. The question I wish to raise is whether the Machiavellian category of princely leader, or ruler, can possibly extend so far as to include rulers of that kind.

III

Rulers include sovereigns, remember—those who claim and are conceded powers to impose lawful social orderings by declaration, regardless of rightness or fitness or anyone's opinion thereof. If you do not count the Supreme Court among the sovereign rulers of this country, you fail to understand how republican government is practiced here, for better or for worse.[17] Now to concede that high court judges can be sovereigns of a sort—hence rulers of a sort—in a republic is not yet to concede that they are welcome to act in the Machiavellian role of liberty-taking prince. Sovereignty is one thing, princely leadership another, and there may be some deep incompatibility between what republics require of those who rule as judges declaring law and what they, by necessity, permit to those who govern as nonsovereign leaders, à la Lincoln. Eventually, we shall have to sort this out. Until further notice, though, I ask you to set aside the question of a special exclusion of judicial rulers from emergency's demands on rulership in general, as Machiavelli would have them.

You may ask, what prompts this line of inquiry? Why bother with it? Machiavelli is dead—meaning, among other things, that our liberalized and democratized notion of republican government is pretty far removed from his. My questions arise in the wake of the temptation many have felt to explain and even justify the Supreme Court's intervention in the 2000 election by casting the Court in what we neatly may depict as a Machiavellian role. Now by "many," I do not particularly mean me. I am not here on some frolic of my own. I follow distinguished guides, of whom I will mention specifically Judge Richard Posner.[18] In a nutshell, and shorn of the Machiavellian trappings I shall add, the hypothesis—or it would be better to say the speculation—is that the Court may be thanked for having acted in December 2000 to save the country from the mushrooming risk of a chaotic presidential selection process headed possibly for the national disaster of a government bereft of legitimacy. Granted it is I and not Judge Posner who hangs the Machiavellian drapery over this speculation. Still the speculation itself, in substance, was his before I ever brought it up, and of course it is shared by many others.

Those who do speculate over this sort of possible explanation for the Court's actions mean generally, I think, by doing so, to place the actions in a relatively favorable light. At least they counter a view of the actions as having been designed specifically to the end of securing the presidency for the candidate of the Republican Party.[19] Absolution of that kind is not my aim. Neither, however, do I mean to presume any particular malignancy in the Court's actions under a Machiavellian construction of them. I want for now to hold that question open. Ultimately, in any event, I am less concerned with how a Machiavellian construction of the Court's actions should make us feel about it than with how it should make us feel about ourselves as republican citizens. For I believe, as I shall explain, that no imputation of Machiavellian motivations to the Court is plausible without a corresponding imputation to us all as citizens, one that I intend my readers to find unflattering. So it will not be the Court's actions standing by themselves that I shall be asking us to ponder. It will rather be the Court's actions considered together with the public's responses to them and also—as im-

portant—considered together with our own several, innermost private responses to these events.

IV

The *Bush v. Gore* judicial majority may have chosen to make their decisive
intervention in the election lacking anything like settled belief in the bare
adequacy—much less in the compellingness—of the legal grounds put
forth by them to explain their actions. Many believe that it did, and I share
the suspicion.[20]

Had the matter at hand been a court-ordered, statewide recount in an
election, say, of the next governor of Oregon, involving ballot-counting
variations among counties or precincts similar to those in *Bush v. Gore*, I
do not believe that an equal protection complaint would have stood a re-
alistic chance of success before the Supreme Court. It almost certainly
would have been rejected by a majority of the justices who supported it in
December 2000—they being justices who had never shown the slightest
interest in an aggressive, expansive use of equal protection to protect voting
rights (except against "benign" race-conscious districting) and most certainly not in an ostensibly nonracial context of alleged vote "dilution,"
which is what essentially was involved in *Bush v. Gore*.[21]

It is entirely reasonable to believe that the equal protection complaint
succeeded in *Bush v. Gore* only because the following additional factors were
present in that case: first, alarm and anger on the part of some justices at
what they saw as outrageous and dangerously provocative conduct by the
Florida Supreme Court;[22] second, a general distaste on the part of some
justices for the relatively, shall we say, energetic aspects—or we could say
the relatively tumultuous or disorderly aspects—of democracy in action;[23]
third, on the part of some justices, a lack of belief in the ability of Congress,
if and when the Florida imbroglio were to fall into its lap, to see the affair
through to a conclusion that the country could respect; and, perhaps,
fourth—a kind of summation of all of the above—a fear that the country
was headed for catastrophe if someone in a position to do so did not act
very soon to bring the election to a clean and decisive end.

Some will have noticed, perhaps with chagrin, an omission from my list
of possible explanations for the Court's adoption of its equal protection
ground in *Bush v. Gore*. I did not include the possibility that any justice
acted out of a personal desire to secure the presidency for the candidate
of the Republican Party. I want to put that possibility to one side, because
an attribution of such a crudely partisan motive to any of the *Bush v. Gore*
majority would subvert the more benign-looking Machiavellian construction of its conduct that it is my purpose here to explore. What we cannot
overlook, though, is the plain fact of *foreseeable suspicion* of this motive. The

Court's majority surely knew it was inviting such suspicion—members have as much as said so[24]—and *that* fact figures centrally in the Machiavellian construction I shall be offering not just of the Court's actions viewed in isolation but of the Court's implicit transaction with what I shall suggest was a willing country.

The plain fact of foreseeable suspicion figures centrally, as well, in a grave charge brought against the Court, a charge that I want to question, much as I may tend to sympathize with it.[25] The charge is one of breach of trust and resulting reckless endangerment of the social contract by the Court's involving itself *at all* in the election controversy rather than leaving the matter to be sorted out and resolved by Congress.

The country, it is said, relies on its independent judiciary to secure its highest political principles and values—the Constitution's principles and values, the principles and values of the laws of the Republic—against debasement by heedless or wayward occasional political majorities. (In Machiavellian terms, that means securing not only the country's values but also its safety, its endurance through time.) The judiciary, controlling neither the purse nor the sword, has nothing but its reputation with which to back its calls for compliance with the values it asserts in the Constitution's name. That means, specifically, its reputation for political detachment, self-restraint, and perhaps above all candor—for restricting its interventions in social and political life to those the judges both honestly find and expressly declare to be compelled by the law as they find it to be, as objectively as they are able. In other words—so runs the argument—the public's willingness to accept in good spirit the judiciary's demands for compliance with the laws of the Republic will sometimes be all that stands between us and majoritarian tyranny (and, in a Machiavellian view, the devolution to chaos toward which that inexorably leads); and since that willingness is underwritten by nothing except the judicial reputation for a certain kind of probity, then that reputation is a national treasure, an entrustment to the judiciary, never to be squandered or placed at risk.[26] It has seemed to many to follow from this view that as the Supreme Court in December was unable to muster clear and compelling legal grounds for intervention, and considering that it was the election of a president hanging in the balance, and especially considering that the five justices who chose to intervene were the very ones who fairly could have been believed to have strong, personal political preferences for the candidate whose victory was cemented by their intervention, then the Court in all probity and decency should have kept itself out of the matter and left it to be resolved by political means, in the democratically accountable forum having a clear constitutional purchase on it, namely, the Congress.

Even granting all its premises, that seems a hazardous line of argument, standing in need of refinement. (Ought judges, as a general rule, to back off from applying what they, to the best of their abilities although with honest doubts, determine to be applicable law, whenever they can foresee embarrassing or even possibly dangerous public misconstructions of their motives? In *Roe v. Wade,* for example? Or *Brown v. Board of Education?*)[27] But let us for now accept the argument as sound as long as its premises are granted. It charges the *Bush v. Gore* majority with having committed a major abuse of office by the very suspiciousness of their conduct. The complaint is that the Court violated the country's trust by recklessly mortgaging its own future ability to perform effectively that highest of its callings, keeping the laws of the Republic, including the Constitution's guarantees of individual rights, effective against hostile or wayward political majorities.[28]

Is there solidity in this complaint? May the complaint possibly proceed from a misconception of the terms of the Court's implicit contract with the country? I raise the question sharing fully the amazement of many lawyers at the transparent weakness of the legal reasoning of the per curiam opinion in *Bush v. Gore* and the suspicion to which it gives rise that the Court's majority acted in the election in a subjectively lawless and hypocritical way—meaning by "subjectively lawless" that they took their decisive action lacking sincere belief in the compelling force and adequacy of the legal grounds they asserted in justification of it and meaning by "hypocritical" that these are justices who posture as judicially restrained, claiming to believe that nothing can move them to intervene in social and political life but the compulsion of what they take to be true reasons of law.[29] But here is the point—the Machiavellian point—that keeps tripping me up. Hypocrisy is one thing, violation of trust another, and maybe, in this case, the twain do not meet. It is conceivable, or so I want to suggest, that hypocrisy of a certain kind is what the country desires of the Court and has bargained with it for.

Consider some polling data. A CNN-Gallup survey taken during the week following the Supreme Court's decisive action in *Bush v. Gore* asked whether respondents believed the justices' votes were "influenced by their personal political views."[30] Half the sample said they did believe exactly that. To the question whether respondents "agreed with" the decision, again just about half (49 percent) answered no. We safely can suppose a substantial overlap between the half of the sample who disagreed with the decision and the half who believed it was influenced by the personal politics of the judges. Yet when the half who disagreed were asked whether they "accepted" the decision, two-thirds of them (32 to 17 percent) said they did.

What are we to make of such results? What does a person mean by saying she "accepts" a judicial decision she not only "disagrees with" but (probably) also believes to have been motivated more by the personal politics of the judge than by any sense on the judge's part of necessitation by justice or law? One doubts that respondents thought they were being asked whether they meant to abide peacefully and calmly by the decision or rather planned on taking to the streets or running in the halls. Instead they must have thought they were being asked whether they felt some genuine sense of reconciliation with the outcome, as one that legitimately demanded their loyalty. The two-thirds of them who answered yes must have been testifying to their own positive dispositions to embrace a procedural system in which the Supreme Court's word is final because it is—in other words, to treat the Court as a sovereign ruler—and to their own positive readiness, for that reason, to treat the matter of the election as not only officially but also rightfully (if not exactly rightly) settled by the Court's dictate. "Acceptance" then would signify a willingness to place procedure—judicial finality— above the substance of rightness or justice, to honor the system of government by judiciary for its own sake and in its own right.

Let us suppose that in December 2000 a fear was astir in many Americans of a "constitutional train wreck." It is not a wild supposition. Judge Posner, not exactly the most panicky fellow I know and expressly taking care not to overdramatize, speaks of a "real and disturbing *potential* for disorder and temporary paralysis."[31] As he puts the matter, "[W]hatever Congress did would have been regarded as the product of raw politics, with no tincture of justice. The new President would have been deprived of a transition period in which to organize his Administration and would have taken office against a background of unprecedented bitterness."[32]

The implication is that an intervention by the Supreme Court may have been our last best hope of salvation, as it were, from ourselves. I am sure many readers shared that intuition at the time, at least to some degree. But now stop for a moment and think. Why would it be *the Supreme Court* rather than Congress that you would think possessed of a unique ability to put a leash on the country and pull it back from the brink of chaos and disaster? Why would an institutionally insulated body of judges be felt better situated than a politically accountable Congress to dictate an outcome—it was a *presidential election* at stake, let us remember—that a professedly democratic country could accept as legitimate and feel bound in citizenship to follow? According to a standard answer, because of the Court's supposed reputation for legalist impartiality and detachment, its supposed reputation not just for standing above personal concerns and partisan politics but, further, for acting only under felt compulsion of reasons of law as honestly seen by the justices, let the outcome be what it may.

What now easily may take shape in the imagination is a suggestively Machiavellian tale. "Machiavellian" does not mean depraved, and it does not mean wicked, at least not in any simple sense. It does mean a willingness on a ruler's part to do what plainly is against good morals—lie, cheat, bully, break faith, sometimes even kill—when and as required for the safety of the country for whose safety that ruler has assumed responsibility. Especially it means a readiness to do such things under cover of a carefully cultivated, if perhaps always slightly uncertain, reputation of not doing them.

Perhaps American Supreme Court justices shoulder consciously the cares and burdens of rulership—they being, as I have said, undeniably rulers in this country. Perhaps, in December 2000, some justices also—if perhaps not entirely consistently—saw themselves uniquely well positioned to secure the threatened safety and welfare of the country, by virtue of their special reputation, as judges, for standing clear of ulterior motivation and limiting their interventions in social and political life to those required by what they honestly find compelling reasons of law. The justices, I am imagining, think that reputation gives them a special ability and hence a special responsibility to get the ominously rumbling country settled down. If they act now and boldly, they can exploit that reputation to save the country from a thickening cloud of danger.

The oh-so-Machiavellian catch is that the action they will have to take will be in violation of the very sort of probity a reputation for which supposedly is what gives them their special ability to act effectively at all. My imagining—and of course it is only an imagining, although a plausible one in my view—is that what actually propelled the Court to its action in December 2000 is not any conviction that the constitutional guarantee of equal protection requires it but rather is a conviction that the welfare of the country requires it, even if the legal grounds for it are weak and would not otherwise have found favor with the Court.[33] The Machiavellian twist is that justices acting for such reasons would have to hide their true motives so as to make good use of their supposed, reputation-based, special ability to call the country to order. Not that necessity and law are irreconcilable opposites, not that necessity is never itself a legal principle. But it sometimes, as in this case, is not. The justices, I am imagining, could not hope to succeed by going openly before the country to say that although they do not see any sufficiently compelling legal grounds for ordering termination of the judicial recount in Florida and would not have done so but for their apprehension of a looming national disaster, they have decided to do it in order to save the country from the colossal mishap of having the election controversy land in the lap of Congress. To make good use of what they take to be their special power to bring the election to a safe end, the justices rather would have to assert belief in the sufficiency of some politically neutral, legal reason or reasons to impel their decision and their resulting orders.

And what if no majority of the justices in fact held such a belief? In that case, either some would have to dissemble or else the Court would have to forgo the project of rescuing the country from the brink of chaos. And yet the Court is the governmental chamber reputed beyond all others never to act for reasons other than the exact ones its members announce for the occasion, and it is on that reputation that the Court, in this Machiavellian scenario I am spinning out, would be staking its hope of the country's acceptance, as legitimately binding, of its dictate to end the Florida recount, thus awarding the disputed presidency to Bush. Hypocrisy, then, will be the very key to success.[34]

And perhaps even the key to keeping faith with the country, because I want to suggest that the license for hypocrisy may not be confined to the Court's end of the bargain. The country is not stupid, and the justices presumably know that it is not. It was obvious in December 2000, given both the novelty and the surprisingness of the majority's announced legal grounds and the glaring suggestiveness of the "ideological" 5–4 split within the Court, that a large fraction of the country simply was not going to believe it really was those grounds that impelled the Court to its action. Inevitably, lawyers by the hundreds would yell the implausibility of those grounds to high heaven, and millions of listening Americans just as inevitably would be prone—would be positively *aching*—to believe the charges. From the Court's standpoint at the moment of action, does this matter? If it happens, will it in the short run ruin the Court's attempt to dictate a clean and quiet settlement of the election? And will it in the long run detract seriously from the Court's ability to enforce its views of the demands of the Bill of Rights against the contrary popular desires of the moment?

To those questions, I believe we have the answers. Because it *did* happen. Lawyers did yell to high heaven. Their charges were widely gobbled up and, I have no doubt, believed. And the legitimacy of the resolution dictated by the Court appears to have been in no way impaired. Remember those poll results I reported earlier? To me they suggest that the proposition of a breach of faith by the Court with the American people is false. To me they speak of an American people smart enough to know, as every lawyer knows, that it simply is not and cannot be true that judicial actions in big, hot cases such as *Bush v. Gore* are controlled by objectively decidable propositions of constitutional law, impersonally derived by judicial science. They speak of an American people knowing that but basically not caring because what is most important is that our long national nightmare ended,[35] thanks to the Supreme Court's use of a special power we grant it to call the fractious country to order. Judge Posner is on the mark, it seems to me, with his observation that the Court's action was "greeted with relief by most of the nation."[36]

V

The 2000 election cases are special, and what we glimpse in them is a swallow, not a summer. But the experience is nevertheless suggestive. It might not be every country on earth, not even every politically decent country, whose people would quietly have accepted the resolution of a closely contested presidential (or equivalent) election by the dictate of a small body of unelected, nonrecallable judges, not to say judges whose actual impartiality in the matter was seriously doubted by half the population. So a question worth raising is this: When Americans do behave this way—when we submit procedurally to government by sovereign judiciary, when we treat the Supreme Court as right because it is final and not final because it probably is right—why do we, or would we, or (possibly) ought we to comport ourselves in such a way?

One possibility, not lightly to be shrugged off, is that we do it for substantive moral reasons, in the pursuit of justice, as part of a strategy we have for advancing as effectively as possible a particular set of ideals we hold about justice, freedom, and human individual rights. People rationally might believe that a general commitment to leaving the Supreme Court with the last word gives us our best long-run shot at this goal and at holding our politics above some level of decency. You do not have to believe that judicial decision making in big, hot cases is generally impervious to the personal convictions, dispositions, and ideologies of the justices to be willing to bet that a system of partial governance by an independent judiciary will do a more reliable job of effectuating the true spirit of the laws of the Republic than popularly accountable legislative and executive branches would do if left to themselves. You could base such a bet on considerations respecting the training, selection, acculturation, institutional situation, and peer relations of judges while quite explicitly allowing for the certainty of occasional lapses or even conscious ditchings of the law by courts including the Supreme Court. Acceptance of the lapses and the ditchings would be a part of the price you are prepared to pay—along with partial relinquishment of popular control over the laws, assuming you consider that a price—for preserving the Court's general power of rule over the country's politics, which you consider to be on balance good over the long run for the cause of justice and human rights.

There we would have a perfectly plausible explanation for the ready acceptance by Americans of even highly suspect judicial actions, such as *Bush v. Gore* is in the eyes of many. But it must be obvious, in our post-Freudian age, that this may not be the full explanation or even the most important part of it. It could be that what Americans want above all else out of the Supreme Court is assurance that someone is there to bring the country to heel when chaos looms or politics threaten to get out of hand; assurance that someone is there to cut short and bring to practical resolution certain kinds of bitter and divisive social controversy that Americans just cannot bring themselves to believe ordinary democratic politics can manage in a way that people will be willing peacefully to accept—in the words of a well-known Supreme Court opinion, "to call the contending sides of an [intensely divisive] national controversy to end their . . . division by accepting a common mandate rooted in the Constitution."[37] It could be that what Americans most deeply count on getting from the Supreme Court is less "law" than it is "order"—is less law in the sense of true rules and rulings of justice than it is finality and settlement, order pure and simple. Or rather—hypocrisy marching always, after all, to virtue's tune—not order pure and simple but order presenting itself more or less plausibly as justice: not just any old judicially uttered "mandate" but a grave judicial pronouncement of "a mandate rooted in the Constitution."[38]

Insofar as there may be truth in that suggestion, it could mean that the Court in the election cases, far from betraying the trust of the country, gave the country exactly what it most deeply wants and counts on getting from the Court. The suggestion makes it a part of the Court's contract with the country to stand ready to assume a kind of Machiavellian princely role if and when it appears that an act of judicial hypocrisy of the kind I have been envisioning—only, of course, as a matter of speculation—is needed to avert a grave danger to the laws of the Republic.

VI

Justices do not openly engage in politics of the ordinary kind. They are not political leaders; probably few are fit to be, and no one wants them to be. Yet undeniably they serve, quite consciously and openly, as rulers—partial rulers but rulers—in the American Republic. A country is not safe, in Machiavelli's view, with rulers who primly refuse involvement with hypocrisy and worse. To the contrary, Machiavellian good rulers stand prepared to sacrifice *everything* to save the imperiled republic—honor, probity, reputation, even salvation or an honored place in history.[39] Judge Posner thus sounds a distinctly Machiavellian note when, speculating along the lines I have been developing about the Court's role in the election, he offers the view that "judges unwilling to sacrifice some of their prestige for the greater good of the nation might be thought selfish."[40]

Is it the thought, then, that in making such a sacrifice the justices may have done a good and a noble thing? Does ours accordingly become a story with a happy ending for the history of republics, even an inspirational one, and even granting the truth of the darkest suspicions of critics regarding the subjective lawlessness and hypocrisy of the Supreme Court's actions in the 2000 election controversy? Why not, if you accept the Machiavellian view that the worst thing that can befall us is for the laws of the republic to be lost, so that the worst rulers to have are rulers who care so much for personal probity that they will not dare to take liberties with those laws, under the pretense of serving them when that is what will work and is required to save the laws from emergency danger of destruction?

I expect most readers are revolted by such a conclusion, as I am. But why, exactly, do we squirm? It might be simply because we do not believe that an impartial, level-headed, noninflamed observer could reasonably have concluded in December 2000 that Congress could not be trusted to bring the country safely through the election. All this talk of grave danger to the Republic may strike us—it does me—as wild exaggeration of the sort Judge Posner commendably aims to avoid. But still we do have to allow that even the best of princes, acting in the best of faith, will sometimes overreach (just as the view that judicial supremacy helps to guide us closer to full adherence to the Bill of Rights must in all reason make allowance for the certainty of judicial misjudgment and even miscreancy).[41] And if perchance the Court did err and overreach, its deeds in consequence seem mild on the Machiavellian scale. Machiavellian princes carry licenses to kill. No one suffered the slightest scratch or material loss in direct consequence of anything done by the Supreme Court in the election cases.

No, the revulsion I am sure many feel to my Machiavellian story is not a simple disagreement with a particular (supposed) judicial (mis)calculation in December 2000; it is to the whole idea of the Supreme Court assuming a Machiavellian princely role. But probably it is not, I hasten to add, a rejection of the Machiavellian argument across the board. I doubt whether all of us, from the bottoms of our hearts, would reject the argument as it might have applied, say, to some of President Lincoln's actions during the Civil War.[42] What I suggest we feel ourselves rejecting, and rejecting rather vehemently, is the infiltration of the Machiavellian argument into our conception of the role in American life and politics of *the Supreme Court,* the "exemplar of public reason,"[43] the department of government that is specially charged with upholding and exemplifying an ideal of the rule of law that we like to regard as absolutely indispensable from any possible conception of decent, constitutional government. As we might think of putting it, a republic in which there is *no* institutional safe haven for the ideal of the rule of law—a republic in which *no one* can be trusted to uphold it and stand up for it come hell or high water—would not be worth saving anyway.

But a claim of that sort, cast in such terms, would be vaporous and, furthermore, wide open to the charge that it misconceives the rule of law as something apart from a concrete particular set of institutionally supported social practices. It is not. To say that the rule of law prevails in a country is to say something about the way in which that country manages to conduct its political affairs, the manner in which the political institutions and mores in that country lead officials there to dispose over the force of the state. The rule of law does not in real life exist *over and above* a country's basic laws-in-fact, its basic laws-in-practice; it is immanent in them. In a republic, the rule of law is immanent in its laws-in-practice. The survival in a republic of the rule of law, in other words, is contingent on—it is tantamount to—the survival of the laws of the republic.

That being so: If indeed it can happen that those whose special reputation in a country is that of upholding the laws might find themselves, by virtue of that very reputational fact, in a position where they can by some jiggering of the law act to save the laws and their rule from threat of destruction, how could we not wish them to do it? I put the question in that form not because I think I have shown that such in reality was the case with this country in December 2000—I do not—but because I think it nevertheless fairly is raised by reflection on the judicial events of that time and the country's apparent response to them.

VII

The question will not yield to facile answers. Let us consider some.

(1) We might ask who ever licensed members of the Supreme Court to be responsible for the country's safety. It is true that with responsibility may come license and Machiavelli, we said, makes rulers responsible to take liberties when and as required for the safety of the country "for whose safety that ruler has assumed responsibility."[44] But where in the Supreme Court's contract do we find a conferral of responsibility to look out for the country's safety, with which a Machiavellian taking-liberties license might come bound up? Judges in the United States are not the equivalents of biblical judges in Israel; they are not Deborah. Their contract is strictly for securing the country's laws. Why expand that to a license to do what is required to secure the country's safety? Is everyone whom you would think fit to appoint to the former responsibility necessarily someone you would want to entrust with the latter? May the Supreme Court declare war?

Formidable as this objection may look, Machiavelli, at any rate the Machiavelli of my mind, has this objection for lunch. The laws are not a suicide pact, he says. Contract—the constructive meeting of the minds—does not rise above reason; it incorporates it. If public expectations of the comportment of the ministers of the laws position those ministers to save the laws and their rule by jiggering some law, then why not, in all reason and in all contract, have them do it? *Fiat iustitia, ruat coelum.* But *fiat iustitia, ruat iustitia?*

(2) And what, then, of the distinction I drew at the start, between rulership in the sense of sovereignty and rulership in the sense of political leadership?[45] What of the fact that Supreme Court justices, however much they may be rulers in the sense of final declarers of the law, are not rulers in

the sense of political leaders? Standing by itself, that fact cannot supply a reason to deny the Court a Machiavellian license appropriate to the judicial station—to jigger some law in order to save the laws. Rather, to the contrary, it seems to make the issue disappear. Sovereign are those whose declarations of what the law is make it be what they declare. Insofar as that is what Supreme Court justices are and are accredited to be, it seems they could not *jigger* the law if they tried—the law then being whatever they say and just because they say it.

(3) You may say that is not what they are accredited to be. You may say Americans ask their judges only to develop and apply, in a principled and honest way, *preexistent* norms—or at any rate norms emergent from preexistent materials—framed in terms sufficiently general to bear the name of law.[46] In the cruder terms of American vernacular understanding: To develop constitutional law as a judge is not to *make* it as a sovereign ruler but rather is to bend and submit one's own judgments to the word of some *other* sovereign ruler, let us say the People. No judge therefore is accredited as sovereign.[47] And since also none are political leaders, then none are rulers in any sense to which a Machiavellian princely license to take liberties need be annexed.

This is too wooden, too brittle, to work. In the face of sometimes radical, persisting disagreement over the true or correct applications of constitutional-legal norms (to affirmative action, say, or political campaign regulation, or abortion, or religious exemption from regulatory legislation) and, indeed, over the method to be used to ascertain correct applications (original meaning?[48] "translated" for changing social facts?[49] "moral reading"?[50] consonance with contemporary community values?[51]), the country requires, or believes it does, decisive institutional settlements of pending social and political disputes in which constitutional-legal meanings are contested.[52] For fulfillment of this need, Americans look to the judicial hierarchy capped by the Supreme Court, treating the Court's renditions as final. And final is not just for the case at hand. What starts out as the law of the case extends itself to become the law of the land. Increasingly, it seems, in recent years the assumption grows that the Supreme Court's renditions of constitutional law, no matter how debatable and contested, are to be controlling on all other officials.[53] And of course the renditions are irreversible by any political means short of an exceedingly onerous, rarely executable process of constitutional amendment. The Court thus *does* rule. Whatever may have been the Court's own role in gathering such a sovereign role unto itself, the country willingly concedes it. Some think for better and others for worse,[54] but none should be amazed if these acknowledged rulers of the republic come to feel themselves beholden for the general care of its safety.

VIII

Quis custodiet ipsos custodes? Why, *nemo.* Or, to speak more exactly, in our country today the question is misplaced and so can beget no answer.[55] Quite in the Machiavellian republican tradition, our people accept the care of lawgivers who are not them: Founders who lay down the country's basic laws and (or including) high judges who construe the laws and maybe from time to time take such liberties with them as may be required (the judges believe) for their preservation and refreshment. Ultimately, Americans do not demand to be their own rulers.

Acceptance of such arrangements may not be the only rational and reasonable choice open to a democratically and constitutionally minded people. That is a matter under debate.[56] On the evidence of *Bush v. Gore* and its aftermath, it is the choice made by Americans, at least those of our generation. We may not all like this fact or feel proud of it. But why, after all, should anyone here and now take Machiavelli to be worth dredging up, long after his death and that of his particular romanist-inspired political ideas, except as possibly a disturber of complacency and cant? Of course, it is hard to come face-to-face with one's own cant.

NOTES

An earlier version of this chapter was delivered as the 2001 Colin Thomas Ruagh O'Fallon Lecture, University of Oregon, April 9, 2001.

1. Hans A. Linde, "A Republic . . . If You Can Keep It," 16 *Hastings Const. L.Q.* 295, 317 (1989) (7th Francis Biddle Lecture, Harvard Law School, October 17, 1988). Linde drew his title from a reputed remark of Benjamin Franklin's. Franklin, having been asked by an acquaintance what sort of government the Philadelphia Convention had decided to propose, reportedly had replied, "A republic, if you can keep it." For Franklin's remark, Linde cited the Papers of Dr. James McHenry on the Federal Convention of 1787, reprinted in *Documents Illustrative of the Formation of the Union of the American States* (Washington, D.C.: GPO, 1927), 952. See Linde, "A Republic," 296.

2. Linde, "A Republic," at 315.

3. Linde, "A Republic," at 303, 307.

4. Linde, "A Republic," at 326.

5. Linde, "A Republic," at 307–8.

6. Linde, "A Republic," at 323 (quoting Theodore C. Sorenson, *Watchmen in the Night: Presidential Accountability after Watergate* [Cambridge, Mass.: MIT Press, 1975], 126).

7. See *id.*

8. Compare Jack M. Balkin and Sanford Levinson, "Legal Historicism and Legal Academics: The Roles of Law Professors in the Wake of Bush v. Gore," 90 *Geo. L.J.* (2001) (asking us to imagine the reaction had the *Bush v. Gore* majority defended

its election orders by invoking the Constitution's guarantee to every state of "a Republican Form of Government").

9. Thus he claimed a power to abolish slave law in certain regions of the country but only by virtue of a commander-in-chief power invested in him by a law he did not make and claimed no power to alter but considered himself responsible to construe. See Sanford Levinson, "Was the Emancipation Proclamation Constitutional? Do We Care What the Answer Is?" (David C. Baum Memorial Lecture Series on Civil Liberties and Civil Rights, University of Illinois School of Law, April 5, 2001).

10. See, *e.g.*, Ronald Dworkin, *Freedom's Law* (Cambridge, Mass.: Harvard University Press, 1996), ch. 1; Jürgen Habermas, *Between Facts and Norms*, trans. William Rehg (Cambridge, Mass.: MIT Press, 1996), 408–9, 417–18, 437.

11. See Frank I. Michelman, "Law's Republic," 97 *Yale L.J.* 1493, 1504–5 (1988).

12. See, *e.g.*, Habermas, *Between Facts and Norms;* William E. Forbath, "Caste, Class, and Equal Citizenship," 98 *Mich. L. Rev.* 1 (1999); Frank I. Michelman, "'Protecting the People from Themselves,' or How Direct Can Democracy Be?" 45 *UCLA L. Rev.* 1717, 1733–34 (1998).

13. Sebastian De Grazia, *Machiavelli in Hell* (Princeton: Princeton University Press, 1989), 163, 421 (translating and quoting from Machiavelli's "Discursus florentinarum rerum post mortem iuneris Laurentii Medices").

14. See, *e.g.*, De Grazia, *Machiavelli,* at 166, 193.

15. See De Grazia, *Machiavelli,* at 236–37.

16. See Levinson, "Was the Emancipation Proclamation Constitutional?"

17. See *infra* Parts IV–V; Frank I. Michelman, *Brennan and Democracy* (Princeton: Princeton University Press, 1999), 25–29 (explaining that judges make law while deciding constitutional cases); Terrance Sandalow, "Judicial Protection of Minorities," 75 *Mich. L. Rev.* 1162, 1170–72, 1185 (same) (1977).

18. See Richard A. Posner, "Florida 2000: A Legal and Statistical Analysis of the Election Deadlock and the Ensuing Litigation," 2000 *Sup. Ct. Rev.* 1 (2001).

19. See, *e.g.*, Alan M. Dershowitz, *Supreme Injustice: How the High Court Hijacked Election 2000* (Oxford: Oxford University Press, 2001).

20. As I have elsewhere summarized the grounds for it, the suspicion

springs initially from the observation that the justices who cast the pro-Bush votes include all and only the five who are commonly identified as composing the conservative wing of an ideologically polarized Court, and it is girded by certain additional observations: the apparent novelty, contentiousness, and narrowness of the legal grounds supplied for the pro-Bush votes by those who cast them; the apparent difficulty of mapping the judicial votes cast, or the legal issues with respect to which they were cast, onto any cognizable grid of constitutional principles and ideals, or competing sets of them, that independently might explain the Court's division over these issues; and the refusal of the conservatives to heed their liberal colleagues' calls for abstention of the Court from substantial involvement in the election controversy when another branch of government was constitutionally available to resolve it—that branch having the clear institutional advantage, with the choice of a president hanging in the balance, of direct accountability to the electorate. (Frank I. Michelman, "Suspicion, or the New Prince," 68 *U. Chi. L. Rev.* 679 [2001])

21. See Michelman, "Suspicion."

22. See David A. Strauss, *"Bush v. Gore:* What Were They Thinking?" 68 *U. Chi. L. Rev.* 737 (2001).

23. See Richard H. Pildes, "Democracy and Disorder," 68 *U. Chi. L. Rev.* 695 (2001).

24. In congressional testimony, Justice Thomas remarked, "I was only interested in discharging my responsibility as opposed to avoiding it and playing it safe" (see *USA Today,* March 30, 2001, at 7A), and Justice Kennedy said that while it may be "easy . . . to enhance your prestige by not exercising your responsibility," taking such a course has not been "the tradition of our court" (see http://www.usatoday.com/news/court/2001–03-election.htm).

25. See Michelman, "Suspicion."

26. See, *e.g.,* the dissenting opinion of Justice John Stevens in *Bush v. Gore* ("The [action] of the majority of this Court can only lend credence to the most cynical appraisal of the work of judges throughout the land. It is confidence in the men and women who administer the judicial system that is the true backbone of the rule of law"); Ronald Dworkin, "A Badly Flawed Election," *supra,* at 93 ("We must try . . . not to compound the injury to the Court with reckless accusations against any of its members. But those of us who have been arguing for many years that the Supreme Court makes America a nation of principle have a special reason for sorrow"). Compare the congressional testimony of Justice Kennedy not long after the events: "Kennedy said the nation's highest court has 'a language, an ethic, a discipline . . . that's different from the political branch.' The Court builds a reservoir of trust with the public over the years, and it 'draws down' on that trust when it makes difficult decisions, he added," *Des Moines Register,* March 30, 2001 (main news section).

27. For a brief attempt to suggest refinements that might distinguish *Bush v. Gore* from *Roe* or *Brown,* see Michelman, "Suspicion," at 682–85.

28. In his Biddle lecture, Justice Linde recalled the fear of Judge Skelly Wright that "if judges did not stay out of institutional disputes, a 'political backlash' might strike at the courts' powers in the area that he thought most essential, equal protection of the law." Linde, "A Republic," at 322 (quoting J. Skelly Wright, "Judicial Review and the Equal Protection Clause," 15 *Harv. C.R.-C.L.L. Rev.* 1 [1979]).

29. See, *e.g., Bush v. Gore:* "None are more conscious of the vital limits on judicial authority than are the members of this Court. . . .When contending parties invoke the process of the courts, however, it becomes our unsought responsibility to resolve the . . . constitutional issues the judicial system has been forced to confront."

30. The poll was reported at http://www.cnn.com/2000/ALLPOLITICS/stories/12/18/cnn.poll/index.html (site visited Feb. 10, 2001).

31. Posner, "Florida 2000," at 64 (emphasis in original).

32. *Id.* Elsewhere, Judge Posner reportedly said that "the Supreme Court spared us from a constitutional crisis." See Frank Davies, "High Court Trying to Leave Election Decision Behind," *Miami Herald,* May 2, 2001.

33. Note that this is not the same as saying that the Court's equal protection holding was "wrong." See Mark V. Tushnet, "Renormalizing *Bush v. Gore:* An Anticipatory Intellectual History," 90 *Geo. L.J.* 113 (2001) ("I think we can expect to see

... progressives asserting that, as a matter of fact, *Bush v. Gore* was correctly decided. As indeed it was").

34. See Niccolò Machiavelli, *The Prince,* trans. David Wooton (Indianapolis: Hackett, 1995), 54 ("[I]t is essential to know how to conceal how crafty one is, to know how to be a clever counterfeit and a hypocrite"); De Grazia, *supra,* at 296 ("The prince cannot govern as the people idealize his governing. Yet he must appear in that light to them if he is to secure their support to work successfully for their good").

35. See Tushnet, *Renormalizing,* at 125 ("The Democratic variant would have it that the real conclusion of the Court's opinion read, 'Our long national nightmare is over'").

36. See Posner, "Florida 2000," at 46.

37. Planned Parenthood of Southeastern Pennsylvania v. Casey, 505 U.S. 833, 866–67 (1992) (O'Connor, Kennedy, and Souter, J.J.).

38. *Id.*

39. See, *e.g.,* De Grazia, *Machiavelli,* at 156.

40. See Posner, "Florida 2000." Do justices talk to judges? Compare the remark of Justice Kennedy in March congressional testimony referring to the election cases: "Sometimes it is easy, so it seems, to enhance your prestige by not exercising your responsibility, but that's not been the tradition of our court" (http://www.usatoday.com/news/court/2001–03-election.htm). For a less rosy view of the tradition and the consistency of its sway over the Court's conduct, see Lisa Kloppenberg, *Playing It Safe: How the Supreme Court Sidesteps Hard Cases and Stunts the Development of Law* (New York: New York University Press, 2001).

41. See *supra.*

42. See Levinson, "Was the Emancipation Proclamation Constitutional?"

43. See John Rawls, *Political Liberalism* (New York: Columbia University Press, 1995 [1993]), 231–40.

44. See *supra.*

45. See *supra.*

46. See, *e.g.,* Lon L. Fuller, *The Morality of Law* (New Haven: Yale University Press, 1964).

47. See Robert Cover, *Justice Accused: Antislavery and the Judicial Process* (New Haven: Yale University Press, 1975), 132.

48. See Antonin Scalia, "Common-Law Courts in a Civil-Law System: The Role of United States Federal Courts in Interpreting the Constitution and Laws," in *A Matter of Interpretation,* ed. Amy Gutmann (Princeton: Princeton University Press, 1997).

49. See, *e.g.,* Lawrence Lessig, "Fidelity and Constraint," 55 *Fordham L. Rev.* 1365 (1997).

50. See Ronald Dworkin, *Freedom's Law: The Moral Reading of the American Constitution* (Cambridge, Mass.: Harvard University Press, 1996).

51. See Terrance Sandalow, "Constitutional Interpretation," 79 *Mich. L. Rev.* 1033 (1981).

52. See Henry M. Hart Jr. and Albert M. Sacks, *The Legal Process: Basic Problems in the Making and Application of Law,* ed. William N. Eskridge Jr. and Philip P. Frickey (Westbury: Foundation Press, 1994), 1–9; Larry Alexander and Frederick Schauer,

"Defending Judicial Supremacy: A Reply," 17 *Constitutional Commentary* 455, 466–67 (2001).

53. See Mark Tushnet, "Shut Up He Explained," 95 *Nw. U. L. Rev.* 907, 916–20 (2001) (remarking critically on the recent, pronounced emergence of a claim by the Supreme Court to have final, sole authority to declare the legal meaning of the Constitution).

54. The controversy is reviewed in Alexander and Schauer, "A Reply."

55. See John Hart Ely, *Democracy and Distrust* (Cambridge, Mass.: Harvard University Press, 1980), 72 ("No answer is what the wrong question begets").

56. See, *e.g.,* Mark Tushnet, *Taking the Constitution Away from the Courts* (Princeton: Princeton University Press, 1999).

Part Five

FOREIGN
PERSPECTIVES

14

A FLAWED YET RESILIENT SYSTEM: A VIEW FROM JERUSALEM

Shlomo Avineri

For an outside observer, the crisis surrounding the November 2000 U.S. presidential election presented a mixed and contradictory picture. On the one hand, it proved beyond doubt the resilience of the American political and judicial system under difficult circumstances, which easily could have led to an intractable constitutional crisis—if not to something even worse. On the other hand, it brought to light, perhaps more than any crisis since the outbreak of the Civil War, some of the internal tensions, contradictions, and political costs involved in maintaining as a functional system a constitutional order built on eighteenth-century republican—and not democratic—principles. The survival of this system was made possible by grafting on the original constitutional principles ideas of universal suffrage and equality of access to political power in a haphazard and unsystematic way. This grafting has been done through a series of constitutional amendments, creative and innovative judicial interpretations of existing constitutional principles, and subsequent legislation, a panoply of overlapping and sometimes contradictory federal and state laws—all coupled with political pragmatic practices anchored in a two-party system aiming at continuity and avoidance of stasis.

Moreover, it was obvious that the crisis seriously tested some seminal aspects of the separation of powers, the principles of federalism and judicial independence, at both the federal and the state level. In other words, the historical U.S. constitutional achievement—two centuries of constitutional continuity, with just one brutal interruption leading to the Civil War—as well as the limits of this achievement and its costs, stood out in the weeks and months of the crisis.

Adjusting an eighteenth-century constitution to the conditions of the twenty-first century cannot be smooth sailing, and some of the costs—and perhaps even the need to cut corners—became crystallized in such a dramatic fashion because of the high stakes involved and the unavoidable salience of the issues through constant coverage by the mass media. It was a civics lesson of history teaching by example, and obviously many Americans learned more about the arcana of their Constitution during the crisis than in all their civics lessons in school.

The crisis may also have helped to demythologize the U.S. constitutional order and present it, warts and all, to a sometimes befuddled American and international audience. If some of what transpired in Florida could have been expected more in Ruritania and Kaffiristan, the ultimate constitutional way in which the crisis has been resolved are two sides of the same, far from perfect yet functioning system.

This has to be pointed out, because before moving to the critical and problematic aspects laid bare by the crisis to at least one foreign observer, the resilience of the system should not be overlooked. After all, for almost two months the U.S. presidency—the most powerful political office in the world—and its legitimacy hung in the balance. One could not imagine a higher degree of uncertainty in a crucial electoral process; there was no obvious let alone universally accepted exit strategy because of the complexity and the confusingly overlapping sets of problems involved, ranging from theoretical issues of constitutional principles to hanging chads; both sides tried legal, political, and public relations maneuvers that sometimes looked, not only to their adversaries, but also to detached observers, more than questionable; and rhetorical flourishes, sometimes underpinned by learned scholarly opinions, cast aspersions on the very legitimacy of the candidate who might ultimately be declared the winner.

Yet during all this turmoil, the country went about its business normally; its foreign relations and strategic standing in the world were not visibly impaired; and—this is crucial—even under the shadow of a possible constitutional crisis, there was no doubt that eventually the issue would be settled peacefully.

It was so utterly clear that there never was or would be a danger of a coup, a military takeover, an autogolpe, or any other variation of a violent and extralegal intervention in what after all was evidently a flawed and controversial process that even mentioning this fact was considered banal. There could not be a greater compliment to the system than this obviousness of the absence of a violent extralegal alternative.

Yet this is not self-evident—one can imagine even consolidated democracies being shaken to their foundations by such a momentous crisis—as can be seen in the French crisis of 1958. It is as much a victory of the constitutional system as a victory of a political culture where, despite a highly competitive winner-takes-all mentality, an overwhelming consensus about civility, rules of the game (even if found out to be highly flawed), and a common interest not to rock the political boat unnecessarily all suffuse the political sphere, for all its cutthroat mind-set, which does, however, rule out violence and the threat of violence. Few countries could present a similar achievement.

Having said this, the following comments are made from the perspective of an outside observer who detected in the 2000 presidential election crisis some expressions of American exceptionalism in the sense of the U.S. system being fundamentally different from other democracies. I do not aim to hold up an ideal-type, or utopian, model of democracy as a yardstick by which to judge the U.S. system's behavior in the crisis and find it wanting. Yet, per contra, the crisis showed that the U.S. system is far from an ideal system: it is deeply flawed, it functions as an uneasy amalgam of conflicting principles and practices, and Americans should be just as humbled as proud regarding the experience of November–December 2000; they may also want to have second thoughts about offering their patchwork system for universal export. I would like to measure the U.S. system not by an ideal yardstick but by a pragmatic comparison of some of its salient features with what can be considered a common denominator prevalent among consolidated democracies. As mentioned earlier, the U.S. system survived what might have been its most serious challenge since the 1860s; yet its imperfections, flaws, and patent absurdities also became evident as never before. As pointed out by Hegel long ago, a crisis—or a war—brings out the best and the worst in humans and in human social systems.[1]

A REPUBLICAN, NOT A DEMOCRATIC, CONSTITUTION

One of the glaring contradictions apparent in the outcome of the 2000 election is encapsulated in the following figures: Al Gore received about 540,000 more votes nationally than George W. Bush, yet the election was decided in the latter's favor by his victory in Florida by 0.009 percent of the certified votes in that state. Significant numerical gaps between the popular vote and the distribution of parliamentary seats occur, of course, in any "first by the post" system and are endemic to the systems in many of the English-speaking countries that base their voting method on single-member constituencies. It is also part and parcel of the way in which the U.S. House of Representatives is elected and is further exacerbated through tinkering by legally sanctioned gerrymandering strategies. In the British case, the outcome is visible in the underrepresentation and virtual parliamentary marginalization of any third party, specifically, the historical Liberal Party and its current offshoot; in France, a slightly different system marginalizes the National Front. Yet in many cases this is at least partly compensated by runoff elections when no candidate receives an absolute majority in the first round in his electoral district, so that the majority principle is somehow maintained.

But if such consequences of a majoritarian system have serious flaws in a parliamentary one, certainly there is no other democratic society in which an executive president can be elected if he receives fewer popular votes than his major contender.

In the United States it happened only twice before that a candidate who won fewer votes than his rival won the election (in the second of these cases, this had far-reaching consequences regarding the democratic culture of the country: it effectively put an end to Reconstruction in the South). The key to this anomaly, of course, is the Electoral College. The paradox is that until the 2000 election, most scholars and commentators viewed its very existence as a picaresque remnant of little consequence; most voters were only vaguely aware of its existence, and certainly there was little public discussion about its significance.

Yet this apparent anomaly, so clearly evident in the 2000 campaign and dramatically etched in the public consciousness through the vagaries of the Florida recount contest and various court cases, is not a mere antiquated quirk; it goes back to a fundamental principle of the U.S. constitutional system and points to a major internal contradiction within the U.S. political system. While for all practical purposes the United States is obviously a democracy, it is so as an outcome of a long series of accumulated political and juridical practices—but not according to its Constitution.[2] As Chief Justice Rehnquist reminded a somewhat stunned public in an unforgettable obiter dictum during the recount contest, there is no constitutional right in the U.S. Constitution to vote for president.[3] Under the U.S. Constitution, the president is elected by the Electoral College—and the procedures and rules relating to this process are vested under the Constitution with constitutional status and hence are privileged.

Despite appearances, the Equal Protection Clause of the Constitution does not mandate as such the right to vote for president, though it guarantees certain procedures connected with this voting, once such voting, direct or indirect, takes place. Yet the very right to vote for president is not constitutionally entrenched.

At first, this may sound a mere technicality—or far-fetched. Yet this is substantially so in a legal and constitutional sense, and it is deeply anchored in the mind-set and ideology of the Framers. As the *Federalist* as well as the constitutional debates at Philadelphia amply attest, the Founders clearly shied away from a democratic constitution, which was usually identified in the late eighteenth century with mass rule by the poor and the tyranny of the majority. This aversion to the principles of majority rule was further strengthened in the American case by the checks and balances necessary to make thirteen somewhat reluctant and virtually independent republics join "a more perfect Union."

Hence the introduction of an indirect system of electing the president through the establishment of the Electoral College—and the constitutional provision that leaves it to every individual state to decide how to select, appoint, or elect its electors. Until the 2000 election, the consequences of this arrangement were never widely discussed in public and were shared by a mere handful of constitutional lawyers, though the specter of not having a majority in the Electoral College while winning a majority of the popular vote did occasionally haunt one of the contenders in 2000 (paradoxically, it was Gore's experts who were disturbed by this possibility).

Because almost all states follow a winner-takes-all system, the composition of the Electoral College usually reflected a gross overrepresentation of the winner in the popular vote—but usually it did not change (except in the two notorious nineteenth-century cases) the outcome of the elections. Because the winner of the popular vote was also the winner in the Electoral College, albeit with an enhanced majority, the College itself could be viewed as a mere formality, somewhat helping to restore the balance between smaller and larger states (as is the aim, in a different way, of the equal representation of the states in the Senate). Moreover, and somewhat paradoxically, endowing the winner of the popular vote with an enhanced majority in the Electoral College even tended to add extra legitimacy to the eventual winner. So-called landslide victories in recent U.S. elections in which the winner appears to carry all states "except Massachusetts and D.C." are far from being landslides in the popular vote. A minuscule marginal win in the popular vote, if more or less randomly distributed among all states, could create the image of a landslide where none really existed. Moreover, in cases in which there was a strong third-party candidate and the winner achieved only a plurality of the popular vote (as did Clinton in both 1992 and 1996), the winner-takes-all composition of the Electoral College helped to eradicate from public memory the fact that he was basically a minority president.

This is all well known and hardly bothered anyone more than marginally (with the exception of some learned punditry after each presidential election musing aloud but not seriously "whether we really need the Electoral College"). Yet the 2000 election brought out the archaeology of how the United States became a democracy. It is true that the civil rights movement effectively used the Equal Protection Clause to sanction the "one person, one vote" formula. Yet it was only in 2000 that many U.S. citizens realized for the first time that nowhere does the U.S. Constitution empower the citizens to elect the president. The indirect system inherent in the idea of the Electoral College was changed over the course of the nineteenth century by introducing democratic principles into the process by which each state made the election of its delegates to the Electoral College. No longer were electors appointed by state legislators or elected by a limited ballot; they were being elected now by the majority of the voters in each state. In this way, the United States became a democracy. Yet this transformation was never directly anchored constitutionally.

In other words, when it comes to the election of the president, the United States is de facto a democracy, but only de facto. Constitutionally there is no provision that the U.S. president has to be elected by the majority or plurality of U.S. voters. It is the patchwork nature of U.S. electoral and political history that transformed the Electoral College from a mediating institution, expressly devised to guarantee a disconnect between voters and the presidency, into a vehicle of popular democratic decision making. To push the argument even further, perhaps to its limits, it could plausibly be argued that if tomorrow state legislatures would decide to select their electors in a different way (by lot, or by direct appointment by the state legislature according to whatever principles the majority there would find fit, or by the state governor), this may not obviously be overruled by the U.S. Supreme Court as being blatantly unconstitutional. The political process would make such a move rather unlikely, however—but not the Constitution per se.

This may sound far-fetched, yet no other consolidated democracy has such a serious idiosyncrasy built into its system. The reason for this is, of course, that the democratization of the American system happened incrementally, not through revolution or rupture; new wine was poured into old vessels (the French, obviously, did it differently). This nonviolent incrementalism is clearly praiseworthy; yet in Florida in 2000 it exacted its price. Procedures about certification, technical deadlines, and other constraints connected with what could justly be considered purely formal aspects of the process were constitutionally privileged and protected and thus could trump substantive democratic principles such as counting the vote, which did not enjoy similar constitutional guarantees.

FEDERALISM, VOTER REGISTRATION, AND BALLOTS

Most democratic societies have a uniform system of voter registration and use uniform ballots. The U.S. federal system prevents, of course, the use of one uniform ballot across the nation, as elections are held at the same time not only for president but also for the House of Representatives, one-third of the Senate, and a plethora of state officials. Yet the peculiar nature of American federalism as well as the fact that universal suffrage is not anchored in the Constitution create a multilayered system of voter registration and ballots. Again, this was well known and never appeared to raise serious objections; only the closeness of this election, especially in Florida, brought out some of the problems inherent in such a decentralized and nonuniform system.

Most countries that practice universal suffrage have a national, central voter registry. In Israel, for example, the Ministry of the Interior keeps a voter registry that lists every person entitled to vote in national elections. Eligibility to vote is regulated by a number of relatively simple legal requirements: you have to be a citizen of Israel, currently resident in the country, and eighteen years of age on election day. There are no overseas absentee ballots, except for diplomats and sailors on Israeli registered vessels; the only in-country absentee voting is that of soldiers on active duty.

The basis for this National Voter Registry is the latest census, plus changes (deaths, coming-of-age, change of address, and addition of new citizens through immigration and naturalization), and it is updated on an annual basis. According to the Election Law, at a set date before an election, each voter receives by mail a notice from the National Election Commission that includes personal data, confirms that he or she is entitled to vote, and provides information about the location of the assigned polling station and the person's place on the polling station's list of voters. In the event a prospective voter does not receive this notice, ads in newspapers and on radio and television inform voters where they may check or file a claim to be added to the voter registry.

As Israel is a highly wired society, since the last election this National Voter Registry has also become accessible online at the National Election Committee Website (www.elections.gov.il). On logging in one's name and ID number, the voter's registration data and the relevant polling station information appear on the screen and can be downloaded.[4] Nothing of this sort exists in the United States. Voters have to register on their own, which obviously disadvantages the weaker sectors of society—those who do not have access to cars, who do not follow public announcements, who do not frequent public institutions such as schools, courthouses, or churches, who may have difficulty establishing a fixed, legal residence, or who may not be fully literate. That registration procedures also vary from state to state adds further complications, difficulties, and inequalities.

The result is a clear class bias, so that almost 30 percent of people who are entitled to vote usually do not register. This has been commented on frequently, but both major parties have their own, divergent yet parallel interests in not creating a national voter registry.

To this one should add the traditional American suspicion, common to both Left and Right, of anything that may look like a Big Brother databank of all citizens. However, both parties seek to register, under party auspices, potential voters who may be likely to vote for the party organizing the registration drive. This, of course, highly politicizes the process of voter registration—which, after all, should be a neutral, politically blind bureaucratic process. In the specific context of the United States, voter registration drives are also race connected. Registering as many blacks as possible (who tend to be underregistered) is one of the main election campaign mechanisms of the Democratic Party.

This is a serious flaw in a process that should be universal and as politically neutral as possible. What became clear in the 2000 election was that in a southern state like Florida, especially in some of the rural counties, some remnants of Jim Crow practices appear to have made it even more difficult than usual for some blacks to have equal access to the process of registration and then actually vote.

Another aspect of the same flaw is the lack of a legally binding universal mode of voter identification at the polling station. There is no national ID document in the United States—because of the same aversion to anything even slightly reminiscent of Leviathan or Behemoth. While drivers' licences are usually considered an adequate substitute, this is not universally so. There is enough evidence to suggest that in some middle-class neighborhoods no great care is taken to establish a voter's identity: you walk in, give your name, and if you appear on the list, you usually will be given the ballot. One can imagine that in some rural southern counties, first-time black voters, who have only recently registered, may be held to higher standards of identification. That many of these poor, rural blacks may not possess a driver's licence underlies some of the dilemmas and resulting inequalities involved.

The introduction of a national ID card would obviously overcome these problems—and even if some of the problems are just imaginary, perception counts. Again, to bring an Israeli example: the only valid identification document at the polling station is the national ID card. A few weeks before the elections, Interior Ministry ads in the media remind voters that they should bring their ID cards with them to the polling station. If the cards have been lost or mislaid, voters are urged to apply for a substitute at the local offices of the Interior Ministry, which in the weeks leading to the elections are open extra hours and hire extra temporary staff.

There is no doubt that the lack of a uniform national voter registry, the consequent need for party-led registration drives, and the haphazard and nontransparent manner of registration and identification at the polling station created disparities in access to actual voting and became crucial in some of the contests about recounts in Florida.

Another aspect of the piecemeal extension of voting rights in the United States, as well as the underlying salience of states' rights in American federalism, is the lack of a uniform ballot or at least nationally binding guidelines for the ballot format, which could then be adapted to local needs incorporating the specific election campaign in each state or county. Alternatively, at least each state could follow uniform practices in devising its own ballot format. The situation in which each county decided on which ballot to use, and what kind of voting machine, created the discrepancies between the rate of overvotes and undervotes in different Florida counties. It was this fundamental diversity—utterly unknown in other democracies—that gave rise to the contentious and confusing "butterfly ballot" used in Palm Beach County. There is no doubt that the disproportionate strong showing for Patrick Buchanan in a county with a large Jewish population was the outcome of this not very helpful ballot, that it complicated the possibilities of a reliable recount, and that it was ultimately one of the determining factors in the election outcome.

Most of the criticism in the media and by political and legal commentators focused on the format of this ballot; few comments addressed the fact that the basic issue was the lack of uniform, universally binding guidelines or standards for ballots.[5] It is highly unlikely that the objection in principle to uniform ballot formats will disappear, and constitutionally there is probably no way to enforce it. Yet there is no doubt that the lack of uniform standards greatly impeded equality before the law and distorted voting significantly.

A similar flaw was caused by the use of different types of voting machines. The old, manual punch-card machines used in some of the problematic Florida counties were just an example of the electoral consequences that this lack of uniformity in what is not a merely technical matter entailed.

Most countries of course use one ballot format. In the Israeli case, paradoxically, while voter registration is done electronically and is available online, voting itself is done the old-fashioned way—by paper ballots, manually counted. It surely does not compare with the sophistication of some of the varied methods used in American voting; but results are easy to check, recounts can be done quickly, no great discrepancies appear, and results from all polling stations are available within a few hours after the polls close.

Furthermore, as the Florida selective recounts proved, different types of voting machines cause highly differentiated ratios of both overvotes and undervotes. Where modern electronic equipment was available, the margin for possible voter error and hence possible invalid votes was obviously lower. A closer scrutiny of Florida counties showed that the richer (mainly Republican) counties used modern, electronic equipment, while poorer (mainly Democratic) counties still used the antiquated machines that created so much havoc and were the center of attention of a befuddled national electorate that became deeply engrossed in the arcana of hanging, dangling, and pregnant chads.

Again, it is the peculiar nature of U.S. federalism that is the cause of these discrepancies, since responsibility for the conduct of elections is not federal but is vested in the states, which delegate responsibility to the counties. This also means that funding is locally based, which again means that richer counties can afford better and more accurate machines. This is a clear class-based bias in favor of residents of richer areas having a better chance that their votes will be adequately counted than those in poorer areas. This is, of course, not the intent of this highly decentralized system: it is, however, an inescapable consequence of it.

All this leads back to a basic flaw—and idiosyncrasy—of the U.S. system: the Federal Election Commission deals mainly with campaign funding, not with the conduct of the election or with setting down uniform rules for voting procedures. As a member of a number of international teams of observers under the auspices of the U.S. National Democratic Institute (NDI), I have participated in a number of election observation teams in postcommunist countries. One of the first issues we raised was the uniformity of election rules and procedures and the integrity of the ballot. What is self-evident for Americans when trying to guarantee elections abroad is not practiced at home.

NATIONAL ELECTION COMMISSION

The lack of a national election commission enforcing uniform norms was clearly visible during the drawn-out period of the recount and contest in Florida. The transparency of the process was greatly vitiated by the lack of such an impartial authority, and it might have contributed to the aura of illegitimacy that accompanied some of the maneuvers involved in the process of certification of the Florida vote.

One of the surprising aspects of the American system as it transpired during the controversy over the Florida vote was that the U.S. Constitution ultimately leaves certification of federal election results in the hands of state officials, themselves politically elected and partisan. That election results would be certified, as they were in Florida by Secretary of State Katherine Harris, a party activist who was also co-chair of the Bush campaign in Florida, would be unthinkable in any democratic society.

The composition of a national election commission, where it exists, as it does in most democratic societies, varies from country to country: it is, however, a mix of public servants, judges, representatives of the contending parties and candidates, and members of other public bodies. To go back to the Israeli example, the National Election Commission is, by law, made up of representatives of the parties as proportionally represented in the outgoing Knesset (plus observers of new parties not yet having parliamentary representation). This commission is presided over by a Supreme Court justice; the full commission lays down general principles, and the chair rules on matters of procedure or legal interpretation. These decisions are open to appeal before the Supreme Court (there are subsidiary regional commissions, with a parallel composition). The National Election Commission has a permanent skeleton staff of Interior Ministry officials, and during elections they are assisted by additional public servants, seconded from other ministries, for a limited period.

That so much of the anger at Katherine Harris's performance was ill placed, malicious, and sexist is repulsive; yet the very role given to her under the U.S. Constitution harks back to predemocratic periods of the American polity. Under normal circumstances, it would be a mere formality—as it was even in 2000 in virtually all the other states. But in a close and contested election, as in Florida, the price paid for constitutional continuity is clearly exposed: the formal and substantive aspects of the American system were clearly divorced from each other. The anomalies thus created have tended this time to bring the system to the abyss and to the brink of a crisis of legitimacy. The resilience of the system eventually overcame its flaws—yet at a very high cost.

INDEPENDENT COURTS? SEPARATION OF POWERS?

Perhaps the most egregious aspect of the Florida recount became the role of the courts. It is a truism of the democratic ethos that regardless of the voting system, the way votes are ultimately counted will be, in the case of a contest, laid at the door of an impartial judicial system that serves as the final arbiter of what is legitimate and what will pass as legal and valid. In the U.S. context, this is in theory apparently enhanced by the doctrine of the separation of powers and the constitutionally guaranteed independence of the judiciary. Again, as a veteran observer for NDI, I can point out that the existence of such an impartial court was always one of the first questions asked in any case of an internationally sponsored observation mission.

It was perhaps this notion that became the main victim of the way in which the 2000 presidential election was ultimately settled by the U.S. Supreme Court. If some of the practices of local and state Florida officials occasionally could be attributed to the usual partisan skullduggery, the way in which the Florida circuit courts, then the Florida Supreme Court, and ultimately the U.S. Supreme Court handled the issues cast a deep—and perhaps lasting—shadow on the notion that the American judicial system is what is professes to be.[6]

Without going into the details of the various decisions handed down by the different courts, which are discussed elsewhere in this volume, the following is clear: this is not the way the U.S. legal and constitutional theory likes to present the American judiciary.

That American federal and state judges and justices are appointed by a process that is not, nor can it be, totally free from political considerations is an inevitable outcome of the procedures prescribed by the U.S. Constitution (and by various state constitutions), as well as by the political practices that evolved within that legal framework over generations. The raucous and confrontational hearings before the Senate and the noisy public debate that accompanied some recent nominations, such as those of Bork and Thomas, only exacerbated the ideological and partisan nature of the process and its perception as such by the public. Yet for all of this partisanship, which the U.S. public takes for granted, one could argue that most observers would still like to believe that while justices and judges could be categorized as "conservative" or "liberal" on most of the contentious ideological issues (such as abortion or prayer in school), when confronted with issues that are of utterly political significance yet also highly technical, relating to election certification, recounts, and so on, they would not vote along discernibly party lines.

Yet this was not the case in the Florida contest. First, when any issue came up before the courts—from Tallahassee through Atlanta to Washington, D.C.—the judges and justices involved were immediately identified according to what could be known about their political sympathies by the simple device of reminding the public by whom they were appointed (a Democratic governor, a Republican president, etc.). Moreover, in choosing which court to approach (in those cases in which such a choice was available), both contending sides decided their strategy along considerations drawn from the known or supposed political preferences of the judges or justices in question, as based on their appointment history and their known previous ideological preferences as expressed in decisions handed down by them in the past.

Yet it was not only the public's or the lawyers' perceptions, but the ultimate outcome, that was so problematic both on the state and federal levels. With a few minor exceptions, the Florida Supreme Court, overwhelmingly appointed by previous Democratic governors, tended to favor Gore on issues of deadlines, mandating recounts in heavily Democratic counties, and so on. Even more egregious were some of the maneuvers in the U.S. Supreme Court, when the conservative majority engaged in a series of tactical moves that could only be called underhanded and that made an ultimate Republican victory unavoidable eventually, on the basis of formal decisions that succeeded in avoiding the democratic substantive issue ("Count the votes"). In all fairness, the liberal minority took the same approach—only they lost. A 5–4 vote in the Supreme Court, so clearly divided along political lines, makes a travesty of judicial impartiality and independence. Furthermore, it could be argued that the December 9, 2000, decision to stop the vote, and Justice Scalia's justification of it, created an effective time trap, motivated by partisan considerations as much as by constitutional logic. It was this time trap from which Gore's lawyers could not extricate themselves, and the foreordained conclusion then appeared as the apotheosis of the December 12 per curiam opinion. Q.E.D.

In this politicized process, conservative justices of the U.S. Supreme Court privileged federal power over states' rights, and some liberal justices became the staunch supporters of the primacy of states' rights. Such an inversion of ideological positions in order to reach partisan, politically desired goals was transparent, especially when the ultimate decision of the U.S. Supreme Court was based on a technical impediment created earlier by the same Court itself. By putting the Gore campaign against a time constraint created by its own previous decision, the Court majority acted not as objective arbiters but as partisan supporters. For the august U.S. Supreme Court to decide in this way by a majority of one was, to say the least, a great disappointment for all who looked up to the highest court in the land of the free and the home of the brave.

THE MEDIA

The role of the media has been extensively discussed during and after the drawn-out contest. There is no doubt that whatever flaws the system produced were gravely exacerbated by the minute and continuous coverage focused on them by the media and the constant barrage of news, comment, spin, and hype involved in what was certainly one of the most dramatic events in modern electoral history. The twists and turns of the story, unexpected and constantly changing, added a dramatic dimension that made this one of the best political thrillers ever to have been produced. If composed by a fiction writer, it would have been dismissed as totally lacking in credibility.

Much attention was drawn to the way the major television networks "called" Florida twice—first for Gore, then for Bush—and how the second "call" established a presumption of victory for Bush that made Gore appear the contester of an outcome that was far from decided; this also sometimes made Gore look like a spoiler whose attempts to achieve an adequate recount could be presented as verging on the illegitimate. In a situation of great volatility and an obviously very close vote, television's proclaiming Bush the winner framed the subsequent discussion as between a president-elect and a challenger.

Yet a situation in which the media call an election before most of the votes, let alone all of them, have been officially counted is now more or less universal; unless the vote is very close, exit polls turn out to be a reliable predictor. But the closeness of the Florida vote made the early calling of the state for Bush more problematic, and it is obvious that the organizational changes the networks will in all probability make in the future in their methodology (especially in not relying on one analytic source) are greatly welcome.

One issue, though, deserves special attention—because it epitomizes a clear clash between the principle of fair reporting and the constitutionally privileged position of free speech in the U.S. context. This is the issue of the networks first having called Florida for Gore when voting was still going on in some counties of Florida's western panhandle, where the polls close an hour later because the counties are in a different time zone. This raises, of course, the wider issue of calling states when elections are still in progress in the western states: voters there may be—or may feel—at a disadvantage and may be discouraged from going to the polls when it appears that the election has already been decided on the East Coast and in the Midwest. The time zones spanning the American continent certainly present a unique problem for which there is no obvious or easy answer.

Most democratic countries are in one time zone, and hence it is easier to try to regulate the way exit polls are broadcast. The general rule would be that the law prohibits the broadcasting of exit polls when the election is still going on. Some countries even prohibit by law publishing public opinion poll results during a designated time immediately before the elections (twenty-four or forty-eight hours). Again, let me refer to the Israeli example: in Israel, all polling stations all over the country close at the same hour, 10:00 P.M.; media sample exit polls (which usually cover about 10 percent of the polling stations) close one hour earlier, at 9:00 P.M., and the polling organizations of both television channels have one hour to work out their calculations. At 10:01 P.M. both channels broadcast the expected results as based on their exit polls and pronounce the winner. In the last two decades, they have been wrong only once, in a very close election, and within the statistical margin of error their estimates have proven accurate as to the distribution of votes and seats in parliament as well.

Announcing the winner in Florida before all polling stations in the state closed was obviously a serious intervention by the media in the electoral process; whether it did or did not affect the final result, eventually so close in Florida, is beside the point. But the absolute protection of free speech under the Constitution makes it extremely difficult, probably outright impossible, to pass legislation that would prohibit a repeat of such an occurrence. Voluntary self-restraint can be an effective substitute and may indeed be achieved next time in the specific case of Florida's two time zones; yet while the major networks may reach an agreement on this, policing it on the Internet may turn out to be difficult.

IN LIEU OF CONCLUSION

The argument I have tried to develop in this analysis is that the Florida case in the 2000 presidential election was not just a freak case or a road accident; its main facets are systemic and deeply anchored in American exceptionalism. Perhaps with the exception of the United Kingdom, the United States is the only modern democracy where universal suffrage is not anchored in a basic, more or less coherent founding document. It is made up of a hodgepodge of incremental changes grafted on a Constitution that while republican is not democratic in the normative and institutional sense. In most cases, the seams of this patched-together garment are not visible and the system works more or less in an orderly fashion.

When the margin of victory is wide, a few thousand overvotes or undervotes caused by faulty machines and other consequences of the lack of a uniform election code do not make much of a difference. But when the margin narrows—as it eventually did in Florida—to a few hundred votes deciding the presidency of the United States in a system whose procedures developed in an eighteenth-century indirect system anchored in an Electoral College trumping the popular vote, which is not equally protected under the Constitution, then the splendid multicolored coat of the American polity was almost torn. Certainly it became clear that it is not as neat as the American self-image would like it to appear.

Given American federalism and the ingrained American aversion to government-regulated overall structures, it is unlikely that a national election commission, regulating through uniform norms voting procedures and certification, let alone voter registration, is likely to emerge. Yet in a well-tried American method of using the powers of the purse to eliminate at least some of the glaring inequalities (in funding, availability of identical equipment, etc.), some tinkering with the system may help to produce not a more perfect Union but at least a less uneven one.

APPENDIX

Printout of Voter's Data, National On-Line Voters Registry,
Israel 2001 (translation)

SPECIAL ELECTIONS FOR PRIME MINISTER, 2001

Enquiry results

PERSONAL DATA:

ID NUMBER: 043000983
FAMILY NAME: Avineri
FIRST NAME: Dvora
FATHER'S NAME: Jonah

POLLING STATION DATA:

POLLING STATION: 407.0
NUMBER ON POLLING STATION LIST: 0015
POLLING STATION ADDRESS: 15 Kovshei Qatamon Street
CITY: Jerusalem
LOCATION: Horev Elementary School
HANDICAPPED SPECIAL ACCESS AVAILABILITY: None

Click here for map of area of Polling Station

NOTES

1. For a collection of some of the salient op-ed pieces, legal commentaries, and court decisions regarding the crisis, see E. J. Dionne Jr. and William Kristol, eds., *Bush v. Gore* (Washington, D.C.: Brookings Institution Press, 2001).

2. Even a political theorist of the stature of Harvey J. Mansfield did not apparently find this significant enough to be mentioned in his defense of the U.S. Supreme Court ruling in *Bush v. Gore*. See his "What We'll Remember in 2050," *Chronicle of Higher Education,* Jan. 5, 2001.

3. The Florida Constitution (Art. I, § 1) does declare that "All political power is inherent in the people," yet even the Florida Supreme Court found it difficult to construe from this a federal constitutional right to vote for the U.S. president. See Palm Beach County Canvassing Board v. Harris, 772 So.2d 1220 (Fla. 2000).

4. See Appendix for the English translation of one voter's data for the February 6, 2001, election for prime minister.

5. *E.g.,* Ronald Dworkin, "The Phantom Poll Booth," *New York Review of Books,* Dec. 21, 2001.

6. Gore v. Harris, 772 So.2d 1243 (Fla. 2000); Bush v. Gore, 121 S. Ct. 512 (Dec. 9, 2000); Bush v. Gore, 121 S. Ct. 525 (Dec. 12, 2000).

15

CONSTITUTIONAL COUNCIL REVIEW OF PRESIDENTIAL ELECTIONS IN FRANCE AND A FRENCH JUDICIAL PERSPECTIVE ON *BUSH V. GORE*

Noëlle Lenoir

At a time when the market economy is on the way to dominating the world, some people are announcing that ideologies are dead and that politics is being ousted by economics. Is this prophecy becoming a reality? There are good grounds for doubting it, considering the excitement that political elections continue to generate in the life of a country. Admittedly there is a general tendency for the abstention rate to rise from one election to the next, although this tendency is appreciably lower in Europe than in the United States. And the younger generation's lack of interest in public life is a genuine source of concern. But let us not be misled: national and even local elections are still the high points in the life of a democracy. This is when the citizens get to choose who will represent them (in France, as deputy, senator, or president of the Republic) or what team (municipal, general, or regional council in France;[1] parliamentary majority), once in place, will have the responsibility of directing the life of the national or local community to meet the aspirations of the country. It is when the citizens choose their political leaders, whom they can then call on to "give an account of their administration."[2]

The right to vote is at the core of democracy. It is the vector through which the people's will is expressed, this "general will" that in the view of Jean-Jacques Rousseau could never do wrong. Conceived as the base for national sovereignty, the general will has a quasi-religious status in France. The right to vote, in France as elsewhere, is the source from which all other rights flow. At the end of the nineteenth century, the United States Supreme Court held that "The right of suffrage is a fundamental political right, because preservative of all rights."[3] In the same spirit, the Constitutional Council (as France's supreme constitutional court, which is the only tribunal that can adjudicate constitutional issues, is called) today ranks

"pluralism in ideas and opinions" among the constitutional objectives forming the "basis for democracy."[4] Without the possibility of access to a wide
range of political opinions there can be no free and enlightened choice by
the voter, guaranteeing the democratic exercise of the right to vote.

Under the current French Constitution, dating from 1958, three principles guarantee the democratic character of the right to vote. The first is
equality of voting rights. "One person, one vote" is the motto of modern
democracies. Irrespective of social or ethnic origin, marital status, or income, each person's vote carries the same weight. The second principle, a
corollary of the first, is the universality of voting rights. No category whatsoever can be excluded from the right to vote: the poor, or women, for
example. Let us recall in passing that the principle of universality applying
to the whole of society took much longer coming in France than in most
other European countries. It was only toward the end of the war, by an
ordinance of General de Gaulle's Provisional Government of April 21,
1944, that French women were given the right to vote.[5] The third principle
relating to the right to vote, anchored in the French political and legal
culture for a long time now, is the secret ballot. In ancient Rome, whose
legal system influenced France so heavily, voting was public in accordance
with a partly aristocratic concept of politics. The least powerful voters were
supposed to accept the influence of their elders and betters. But in this
respect France did not follow Rome's example, and already in the Middle
Ages the principle of the secret vote was adopted for the designation of
certain deputies representing the Third Estate.[6] Voting booths, a practice
first used in Australia at the 1856 elections in the state of Victoria, constitute a formality now made mandatory by the Electoral Code. And the secret
vote is not only intended to protect voters against the possibility of pressure.
Its significance is broader. It means that voting is the expression of a truly
free choice, deferring to a liberal vision of the relationship between the
citizen and politics. This design always prevails, even if, in France as elsewhere in Europe, voters' minds nowadays are made up primarily by party
machines, far more highly structured than in the United States. The introduction of the secret vote on the Australian model (with voting booths)
could at certain times and in certain countries be deflected from its true
aim, as it was, for example, in the southern United States to restrict the
black turnout in the elections of 1888.[7] But in France the voting booth
genuinely protects the constitutionally entrenched freedom of the vote. In
the event of failure by a sufficient number of voters to comply with the
obligation to use voting booths, the electoral court considers whether this
breach of the Electoral Code may or may not have influenced the outcome
of the ballot. In the affirmative, it can go as far as to annul the votes cast
at the relevant polling station.[8] Clearly, then, the principles stated by Article
3 of the French Constitution of 1958, namely, that "Suffrage may be direct

or indirect as provided by the Constitution. It shall always be universal, equal and secret," are at the core of electoral litigation.

In France, it was not always for the courts to enforce the principles of electoral law. In local elections judicial review has for a long time been exercised by the administrative courts, the highest of which is the Council of State.[9] With regard to national and more particularly parliamentary elections, however, the tradition until 1958 was, as in the United States, to allow Parliament itself to certify that its members had been properly elected. After each general election, for instance, the National Assembly[10] would check the validity of the election of deputies (elected by direct suffrage), and after each senatorial election the Senate did likewise for senators (elected by indirect suffrage by a college of "grand electors").[11] Just as the American Constitution (Art. I, § 5) provides that "Each House shall be the judge of the Elections, Returns and Qualifications of its own Members," so successive Republican constitutions of France provided that "The legislative body alone shall rule on the validity of operations of the primary assemblies" (Constitution of 5 Fructidor, Year III, Art. 23, under the Revolution), that "Each House shall be the judge of the eligibility of its members and of their proper election; it alone may receive their resignation" (Constitutional Act of July 16, 1875, Art. 10, of the Third Republic), and that "Each of the two Houses shall be the judge of the eligibility of its members and of their proper election; it alone may receive their resignation" (Constitution of the Fourth Republic, October 27, 1946, Art. 8). The country that symbolizes the parliamentary system in its purest form—the United Kingdom—abandoned this procedure of "verification of credentials" by the houses of Parliament in the nineteenth century and transferred electoral litigation to the ordinary courts.[12] But it seemed out of the question for France ever to give up a system that clearly illustrates the primacy of the political over the legal, a dogma that is so dear to French culture. Yet the profound changes introduced by the 1958 Constitution succeeded in doing away with this procedure, which had admittedly come under serious strain several times in the Fourth Republic. Certain decisions of the National Assembly, manifestly partial and unjust, had greatly shocked public opinion and provoked reactions in the press.[13] So the authors of the Constitution of 1958 decided to assign to a court—the Constitutional Council—responsibility for settling litigation surrounding parliamentary elections.[14] The Council was also given jurisdiction to oversee referendums. Referendums, like the Constitutional Council itself, are among the great innovations of the 1958 Constitution that testify to the scale of the institutional changes made by it. By conferring on the Constitutional Council the jurisdiction of an electoral court (and more besides, as will be seen), the 1958 Constitution exemplified here as elsewhere the reduction in the powers of Parliament. The concept of "rationalized parliamentarianism" is commonly used to reflect the predominance of the executive branch over the legislative branch that is the leading feature of the current political setup in France. The aim of "rationalizing" parliamentarianism was in this case fully attained; Parliament saw itself not only as dispossessed of the power it had in previous Republics to check the status of its members but also as subject to competition in the exercise of its legislative power by the possibility henceforth offered to the people to enact legislation directly by way of referendum.[15] In accordance with the will of General de Gaulle, the chief inspirer of the 1958 Constitution, the people were thus rehabilitated. In particular, there was an end to the "exclusively party-based system" to which de Gaulle attributed the serious failures of French politics (in particular, the fact that from the 1950s, successive governments of the Fourth Republic were unable to resolve the Algerian crisis). Curiously enough, constituent assemblies in France and the United States proceeded from the same aim of avoiding giving an excessive influence to the political parties to establish radically different electoral systems. As Bruce Ackerman shows in chapter 10 of this volume, the fear that the party system might be abused was behind the system whereby the president of the United States is elected by grand electors designated by each state and capable of filtering the popular vote: "The prevailing ideology regarded political parties as dangerous, and it seemed risky to allow them to engage in demagogic campaigns in support of their presidential favorites. Why not trust the legislature to select men of probity who might wisely cast the state's electoral votes without populist pandering?" In France, the best antidote to the reign of the political parties seemed, on the contrary, to allow the people to express their views directly ("national sovereignty," which "belongs to the people," is "exercise[d] . . . through their representatives and by means of referendum," according to the first paragraph of Article 3 of the Constitution of 1958) and at the same time to withdraw the power to review elections from the houses of Parliament and entrust it to an independent, impartial body, the Constitutional Council.[16]

But the political change brought about by the Fifth Republic was far from completed in 1958. The institution of the election of the president of the Republic by direct universal suffrage in 1962 is an equally important date in the constitutional history of France.[17] With this reform, France reverted to a certain tradition of allegiance to a charismatic leader in direct contact with the people and officially in charge of its destiny. De Gaulle had never hidden his distaste for the previous Republics, in which the president—exercising symbolic rather than real powers—was designated by the two houses meeting together. In a speech at Bayeux on June 16, 1946, which is regarded as expressing his constitutional doctrines, he argues that "From a bicameral Parliament exercising the power to enact legislation, it goes without saying that the executive power cannot proceed without running the risk of creating a confusion of power in which the government would soon be no more than a bundle of delegations." In 1958 the first step was taken toward making the president of the Republic less dependent on Parliament and political parties represented in it. The Constitution provided for a president of the Republic no longer elected by Parliament but by a broad-based college including the members of Parliament and a number of elected local representatives (80,000 grand electors in all). Three years later, the last stage of the process was launched: de Gaulle decided to put to a referendum a constitutional bill[18] providing for the election of the president of the Republic by direct universal suffrage. In his last address before the referendum, on October 8, 1962, de Gaulle stated the issue clearly: "If you answer No, as the old parties would all like you to so that they can restore their terrible system and all the faction leaders would like so that they can set out on their subversive paths, or if there is a majority Yes vote, but a weak, mediocre, unreliable one, it is obvious that my term of office will immediately and irrevocably expire."[19] He did not have to carry out his threat; the reform was approved by nearly a two-thirds majority. The reform in question gives the Constitutional Council the power to certify the regularity of the presidential election, with wider and especially more diversified powers than those it possesses regarding general or Senate elections. With respect to the latter, the Council exercises the traditional jurisdiction of an electoral court. When deciding on a referral concerning the election of a member of Parliament, the Council can declare the election invalid several months into the member's term of office, well after the new Parliament has opened, if it finds that irregularities or fraud has affected the fairness of the ballot. With regard to presidential elections, it does not act solely as a court but also as an administrative authority. It monitors the whole chain of electoral operations from the beginning of the preparation of the instruments organizing the election to the declaration of the final results and the name of the elected president. Article 58 of the Constitution is explicit: "The Constitutional Council shall ensure the proper conduct of the election of the President of the Republic. It shall examine complaints and shall declare the results of the vote." This role of guarantor of the proper course of electoral operations entrusted exclusively to the Constitutional Council underlines the fundamental difference in inspiration between the French constituent assembly and the Founding Fathers of the American Constitution. In the United States, all is done to mitigate the risk of a monarchist tendency connected with a direct election of the head of state by the people. As Denis Lacorne states in an article on the presidential elections of November 2000,[20] the mechanism of the grand electors satisfied the republicanism of the time, based on a certain mistrust of popular suffrage. Witness the famous *Federalist* papers. This document, designed to convince the states' delegates to the ratification conventions of the cogency of the political regime defined in Philadelphia, stresses the guarantees offered by filtering the popular vote by electors. "A small number of persons," wrote Hamilton,

> selected by their fellow-citizens from the general mass, will be most likely to possess the information and discernment requisite to such complicated investigations. . . . And as the electors, chosen in each State, are to assemble and vote in the State in which they are chosen, this detached and divided situation will expose them much less to heats and ferments, which might be communicated from them to the people, than if they were all to be convened at one time, in one place.[21]

In France, by contrast, the constituent assembly of the Fifth Republic wanted to confer the most undeniable legitimacy possible on the president of the Republic while putting him in direct contact with the people. "Nowadays direct agreement between the people and the person who has the responsibility of leading them have become fundamental to the Republic," de Gaulle stated in a television speech (June 8, 1962), a few months before submitting his project to a referendum.

It is an irony of history that in France where the constituent assembly wanted to place the president of the Republic "above the parties," as de Gaulle put it,[22] the effect of divided government, known as the "cohabitation" situation, is to deprive the head of state of the effective enjoyment of the majority of his powers. This goes to show that France remains a parliamentary system; even if there is now a strong presidential element, this is a parliamentary system in which elections to the National Assembly are the dominant fact of political life. It is these elections that set the rhythm of government policy. If the majority in the National Assembly is of the same political stripe as the president of the Republic, then the president is in control of the policy of the nation, whatever Article 20 of the Constitution says about this being the prime minister–led government's job. If after the general election the majority in the National Assembly does not consist of parties supporting the president of the Republic (as has been the case several times since 1986, notably since the elections that followed the dissolution of the National Assembly by Jacques Chirac in 1997), a period of cohabitation then begins during which it is indeed up to the prime minister to direct the government's action. Presidential elections in France thus do not always have the structural effect they have in the presidential regime in the United States.[23] This is not to say that in France presidential elections are ever, as in some countries, a minor fact of political life. Indeed, whenever the president of the Republic and the majority in the National Assembly belong to the same political family, the powers of the French head of state are considerable, even more important than those of the president in the United States.

With that in mind, let us now consider the central question: is it conceivable that the Constitutional Council, as an electoral court reviewing the presidential election, might take a decision similar to that taken by the U.S. Supreme Court in *Bush v. Gore* on December 12, 2000? Formulated in this way, the question must be answered in the negative, as there are so many legal problems specific to the United States that do not arise in France. For one thing, the Constitutional Council is the only court with jurisdiction over presidential elections. The Council, operating in a unitary rather than a federal state, enjoys exclusive jurisdiction under the Constitution to review presidential elections. It does not therefore, by definition, have to consider the extent of its jurisdiction, as the U.S. Supreme Court had to do in relation to the Florida Supreme Court. It does not have to consider its jurisdiction to interpret state electoral law, as there is only one electoral law, valid for the entire country. According to this legislation, the Constitutional Council is required to count all the votes cast, from the first to the last. It is indeed for the Council to declare the results of the election after making any necessary corrections in the light of any complaints that it considers founded. It would be unthinkable for the Constitutional Council to certify these results (and therefore the name of the elected president) without first calculating the exact number of voices obtained by each of the candidates.[24]

For all that, is it possible that the Constitutional Council might one day be faced with difficulties similar to those met by the U.S. Supreme Court? The answer to this question is yes, assuming that these difficulties were of a political as much as a legal nature. How to arbitrate a particularly close election? What would happen if on the evening of the second ballot the television networks announced that this or that candidate had won a presidential election in France by a margin of just a few votes? If there was an action contesting the election on the basis of serious arguments, would the Constitutional Council not be, like the U.S. Supreme Court, in a crucial arbitration situation? Indeed it would, and there would be no way out. It could not decline the jurisdiction and pass the buck to another court or to Parliament, which no longer has a role to play in the process of electing the president of the Republic. So what line would it take? Would it opt for a position of "self-restraint" so as to be above all suspicion of politicization? Would it take a more activist approach and cause the scales to lean more heavily to one side than the other? Another, related question is this: would the nine members of the Constitutional Council cast their votes in accordance with their respective political sensibilities?[25] Or would the Council, in a case with such a political dimension, be at pains to find a consensus at all costs in order to better protect the institution?[26] The answers to these questions are bound to be purely hypothetical as it is always hard to predict the decisions of a supreme or constitutional court, inevitably more sensitive than other courts to the political impact of its decisions.

Before I go on to analyze the Constitutional Council's role in administrative decisions and litigation in reviewing presidential elections, a brief description of how candidates are selected and the poll conducted might be helpful. In France, the job of president of the Republic is not open to just any man or any woman who wants it. Every candidate for the presidency must receive a number of nominations, the validity of which must be verified by the Constitutional Council. France does not have a system of primaries[27] but a "nomination" system. The aim is to filter candidacies without jeopardizing the principle of the popular vote. Under the Decree of March 14, 1964 (amended several times), which is the basic instrument governing the election of the president of the Republic by universal suffrage, a candidate for the presidency must be sponsored by at least five hundred citizens exercising an electoral office and coming from at least thirty departments or overseas territories,[28] no more than one-tenth of them being the elected representatives of the same department or overseas territory. These "nominating citizens" are therefore all national representatives (deputies and senators) or local representatives (regional or department councillors, members of the Paris Council, members of the assemblies of the overseas territories, mayors, etc). The list is updated periodically, to take account of the developments in administrative structures and electoral representation. An act of February 2001, for example, added to this list the mayors of the districts of the two largest cities outside Paris (Lyon and Marseilles) and members of the European Parliament having French nationality and elected in France. The lists of nominated candidates must be sent no later than eighteen days before the first ballot to the Constitutional Council, which forthwith checks whether nominations indeed come from proper representatives who have personally signed the form provided for this purpose. In addition, these forms, printed by the administration, must be in conformity with a model approved by the Constitutional Council.[29] The name and status of the nominating citizens are made public by the Constitutional Council, no later than eight days before the first ballot, at the same time as the list of candidates. The latter can be contested by any person having received at least one nomination. Deadlines are extremely tight: candidates have only until midnight the day following publication of the list to refer the matter to the Council, and the Council is required to rule "without delay."[30] Cases can now be referred to the Constitutional Council concerning not only the nomination but also the eligibility of candidates. In 1969, for example, the eligibility of one of the candidates for the presidency, Alain Krivine, leader of a Far Left party, was contested on the grounds that he had not fully discharged his obligations with respect to military service.[31] The Council ultimately upheld his eligibility and confirmed his candidacy.[32]

Regarding the balloting technique, it meets the overall objective of consolidating the popular legitimacy of the president of the Republic. The poll involves voting for individual candidates, who must obtain a majority, and there are two ballots. A candidate who obtains an absolute majority of the votes cast at the first ballot is elected. If no candidate obtains this majority at the first ballot, a second ballot is held no more than fifteen days later, when only the two "candidates who, in appropriate cases after better-placed candidates have withdrawn their candidacies, have received the largest number of votes at the first ballot" remain eligible. The idea is to prevent the president of the Republic from being elected by only a small percentage of voters, which might be the case with a single ballot. Even so, if there is a low turnout or a large number of blank or spoiled votes, the elected president may have received the votes of only a minority of the electorate. At the presidential election of June 1 and 15, 1969, when two right-wing candidates remained at the second ballot—a Gaullist, George Pompidou, and a Centrist, Alain Poher, at the time president of the Senate—the left-wing parties invited their voters to abstain or cast blank or spoiled votes. Result: George Pompidou obtained a comfortable majority, 58 percent of the votes cast, corresponding, however, to only a minority of the registered voters; even disregarding the blank votes, the abstention rate, abnormally high for France in a presidential election, had amounted to more than 30 percent. Another example is the presidential election of 1995. Rivalry between the two Gaullist candidates standing at the first ballot, Jacques Chirac and Edouard Balladur, upset a good number of right-wing voters. At the second ballot Jacques Chirac was now standing alone against Lionel Jospin, the Socialist candidate, but some of these voters decided to cast blank or spoiled votes; these accounted for almost 5 percent of the votes cast, so that Chirac obtained almost 53 percent of the votes cast but not an absolute majority of the potential votes. But this is not comparable to the American situation, where, through the system of electors representing their individual states, a candidate can lose the election even after having received more votes in the country than his opponent, as was the case of Al Gore in November 2000.[33]

The mechanism in France is as follows: if no candidate receives an absolute majority of the votes cast in the first ballot, the Constitutional Council, no later than 8:00 P.M. on the Wednesday following the Sunday when the ballot took place,[34] declares the number of votes cast for each candidate and publishes the names of the two best-placed candidates[35] remaining for the second ballot. If contentious questions arise at this stage, the Constitutional Council's decision is final and there is no appeal. The declaration of the results of the second ballot likewise compels the Constitutional

Council to settle once and for all any complaints about the election. It is said that this declaration "clears the litigation table." This procedure may seem somewhat expeditious, but it actually aims to reconcile exhaustiveness of the calculation of votes with speed in the installation of the newly elected president.[36] The discussion between the two candidates, George W. Bush and Al Gore, on the validity of the extension by the Florida Supreme Court of the time allowed for the recount in certain counties of the state was influenced by the question of how the public would react to a longer electoral process. In France, the legislation also sets time limits. Under the Decree of March 14, 1964, all complaints to the Constitutional Council about the results of the votes must be examined by it within ten days following the election.[37] To stay within a deadline that is so tight for such an important election in a country with an electorate of more than 42 million is quite a challenge.[38] Certainly the exercise is not easy; but it is possible because the Constitutional Council is involved far upstream of the actual election, even before the campaign officially opens.[39]

The Constitutional Council, as we have seen, does not just review the presidential election but acts as a veritable election monitor, whereas the American courts (right up to the U.S. Supreme Court if necessary) act only to settle litigation. Moreover, and this is another essential difference between France and the United States, the electoral legislation in France applies throughout the country. Even the practicalities of how votes are cast are strictly uniform for all elections, be they national, European, or local. There is complete judicial review of the presidential election in France, as the Constitutional Council must recount all the votes in order to be able to declare the results. In the United States, in contrast, a president may very well be declared elected without anyone being able to determine the exact number of votes cast for him or her.

The Constitutional Council's review of the presidential electoral process is decidedly original. The Council is consulted on the drafting of the instruments (decrees and circulars) organizing the relevant election on the basis of the general electoral legislation.[40] These instruments govern both the practical organization of the campaign and the electoral operations themselves. They specify, for example, the conditions of production and distribution of programs relating to the official television campaign.[41] The Council is also asked to state an opinion on the standard forms used in organizing the election, checking, for example, whether they are understandable enough for those who fill them in to discharge their legal obligations. Such is the case in particular for the forms used by the nominating citizens who sponsor a candidate. The Council's opinion on these forms is advisory and therefore has no judicial status. But the Council can receive references in a judicial capacity concerning complaints about preelectoral operations. Its case law in this area is decidedly subtle, because it must take account of two contradictory imperatives: on the one hand, it cannot open the floor of the court too generously to applicants who, in contesting the decree organizing the election or determining the date, are using delaying tactics to try to postpone or block the election; on the other, it is bound to respect the "right to an effective judicial remedy," which it has held to be a constitutional right on the basis of the case law of the European Court of Human Rights in Strasbourg. The solution selected is to admit references contesting preelectoral operations in borderline cases; that is, when declaring the reference inadmissible, as the Council has held, "there would be a risk of seriously compromising the effectiveness of its review of referendum operations, vitiating the general ballot procedure or jeopardizing the proper functioning of the public authorities."[42] Otherwise, applicants are left with the prospect of a safer reference to the Council of State. In March 2001 the Constitutional Council accordingly rejected as inadmissible a reference made on what it held to be inadequate grounds contesting a decree concerning the drawing up of the lists of candidates for the presidential elections scheduled for 2002.[43] The dividing line established by the Constitutional Council between the cases it considers it must try itself, having regard to the serious character of the grounds relied on, and those it refers back to the administrative courts might imply a comparison, albeit a rather audacious one, with decisions of the U.S. Supreme Court holding that it has jurisdiction to interpret state law on the ground that the alleged violations are especially serious.[44] But the analogy goes no further, as the two Courts—the Constitutional Council in France and the Supreme Court of the United States—have neither the same function nor the same status within their legal system. The Constitutional Council is further involved, it has been seen, at a third level (under the conditions specified above)—the nomination of candidates. It is therefore only at the end of the electoral process, and for what is in theory a very short period, that it is required to play the traditional role of an electoral court with jurisdiction over applications contesting the election. It is then said to be a "court of full jurisdiction" having the power to rectify the results of the poll by substituting its own count for that temporarily established on the day after the election. It is on the basis of this count that it declares the results. Before this proclamation, there cannot be an officially elected president.

The second major feature of the organization of the presidential election in France is centralization. The presidential election, like all other elections, is organized in the same way throughout the country and is the responsibility of the state.[45] For example, the form and presentation of the electoral documents (information sent to voters' homes, setting out the candidates' programs; electoral posters at certain reserved sites; ballots; envelopes containing the ballots; etc.) must meet criteria defined uniformly for the whole country. The way in which votes are cast is also the same everywhere, whether the polling station is in Paris or in a rural district with a tiny population. There are no voting machines in France; votes are cast by hand, and the voter must follow a signposted path from entry to exit at the polling station. When the voter enters the polling station of her commune, presided over in general by the mayor or a mayoral assistant, she must in theory submit an identity card making it possible to check her registration on the electoral rolls.[46] Then, having been given an envelope by one of the officers of the polling station, she must go to the voting booth and place her ballot paper in it.[47] Leaving the voting booth, she places her envelope in the ballot box under the watchful eye of the presiding officer. For the last twenty years or so, the voter has had one last formality to perform—signing the "register of signatures" attesting that she has actually voted. This ritual is strictly the same in each of the fifty-five thousand polling stations in France. There is only one trifling exception that can be made: the prefect (the representative of the state in the department)[48] may allow the closing time of polling stations in certain major conurbations to be delayed by up to two hours (8:00 P.M. instead of 6:00 P.M.)! Another illustration of the centralization of the system: the proper functioning of electoral operations is not monitored principally by the local authorities but by the Constitutional Council, which designates delegates for the purpose. There are approximately fifteen hundred Council delegates chosen from among judges at the administrative courts; their role is to travel to the polling stations in their departments and report to the Council on incidents that they witness or difficulties that they encounter. The Constitutional Council takes their comments seriously, as it may subsequently hear and determine litigation relating to the poll. If it finds that the president of a polling station declined to act on a request by a delegate to remedy an irregularity, the Council penalizes this behavior by annulling the votes cast in the relevant polling station.

The last specific feature of the review of presidential elections in France is its exhaustiveness. This is made possible through a rigorous mechanism whereby results are transmitted from bottom up as follows: once the electoral operations are over, each polling station counts the votes. Envelopes are opened one after the other in the presence of the public and their contents read aloud. The overall results for each commune, recapitulated on forms provided for this purpose, must reveal the votes cast and the abstentions and spoiled votes.[49] The results are then passed on to an administrative "counting committee" for the department, made up of three magistrates, where the results for all the polling stations are added up[50] after corrections if necessary and then passed on by each departmental committee to the Constitutional Council. The Council is the final link in the chain, pooling the counting of votes at the national level. This design in France of an electoral court that both counts and reviews is not entirely new. In the nineteenth century the Council of State, the only electoral court at the time, had jurisdiction in disputes relating to local elections but was already regarded as an "accounting office" and therefore as entitled to "check all operations" connected with the election.[51] At the same time, Jules Laferrière,[52] deputy chairman of the Council of State, stated that the electoral court "can therefore, and sometimes indeed must, change the outcome of the election. . . . The mere fact of discussing a question of majority means that the count is up for debate; and once that operation is submitted to the court, the entire operation is submitted to it as it is indivisible and that all the components of it are connected as so many factors in the same equation. . . . [A]llegations are made about the accuracy of the count, so it must be checked and redone from scratch." These considerations apply all the more to litigation regarding presidential elections, where the Constitutional Council is responsible for declaring the results to within one vote. This applies, of course, both to votes cast personally by voters and to proxy votes.[53]

Although the Constitutional Council receives references on every aspect of the presidential election, it nevertheless considers each reference individually. This is the most important of its functions, even though in theory it has only ten days to consider all references. Because this period is very short and it is important to avoid a proliferation of references, the possibilities of referral to the Council are tightly circumscribed. With regard to general and Senate elections, references may be made to the Council by any candidate or any voter in the district within ten days of the election, without any other special condition. And it has several months to rule after having gathered all the information it needs for its judgment. The right to contest a presidential election is open to voters or to candidates' representatives only if they take the precaution of registering their complaint in the official report of the operations of the relevant polling station.[54] Admittedly, prefects and the candidates themselves, who can also contest the election, are exempted from this formality; but they have only two days to bring their case. Apart from these procedural constraints, applicants are obviously free to rely on whatever grounds and arguments they wish; for example, maneuvers designed to prevent certain voters from going to the polls are denounced before the Council. As in the United States, intimidation to dissuade black voters from turning out have sometimes been observed in New Caledonia, a French overseas territory, and similar allegations were made at the first ballot for the presidential election of 1988. In particular, because barricades had been put up on the public highway, many polling stations had been unable to open. Given the political circumstances of the election in this territory and to avoid fueling the climate of violence prevailing at the time between separatist and antiseparatist movements, the Council was content in its decision on the presidential election to underscore the gravity of the facts without annulling the vote in the territory, as the law required it to.[55] At the presidential election of 1995, in contrast, it annulled the results at the polling station in a village in central France that closed for lunch[56] and thus deprived the electorate of the chance to vote for part of the day. With the same "educational" aim, the Council is at pains to enforce certain formalities that it regards as substantial because they are intended to avert the risk both of fraud and of attempts to pressure voters. In 1995, for instance, the Council annulled the results of a polling station where the official in charge of the station—in this case the mayor of the commune—had refused to submit to the delegated magistrate's request that he check the voters' identity as required by the Electoral Code.[57]

Votes are also invalidated when the ballot box is not transparent, because the Council considers that there is a risk of fraud in this case. And if there is a serious discrepancy between the number of ballots found in the ballot box and the number of voters who signed the register, the Constitutional Council will have no hesitation about annulling the results at the polling station.[58]

Apart from anomalies—formal irregularities, maneuvers, and fraud— that might adversely affect the outcome of the election, the Constitutional Council, like any electoral court, will sometimes have to determine a voter's intention in order to assess the validity of votes cast. The situation that arose in Palm Beach County in the American presidential election of 2000, where more than twenty thousand voters thought they were voting for Al Gore but unwittingly voted either for both Al Gore and Pat Buchanan or for Pat Buchanan alone, is most unlikely to arise in France. In France, voters have no machines to operate; they simply select among the ballots placed before them the one that bears the name of the candidate of their choice.[59] But the fact remains that the validity of certain ballots may have to be assessed in France as in the United States. This is a purely factual assessment, but that makes it all the more delicate. In theory, any ballot will be excluded if there is the slightest means of recognizing it and therefore a possibility of camouflaging fraud. The courts have held in a long line of cases that ballots with erasures, overwriting, holes, tears, or whatever are spoiled votes. But however clear and constant the case law may be, its practical application can raise difficulties of assessment as to whether certain ballots should be annulled. The Constitutional Council faced such a dilemma on the occasion not of a presidential election but of a Senate election in 1996. The two candidates still standing at the second ballot received equal numbers of votes, so, in accordance with the Electoral Code, the older of the two was declared elected. On a reference from the unsuccessful candidate, the Constitutional Council acknowledged that one of the ballots it had annulled might possibly have been regarded as valid, which would have changed the outcome of the election. Having doubts, the Council annulled the election[60] (at the subsequent by-election the older candidate's success was confirmed beyond a shadow of a doubt). A similar situation could easily arise at a presidential election if there was a narrow gap between the numbers of votes cast for the two candidates at the second ballot and doubts arose as to the validity of certain ballot papers. How would the Council discharge its constitutional duty to declare the results of the election? So far it has had to make only minor corrections to the numbers of votes cast,[61] which would never have had any influence on the designation of the candidate declared elected once the results of the ballot had been declared on the same evening. But what attitude would the Council take if the corrections were capable of reversing the outcome? If in doubt as to the reality of the results,[62] would the Council annul the election? According to a traditional rule of electoral litigation, there is no need for it to be certain that the results of the election are distorted in order to cancel an election;[63] it is enough for there to be a probability.

Let us imagine for a moment, then, that the gap between the votes cast for the two candidates at the second ballot is down to a few hundred, and the Constitutional Council observes irregularities affecting the validity of far more ballot papers than that. Let us imagine another hypothetical case, in which the Council has serious doubts as to attribution to one or the other of the two candidates at the second ballot of a no less significant number of ballot papers. What solution would it adopt? In the first hypothesis, strict attachment to principles would suggest that it should reverse the results and declare elected the candidate who was thought to have been the loser. But it has never gone that far in a parliamentary election,[64] and it is therefore unlikely to do so in a presidential election. The second solution would be for the Constitutional Council to turn a blind eye to the anomalies it has observed and to confirm the results as announced by the media on the evening of the election. But would this not perhaps tarnish its image and affect its authority and possibly even weaken the president? That leaves only the possibility of annulling the election. As Guy Carcassonne argues in an enlightening commentary, while there is no doubt that this is legally a valid option for the Constitutional Council, "politically, things are very different."[65] But would it really have the option of proceeding differently if the results of the voting were seriously contested? The possibility of annulling the presidential election is expressly provided for by the legislation. An institutional act[66] applicable both to referendums and to presidential elections provides that "if the Constitutional Council observes irregularities in the course of electoral operations, it must assess whether, given the nature and gravity of these irregularities, those operations should be confirmed or annulled in whole or in part." The reconciliation of these provisions, in the event of total annulment of the results of the presidential election, with those requiring the Constitutional Council to declare the results within ten days following the second ballot can be problematic. How can a decision annulling a presidential election, with its enormous political impact, be made in such a short time without jeopardizing its credibility? It might be thought that in such a case of force majeure the Council would take the liberty of exceeding the time allowed under the Decree of March 14, 1964 (a simple decree), so that it can undertake an in-depth assessment before coming to a decision. The most elementary precaution would also be for the Constitutional Council to give thorough and exhaustive grounds for its annulment decision, unlike its decision proclaiming the results of the presidential election, for which only scant grounds are generally given. The final difficulty lies in the fact that there is no provision in the Constitution for extending the term of office of the president of the Republic.[67] The Constitutional Council would accordingly have to apply Article 7 of the Constitution, declaring a vacancy in the office of president of the Republic and launching the interim period in which the president of the Senate holds the office. The same article of the Constitution then requires that a new election be held within twenty to thirty-five days. Reasonable solution or disaster scenario? The Constitutional Council is the judge of that, but history will then be the judge of the decision it opts to take.

By way of conclusion, several points come to mind. First, in the way they are organized and reviewed, presidential elections in the United States and France have little or nothing in common. The American system admits differences according to the voters' geographic location, whereas French legislation is designed to secure as scrupulously as possible the principle of equal protection of the law; moreover, this legislation, however recent (forty years), is constantly being adapted so that it can better match the challenges of a modern presidential election. The law is regularly amended, in preparation for each new election, among other things to take account of the "observations" (published in the *Official Journal*) that the Constitutional Council addresses to the government to review the previous presidential election and prepare for the next one.[68]

In France, the events that marked the American presidential election of November 2000 are simply impossible. Everything is done to allay all possible doubts as to the exactness of the results as declared by the Constitutional Council. No detail of the organization of the election is left to chance: neither the presentation of forms for nominating candidates, nor the size of the posters and the color of ballot envelopes, nor even the smallest detail of the voter's conduct. All in all, presidential elections in France, being subject to permanent vigilant monitoring by a single authority—the Constitutional Council, which operates either as an advisory authority or as a court, depending on the question—are based on a more reliable and rigorous system than the American system. In 1980 Marie-France Toinet, a French political scientist specializing in the United States,[69] already noted how dissatisfied the Americans were with their presidential election process, seen by many as an "old badly maintained machine." She quoted several critical comments denouncing the fact that the result of the election of the president of the United States "is the effect of chance, money, advertising and luck."[70] Neither chance nor luck should come into play in France, where the presidential election system claims to be perfectly under control from the beginning to the end of the electoral process.

Even so, this system is not wholly protected from unpredictable events like those involved in the U.S. Supreme Court decision in *Bush v. Gore*. The paradox is that the Constitutional Council is at even greater risk than the U.S. Supreme Court, which apparently did not actually have to rule directly on the election itself but could have left it to Congress. In France, this would not be possible. The Constitutional Council is bound by the Constitution to have the last word. If it has doubts as to the results, it must consider every possible and every conceivable legal argument and then come to a final decision. The principles of electoral law in this situation should prompt it to annul the election. But can one ever know in advance what a supreme or constitutional court will decide to do in a given political configuration? "I never promised you a rose garden. I never promised you a perfect justice," wrote the American author Hannah Green. All we can hope is that an electoral court that is forced to intervene directly in such a political process (a situation that the Constitutional Council has not experienced since it was established) will above all resist the temptation of politicization.

NOTES

1. France, a unitary state, comprises three territorial levels of administration: the commune, whose decision-making body is the municipal council chaired by the mayor; the department, whose decision-making body is the general council; and the region, whose decision-making body is the regional council. All these territorial bodies are elected by direct universal suffrage.

2. Article 15 of the Declaration of Human and Civic Rights of 1789, which is part of the "corpus of constitutional law" in France, provides expressly that "Society has the right to ask a public official to give an account of his administration."

3. Yick Wo v. Hopkins, 118 U.S. 356, 370 (1886).

4. See in particular Decision 89–271 of January 11, 1990, on the law concerning the limitation of electoral expenditure and the clarification of the financing of the political activities, *Recueil*, 21.

5. See Noëlle Lenoir, "Parity in France, or Increasing Women's Electoral Representation," *International and Comparative Law Quarterly*, April 18, 2001.

6. In the ancien régime, society was divided into three estates: the Aristocracy, the Clergy, and the Third Estate (the middle class).

7. See Martin Pierre, *Les systèmes électoraux et les modes de scrutin,* 2d ed., Collection Clés (Paris: Montchrestien, 1997).

8. The case law of the two principal electoral courts in France—the Council of State, which reviews local elections and elections to the European Parliament, and the Constitutional Council, which reviews general elections—is nevertheless different. The Council of State is stricter and considers that if a substantial number of voters fail to use the voting booth, the election must be annulled (Judgment of February 12, 1964, *Bonneuil-sur-Marne Municipal Elections, Recueil,* 101), whereas the Constitutional Council is more flexible.

9. Created by Napoleon I in 1800, the Council of State plays the role of supreme administrative court. It is also the legal adviser to the government, which must submit all government bills to it for mandatory opinions before they are adopted by the Council of Ministers and laid before Parliament.

10. Called the "Chamber of Deputies" under certain Republics.

11. Note that the Senate, which by Article 24 of the Constitution ensures "the representation of the territorial units of the Republic," is part of a unitary state. Consequently, the number of senators per district is not the same everywhere but depends on the local population figures.

12. The High Court for England and Wales, the Court of Session for Scotland, and the High Court of Justice for Northern Ireland. Their judgments can be appealed to the House of Lords, which gives final judgment.

13. The history of successive Republics shows that Parliaments did not hesitate to exercise this power and allow political objectives to prevail over legal imperatives. When Blanqui was to be disqualified as a deputy, Clémenceau stated: "This House is neither a jury, nor a court: we are the Chamber of Deputies, i.e., a political body ruling on an election, i.e., a political measure," in *Journal officiel des débats de la Chambre des Députés,* 4.6.1879, p. 4618.

Even more blatantly, the Chamber had discredited itself at the time of the general election in 1956 by disqualifying, without genuine legal grounds, eleven deputies of the new "poujadist" party (a party set up to defend small tradesmen against excessive taxation) to replace them with deputies of the more traditional parties, in particular Socialists, Radicals, and Christian Democrats. See Loic Philip, *Le contentieux des assemblées politiques françaises* (Paris: LGDJ, 1961).

14. Other countries in Europe give their Constitutional Court jurisdiction in electoral litigation. Austria is a case in point. In other countries, Constitutional Courts are also involved but more indirectly (the Portuguese Constitutional Court) or less completely (the German Constitutional Court). In most countries, however, apart from Ireland and the United Kingdom, where electoral disputes are within the jurisdiction of the ordinary courts, it is the Houses of Parliament that are judges of the validity of the election of their members. See Francis Delpérée, *Le contentieux electoral,* Collection Que Sais-Je? (Paris: Presses Universitaires de France, 1998).

15. Thus Article 11 of the Constitution of 1958, as most recently amended, provides that

The President of the Republic may, on a proposal from the Government when Parliament is in session or on a joint motion of the two assemblies, published in either case in the *Journal officiel*, submit to a referendum any government bill which deals with the organization of the public authorities, or with reforms relating to the economic or social policy of the Nation and to the public services contributing thereto, or which provides for authorization to ratify a treaty that, although not contrary to the Constitution, would affect the functioning of the institutions.

Where the referendum is held in response to a proposal by the Government, the latter shall make a statement before each assembly which shall be followed by a debate.

Where the referendum decides in favor of the government bill, the President of the Republic shall promulgate it within fifteen days following the proclamation of the results of the vote.

(The referendum procedure can also be used to amend the Constitution in the circumstances envisaged by Article 89.)

16. "The Constitutional Council shall rule on the proper conduct of the election of deputies and senators in disputed cases" (Article 59) and "shall ensure the proper conduct of referendum proceedings and shall declare the results of the referendum" (Article 60)—the two forms of words conferring powers of different extent, as will be seen.

17. See "Elections présidentielles," in Pascal Perrineau and Dominique Reynié, eds., *Dictionnaire du vote* (Paris: Presses Universitaires de France, 2001), 386.

18. There is no need here to go into excessive detail on the legal problems posed by the procedure chosen for this referendum, which was not that required for amendment of the Constitution (Article 89) but for the adoption of certain ordinary or institutional acts (Article 11). It is probable that if the government had followed a proper procedure, it would not have managed to get its reforms adopted. At all events, on a reference contesting the statute enacted by referendum with a majority of 62.2 percent in favor, the Constitutional Council, in a Decision of November 6, 1962, held that it had no power to declare unconstitutional a statute that was "the direct expression of national sovereignty."

19. Quoted by Dimitri Lavroff, in "Le Droit Constitutionnel de la Vème République," in *Collection droit public et science politique*, 3d ed. (Paris: Dalloz, 1999), 450.

20. "Sur l'Election Présidentielle Américaine. Vestiges d'un âge prédémocratique et antimonarchique," *Le Débat*, January–February 2001, no. 113: 15.

21. *The Federalist*, ed. Benjamin F. Wright (Cambridge, Mass.: Harvard University Press, 1961) (A. Hamilton, No. 68), 441.

22. This role of neutral arbiter responsible for the general interest of the country is conferred by Article 5 of the Constitution of 1958, whereby "the President of the Republic shall see that the Constitution is observed," whereas that task is not expressly entrusted to the Constitutional Council, though it is its main function. This provision, which might appear astonishing in a state based on the rule of law, accurately reflects the nature of the presidency in the Fifth Republic.

23. That is the question raised by the electoral deadlines of 2002. The dissolution in 1997 upset the date scheduled for parliamentary elections so that, contrary to the practice since the beginning of the Fifth Republic, the general election should now intervene a few weeks before the presidential election. Hence the proposal of

the Socialist prime minister, Lionel Jospin, to reverse the schedule so that the presidential election can precede the general election.

24. The *New York Times* of November 27, 2000, reports remarks made by Al Gore whereby "[i]gnoring votes means ignoring democracy." This formula corresponds to the idea of certification of the presidential election by the Constitutional Council to ensure that the newly elected president enjoys full popular legitimacy.

25. The members of the Constitutional Council in France are appointed by political authorities; three members, including the president, are appointed by the president of the Republic, three by the president of the Senate, and three by the president of the National Assembly.

26. The distribution of the votes within the French Constitutional Court is not revealed, for in the French courts—the Constitutional Council being no exception—the practice of dissenting and competing opinions is unknown. Any judgment is strictly collegial, and although the names of the judges contributing to it are quoted in the decision, their individual positions remain secret.

27. At the urging of Charles Pasqua, several times a Gaullist minister, there was a plan in 1990 to adopt the system of primaries in France. The idea was that the right wing should overcome its internal divisions with a view to the presidential elections of 1995. The first primary system envisaged is set out in an internal charter of the two main right-wing parties (the UDF and the RPR), signed by them on April 10, 1991. The second system is presented in a draft bill submitted by Charles Pasqua to the prime minister at that time, Alain Juppé, on June 27, 1994. This would have provided for a consultation of all the registered voters on an electoral roll on the same day. It should be noted that François Mitterrand was in favor of primaries in France in 1969. Ultimately, the idea never took off. See Pierre Esplugas, "Le système des élections primaires est-il transposable à l'élection présidentielle française?" *Revue Française de Droit Constitutionnel*, No. 25, 21 (1995).

28. New Caledonia and French Polynesia are the main overseas territories.

29. Since 1988 the Council has produced the list of nominators on the basis of a computerized process, which is essential as there are more than sixteen thousand nominations in any presidential election.

30. At the 1995 elections, the Council received eleven referrals, some of which were declared inadmissible and the others rejected on the merits.

31. Military service has now been abolished, and France has a purely professional army.

32. Krivine was actually performing his military service at the time, and the Council followed its usual practice of preferring a strict interpretation of the relevant ground of ineligibility. See Ducatel v. Krivine (decision given on May 17, 1969), *Recueil*, 78.

33. This situation can occur at the general election. The coalition parties having obtained a majority of the seats in the National Assembly might have only a minority of the votes in the country. This happened to the left-wing parties at the general election of 1978; they received a majority of the votes but a minority of the seats.

34. In France, elections are always held on Sundays.

35. The best-placed candidates can withdraw their candidacies at the second

ballot. In this case, it is the next following candidate in terms of the number of votes obtained who replaces the candidate withdrawing. This has never yet happened.

36. It is hardly likely that a president of the Republic would be forced out of office because his election was annulled. That would place him in such an uncertain position as to make it difficult for him to do his job.

37. In practice, the results are declared even sooner, on the Wednesday or Thursday following the second ballot.

38. The electorate represented less than 40 million people at the time of the general election on May 1997. This was not important as many young electors did not register on the electoral roll. New legislation of November 1997 provides for an automatic enrollment, which gave an electorate of more than 42 million.

39. For an assessment of the review of the presidential election of 1988, see Bruno Genevois, "Le Conseil Constitutionnel et l'élection présidentielle de 1988," in *Revue de Droit Public,* 1989, 19, and Bernard Malinier, "Les aspects contentieux de la proclamation de l'élection présidentielle de 1988," *Les Petites Affiches,* July 6, 1988. For an assessment of the review of the 1995 election, see Olivier Schrameck, "Le Conseil Constitutionnel et l'élection présidentielle de 1995," *Actualité Juridique de Droit Administratif,* July 20, 1995.

40. With respect to electoral legislation, the Council plays its role of Supreme Constitutional Court. It can receive references contesting ordinary statutes, which it reviews for constitutionality like any other statute. Consultation by the government on institutional statutes is mandatory under the Constitution. Institutional statutes are so defined both by their contents (they apply constitutional provisions directly) and by the adoption procedure (they can be enacted by the National Assembly, which has the last word, only if there is an absolute majority of its members in favor).

41. In France, all commercial advertising techniques via the press or the audiovisual media are prohibited at the time of election campaigns.

42. Decision of July 25, 2000, on a referral by Stephane Hauchemaille, *Recueil,* p. 117.

43. Decision of March 14, 2001, on a referral by Stephane Hauchemaille (to appear in the 2001 *Recueil*).

44. In theory, as Judge Edmondson states in his dissenting opinion in Roe v. State of Alabama, 43 F.3d 574, 585 (11th Cir. 1995), to protect the boundary between constitutional law and dispute resolution processes for state elections, the federal intervention requires "extraordinary circumstances affecting the integrity of the state's election processes."

45. Including financially: the state refunds to candidates who obtain at least 5 percent of the votes at the first ballot half of the electoral expenditure incurred by them, subject to the ceiling provided for by law.

46. Electoral rolls are kept by each of the thirty-six thousand communes in France.

47. Voters are supplied with adequate numbers of separate ballot papers for each candidate at each polling station. They also receive them by post in the days before the poll.

48. In Metropolitan (= European) France, there are 36,000 communes, 100 departments, and 22 regions.

49. Blank votes are those where no candidate is actually voted for. Spoiled ballots are those that are somehow identifiable by means of, for example, erasures, corrections, perforations, or tears and, consequently, cannot be taken into account.

50. Each counting committee adds up the vote (as summarized in the official reports drawn up by the communes) in the presence of the candidates' representatives who can ask for complaints to be recorded in the official report of the counting committee (see hereafter).

51. See Romieu, President of the Litigation Department of the Council of State, in *RGA*, 1887, vol. 2, p. 426.

52. See his *Traité de la juridiction administrative et des recours contentieux*, 1887, vol. 2, p. 318, quoted by Jean Pierre Camby, in "Elections: Contentieux électoral relevant du Conseil Constitutionnel," part of *Répertoire du Contentieux Administratif Dalloz sur les élections*, Paris, October 2000.

53. Voters who are temporarily absent from France or unable to vote can have their vote cast by proxy at the polling station.

54. Or in the case of a candidate's representative, in the official report of the departmental counting committee (see note 50).

55. At elections, it is quite common for the Council of State to annul the results. See in particular the judgment of June 2, 1967, *Elections at Ghisoni, Recueil*, 233.

56. See the decisions of May 10, 11, and 12, 1995, declaring the results. The Council was manifestly keen to take a didactic decision in order to avoid the generalization of the very French practice of closing down during the lunch hour.

57. Identity checks are obligatory in communes of more than five thousand inhabitants. In accordance with what was indicated above, this decision takes account primarily of the behavior of the presiding officer with respect to the magistrate delegated by the Constitutional Council.

58. See the declarations of the results of May 15, 1981, and May 11, 1988.

59. It is only at elections to Parliament that the Constitutional Council has had occasion to invalidate ballot papers bearing indications that might give rise to confusion. For example, it annulled ballot papers in the name of a party called the "Green Generation," whose logo was likely to cause confusion with the existing ecological parties (Ecology Generation and Greens). Decision 58 110/128 of April 23, 1959, National Assembly, Guadeloupe, Constituency 2, *Recueil*, 209.

60. Decision 95–2062 of May 3, 1996, Senator elections, Vaucluse, *Recueil*, 69.

61. In 1995 it annulled approximately 18,000 votes and restored 572 votes invalidated by a departmental counting committee at the first ballot. At the second ballot, it annulled approximately 11,000 votes and restored 12 votes also wrongly invalidated by a counting committee.

62. This article does not mention the question of the review—also exercised by the Constitutional Council—of the campaign accounts of candidates at the presidential election in France. The management of these accounts is now subject to rigorous conditions. The nature of income is limited as, since 1995, candidates have no longer been able to enjoy financing other than subsidies or loans from their political party, bank loans and advances and contributions from their members not being bodies corporate (in modest amounts). The parties themselves are financed only by the state and their individual members. Last, the amount of electoral ex-

penditure has remained stationary for each candidate to the presidential election at Fr 13.7 million at the first ballot and Fr 18.3 million at the second. This is far from the astronomical amounts spent to finance the last presidential electoral campaign in the United States. But reviewing this new mechanism of financing of the presidential campaign in France does not raise the same difficulties for the electoral court, in this case the Constitutional Council, as reviewing the proper conduct of the poll. In the case of presidential elections, unlike other elections, the penalty is not the annulment of the election and ineligibility for one year but the imposition of financial penalties. (But these can be heavy and provoke doubts as to the legitimacy of the elected president.)

63. There is an abundance of case law along these lines as regards local elections.

64. Unlike the Council of State in relation to local elections.

65. See "Thalassee, Paris," *Revue Dalloz*, No. 5, 2001.

66. Section 50 of Ordinance 58–1067 of November 7, 1958, relating to referendums, made applicable to presidential elections by Act 62–1292 of November 6, 1962, on the election of the president of the Republic by universal suffrage.

67. This term of office was seven years until recently but was reduced to five years by a constitutional amendment on September 24, 2000.

68. For instance, at the end of 2000 the government laid before Parliament a bill eventually enacted as the Act of February 2001 referred to above.

69. See her article "La désignation des candidats présidentiels aux Etats-Unis," *Pouvoirs*, No. 14, 1980, Paris.

70. Editorial by James Reston in *International Herald Tribune*, February 9–10, 1980, quoted by Marie-France Toinet.

16

SEVEN REASONS WHY *BUSH V. GORE* WOULD HAVE BEEN UNLIKELY IN GERMANY

Dieter Grimm

1. NO PRESIDENTIAL ELECTION

A direct parallel between the events of November and December 2000 in the United States and the situation in Germany cannot be drawn. The systems are too different. Whereas the United States is a presidential democracy, Germany can be characterized as a parliamentary democracy. The federal president, whose functions are more representative than political, is not elected by the people but by a special organ, the *Bundesversammlung,* composed of all members of the *Bundestag* (federal Parliament) and the same number of electors named by the parliaments of the various states *(Länder).* The chancellor is elected by the *Bundestag.* The people elect only the members of Parliament. This election is a direct one. The voters decide about the composition of Parliament without the intervention of electors nominated by the *Länder.*

2. ONLY FEDERAL LAW

Although German federalism is, generally, less dualistic than American federalism, it strictly separates federal and state spheres in matters relating to elections. The federal election is regulated by a federal law, the *Bundeswahlgesetz* (BWG). This law contains provisions as to suffrage requirements, composition and appointment of local, state, and federal election authorities, admission of candidates and parties, ballots, voting and counting procedures, control mechanisms, and so on. The technical details can be found in the *Bundeswahlordnung* (BWO), a regulation issued by the federal government. Another law, the *Wahlprüfungsgesetz,* regulates control of the legality of parliamentary elections. States and local communities have no regulatory power over national elections. National elections are held under the same conditions throughout the country. When organs of the *Länder* or of the local communities are involved they have mere organizational functions and act on behalf and under the control of the Federal Republic. All costs that may arise for the *Länder* or the local communities in connection with a national election are covered by the national budget.

3. IDENTICAL BALLOTS

The design of the ballot is stipulated in the BWO. The ballots are printed under the responsibility of the federal government and have the same format in every *Land* and in every precinct. The ballot leaves little room for doubt about the voter's intent. After each candidate or political party there is a circle the size of a quarter. The voter marks, usually with a cross, the circle following the name of the candidate or party he or she wants to vote for. There is sufficient space between the circles to exclude unclear votes. Manual marks are the rule. Voting machines may be allowed by the Federal Ministry of the Interior in individual precincts, but each type of machine must be approved by the ministry. Section 39 of the BWG contains a list of circumstances under which an individual ballot may be ruled invalid. The decision about invalidity is made by the board of each polling station. The electoral board of the precinct has the power to review the decision of the station's board. All higher electoral authorities (head and board of each *Land* and head and board of the Federal Republic) are bound by the local decision and may only correct obvious counting errors. A review of the decisions is reserved for a special procedure *(Wahlprüfung)* that can be initiated only after the election.

4. EASY COUNTING

The ballots are opened and counted in every polling station by its electoral board immediately after the polls close. The manner of counting and, if necessary, recounting is prescribed in great detail by the BWO. Counting is open to the public, and the results at each polling station are known one to two hours after the polls close. Results are first reported to the local community where the polling station is located and then to the head of the electoral board of the precinct, which may review the results. This board's decision can be challenged only through the *Wahlprüfung* before the newly elected parliament whose decision is subject to review by the Federal Constitutional Court. The precinct authorities report the result to the head of the electoral office of the state, who in turn reports the result within the *Land* to the head of the federal election office. The provisional official result for the whole Federal Republic is usually announced about four hours after the polls close. The final result may follow some days later.

5. LIMITED POLITICAL INFLUENCE

The counting and determination of the results of an election cannot be influenced by politicians. Direct political influence is limited to the appointment of the head of the electoral office. Historically, the head of the federal office has been the president of the Federal Bureau of Statistics. Likewise, the heads of the states' offices are usually the presidents of their various statistical bureaus. The heads appoint the members of the boards. Political parties that have candidates in a given precinct are represented on the board of that voting station. Cabinet members or other political officeholders are not involved in further electoral procedures. The question of whether a recount is necessary and how long it may last belongs exclusively to the board of the polling station and the board of the precinct. Political interference would be illegitimate.

6. NO JUDICIAL REVIEW BEFORE DETERMINATION OF THE FINAL RESULT

Voters, groups of voters, the heads of the electoral offices of the *Länder* and of the Federal Republic, and the president of the *Bundestag* have the right to challenge an election. The legality of the election is, in the first instance, controlled by the *Bundestag* itself, which has a special committee for this purpose. This means that doubts as to the correctness of the counting do not hinder the formation of the newly elected *Bundestag*. The decision of the *Bundestag* can be reviewed by the Federal Constitutional Court. Should an election be declared invalid, either totally or in part, it will be repeated nationwide or in those precincts where an irregularity occurred.

Thus far no national election has ever been declared invalid. Litigation in electoral matters usually concerns conflicts preceding the election (such as the admission of candidates or parties to the ballot, reapportionment of precincts, the principle of government neutrality in the campaign and of equal chances for the competing parties) or doubts as to the constitutionality of certain provisions of the election laws. The counting of votes has not been the subject of litigation, which would come before the Constitutional Court.

7. INTENT VERSUS TIME

Given the situation in Germany that has been described above, it is almost impossible that a case like *Bush v. Gore* could have reached the Federal

Constitutional Court. Had it reached the Court, it is unlikely that it would have been decided in the same way. I make this assertion, of course, on the assumption that the Federal Constitutional Court would adhere to the principles that have guided its jurisprudence so far.

The German court would agree with the U.S. Supreme Court that, in electoral matters, equal protection applies, not only to the initial allocation of the franchise, but also to the manner in which it is exercised. This forbids any arbitrary or disparate treatment of voters. Yet, as neither state law nor state courts are involved in federal elections, the question of whether a state court met these requirements in its judgment could not have arisen. Had a lower court ordered a recount, as the Florida Supreme Court did, but failed to supply specific standards to ensure uniform treatment of the voters, this failure would not have rendered the decision defective because the standards are set forth in the Federal Election Law. Accordingly, there would have been no danger of different treatment.

According to its majority opinion, the U.S. Supreme Court did not remand the case with instructions on recounting because of the lack of time. It is most likely that this question, if it could have come up in the German Constitutional Court, would have been decided differently, provided the Court adhered to the principles it usually applies when it comes to a conflict of different constitutional requirements. In *Bush v. Gore* the conflict was between the requirement to ascertain the intent of the voters, on the one hand, and to meet the deadline for returns, on the other. Conflicts of this type are resolved in Germany by a balancing method. The respective weight of the competing requirements is determined, and then a decision is made as to which one prevails in the case at hand.

The first requirement is a material one of the highest order. In elections, the intent of the voter counts. The most important element to be secured by the election laws and the manner of their application is to determine the voter's intent. Otherwise the final result of the election would not be compatible with the intent of the voter, and the legitimizing bond between the people and the officeholders would be cut. The time limit, in contrast, is a formal requirement without a basis in the constitution. The reason behind it is not a principle of the highest order but of mere expediency. Evidence that failure to meet the deadline would result in a constitutional crisis, like creating an interregnum without a president, did not exist. Weighing the competing requirements thus, there can be no doubt that the German Constitutional Court (provided that it did not depart from established principle in a highly politicized matter) would have ordered that each voter's intent must be ascertained as accurately as possible.

17

BUSH V. GORE: A VIEW FROM ITALY

Pasquale Pasquino

Il n'est presque pas de question politique, aux États-Unis, qui ne se résolve tôt ou tard en question judiciaire.
ALEXIS DE TOCQUEVILLE

Electoral systems are algorithms that permit the transformation of a number of votes *(N)* into a smaller number of seats *(n)*. Since the beginning of representative government, this essential mechanism of democratic states, like the right of suffrage, has been discussed extensively.[1]

Very little attention has been given, however, to each electoral system's point of departure, perhaps because the question of how to obtain *N* seems settled and unproblematic. This is the problem that emerged with unsuspected virulence during the very long month from November 7, 2000, election day, to December 12, 2000, when the U.S. Supreme Court decided that the American presidency should go to George W. Bush.

The question is how the votes are counted, not how they are transformed into a very small number of seats, or just one seat, as in the American presidency. It is on this seemingly banal question that the world's only superpower at the end of the second millennium got stuck, as in a giant swamp. The solution that lifted the aircraft carrier named *America* over the treacherous waters of the Florida count threatens, however, to discredit one of American democracy's most prestigious institutions: on December 12 the Supreme Court decided that it was too late to complete the ongoing manual vote count.

The Court's decision in *Bush v. Gore* is a strong candidate for being among the most incongruous and negative opinions it has issued. In Europe it has provoked a very negative opinion of American constitutional justice.

MEN, MACHINES, AND HOLES:
THE FIRST DECISION OF A FEDERAL COURT

Most attentive scholars of the American political system expected both a narrow electoral victory and a discrepancy between the popular vote and the Electoral College majority. Presidential elections are indirect elections that may result in a candidate winning the election without obtaining more votes than his closest competitor. Similar distortions may be seen in almost every method of determining the victor in an election.[2] The 1996 elections in Italy produced a comparable phenomenon: the center-Left obtained a greater number of seats in Parliament, even though the center-Right obtained a greater number of the popular votes. But no one could have expected what actually happened in Florida.

On November 8 the Florida Division of Elections gave Bush a 1,784-vote advantage over Gore. The next day, the mechanical recount reduced the Republican candidate's lead to 327 out of a total of about 6 million votes. Florida election law mandates that a mechanical recount of the votes be carried out when the leading candidate has an advantage of less than 0.5 percent of the votes. The difference between the two candidates given by the first official figure (1,784) amounted to 0.0299 percent of the total votes cast. This triggered an automatic mechanical recount. The law setting forth the procedures for protesting electoral results, Florida Statutes § 102.166 (2000), provides that within seventy-two hours of the election any candidate may request that the canvassing board in the county where the protest arises conduct a manual recount.

At this point, we Europeans discovered, with some surprise, that voting systems in the United States vary significantly from one state to another. For example, we became aware that Oregon recently introduced voting by mail for all its residents, which explains why its results were delayed for several days. Moreover, in Florida voting procedures vary from one county to the next. Of the state's 67 counties, one uses manually tabulated paper ballots (as in Italy), another uses a lever machine (as in New York City), 39 use a ballot requiring that the voter fill in the circle corresponding to the names of the candidates to be read by an optical scanner, and 26 use punch-card ballots. Experts have suggested that the margin of error in the Florida vote was on the order of 5 percent.

Between November 7 and November 11 the Democratic Party, on behalf of Gore, filed protests with the canvassing boards of four counties. Three of the four immediately ordered manual recounts.[3] On November 11 Bush's lawyers appeared in the U.S. District Court for the Southern District of Florida to ask for an injunction against these manual recounts. On November 13, Judge Middlebrooks denied the request.[4] The reasoning behind this decision is particularly interesting and helps us to understand a number of important aspects of the legal and constitutional dispute surrounding the election.

The judge had to decide on an emergency motion for a temporary restraining order and a preliminary injunction against the manual recounts on the grounds that § 102.166(4) of the Florida election law, pursuant to which the recounts were proceeding, violated the First and Fourteenth Amendments of the U.S. Constitution, in particular the Equal Protection Clause, which roughly corresponds to "the principle of equality" under the Italian constitution. Judge Middlebrooks carefully considered the constitutional issue arising under the principle of equality:

> The thrust of Plaintiffs' position is that Florida's decentralized county-by-county electoral system can yield disparate tabulating results from county to county. For instance, similarly punched ballots in different counties may be tabulated differently in a manual recount due to the introduction of human subjectivity and error.[5]

It is well known that three of the counties at the heart of the electoral protest (Palm Beach, Broward, and Miami-Dade) use perforated ballots, where the voter uses a stylus to punch out a perforated square of paper corresponding to the name of the chosen candidate. If all goes well, a little square of paper (called a "chad") completely detaches from the rest of the ballot, resulting in a hole that the optical scanning machine counts as a vote. But it is possible that the voter, unskilled in the use of the stylus, inadvertently detaches three, or two, or just one side of the chad. The machine interprets some of these as holes and others not. How do those who recount the ballots, applying Florida law, define a "hole"?[6] Is there a standard, unambiguous, universally accepted definition of what kind of a hole, or vote, is valid in the specific case for every canvassing board charged with the manual recount? And if there is not, and equal holes may be counted differently or different holes may be counted equally, would this be a violation of the principle of equality, understood as granting each citizen an equal vote?

Judge Middlebrooks, considering these objections, which would later be tackled by the U.S. Supreme Court, reasonably asserted:

> These concerns are real, and, in our view, unavoidable, given the inherent decentralization involved in state electoral and state recount procedures. For instance, at least 48 states employ recount procedures—many of which differ in their methods of tabulation. . . . Unless and until each electoral county in the United States uses the exact same automatic tabulation (and even then there may be system malfunctions and the like), there will be tabulating discrepancies depending on the method of tabulation. Rather than a sign of weakness or constitutional injury, some solace can be taken in the fact that

no one centralized body or person can control the tabulation of an entire statewide or national election. For the more county boards and individuals involved in the electoral regulation process, the less likely it becomes that corruption, bias, or error can influence the ultimate result of an election.[7]

Judge Middlebrooks stated further that the plaintiffs failed to demonstrate how and why the manual recount is so unreliable as to constitute a violation of the constitutional principle of equality, especially taking account of the fact that the electronic tabulation has a margin of error of about 5 percent. In the end, Judge Middlebrooks refused to enjoin the manual recount because "we do not find sufficient evidence to declare a law authorizing the use of a manual recount to be unconstitutional on its face."[8]

It is worth dwelling on this ruling because its conclusions are the ones that were to be overturned by the U.S. Supreme Court. Three general observations may be made. The 2000 presidential election revealed some problems with democratic electoral mechanisms. The first concerns the United States in particular: namely, the extraordinary disparity of voting mechanisms, tabulation, and protest procedures dramatically revealed in Florida. This produces uncertainty concerning the fairness and clarity of the results. One hopes Congress will encourage the states, charged by the Constitution with making election law, to unify these procedures.

The second problem is a general one concerning *all voting systems.* In every computation of a great number of entities, whether ballots, holes, or anything else, there exists, as statisticians tell us, a certain margin of error.[9] In the case of elections, the gap between the various candidates is generally significant enough to make us forget that a situation may arise in which the numerical difference is minimal and falls *within the margin of error.* This opens two, not necessarily alternative paths: fix the voting and vote tabulation systems to minimize the margin of error; or accept that in some very rare cases elections will *not* succeed in choosing a candidate. At first glance, the second alternative seems unacceptable. The first alternative suggests using an electronic vote, which easily permits checks by both the voter and the institution in charge of the count.[10] The electronic vote naturally presents the problem of protecting the secrecy of votes.[11] But this simply demonstrates that there is no perfect solution to the problem under discussion and that it merits much more attention, discussion, and research than it has been given in the past.

The third problem is that political science research, long focused on the study of electoral systems, has not, to my knowledge, addressed the mechanics of voting and the methods of vote counting in different countries. There is a legal literature dealing with the norms regulating contests of electoral results,[12] and this ought to be developed with a comparative view to other systems. For instance, in Italy, Parliament has competence over the contestation of legislative elections (modeled after the French Revolution);[13] in France, since 1958, contests are decided by the Conseil Constitutionnel; in Germany, by an ad hoc commission of specialists; and in the United States, by the courts.

A COURT OR A PARLIAMENT?

The U.S. Supreme Court's first intervention in the electoral contest seemed to me ambiguous and, to a certain extent, inconclusive. It is a fact that the Court decided to accept the case on November 24, surprising many observers (and notwithstanding the opposition of some of its members) and transforming a political question—the choice of the president of the United States—into a legal one. It is also a fact that from November 24 until the Court's final decision on December 12, the Court became the center of the attention of the country, the press, and the mass media, even as the conflicts in Florida were intensifying.

Bush's lawyers aimed with their petition to overturn both the decision of Judge Middlebrooks and that of the Florida Supreme Court, which seemed too favorable to Gore.[14] The Supreme Court's per curiam December 4 decision paid the price of opacity for painfully achieved unanimity.[15] The Court vacated the decision of the Florida Supreme Court and asked it to justify its decision in a more satisfactory way, apparently maintaining an interlocutory stance.[16]

This gave the Florida Supreme Court one week to clarify its position. On December 6, the Eleventh Circuit Court of Appeals rejected Bush's appeal of Judge Middlebrooks's decision. By November 26 Secretary of State Harris had already certified Bush the winner of the Florida election. On December 8 the Florida Supreme Court—this time split four justices to three[17]—handed down a new opinion, insisting that the manual recount of the nine thousand ballots in Miami-Dade County be continued and requiring Harris to add votes identified by the manual recounts to those officially attributed to Gore. Bush's lawyers then filed an emergency application for a stay of the manual recounts, and the U.S. Supreme Court, in a 5–4 decision, issued its December 9 stay suspending the recounts.[18]

At that point the alignments within the Supreme Court became clear. What most surprises an observer of constitutional courts, which usually deliberate in secret and without dissenting opinions, like the French and Italian courts, is that the U.S. Supreme Court, like a nineteenth-century parliament, is divided into a liberal Left, a conservative Right, and a powerful "swamp" of the center, the *median justices* in the language of political science, on whom the essential decisions depend. The oldest justice on the Court, Stevens, in his dissenting opinion of December 9, declared that the majority's decision "departs from . . . venerable rules of judicial restraint that have guided the Court throughout its history." "The majority," Stevens asserted, "acted unwisely." He added that to obtain a stay the applicant must make a substantial showing of the likelihood of irreparable harm and that the applicant failed to carry that burden. Most important, "[c]ounting every legally cast vote cannot constitute irreparable harm. . . . Preventing the recount from being completed will inevitably cast a cloud on the legitimacy of the election."[19] On this point it is hard to disagree with him.

Faced with such an explicit attack, which threatened to disqualify the majority's decision in the eyes of the public and accused it above all of abuse of power, Justice Scalia, ideologue of the conservative wing of the Court, felt obliged to defend the majority decision, a highly unusual practice in the context of granting a stay. In his brief concurrence, Justice Scalia tried to counter the legitimacy of counting every valid vote by arguing that the important issue is the very validity of such votes and that they cannot be counted first, leaving for later what the criteria of validity ought to be. It is this way of proceeding, he stressed, that would undermine the public acceptance of the results that democratic stability requires. In contrast to Judge Middlebrooks's opinion, Justice Scalia insisted on the fact that the standards for the determination of the intention of the voter must be the same in each county (which provides a ground for declaring Florida law unconstitutional for violating the principle of equality).

It is clear that the majority and the dissenters were divided on an important and complex question: May the contested votes be manually counted, leaving the criteria of validity (or, more concretely, when a hole is a hole) to the individual county canvassing boards, or must such criteria rather be fixed and objective and binding on all boards before counting begins? And who must fix these criteria?

Naturally, it is doubtful that there are such objective standards; certainly, homogeneous criteria may be authoritatively fixed, but unless one trusts the canvassing boards, what way is there to make sure, for example, that the homogeneous standards are uniformly applied? The Court may have had other ways out of this problem, to which I shall return in the conclusion.

The December 12 per curiam opinion probably expressed the positions of Justices O'Connor and Kennedy—the two justices who de facto decided the forty-third president of the United States. This decision turned on the Equal Protection Clause, a constitutional provision introduced after the Civil War to protect the "new" American citizens created by the abolition of slavery. The point again is that of the need for equal standards to be used in ascertaining the voter's intention. The majority opinion argues that it is possible to set these general criteria and, simultaneously, that there is no time to do so. These, essentially, are the reasons that led to overturning the decision of the Florida Supreme Court and the final acceptance of Secretary of State Harris's November 26 certification.

In the course of oral argument, the justices did interrogate Gore's law-yers on the possible homogeneous criteria for a manual recount of the ballots, though without obtaining a response. It also seems that Justices Breyer and Souter attempted to strike a compromise within the Court on this point but without success. My impression is that the Court's use and abuse of dissenting opinions discourages discussion and internal deliber-ation. It also dedicates very little time to the "Council Chamber,"[20] another factor making compromise very difficult. More than a judicial body, the U.S. Supreme Court seems, at least to European eyes, like a mini-parliament, with its majorities, minorities, and ideological contests.

Applying the Humean principle of tolerance,[21] one may argue that the majority's choice was guided by the will to avoid a constitutional crisis.[22] But this crisis would have been a perfectly manageable one. Effective laws and a certain number of historical precedents[23] enable us to imagine an alternative scenario to that imposed by the Supreme Court majority. First of all, it is not at all evident that the final result of the manual count would have been unfavorable to Bush. With their decision, the (conservative) ma-jority justices gave the unpleasant impression of wanting to protect Bush from every risk. Suppose that the Florida vote favored Gore in the end. On December 18 the Electoral College would probably have received two lists of electors from Tallahassee, the Republican one sent by Secretary of State Harris and a Democratic list certified by the Florida Supreme Court. In this case, the Electoral College would not have been able to reach a clear ma-jority and would have had to defer the final decision to Congress.

Certainly this solution would have kept the country in relative uncer-tainty for yet another month. And it would have assured the White House for Bush, given that the House of Representatives, which had a clear Re-publican majority, decides the presidency. But perhaps it would have led to Lieberman's selection as vice president, since the vice presidency is de-cided by the Senate, which at that point had fifty Republicans and fifty Democrats and would have been subject to a tie-breaking vote by the vice president, Gore.

But the vote of just one justice was enough to elect Bush the forty-third president of the United States. The arguments used to justify this choice are highly contestable and have been contested. But the fact remains: the majority of the Court arrogated to itself the right to choose the president, who is the one who chooses (with the consent of a simple majority of the Senate) the members of the Court. Beyond the difficulty in considering the majority's arguments irrefutable, it is difficult to say that the justices behaved in an elegant fashion. Leaving the choice of the president to Con-gress, the justices would have given to Caesar that which is Caesar's: *to a politically responsible body, the burden of a choice that falls, in principle, to the electors but could not be made in an unequivocal way due to intrinsic difficulties in the way the votes are counted.* For an institution like the Supreme Court—not subject to popular control and a body that unlike Congress cannot be punished by means of elections—to take this decision upon itself is an encroachment on a constitutional state that is hard to defend. A similar conception is defended in Italy, which does not consider popular suffrage as the sole or the last word in the political process. But "governing with judges" is not the same thing as letting "irresponsible" judges choose the holders of elective office.

The U.S. Supreme Court, in deciding to choose he who will choose its own future members, consumed an enormous amount of credibility as an impartial organ. "Millions of Americans," wrote Cass Sunstein at the end of the struggle (and surely millions of Europeans think this as well), "believed that the court had acted in an unacceptably partisan manner. . . . *Bush v. Gore* raised widespread doubts about the neutrality of the Supreme Court."[24] Considering the very high institutional cost of this likely consequence, Justice Breyer wrote in his dissenting opinion that "the Court was wrong to take this case."[25] In *Bush v. Gore* everything leads to the thought, at least on the other side of the Atlantic, that the Supreme Court abused its power, substantially harming its image as an institution *super partes.* Unless there is a more profound misunderstanding, Americans are in fact disposed to accept the partisan political character of their judicial power.

In a recent book on justice, a prominent scholar of the Italian judicial system writes aptly that the judge, a neutral third with the job of resolving a conflict between two parties, must convince them that he or she is not taking sides. "His or her impartiality—and above all his or her image of impartiality—is thus preserved and, moreover, strengthened as much as possible."[26]

Whatever the reasons motivating the individual justices, the majority's decision cannot be seen as illustrating the indisputable prestige and impartiality of the supreme organ of judicial power in the United States. It seems, unfortunately, to have behaved like a politically irresponsible miniparliament rather than as a high court of justice.

NOTES

Epigraph: *De la démocratie en Amérique,* vol. 1 (Paris: Gallimard, 1986), 401 (De l'esprit légiste aux États-Unis, et comment il sert de contrepoids à la démocratie): "Scarcely any political question arises in the United States that is not resolved, sooner or later, into a judicial question" (*Democracy in America* [New York: Vintage, 1945], 290). I owe this quotation to John Ferejohn, whom I thank.

1. See, *e.g.*, Pierre Rosanvallon, *La rivoluzione dell'uguaglianza* (Milan: Anabasi, 1994); and Pierre Martin, *Les systèmes électoraux et les modes de scrutin* (Paris: Montchrestien, 1994).

2. Taking this into account, the diffuse criticism of the institution of the Electoral College (I am thinking of the pieces by Ronald Dworkin, chap. 4, this volume; and Akhil Amar, *New York Times*, November 9, 2000) does not seem particularly pertinent, especially a posteriori. Furthermore, to abolish it and introduce the direct election of the president would require a constitutional amendment, very difficult to obtain given the opposition of the small states that have the right to veto any constitutional reform (see the fine interview of Kathleen Sullivan on the editorial page of the *New York Times*, November 15, 2000).

3. In particular, on November 13, as we shall see in looking at the first important legal decision, a manual recount had been authorized in three districts in Broward County. The decision was being awaited in Miami-Dade County. In Palm Beach County the authorization had been given for all the districts. And finally in Volusia County, after the confirmation in district 216 of the poor functioning of the floppy disk containing the program for the electronic count of the votes and its replacement, a manual recount of all the ballots in the county was authorized.

4. Siegel v. LePore, 120 F.Supp.2d 1041 (S.D. Fla. 2000).

5. 120 F.Supp.2d at 1051.

6. On the not so simple ontology of the same, see R. Casati and A. Varzi, *Holes and Other Superficialities* (Cambridge, Mass.: MIT Press, 1994).

7. 120 F.Supp.2d at 1051.

8. *Id.*

9. I am indebted to Molly Przeworski for this observation.

10. The voter may check the accuracy of his or her vote on the screen before finally confirming it; furthermore, a computer system can quickly recount the electoral results many times, reducing the margin of error.

11. Electronic voting has been instituted in Belgium, and the German government proposes its introduction on a national scale in 2002. On some of the problems posed by this type of voting, see "County in California Touches Future of Voting," *New York Times*, February 12, 2001 (discussing the experience of Riverside County). Note that 9 percent of American citizens already vote with an electronic touch screen. On electronic democracy more generally, see S. Rodotà, *La démocratie électronique* (Paris: Apogée, 1999).

12. I am familiar with the work of Maria Vicenta Garcia Soriano, *Jueces y magistrados en el proceso electoral* (Madrid: Centro de Estudios Políticos y Constitucionales, 2000).

13. In regional elections, administrative courts and the Council of State are competent.

14. Italians were negatively struck by the fact that all seven justices of the Florida Supreme Court are Democratic nominees and, moreover, by the fact that in America all federal judges are chosen by a simple political majority—in contrast to Kelsenian systems of constitutional justice, in which the nominations for a super partes organ are exempt from the majoritarian principle.

15. Bush v. Palm Beach County Canvassing Board, 121 S. Ct. 471.

16. See, *e.g.,* the comment on this decision published by Cass Sunstein in the *New York Times,* December 5, 2000.

17. Gore v. Harris, 772 So.2d 1243 (2000).

18. Bush v. Gore, 521 U.S. 98 (2000).

19. *Id.* at 513 (Stevens, J., dissenting).

20. The Italian Constitutional Court discusses all of its decisions collectively, and the most important ones at length, in collegial meetings (called the jurisdictional chamber councils) that occupy the justices for twenty-one weeks a year.

21. As did Burt Neuborne so elegantly in a series of fictitious opinions that develop the justices' opinions; see chap. 9, this volume.

22. This is the argument made by Richard Pildes, in chap. 3, this volume.

23. For example, the Tilden-Hayes presidential election of 1876.

24. Chronicle of Higher Education, January 5, 2001 (reprinted in E. J. Dionne and William Kristol, eds., *Bush v. Gore. The Court Cases and the Commentary* [Washington, D.C.: Brookings Institution Press, 2001], 339–40).

25. In *Bush v. Gore. The Court Cases and the Commentary,* 132.

26. Carlo Guarnieri, *La giustizia in Italia* (Bologna: Il Mulino, 2001), 14.

DEMOCRACY IN AMERICA: A EUROPEAN PERSPECTIVE ON THE MILLENNIAL ELECTION

Mattias Kumm

There are still many for whom the basic constitutional structure of the United States is regarded as an attractive model for what the European Union ought to become. The attraction of the United States in this respect is obvious. The political structure established by the U.S. Constitution is perceived as having provided a remarkably stable institutional framework over a span of more than two centuries. During this time, the United States was able to develop from little more than a coalition of rebellious colonies into a global power whose cultural appeal, scientific prowess, economic prosperity, political clout, and military might have few if any historical equals. Most important, the U.S. Constitution as it is understood and interpreted today has established a federal system based on the universally appealing principles of liberty, equality, democracy, and the rule of law—the very principles the European Union professes to be based on. From this point of view, when the presidential election gives rise to intense public debate and a barrage of litigation, ultimately resolved by the Supreme Court on constitutional grounds, important lessons of principle promise to be learned. Given the extensive debates in Europe about how to constitutionally organize democracy on the level of the European Union, such lessons would promise to be both timely and useful.

There are a variety of claims that undermine the idea that there is anything of interest that could be learned from looking at the United States generally and the events surrounding the 2000 election specifically. They all have in common that they are based on an *exceptionalist* account of either American democracy or European constitutionalism. First, there are two kinds of exceptionalist claims focusing on *political culture*. According to these accounts, nothing can be gained by engaging in a comparative endeavor because American democracy is exceptional. American democracy is sustained by a particular political culture that is unique to the United States and that once again became apparent in all its glory (according to one account) or all its monstrosities (according to another account) during the postelection battles of the last presidential election. Second, there are exceptionalist accounts focusing on the *institutional structure* of the respective constitutional orders. According to the first, the U.S. electoral system is tied to a highly idiosyncratic, historically contingent, constitutionally entrenched procedure, the study of which could not possibly be helpful to illuminate anything except the quirks of American history. According to the second, the European Union is an entity that should not be thought of as a federal structure, nascent or otherwise, because European integration is a project sui generis, whose specific features are not appropriately understood when grafted on to a federalist conceptual map.

In the following I briefly describe these positions in greater detail. As will become clear, the 2000 election has thrown light on some basic features of constitutional democracy in federal systems that challenge widely held views about U.S. constitutionalism and undermine exceptionalist accounts of European constitutionalism. As the responses to the election indicate, it is no longer obvious whether the conception of constitutionalism that underlies American constitutionalism today should be conceived as a federal one properly understood, whereas there are no such grounds for doubt on the level of the European Union.

POLITICAL CULTURE, EXCEPTIONALISM, AND AMERICAN ELECTIONS: THE GOOD, THE BAD, AND THE UGLY

If one were to follow the general public reaction, as it is reflected in countless articles in journals and newspapers throughout the European Union, there would not be much beyond voyeuristic curiosity warranting an examination of the events surrounding the last U.S. presidential election. The only thing that could be learned is that the United States is not like Europe: Exceptionalist interpretations of the events surrounding the election dominate. Whether the accounts are respectful and even admiring or aggressively contemptuous and condescending, the United States is cast as the Other: a peculiar political creature, suitable either to marvel at in wonder or to exhibit and make fun of at a freak show but not something to relate to and learn from. Simplifying somewhat, it is possible to distinguish two kinds of exceptionalist interpretations. A stylized rendition of both follows.

1. The Postelection Drama as Ritual: Affirming the Democratic Faith

The first interpretation is generally positive. The drama surrounding the election made visible all those traits of American political culture described with respect and admiration by Alexis de Tocqueville almost two centuries ago. In this view the postelection spectacle was a ritual in which Americans reasserted their faith in a strong form of deliberative democracy.

After it becomes clear that the outcome of the election remains uncertain, an intense and widespread, in part even obsessive, public debate ensues about how the winner should be determined. As recounts and litigation take their course it is not only the law professors and other talking heads appearing on the national networks who put their lives on hold. Intricate electoral details are the stuff of water cooler exchanges in offices throughout the European Union. Conversations easily move from issues of fundamental principle to arcane details concerning the state of chads, ballot design, or voting machines. As the recounts proceed, the ticker tapes running on personal computer screens no longer reflect the performance of investment choices and market developments. Instead the streams of numbers flowing by are likely to be the latest ballot counts, as they come in district by district. Debates over legal technicalities concerning procedure and litigation strategy abound in public forums and private conversations. Newspapers are full of unedited court decisions dealing with various aspects of the election, to be devoured, dissected, and debated by the populace.

Yet even though the election outcome determines who is to become the most powerful public official in the most powerful nation on the globe, there is no real sense of constitutional crisis, punditry rhetoric to the contrary notwithstanding. Citizens do not for a minute start wondering whom the Pentagon will support. No generals in uniform give press conferences expressing their concerns and willingness to assume responsibility at a time of national crisis. No armed militias gather to do battle on the streets in defense of a just cause. Except for some noisy demonstrations outside counting rooms, all remains calm. The president in power does nothing to seize the moment to extend the length of his term. He does not wag his mighty finger announcing to the nation that "these candidates Mr. Bush and Mr. Gore" would both be unfit to assume the presidency in circumstances that amount to an electoral tie. He does not proclaim that, in the interest of national unity, a new election would be necessary and that it would take place after substantial electoral reform had occurred, to be undertaken with great care, all deliberate speed, and in the fullness of time.

What is more, when the highest court in the country in substance hands down a decision that declares the winner, there is a widespread consensus not only that the decision is seriously flawed but also that it should be accepted as authoritative. Calls to end the dispute prevail. The candidate declared defeated puts on a good face and makes a valiant concession speech. The new leader assumes his role, as the citizenry lets go and moves on. One hundred days after his inauguration the new president enjoys an approval rating of about 60 percent, higher than that of his predecessor at the same stage of his first term. At the same time electoral reform in many states is proceeding. America has mastered one more political conflict, as strong and as united as ever.

2. The Postelection Drama as a Strategic Struggle for Power: American Hypocrisy

A second account is less flattering but more frequently found. According to this account, the United States should no longer be regarded merely as an imperial power that executes juveniles, imprisons a fair segment of its population, celebrates guns, ignores its poor, and yet has the audacity to lecture other countries on democracy. Following the election, it also stands revealed as incapable of organizing its own electoral process in a way that plausibly meets the standards to which third world countries are held. Not least among the long list of deficiencies ranks the fact that some of the most consequential decisions were made by political officials who were anything but impartial. Instead they were intimately involved in the campaign and their political future closely connected to the outcome of the election. Does a country's democratic process deserve to be taken seriously when the state officials ultimately making the decisions in a close election are the co-chair of one candidate's state campaign (Katherine Harris) and the same candidate's brother (Jeb Bush)?

The whole debacle ends when the Supreme Court, sharply divided along political lines, declares the winner by judicial fiat. It does so in a decision that is scandalous from the perspective of legal integrity. Had the factual situation underlying *Bush v. Gore* been used as a hypothetical in law school examinations before the election few self-respecting law professors in the United States, including conservative ones, would have given passing grades to the majority opinion. Furthermore, no one acquainted with the jurisprudential sensibilities of the justices in the majority seems to seriously believe that the same outcome would have been reached if the positions of Gore and Bush had been reversed.

If this is true, so the argument goes, much of what America purports to be standing for on the level of political ideals stands revealed as hypocrisy. The commitments to democracy, the ideal of a constitutionally based rule of law, and the ideal of judicial integrity have all been undermined by the spectacle of the postelection quagmire. The case not only explains the peculiar resonance that critical legal scholars have had with their spectacular claims in American legal culture. It also explains the increasing tendency to use a rational-choice approach to explain and predict judicial decision making. Furthermore, the events surrounding the millennium election exemplify in the realm of domestic politics what is also frequently thought true for American foreign policy. Beneath the thin veneer of a value-laden political rhetoric—a world in which principle is ostensibly celebrated—political hacks of all shades and institutional affiliations devise and execute Machiavellian strategies to secure and expand their hold on power and further their own partial political agendas. From this perspective the most positive aspect of Bush's first hundred days in power is that he fails more obviously than others to hide this fact as he pursues unapologetically unilateralist foreign policies and straightforwardly oligarchic domestic policies. In terms of policy, America, in this view, has turned to embrace explicitly its ugly side, after an election process that had failed badly to cover it up.

FROM CULTURE TO INSTITUTIONS: CONSTITUTIONAL EXCEPTIONALISMS

1. American Exceptionalism as Constitutional Historicism?

Even those who remain unimpressed by these somewhat rough-grained interpretive renditions of the events have reasons to doubt the idea that there is something of interest that can be learned by studying the 2000 election. Many Americans believe that the events surrounding the election cannot be appropriately understood as a debate between different institutional actors on how to apply complex constitutional principles to a hard case. Generally, however, they do not believe in the fundamental corruption of their public institutions either. Instead they believe that the elections have brought to light the *discrepancy between the electoral system as it is constitutionally entrenched and the principles that today are thought to underlie presidential elections.* The disconnect between the principles generally thought to underlie presidential elections and the specific legal rules governing presidential elections established by the Constitution makes apparent the urgency of reform. More specifically, the Electoral College and how it is constituted is thought an outdated eighteenth-century relic. It is based on an elitist conception of government that no politician would dare endorse today. The point of elections, particularly the election of a national president, is to determine and reflect the will of the people. No one today would seriously defend the proposition that the people cannot be trusted to directly elect the president; that instead a college of distinguished and independent citizens should determine who the president and the vice president should be after deliberating the issue by themselves. Furthermore, it is today considered odd that state legislatures have the power to determine how the electors are to be chosen. According to Article II of the U.S. Constitution, state legislatures even have the powers to cancel presidential elections in their states and determine their electors. It is these kinds of anachronisms that, because they lack grounding in plausible principle, generate legal complexities that become susceptible to partisan manipulation. In the cases surrounding the Florida recount litigation, various deadlines concerning certification, meetings, and pronouncements took center stage, even though these baroque procedural hurdles had little or no connection to anything that is thought to matter today. Yet it was the Supreme Court's view of the role of these various deadlines in the general design of the election that determined the outcome of the opinion that determined the outcome of the election. Under these circumstances anyone interested in how democratic elections should be organized in federal systems would have little to gain by studying the rules governing presidential elections in the United States. Only after constitutional reform or other measures achieving similar effects have been implemented, only after a way has been found to regulate elections in a way that more closely reflects the political principles the American people endorse, does the comparative study of American elections promise to be a fruitful exercise.

2. European Exceptionalism as Constitutional Supranationalism?

Skepticism is further compounded by a view that is increasingly gaining acceptance in the European Union. According to this view, the federal system as it has matured in the United States should not be regarded as a model for things to come in the European Union. The reasons invoked by proponents of this view have nothing to do with the American exceptionalist accounts sketched above. Instead proponents of this view insist on the specific nature—the sui generis character—of the European Union. The European Union is described as a historically unprecedented supranational experiment in which member states collectively pool their sovereignty at the supranational level. They create institutions that—for reasons of regulatory efficacy—have the power to enact legislation that is directly effective in the legal orders of member states and generally takes precedence over national laws. Member states are not, however, creating a new sovereign entity legitimated by a European People. National traditions—so the argument goes—are too diverse, run too deep, and are ultimately too valuable a cultural asset to sacrifice on the altar of European integration. It is neither feasible nor desirable to achieve the kind of homogenization of political culture and civil society that sustains independent representative political institutions and democratic processes on the central level.

Since democratic legitimacy cannot effectively be achieved on the level of the European Union by the establishment of democratically effective representative institutions, decision making on that level is limited in a variety of ways in which decision making in mature federal systems such as the United States are not. First, the European Union should act only when member states cannot do so effectively. To implement this basic idea, the principle of limited and enumerated powers is complemented by the principle of subsidiarity, which further limits the exercise of the European Union's regulatory authority. Second, the political process on the level of the European Union is and ought to be linked closely to democratically accountable state institutions. This link is established by insisting on the central role that state ministers and government officials play in the European legislative process—most important, in the Council of Ministers. Third, member states collectively are and must remain the "Masters of the Treaties" that constitute the European Union. The plurality of peoples of member states that govern themselves through the institutions and processes established by their respective national constitutions remain the ultimate source of legitimacy. Conversely, the United States cannot be regarded as a model, because it exhibits three features that from this point of view are undesirable for the European Union. First, the United States is a polity in which most of the pressing problems of the day are dealt with by a central government. Second, the institutions of central government are thought to operate largely independently of state institutions. Third, those who hold public office in those institutions are accountable to the American people as a whole and not to the states.

THE LIMITS OF EXCEPTIONALISMS AND THE LESSONS OF THE ELECTION: FEDERAL CONSTITUTIONAL DEMOCRACY AND THE ROLE OF STATES

Of course, much would need to be said about such an account of the European Union and much would need to be said about the particular conception of U.S. federalism that is cast in the role of a counterexample to illustrate the specifics of the European supranational model. Ultimately, the European exceptionalist account in the form I have briefly sketched above fails to provide either a normatively convincing model of the European Union or a convincing account of federalism in the United States. All that can be done in what follows, however, is to briefly illustrate how the 2000 election has brought to light an important feature of federal elections that tends to undermine the kind of accounts provided by European constitutional exceptionalists and American constitutional exceptionalists. My argument proceeds in three steps. First, I point out some striking and generally ignored institutional features of the electoral process in the United States that the election has highlighted. Second, I briefly discuss the significance of these features for a normatively appropriate understanding of federal constitutional democracy. Third, I discuss some implications of federal constitutional democracy thus conceived for understanding European constitutionalism. More specifically, I argue that federal constitutional democracy provides a more appropriate conception of European constitutionalism than exceptionalist accounts. On the other hand, the current debates concerning federalism in the United States and the responses to some features of the electoral system indicate that there is no longer a consensus in the United States that current constitutional practice should be informed and guided by a federalist conception of American constitutionalism properly understood.

1. The Role of the States in the Presidential Elections: Beyond the Popular Vote

Perhaps the most striking feature of the American presidential electoral process is the role of states. To start, there are two ways in which the makeup of the Electoral College takes account of the special role of states, each of which creates the possibility of winning the presidency while losing the popular vote. First, there is some deviance from the principle of straightforward majoritarianism in favor of equality of states by giving small states a proportionally larger say in the makeup of the Electoral College. Second, the winner-takes-all system that applies to each state's electoral votes is also geared toward strengthening the role of the states. The system is thought to provide an incentive for candidates to campaign in smaller, less populous states rather than focus their resources on the more densely populated urban areas. Furthermore, states are responsible for drafting the laws governing election to national office. Finally, it is also the case that political parties and the political machinery that supports them are largely rooted in state politics, requiring candidates for national office to establish close connections to a state's party apparatus.

2. Federal Constitutional Democracy and the Will of the American People

Although there is no doubt that some aspects of the system, the Electoral College specifically, are outdated, some continue to believe that it is a good thing for states to have an important role in the electoral process. Of course, the president, perhaps more than any other federal officeholder, is thought to represent the American people as a whole. The outcome of the elections, therefore, should also be geared toward reflecting the will of the American people as a whole. But *even though the point of the election is to ascertain the will of the American people as a whole, there are consequences for the kind of electoral procedure that is appropriate to articulate and define what is to count as the collective will, given that the American people are organized in a federal structure.* Conversely, the ideal underlying elections to federal office in federally structured entities is not necessarily to determine which candidate gets the relative majority of the popular vote. *An appropriate construction of the will of the American people through the electoral process need not be identical with a straightforward determination of the will of the relative majority of voting citizens.* To define and articulate what is to count as the collective will of citizens in a federal structure, institutional mechanisms may well be desirable that leave an important role to states in the process of legitimating federal institutions.

This is so because *it may be desirable to bring to bear on the political process the significance of the fact that American citizens are also citizens of a constituent state.* Is there anything in this claim we have reason to be puzzled about?

If the U.S. Constitution is best understood as an institutional framework through which the American people govern themselves, this does not imply—as Rousseau had thought—that popular majoritarianism would have to be the central organizing principle for political decision making. Instead the ideal of self-government is a complex one and integrates a wider range of principles. The possibility of legitimate countermajoritarian decision making has long been discussed and is no longer thought to present a major issue. Just as judicially enforced fundamental rights can be countermajoritarian and just as congressional decision making can be countermajoritarian, it can also be the case that electoral procedures may legitimately provide for outcomes that are countermajoritarian.

It should also not be regarded as particularly puzzling as a matter of principle that in some way or another, the reasons justifying deviance from majoritarian decision making are not restricted to the protection of fundamental rights. Instead *deviance from majoritarian decision making is, in many instances, constitutionally justified, because it gives expression to the significance of the fact that American citizens are also citizens of a constituent state.* Just as the regulatory authority of the federal government is limited in order to protect the autonomy of states and just as the makeup of the Senate reflects respect for the equality of states on the level of federal decision making, there is nothing surprising about having states play a role in federal presidential elections. *All of these institutional devices are means to protect, enhance, and bring to bear on the political process the significance of the fact that American citizens are also citizens of a constituent state.*

Of course, this begs the normative questions: What is the normative significance of the fact that American citizens are also citizens of constituent states? And how does this significance relate to specific questions of institutional design? These are questions that cannot be dealt with here. It is sufficient to point out that something that at first may appear a peculiar quirk in the electoral regime fits into the federal constitutional design generally. It is a pervasive feature of the constitutional structure of the United States that it acknowledges the significance of the fact that American citizens are also citizens of constituent states. As such it is a principle that should be regarded as a constitutive part of any plausible account of federal democratic constitutionalism.

3. Federal Constitutional Democracy: Conceiving European Constitutionalism

If this is so, are there any reasons why constitutionalism in the European Union should be understood in a fundamentally different way? The main reason why many European scholars feel uneasy about using the language of federalism to describe the constitutional structure in the European Union is that national identities generally remain strong and deeply rooted in the member states. A complementary European identity is emerging only slowly and is not likely to have the cohesiveness and robustness of national identities anytime soon. There are two ways this fact is thought to be relevant for questions of institutional design. According to the first, the plurality of *national identities are an asset and have inherent normative value*. They deserve to be cultivated and enhanced, not gradually undermined and ultimately abolished. Because identities can be fostered by political practices that involve national institutions and tend to be undermined by political practices on the European level in which no reference to national identities is made, national institutions should continue to play an important role on the level of the European Union. A second argument does not make a normative claim about the inherent value of this or that identity but focuses on the *empirical features of the democratic process* that are claimed to be necessary for generating legitimacy and sorely missing on the European level. The claim is that because of the lack of a robust civil society on the European level and the lack of the necessary infrastructure of intermediaries between European institutions and European citizens—a European press, European political parties, and European public policy groups; in short: the lack of a well-constituted European public sphere—supranational electoral procedures and institutions are unlikely to be democratically meaningful. Because of this, democratic legitimacy is thought to remain closely tied up with efforts to link decision making to national actors and institutions. For these reasons the normative significance of the fact that European citizens are also citizens of constituent states is not puzzling in the European Union. What follows from this?

If, contrary to the federal democratic constitutionalist account provided above, one believed that a mature federal system is a strongly nationalized system in which the role of states is generally restricted to one of little more than administrative convenience, then the argument that the European Union is not and should not develop into a mature federal system would be very strong. Under this scenario there would seem important differences between Europe, where the role of states is significant for good reasons, and the United States, where the role of states is comparatively insignificant. If the United States were conceived as such a strongly nationalized system, not just the Electoral College but even the Senate as an institution—and certainly the ideas of substantive limits on congressional authority to legislate and of a role for states in the electoral process—would qualify as anachronisms. Many scholars in the European Union seem to think of the United States in this way. There are some constitutional scholars in the United States who endorse positions not unlike it. Much of the influential tradition of philosophically sophisticated liberal constitutional theory that has flourished in the United States in past decades has generally ignored the federal structure of the U.S. Constitution. Under these circumstances it is not surprising that European scholars believe that an alternative conceptual framework has to be found to appropriately deal with institutional and doctrinal issues as they arise in the European Union. There is much disagreement among European scholars on basic constitutional issues. There is certainly disagreement on a great variety of specific issues concerning the allocation of decision-making authority between member states and the community. But there is no disagreement about the fact that these are issues of central importance and need to be addressed. No one would describe them as mere ploys to further a particular substantive political agenda. If a mature federal system is equated with a strongly nationalized system, it is not surprising that many European Union lawyers and most national politicians in the European Union dislike the F-word and prefer an exceptionalist, sui generis account of European constitutionalism.

If, however, a very different account both of U.S. constitutionalism and of mature federal systems generally is more plausible, the case for an exceptionalist account of European constitutionalism may lose its bite. If, as suggested above, *federalism refers to the idea of a multilevel political structure, in which respect for the relative independence of constituent states is taken seriously across the whole range of issues in which it is implicated, giving expression to the normative significance of the fact that a federal citizen is also a citizen of a constituent state,* then it is a mistake not to conceive of the European Union in federal terms. It is important to clarify what this means. It does not mean that the European Union should become like the United States with regard to particular institutional arrangements. It does not mean that legislative decision-making authority should be allocated in the European Union the way it is allocated in the United States or that elections should be organized along similar lines. It does mean, however, that the basic conceptual framework in which questions of constitutional design and allocation of decision-making authority are addressed should be the same. This implies that *European constitutional practice ought to be conceived as the self-government of European citizens, just as federal decision making in the United States is appropriately conceived as the practice of American citizens governing themselves through the institutional framework the Constitution has established.* Of course, citizens of the European Union, like citizens of the United States, are also citizens of constituent states. This has implications for the kind of institutions, electoral processes, and regulatory authority that are appropriate for federal decision making. What exactly the role of the states should be depends, of course, on a variety of historically variable features.

It is very probable that the role of states in the federal process and the significance of legislative jurisdictional limits to central legislation should be significantly greater in the European Union than in the United States. The deeply entrenched cultural differences between European states, the comparatively strong sense of national identity, and the comparatively weak development of a European identity may well be valid reasons to insist on a more significant role for states in the context of the European Union.

Conversely, it is also the case that the nationalization of much of public life during the twentieth century and the absence of deep cultural differences reflected in the geographic boundaries of states justify political and legal practices in the United States that would not be tolerable in the European Union. Indeed, in the United States it is no longer obvious that there is *any* normative significance at all attached to the fact that American citizens are also citizens of constituent states. Some would go so far as to argue that the United States has in fact become a polity in which the federalist elements have lost their normative significance altogether. But if this were to be the case, then all this would imply is that the idea of federalist democratic constitutionalism as described above no longer fits the United States. Except for some constitutionally entrenched anachronisms burdening the political process and best left ignored by the federal judiciary, the United States would have become an entity resembling a unified national polity. Of course, the constitutional relics would be misused and abused by political actors for strategic purposes, thereby corrupting the political process. And the government would, for reasons of administrative efficiency— at its political discretion—leave the issues it would not want to deal with to the states. But even if this were a normatively convincing account of American constitutionalism, the reason why the European Union should not become like the United States so conceived is that the European Union has a reason to insist on its federalist constitutional structure, whereas the United States has long given up on it or may have reasons to move beyond it.

If the above account is correct, European constitutionalism is misconceived as an exercise of states pooling their sovereignty leaving national *demoi* the task of legitimating European political decisions. It is neither the states nor the national *demoi* that, under a federalist democratic constitutional conception of the European Union, are the Masters of the Treaties. That role is reserved to European citizens, who also happen to be citizens of the constituent states. Because citizens of federal polities are also citizens of constituent states, state institutions can and should have a role in the process elaborating and defining the will of the wider citizenry in federally structured polities.

Given the situation in the European Union, there are good reasons why states continue to play a significant role in its constitutional structure. How to understand the constitutional role of states in the United States at the turn of the millennium is a more difficult question. That states actually have a central role to play in federal presidential elections in the United States is a fact the presidential elections drew attention to.

Part Six

REFORM?

19

WEIGHING THE ALTERNATIVES:
REFORM OR DEFORM?

Judith Best

Alexander Hamilton began Federalist No. 68 by awarding Electoral College credits to the Framers. He noted, "The mode of appointment of the Chief Magistrate of the United States is almost the only part of the system, of any consequence, which has escaped without severe censure or which has received the slightest mark of approbation from its opponents." The modern reader is astonished! Since then, there have been more than seven hundred proposals to change or abolish the Electoral College. In fact, more constitutional amendments have been proposed on this subject than for any other part of the Constitution.

At the time Hamilton was right, because the Electoral College was that rare type of compromise that actually addressed the concerns of all. For those who wanted an independent and energetic executive, it provided a method of selection that left the president independent of any unified and continuously existing body—such as Congress. The College exists for only one day, each set of electors meeting separately in its own state capital. Thus it addressed the concerns of those who feared corrupt bargains between candidates and the selecting body. It also eliminated the need to limit the president to one long term in order to preserve the energy of the office. By requiring electors to cast two votes for president, one for a man not from their own state, it addressed the favorite son problem and gave the College a nominating function as well as a selecting function. By tying the number of electors to a state's congressional representation and by establishing the state unit rule in the House contingency election, it addressed the fears of the small states. Special state electors also answered the objections of Southern states where the right to vote was limited by slavery. And supporters of popular choice, such as James Wilson and James Madison, correctly anticipated that the states would soon use popular votes to select state electors. No wonder men of the time considered it ingenious.

However, the Framers failed to anticipate the emergence of political parties, and the result was that the method had to be changed early in our history, with the Twelfth Amendment, to create separate votes for president and vice president. This meant the College lost its nominating function. And where there is a will, there is a way. The large, populous states and the two major parties had the will to increase their influence and found the way in the unit rule, giving all of a state's electoral votes to the candidate who won a statewide plurality. The electoral system evolved and grew in a symbiotic relationship with the two-party system. The system as we know it fully emerged in the 1830s, by which time all the states except one used the unit rule and the political parties had developed national nominating conventions.

Attacks on the College began early, and Election 2000 has renewed demands to change or abolish it. According to its critics, the defects of the system are as follows: it can produce a runner-up president; it has a bias in favor of a two-party system; faithless electors could subvert an election; the House contingency election is at best awkward, at worst a potential source of corrupt deals or deadlock; and finally, because it is federal, because people cannot combine their votes with those of like-minded partisans across state lines, and because almost all states use the unit rule, it is unfair and undemocratic. A constitutional amendment would be necessary to abolish the Electoral College, and there are four such proposals on the table today: direct election, the national bonus plan, instant runoff balloting, and the automatic plan. In addition, there are two proposals that could be put into effect by state legislatures: the district plan and the proportional plan.

No election system is perfect—nothing made by men ever is. Every election plan has its own costs and benefits. Nonetheless, the Electoral College has borne the test of time. Its defects are few, its virtues many. Through two world wars, a great depression, and even a civil war, it has produced a constitutionally elected and constitutionally recognized president. This is rare stability. It is not perfect, and it may be possible to improve it. However, we must weigh the benefits against the costs of change.

The first step in cost-benefit analysis is to carefully define your goals. A presidential election is not simply a popularity contest or an exercise in self-expression. Selecting a president is not like choosing a king's champion or a prom queen—as if we had only one goal, choosing the strongest or the most beautiful. The goals of the election are many. The immediate purpose of the election is to fill the office—but more, to fill it with a president who can *govern* a continental, heterogeneous country because he can build a broad, inclusive, cross-national coalition. This requires a political process, and a head count is not a political process. If just filling the office were the only goal, we could hold a national lottery and pick a name; that would be the most democratic method. And, of course, we want to reduce the potential for fraud, if we can. Then too we want to avoid recounts, court challenges, and contingency elections because delay and uncertainty reduce the time for transition and could lead to corrupt deals or tempt foreign enemies. And most of us want to preserve our moderate, stabilizing two-party system that performs the crucial task of building majorities. The will of the people is not "out there" like some unsurveyed land to which we need only send surveyors with accurate instruments. The will of the people must be constructed and reconstructed; this is the task and the benefit of our two-party system. And that means that the coalition-building system must be sensitive to the interests of minorities of all kinds—not just racial, religious, and ethnic but also local and regional minorities.

Reform has an evil twin called Deform. Since the presidency is but one part of a complex and coordinate governing structure, all reformers must test their reforms against the fundamental structures they propose to change. Our Constitution is an organic arrangement of interdependent parts. It is like the solar system where the whole is dependent on each planet being in its place, and if you change a part, you change the whole. The separation of powers and the federal system, the fundamental structural principles of the Constitution, are the center, the sun, around which everything else in the Constitution rotates. The electoral vote system is the paradigm of that solar system because it is both democratic and federal. We do have a popular vote system *in the states*. The solar system test is the test that all reform plans must pass.

THE DIRECT ELECTION PLAN

The most popular reform plan is direct election;[1] polls indicate that 60 percent of the people support it because they think it is more democratic. Every vote would be cast and counted as if there were one big national ballot box. The plan would establish a direct, nonfederal election, and the candidate who won the most popular votes, aggregated nationally, would be president if he achieved a 40 percent plurality. If no candidate attained the 40 percent plurality there would be a popular vote runoff election between the top two candidates. This runoff provision is included because the plan empowers multiple "third" parties. Without some minimum percentage, a candidate with a 30 or 20 percent plurality could win—not enough for a president to govern.

Its advocates argue that it prevents runner-up presidents and faithless electors, has a better contingency system, and is more fair and democratic because it is a national head count undistorted by state boundaries, by the census, by voter turnout, and by the guaranteed three electoral votes for each state—which gives an advantage to small states. Most especially it is not distorted by the unit rule—which gives an advantage to large states, the two major parties, and organized minorities in competitive states.

What could be said against such a plan? Actually quite a lot. It is true that it gets rid of the faithless electors, but there are less drastic ways to accomplish that. It is true that direct election would prevent a runner-up president, but that is rare and occurs only sometimes when the election verges on a draw. We have had six such elections and only two runner-up presidents. (The first time, in 1888, there was no outcry. The second time, in 2000, within a month after the inauguration, President Bush had high approval ratings, and most reformers were focusing on updating voting machines, creating a uniform ballot, and setting uniform closing times.) It may not happen often, but why not make it impossible? The answer is, direct election may get rid of the possibility of runner-up presidents but at rather great costs.

Too many people think that if you have a direct election all you do is assure that the man with the most votes wins and just about everything else will remain the same. But as every sports fan knows, when you change the rules you change the game; you change how and where it will be played; you change the game strategies and the talents of those who can play it well. In politics as in physics there is such a thing as a critical mass. In presidential elections numbers of votes are necessary but not sufficient. To create the critical mass necessary for a president to govern, his votes must be properly distributed. He cannot simply promise everything to one region or group (the populous eastern megalopolis, or white Christians) and ignore the rest of the country. To illustrate: Why are professional football teams required to win games in order to get into the playoffs and win the Super Bowl? Let's change the rules for the playoffs and select the teams that have scored the most points during the regular season. Football fans can tell you what would happen. Teams would run up the score against their weakest opponents, and the best teams in the most competitive divisions would have the least chance to get into the playoffs. The win-games principle is the best test of the teams' talents and abilities. The win-states principle is the best test of the candidates' abilities to govern.

As direct election removes the state barriers to combining votes, it removes the quarantine on fraud and court contests. If the direct election plan had been in effect in Election 2000, we would have had fifty Floridas. The conventional wisdom is wrong: the Florida problem was not caused by the Electoral College; rather it confined the interminable recounts and court challenges to one state. In any close election, direct election would mean every ballot box in the country would be opened for multiple recounts and court challenges.

As for contingency elections, we have not had one since the current system evolved in the 1830s. Under direct election they would be the norm. This is because direct election will destroy the two-party system. The win-states requirement of the Electoral College discourages national, regional, and sectional third parties as well as single-issue and ideologically extremist candidates because their supporters cannot combine their votes across states lines. It provides a carrot and a stick for national coalition building. The carrot is the incentive it gives the major parties to respond to the complaints voiced by or the new ideas advanced by third parties. Doing so helps them to build a majority and thus to win. It provides a stick compelling third parties to compromise some of their more radical views in order to become part of a major-party coalition. If they refuse to compromise they get nothing. Compromise is the lifeblood of politics.

A plebiscite alone encourages third parties because now they can combine the votes of their supporters across state lines and thus make a clearer statement. Add to this a 40 percent runoff rule, and you have a recipe for a multiparty system with frequent contingency elections. The popular runoff allows many third parties to win something in return for their support in the runoff—a seat on the Supreme Court, a cabinet post, a promised veto on some policy. And such deals could be cut in secret. So we would have candidates of the black party, the Hispanic party, the gay rights party, the labor party, the pro- and antiabortion parties, the military party, and the left-handed vegetarians party. Not only is this likely to deepen our political divisions, we would see recounts and court challenges in all the states, first to determine if any candidate won 40 percent of the national popular vote and if not, which candidates would be in the runoff. Then there would be more recounts and court challenges to determine who won the runoff. Probably the Speaker of the House would become acting president because no winner could be declared by January 20.

The reason the Electoral College does not produce contingency elections and supports the two-party system is the magnifier effect of the unit rule. To illustrate: in 1992 Clinton won the popular vote by 43 percent, but this was magnified by the unit rule to 69 percent of the electoral vote. Perot, who won 19 percent of the popular vote, did not win a single electoral vote because he did not win a single state. We have had five elections when there were strong third-party candidates, and in each one the magnifier effect produced an electoral vote landslide for the winning candidate. Even when the popular vote verges on a draw, in all but two cases it produced an electoral vote winner. And it has never denied victory to a candidate who won a majority of the popular vote.

The unit rule does give an advantage to large states, but that is somewhat balanced by the guaranteed minimum of three electoral votes to small states. It also increases the influence of minorities who are often the swing votes in closely divided states—groups like farmers, who constitute only 2 percent of the national population, or blacks, who constitute about 12 percent. It gives minorities of all kinds many opportunities to be part of a statewide majority. And because presidents are required to win states, it is part of a system designed to balance national and local interests. It makes presidents sensitive to state and local issues. It creates a moderate politics. Just about everybody gets something.

The unit rule does not misrepresent the popular vote because that is recorded and published for all the world to see. So we know that Clinton was a two-time minority president: in neither election did he achieve the support of a popular majority. Instead it gives us a swift, sure decision, filling the office in a timely manner.

The major argument against direct election is that it does not pass the solar system test because it destroys the balance in our entire Constitution. The Constitution created a democratic, federal republic. To say that our government is federal is to say that the national government is constructed from representatives of people who live in and vote in separate states. It is to say that no votes in any national election can be combined across state lines. The Constitution itself was ratified under the federal principle. We are a nation of states. We have a community-based politics, not an identity-based politics. This system makes the distribution of the votes as important as the number of votes. The Framers wanted a president who could unite the nation, one whose popular vote support was both sufficient and properly distributed so that he could govern the whole country. They did not want a system in which the people in the largest and most populous states would choose the president without regard for the people in the smaller states.

The principle underlying the direct election plan is the assertion that the federal principle is unfair and undemocratic in presidential elections. But this means that the entire Constitution is undemocratic and unfair. Attacks on the legitimacy of the federal principle cannot be confined. They must and will extend to the Senate and the House and to the amendment process. Why should a state with half a million people have the same representation in the Senate as a state with twenty million? And why should a state with half a million people have a vote equal to a state with twenty million people on constitutional amendments? If the president should be elected by national plebiscite because he represents us all, why shouldn't we have a national plebiscite on constitutional amendments that rule and limit us all? And why shouldn't we have a national plebiscite on Supreme Court justices who interpret *our* Constitution?

The Framers knew the answer to these questions: majority tyranny. The will of the people is not the same as the will of the numerical majority, for the majority is only a part of the people. The Framers wanted to prevent majority tyranny; they wanted majority rule with minority consent. They asked: Why and when would the minority consent to majority rule? They answered: Only if the minority could see that on some occasions and on some issues it could be part of the majority. The federal principle provides multiple opportunities for minorities to be part of a state or district majority. Minorities of all kinds can be the key factor in a statewide coalition. As all our national officers are chosen directly or indirectly on the basis of state citizenship, minorities of all kinds must be consulted and their interests considered in all branches of the national government.

Because the foundation of all three branches of the national government is federal, the system is in balance and the separation of powers is preserved. If the president alone were exempted from the federal principle, he would be a Caesar. He could claim to be the only authentic voice of the people, and the balance of power would tip dangerously to the president and away from Congress. Further, if the president were exempted from the federal principle, he would be insensitive to state and local issues, thus destroying the balance between legitimate local and national interests. The federal principle is essential to the solar system of checks and balances that supplies "by opposite and rival interests, the defect of better motives." The attack on the federal principle in presidential elections is an attack on the entire Constitution.

THE NATIONAL BONUS PLAN

Another reform, proposed by a task force of the Twentieth Century Fund, is the national bonus plan.[2] The supporters of this plan want to prevent a runner-up president, get rid of faithless electors, support the two-party system, and preserve the federal principle of the Constitution. The plan would abolish the office of elector, and the electoral votes would be cast automatically. It would create a bonus of 102 electoral votes (two for each state and the District of Columbia) to be awarded to the winner of a plurality of the national popular vote. The unit rule would be mandated for the state electoral votes. The national electoral votes and the state electoral votes would be added together, making a new total of 640 electoral votes, and an absolute majority of 321 would be required to win. If no candidate won an absolute majority, there would be a runoff between the two top candidates within thirty days, and the candidate who won the electoral vote majority in the runoff would be president.

All the goals of this plan are desirable. The question is whether the plan could actually achieve these goals. Remember, when you change the rules, you change the game. This plan surely would change campaign strategies, and it could do so in a way that undermines the federal principle. If you need 321 electoral votes to win, and you can get 102 by winning the national popular plurality, you need only 219 of the state electoral votes. In Election 2000, the eight most populous states had 228. So you run a campaign designed to maximize your votes in those few largest states. The small states will be totally neglected—unneeded when you win the bonus votes— and the incentive the current system gives to candidates to create broad, cross-national, federal support disappears. As we saw in Election 2000, under the existing system, small states can be important in close elections. Gore could have won without Florida if he had won West Virginia, or New Hampshire, or Arkansas, or Tennessee.

This plan could produce a president who won far less than 40 percent of the popular vote. A candidate could do this in a multicandidate race if he won the eight largest states and the bonus votes with pluralities of 33 to 35 percent. Instead of isolating and limiting the recount and court challenges problem, this plan makes it pandemic. The 102 electoral vote bonus for winning the popular votes means that in close elections every ballot box would be infected. The bonus votes are well worth the demand for recounts and court challenges. And we already know that this problem could not be resolved in thirty days in the single state of Florida. Imagine the time it would take in the entire country.

And there could be many close elections because, despite the intention to support the two-party system, the plan could undermine it. It does this with its national runoff provision. It is the very existence of a runoff election that provides the incentive for multiple parties to enter the race. They can win something by trading on their support in the runoff. A runoff creates a second-chance psychology among voters: I'll cast a "send-them-a-message" vote in the general election because there's a reasonable possibility I'll have a second chance in a runoff. The "win-something" and "second-chance" psychologies can destroy the two-party system.

The bonus plan has been around for more than twenty years, and it has not picked up much support because it reduces the value of the electoral votes of the small states. The bonus votes are more valuable than the combined votes of twenty-two states and the District of Columbia. Because it only takes thirteen states to defeat a constitutional amendment, its chances are slim and none.

INSTANT RUNOFF VOTING

The latest fad reform proposal is instant runoff voting, sometimes called the Irish Ballot.[3] Former presidential candidate John Anderson is a leading advocate of this plan. Under this plan, the Electoral College would be abolished, and voters would rank their preferences for all candidates—first choice, second choice, . . . fourteenth choice. If no candidate wins a majority of the popular votes, the last-place candidate is eliminated, and the votes of his supporters are switched to their second-place choices. If no candidate still has a majority, the reallocation continues. The idea is to avoid the runoff problem that most other direct election plans produce. Also, it is supposed to save time and money.

This may work well enough in a small homogeneous country such as Ireland, but could it work here, in a heterogeneous continental country? Would people who could not handle the butterfly ballot have a chance of getting this right? We usually have twelve to fifteen candidates on the ballot. Most are fringe candidates who poll less than fifty thousand votes. In a close election do we want the supporters of these candidates to decide the winner? And are the supporters of such candidates likely to have picked one of the two major party candidates as their second choices?

Further, are we going to require people to cast second, third, and fourteenth choices? Given a secret ballot, how would you enforce this? Suppose many people refused to list any second choice. Or suppose they cast their second-choice votes for some total nonentity candidate, votes not even for a Nader or a Buchanan but for one of the twelve or more truly fringe candidates. This plan destroys a two-party system because it encourages and empowers small parties and gives fringe party voters a strategic advantage. This system is mind-bogglingly complicated. No one will be surprised to learn that the plan was invented by an MIT professor in 1870. It raises concerns that the candidate who wins may not be the candidate who got the most votes or who really was the second choice of most people in the country.

THE AUTOMATIC PLAN

The automatic plan[4] is designed to remove one danger in the existing system—the faithless elector. It would abolish the office of elector, and the electoral votes would be cast automatically. For almost all of our history the office has been ministerial and ceremonial, and the clear expectation of the voters has been and is that the electors must be faithful. The first faithless elector was Federalist Samuel Miles, in 1796, and he provoked the now famous retort: "Do I chuse Samuel Miles to determine for me whether John Adams or Thomas Jefferson shall be President? No! I chuse him to act not to think." One hundred million voters today would agree.

There have not been many faithless electors; out of approximately twenty-one thousand electoral votes cast, only twelve to fifteen have been faithless. Faithless electors have acted to protest or to advocate some policy or simply to get their names in the papers. Nonetheless, the office is potentially dangerous and unnecessary. The parties have taken over their nominating function, and modern communications have destroyed the argument that the people do not know enough about candidates from other states to make a choice. Most of us now know more about the candidates than we want to know. To date, no election has been stolen by a faithless elector. If it happened, the outrage would be deafening. The words *perfidy* and *treachery* come to mind. If I were a such faithless elector, I would want to have a seat on the next moon shot.

This reform passes the solar system test because it upholds both the separation of powers and the federal principle. It would simply turn what has been, since the 1830s, a de facto, direct, popular, federal election into a de jure one. I strongly support this reform, and almost no one opposes it in principle. It has not picked up steam because some think the problem can be addressed by the political parties, who choose their candidates for the office of elector and should take care to guarantee their loyalty. They conclude that it is not worth the effort to pass a constitutional amendment. Others want to abolish the federal principle in presidential elections, and this proposal not only falls far short of their goal, it also might destroy any momentum for more radical change. Further, most versions of the automatic plan would constitutionalize the unit rule and thus lose the support of proponents of the district and proportional plans. Finally, it would mean a loss of power for the state legislatures, and some are jealous of their presidential selection prerogatives.

THE DISTRICT PLAN

There are two reforms that do not require a constitutional amendment because they would not abolish the Electoral College: the district plan and the proportional plan.[5] The common purpose of these plans is to prohibit the unit rule. The states are free to choose either plan, since the state legislatures have plenary power to decide how their electoral votes will be cast. Very few have done so. To be effective, these plans would have to be imposed by a constitutional amendment.

The district plan gives one electoral vote to the candidate who wins a popular vote plurality in each congressional district and two electoral votes to the candidate who wins a popular vote plurality in the whole state. Two small states, Maine (four electoral votes) and Nebraska (five), used this plan in Election 2000.

Proponents of this plan say that it more accurately reflects the popular will in the state and encourages voter turnout. They say supporters of the minority party in a state may be discouraged by the unit rule. Take, for example, New York: before Election 2000, it was clear that Gore would win the state: the votes of Bush supporters in the rural upstate counties would be overwhelmed by Gore's strong support in New York City. Proponents of this plan conclude that the supporters of a statewide minority candidate are disfranchised by the unit rule and that it increases the influence of large states. The district plan was used by a number of states in the first presidential elections but was soon abandoned by almost all the states because it disperses a state's votes, while the unit rule consolidates them, thus giving a state more leverage in the election. It was for this very reason that Madison introduced a bill in the Virginia legislature to shift from the district plan to the unit-vote system.

One objection to the district plan is the odious and probably insurmountable problem of gerrymandering the districts. Many forms of gerrymandering have been prohibited by law and by decisions of the Supreme Court, but gerrymandering is still practiced today, and now the legislatures have computers to find ways around the laws. Other problems are that it is more likely than the current system to trigger a contingency election in the House of Representatives or to produce a runner-up president. A *CQ Researcher* analysis in December 2000 of the ten elections from 1960 through 1996 pointed out that if it had been in place, the district plan would have elected runner-up Nixon in 1960 and would have produced an electoral vote tie between Ford and Carter in 1976, thus sending the election to the House of Representatives. If this were not enough, the district plan would undermine the two-party system because it is much easier for multiple third parties to win electoral votes in a district system than under the unit rule. Finally, it makes recounts and court challenges more likely in close elections—first statewide to determine who won the constant two statewide electoral votes and then in multiple districts.

The district plan may be adopted by a few more states, but it is not likely to be adopted widely. Democrats will not support it because it currently favors Republican candidates in close elections. The 2000 election revealed a deep urban/rural divide in the country. Gore won by big percentages in urban areas, in a mere 676 counties; Bush won in 2,477 counties. Further, most medium and large states will not adopt this plan because they know that the unit rule does in fact increase those states' influence in presidential elections, thereby balancing the advantage the small states have with the constant minimum of three electoral votes. Many small states will soon understand that scattering their votes in districts only reduces their impact on the election. Unless the district plan were mandated for all states by a constitutional amendment, which is not going to happen, it is going nowhere.

THE PROPORTIONAL PLAN

The proportional plan has had its adherents for some time and for the same reasons given by supporters of the district plan—more accurate reflection of the popular vote and encouraging participation. It would assign a state's electoral votes on the basis of the percentage of the popular votes a candidate won in that state. The percentages would be calculated out to three decimal points, making this the kind of plan that accountants love. In many elections this plan would produce fifty Floridas, as if one weren't enough. With 50 electoral votes in play, depending on decimal point percentages, every ballot box in the country would be subject to recounts and court challenges to determine if any candidate achieved the 270 electoral vote majority and, if not, which three would be considered in the House contingency election. And it would make contingency House elections very common. In its analysis of the ten elections from 1960 through 1996, *CQ Researcher* found that under the proportional plan four of the ten elections would have gone to the House: 1960, 1968, 1992, and 1996. Like the district plan, this plan abolishes the magnifier effect of the unit rule, which is the reason we have not had a House election since 1824. The unit rule is preventive medicine. In 1992 Perot won 19 percent of the popular vote, but since he won no states, he won no electoral votes, and there was no contingency election.

And it would destroy our two-party system because it feeds and nourishes multiple third parties. Many third parties would win electoral votes. It is likely that Nader would have won some in Election 2000, and certainly Perot would have won many in 1992. Given the deep anger of many Democrats at Ralph Nader, who, they believe, was a spoiler candidate in 2000, it is likely the proportional plan will embitter many people and widen our political divisions. Like the district plan, this plan has no real chance of being widely adopted and for the same reasons.

CONCLUSION

The question is: does our presidential election system have a sound heart, or does it need major surgery? On the basis of cost-benefit analysis, it beats all but one of the alternatives. All of the reforms, except the automatic plan, create more problems than they solve. All the others undermine or destroy our moderate, stabilizing two-party system. All the others open the door to multiple recounts and court challenges. All, except the automatic plan and instant runoff voting, make contingency elections more likely. All, except the automatic plan, abolish the unit rule. This rule is a majority forcing and shaping device that gives candidates the incentive to build broad, cross-national, inclusive political majorities that allow a president to govern.

On the basis of fundamental principle it is the clear winner. All of the reforms, except the automatic plan, fail the solar system test. All the others would deform our Constitution because they all abandon or weaken the federal principle in presidential elections. The federal principle is the fulcrum of our entire national government. It puts a geographic community rider on the formation of majorities recognizing that people who must obey the same state laws, who live together sharing the same roads, parks, schools, climate, natural resources, and local economy do have common interests that must be represented in a national government. The federal principle in presidential elections serves to make presidents sensitive to state and local issues, supports the separation of powers by producing an independent, energetic presidency but not a Caesar, and promotes majority rule with minority consent. To abandon this principle in presidential elections is to call the Senate, the House, and the amendment process into question. It is to call the Constitution itself into question.

Alexis de Tocqueville called the federal principle "a wholly novel theory which may be considered as a great discovery in modern political science." The federal principle is an alloy. We create alloys because we want to combine the advantages and avoid the weaknesses of two different things. Steel alloys can make things simultaneously stronger, lighter, and tougher. Tocqueville intuitively understood the federal principle is an alloy because he says its advantage is to unite the benefits and avoid the weaknesses of small and large societies. It unites the strength and wealth of large societies with the liberty found in small ones. In fusing the two it creates a flexibility and diversity otherwise not found in large powerful societies. Tocqueville was right. It was "a great discovery." Let us preserve it.[6]

NOTES

1. On the direct election plan, see Judith A. Best, *The Case against Direct Election of the President: A Defense of the Electoral College* (Ithaca: Cornell University Press, 1975); Judith A. Best, *Choice of the People? Debating the Electoral College* (Lanham, Md.: Rowman and Littlefield, 1996); Neal Peirce and Lawrence Longley, *The People's President: The Electoral College in American History and the Direct-Vote Alternative* (New Haven: Yale University Press, 1981).

2. On the national bonus plan, see Twentieth Century Fund, *Winner Take All: Report of the Twentieth Century Fund Task Force on Reform of the Presidential Election Process* (New York: Holmes and Meier, 1978); Best, *Choice of the People?* 62–63.

3. On instant runoff voting, see David Wessel and James R. Hagerty, "Tired of Recounts? Try Ireland's Approach to Runoff Voting," *Wall Street Journal,* Nov. 14, 2000, at A18.

4. On the automatic plan, see Best, *The Case against Direct Election of the President,* 21, 43–44; Peirce and Longley, *The People's President,* 177–81.

5. On the district and proportional plans, see Best, *The Case against Direct Election of the President,* 17–19, 43–44; "Electoral College: Should It Be Abolished? Should It Be Changed?" *CQ Researcher,* vol.10, no. 42 (Washington, D.C.: CQ Press, December 8, 2000); Michael J. Glennon, "When No Majority Rules: The Electoral College

and Presidential Succession," in *Congressional Quarterly* (Washington, D.C., 1992), 71–75.

6. Other sources include *After the People Vote,* ed. Walter Berns (Washington, D.C.: AEI Press, 1992); "Electoral College: Anachronism or Bulwark of Democracy?" *Congressional Digest,* vol. 80, no. 1 (Washington, D.C.: Congressional Digest Corp., January 2001); *The Electoral College and Direct Election of the President: Hearings before the Senate Comm. on the Judiciary, Subcomm. on the Constitution,* 102d Cong., 2d sess. (1992).

20

THE ELECTORAL COLLEGE:
A FATALLY FLAWED INSTITUTION

Lawrence D. Longley

The Electoral College is a highly imperfect method of electing the president of the United States. At best it distorts campaign strategy and poorly represents the popular will. At worst it can create a political and constitutional crisis in determining who should be president. My argument is simple: the 2000 election, like any election, vividly illustrates the distortions and imperfections of this fatally flawed means of determining the American president. Further, as in 2000 or a future election, the Electoral College has the potential for creating a serious electoral crisis, deeply eroding the security of our democratic processes.

THE ELECTORAL COLLEGE AT ITS BEST

The Electoral College means of presidential election is of great significance, even when it produces a clear decision. The Electoral College is not a neutral and fair counting device for tallying popular votes cast for president in the form of electoral votes. Instead it invests some votes with more significance than others, according to the state in which they are cast. As a result, these distortions of popular preferences greatly influence candidate strategy: certain key states, their voters, parochial interests, political leaders, and unique local factors, are favored. This focusing on certain key battleground states—and the writing off of other states—could be easily observed in the recent 2000 presidential campaign.

The Electoral College election of the president also discriminates among types of candidates. Independent or third-party contenders with a regional following have great opportunities for Electoral College significance, while independent or third-party candidates with broad-based but nationally distributed support may find themselves excluded from winning any Electoral

College votes, as in the case of Perot and Nader. Even without receiving electoral votes, however, such candidates can prove decisive in terms of swinging large blocs of electoral votes from one major party candidate to the other. Finally, the Electoral College can reflect the popular will inaccurately because of the actions of faithless electors—individual electors who by their votes contravene the will and expectations of those who elected them.

In short, at best the Electoral College is neither neutral nor fair in its counting of the popular votes cast for the president of the United States. The problems of the Electoral College at its best can be summarized as follows.

1. The electoral college is a distorted counting device.

There are many reasons why the division of electoral votes will always differ from the division of popular votes. Among these are the apportionment of electoral votes among the states on the basis of census population figures that do not reflect population shifts except every ten years or more; the assignment of electoral votes to states on the basis of population figures rather than on a voter turnout basis; the allocation of a "constant two" electoral votes equally to each state regardless of its size; and the winner-take-all system for determining a state's entire bloc of electoral votes on the basis of a plurality (not a majority) of popular votes.

The census-based determination of electoral votes allotted each state ensures, for example, that the Sun Belt states of Arizona and Florida, which grew rapidly during the 1990s, will not have this new population growth reflected in their electoral vote total until the presidential election four years after the 2000 census—or fourteen years later. The Electoral College vote's neglect of voter turnout, either over time or among states, maintains the same number of electoral votes for each state despite possible increases in voter participation or, alternatively, continued low levels of voter participation. It is a curious feature of the Electoral College that high turnout in a state is ignored while low levels of voter participation are rewarded.

It is the constant two and winner-take-all characteristics of the Electoral College, however, that are the sources of its most significant distortions. The extra two electoral votes, regardless of population, which correspond to each state's two senators, provide an advantage to the very smallest states by giving them at least three electoral votes, whereas their population might otherwise entitle them to barely one. The importance of the winner-take-all feature overshadows all the other distortions: by carrying New York or California—even by the narrowest margin of popular votes—a candidate will win all of that state's thirty-three or fifty-four electoral votes. As a consequence, the Electoral College greatly magnifies the political significance of the large electoral vote states—even out of proportion to the millions of voters living there. This is even more the case should a large state also be a swing state—one thought likely to go either way in the presidential election.

2. Candidate strategy is shaped and determined by these distortions.

Strategists for presidential candidates know well the importance of these distortions of the Electoral College: any serious presidential candidate will spend inordinate time in the largest states. An additional day of campaigning, an extra expenditure of money, a special appeal—any of these might be pivotal in terms of winning an entire large bloc of electoral votes—in the case of California in the 2000 election, fully 20 percent of the 270 electoral votes needed to win. Candidates and their strategists do not look at the election in terms of the national popular vote but rather in terms of popular votes that might tilt an entire state's winner-take-all bloc of electoral votes.

In a race involving three significant candidates—as was the case in both 1992 and 1996 (especially 1992)—the plurality win and winner-take-all features take on special importance. A candidate in a three-way division of the vote does not need 50 percent of California's votes to win its huge bloc of 54 electoral votes. Forty percent or even 35 percent might well do it. A close three-way division of popular votes in a large state increases even further the pivotal value of that state.

3. The importance of a state's parochial interests, political leaders, and unique local factors is magnified by the Electoral College.

The distortions of the Electoral College lead candidates to focus on large, swingable states in order to win their large blocs of electoral votes, and the best way of appealing to these states is, of course, to concern oneself with the issues and interests specific to that state. As a consequence, candidates always will be exceedingly articulate about the problems of Pennsylvania's coal fields or California's defense industry or New York City's crime rates. A special premium is also placed on the role of key large-state political leaders whose enthusiastic efforts might be significant in determining that state's outcome. In the 2000 election, Mayors Rudolph Giuliani of New York, Richard Daley of Chicago, and Richard Riordan of Los Angeles as well as Governors George Pataki of New York, George Ryan of Illinois, and Gray Davis of California were consulted—and courted—by the candidates, as were the leaders of the California Hispanic and the New York Jewish communities. Political leaders, local factional feuds, and diverse issues in the large pivotal states play an unusually central role in presidential campaign politics.

In contrast, other states and their distinctive interests are neglected. Smaller states, where candidate effort resulting in a narrow plurality win could at most tilt only three or four electoral votes, generally are ignored. There is also a lack of candidate attention to states of any size that are viewed as "already decided." Candidates have no incentive, under the Electoral College, to waste campaign time or resources on a state or region already likely to go for—or against—them. In short, Delaware, for example, a very small state, is unlikely to be contested vigorously by any candidate because of its size; likewise, many of the southern and Rocky Mountain states may well be conceded to the Republican candidate and many of the northeastern and Pacific Coast states conceded to the Democratic contender as a consequence of being "written off" by all the candidates.

In short, the Electoral College focuses candidates' attention and resources on those large states that are seen as pivotal and away from voters in other states that are too small or that are seen as too predictable in outcome. The political interests of the large, swingable states are more than amply looked after; those of the other states are relatively neglected.

4. The Electoral College differs in impact on different types of candidates.

Besides distorting vote counts, the Electoral College discriminates among candidates. The two major party nominees start off on a relatively equal footing as far as the Electoral College goes; each enjoys roughly comparable potential in the large, swingable states (the much-heralded Republican "Electoral College lock" having been picked and thus effectively junked by Bill Clinton's decisive Democratic Electoral College successes in the 1992 and 1996 presidential elections). Independent or third-party candidates, however, differ greatly in their potential in the Electoral College.

Regionally based independent or third-party candidates—for example, Strom Thurmond in 1948 and George Wallace in 1968—can enjoy real benefits from the Electoral College. Because of their concentrated regional strength, they can hope to carry some states and, with these popular vote pluralities, their entire blocs of electoral votes. Their popular vote need not constitute even an absolute majority in a state: a simple plurality of votes will suffice.

Independent or third-party candidates with broad-based but nationally distributed support, in contrast, are sharply disadvantaged by the Electoral College. Without plurality support somewhere, such a candidate may be completely shut out from any electoral votes. Such was precisely the case of independent candidates John B. Anderson in 1980 and H. Ross Perot

in 1992 and 1996. Unless their support was sufficiently unevenly distributed among the states to allow Anderson or Perot to win in some states,
their voter support—even when it was as high as 20 to 30 percent—was
destined to result in total eradication in the Electoral College.

The problem here is more than just a profound unfairness to nationally
based independent or third-party candidates when their millions of popular votes result in no electoral votes. A major factor limiting the support
of these very same contenders is the view that a popular vote for them is
wasted. As the campaign comes to its conclusion, millions of voters who
might be inclined to vote for these candidates may well decide not to do
so because of the Electoral College. Voters may reason, My preferred candidate isn't likely to carry my state. Instead, one of the other, major party
candidates certainly will. I had better vote for one of them (or against one
of them by voting for the other). I want to have my vote mean something
in the election.

There is, however, a way that a "third-place" contender with wide national appeal can be of significance in a presidential election, even should
he or she not be in a position to win electoral votes. The candidate's votes
may be decisive in tilting some of the large, closely competitive states and
thereby tilting the outcome of the national election between the major
party candidates, as Ralph Nader did in 2000.

In short, the electoral college at best treats candidates unequally and
creates enormous potential difficulties for many independent or third-party
candidates, difficulties that a possible additional candidate may or may not
be able to overcome in subsequent elections. Whatever their level of success, however, independent or third-party candidates can have great significance in electoral outcomes because of the powerful impact of relatively
few popular votes in tightly contested large, marginal states, where the determination of blocs of electoral votes may ride on small and shifting state
pluralities.

5. Faithless electors may further distort the popular will.

The last problem of the Electoral College at its best—in other words, while
still producing a clear decision—is the potential occurrence of faithless
electors. In eight of the fourteen most recent elections, we have seen electors deciding, after the November election, to vote for someone other than
the candidate for whom they were expected to vote. In each of these instances, however, the defections were both singular in occurrence and insignificant in outcome. Nevertheless, they constitute a disturbing distortion
of the popular will. When one of the District of Columbia's three Democratic electors decides, as in 2000, not to vote for the District's popular vote
winner, Al Gore, the voters of D.C. have lost a portion of their franchise.

Individual electors who defect for whatever reason—strongly held issues or personal whim—have been of minor significance in the past. Faithless electors, however, might proliferate in an election, producing a very close electoral vote tally in which a few shifting electoral votes could change the outcome, as in 2000. In any case, the occurrence of faithless electors, even on an occasional basis, is one more way in which the Electoral College fails—even when definitive in its choice—to reflect the popular vote faithfully and accurately. The Electoral College is not a neutral and fair means of electing the president. Neither, as we shall now see, is it a sure way of determining who shall be president.

THE ELECTORAL COLLEGE AT ITS WORST

The Electoral College does not result inevitably in a clear determination of the election outcome. Rather, the result of the popular vote, when transformed into the electoral votes that actually determine the president, may be uncertain and unresolved through December and even into January.

1. In a very close electoral vote count,
ambitious electors could determine the outcome.

Individual electors have defected from voter expectations in the past for highly individual reasons. In the case of an Electoral College majority resting on a thin margin of a few votes, electors seeking personal publicity or wanting to bring attention to a pet cause could withhold—or threaten to withhold—their electoral votes from the narrow electoral vote leader. Uncertainty and suspense over whether there would be an actual electoral vote majority when the electors voted in mid-December could, as in the election of 2000, make the period of forty or so days following the November election a period of political disquiet.

2. An election can produce a divided verdict, one candidate receiving the most
popular votes and the other candidate winning the election in electoral votes.

An electoral outcome with a divided verdict might be conclusive in the sense that the candidate with the majority of electoral votes would become president, with little question of outright popular upheaval. The Electoral College would be seen at its worst, however, in the effect of such a "divided-verdict" election on the legitimacy of a president. Should, as in the election of 2000, a person be elected—or reelected—as president despite clearly having run second in popular preference and votes, the result would be a presidency weakened in its ability to govern and lead the American people. A divided-verdict election is, of course, entirely possible in any election with either two or three major candidates, if at least two of the candidates run close to each other in popular votes, as in 2000.

3. An election that is undecided on election night may be decided through deals and actions by the electors at the mid-December Electoral College meetings.

The most frequently expressed fear about the Electoral College concerns the possibility of a deadlock in which no candidate wins an electoral vote majority on the basis of the election night popular vote results. Most analysts assume that in this case an undecided election would go directly to the House of Representatives in January. In fact, it is entirely possible that an apparent Electoral College deadlock, based on the November returns, would set off a sequence of unsavory deals and actions involving the electors themselves.

Should an election produce an apparent election night Electoral College deadlock, a dramatic chain of events dictated in large part by the Constitution would be set into action. The forty-odd days between the election day, in early November, and the day on which the electors meet in their respective capitals in mid-December, would be a period of speculation, conjecture, and crisis. Most electors would certainly follow party lines, but some might deviate from party expectations and vote for a clear popular vote winner or to help a candidate (even one from the opposing party) who had almost achieved an electoral vote majority, in order to resolve an otherwise deadlocked election. Certainly, these nearly six weeks would be a period of intense uncertainty and unease as obscure presidential electors decided the outcome of the presidential election.

Such an occurrence is entirely possible in any close election, especially should a third-party or independent candidate be able to carry one or more states (even by thin pluralities) and thus remove that state's electoral votes from those available to the major party candidates to forge an electoral vote majority. The presidency then would be decided not on election night but through deals or switches at the Electoral College meetings in mid-December or on the basis of the later uncertainties of the House of Representatives.

4. If the Electoral College fails to produce a majority in December, the election of the president will take place in January under the extraordinary procedure of selection by the House of Representatives.

Election of the president by the House of Representatives would be an exceedingly awkward undertaking. According to the Constitution, voting in the House would be by equally weighted states, with an absolute majority of twenty-six states needed for a decision. The House would choose from among the top three candidates in electoral votes; no other compromise candidate could emerge or be considered.

Representatives would be in a great quandary as the House started to vote on January 6. Many would vote strictly along party lines, totally ignoring any strength that might have been shown by an independent or third-party candidate. Other House members might feel it appropriate or even politically necessary to vote for the candidate (the opposing major party contender, or even an independent candidate) who had carried their districts. Some members might even feel influenced by the national popular vote result or by who had received the most popular votes in their states. In other words, should an election be thrown into the House, representatives would vote in different ways for a number of different reasons. A final outcome would be difficult to predict, despite whatever partisan divisions existed.

As a result of the 2000 congressional election, the House is controlled by the Republican Party both narrowly through its total number of seats and, more important for our purposes, in terms of state delegations. Twenty-eight state delegations (the absolute constitutional minimum necessary for presidential election is twenty-six) have Republican majorities. Despite this majority of state delegations controlled by Republicans, House voting for president following the 2000 election would have been at best confused and unpredictable as members sorted out conflicting pressures of party, constituency, political self-interest, and personal preference.

Personal preference would have been especially significant in the case of representatives from the smallest states. Seven states (Alaska, Delaware, Montana, North Dakota, South Dakota, Vermont, and Wyoming) have but one representative; each would be able to cast one of the twenty-six House state votes that could elect the president. These seven individuals, representing slightly more than 4 million citizens, would be able to outvote the 177 House members from the six largest states—California, Florida, Illinois, New York, Pennsylvania, and Texas—who represent a total of more than 100 million citizens—twenty-five times more. The inequities are even starker for the 600,000 residents of the nation's capital, the District of Columbia. Lacking any voting representation in the House of Representatives, they would have no votes at all in the House election of the president of the American people.

5. A final and definitive decision by the House in January is by no means certain.

If called on to choose a president, the House would commence its deliberations and voting on January 6, only fourteen days before the constitutionally mandated inauguration day, January 20. Such a House vote would be between the Republican nominee, the Democratic contender, and whatever additional candidate had received the greatest number of electoral votes (assuming at least one additional candidate had received electoral votes). No matter how the House vote split, no matter how many state delegations were evenly divided and consequently unable to cast a vote, the constitutional requirement of twenty-six state votes would remain. The House of Representatives might well find it difficult—or even impossible—to decide on a president as inauguration day inexorably approached. It is entirely possible that the result of the presidential election could be continued deadlock in the House of Representatives past the immovable date of January 20.

If no president has been elected by the House of Representatives by noon on January 20, the Twentieth Amendment provides that the vice president–elect shall "act as President." This assumes, of course, that a vice president–elect in fact had been chosen by the U.S. Senate by receiving a majority of votes there. This would be a likely outcome, of course, since the voting there is one vote per senator and, most important, is limited to the top two contenders. It should be noted, however, that an exact tie in the Senate vote is also a possibility should the Senate be divided along precisely balanced party lines, as in 2001 (the outgoing vice president would be unable to break such a tie because Senate voting for the election of a vice president is limited to the one hundred members of the Senate). If both the House and the Senate should deadlock and be unable to resolve their stalemates by January 20, then the Automatic Succession Act of 1947 would apply. In case of a vacancy in both the presidential and vice presidential offices, the act places the Speaker of the House, the president pro tempore of the Senate, and the various cabinet officers in the line of succession to the presidency.

Another astonishing situation might arise uniquely in the Senate in the admittedly unlikely case that either the Republican or Democratic presidential–vice presidential ticket should run third in electoral votes (such was, in fact, the fate of the regular Republican ticket headed by incumbent President William H. Taft in 1912). If, for example, the Republican ticket were in the third-place position and no ticket won an outright electoral vote majority, a Republican-controlled Senate might be faced with a most curious choice for vice president—between the Democratic vice presidential nominee and the independent candidate's running mate—with the winner also being called on to serve (should the House deadlock) as acting president.

The result of a presidential election giving rise to the necessity of House and Senate decision, then, might itself not be a decisive, even if delayed, determination of a president but rather the designation of a vice president (or other official) who would only act as president. This person would fill that office for an uncertain tenure, subject to possible removal at any time by renewed House voting later in his or her term—especially following the midterm congressional elections, when the partisan balance in the House might well shift to the disadvantage of the troubled acting president. Such a presidency would be at best unhappy and weakened, subordinate to Congress because of the administration's congressional creation and possible termination, limited by the nonexistence of an electoral mandate, and crippled by uncertainty as to how long the temporary presidency could continue.

The Electoral College in future elections may, happily, exhibit few if any of these extremely serious shortcomings. Or the American people may be unlucky in an election year to follow and be faced, as in 2000, by a clear crisis in the Electoral College. At the least the Electoral College was a crucial factor in shaping and distorting the popular will in the 2000 election, and if not reformed, it will be of unhappy significance in subsequent elections.

At its best, the Electoral College operates in an inherently distorted manner in transforming popular votes into electoral votes. In addition, it has enormous potential to be a dangerous institution threatening the certainty of our elections and the legitimacy of our presidents. The defects of the contemporary Electoral College cannot be dealt with by patchwork reforms such as abolishing the office of presidential elector. This distorted and unwieldy counting device must be abolished entirely, and the votes of the American people—wherever cast—must be counted directly and equally in determining who shall be president of the United States. The election of 2000 has finally provided the American public with indisputable evidence of the failings of the Electoral College as a means of electing the people's president: the barnacles of the Electoral College should be scraped from the ship of state.

21

THE ELECTORAL COLLEGE:
A MODEST CONTRIBUTION

Keith E. Whittington

If one were to make a list of the most valuable elements of the United States Constitution, ranking them according to the importance of their contribution to preserving constitutional values, the Electoral College would fall rather low on the list. It is doubtful that we would design such an institution today if we were writing a constitution from scratch, and even the Founders came up with the device rather haphazardly. Unsurprisingly, it has been among the most frequent targets of reform, with hundreds of proposed constitutional amendments having been introduced in Congress to alter the presidential selection process. Nonetheless, the Electoral College makes a modest contribution to our constitutional and political system, and it would be unwise to tinker with it.

BUILDING THE ELECTORAL COLLEGE

Before considering the contribution of the Electoral College, it is worth specifying the matter for consideration. There are several important elements to the constitutional scheme for presidential selection.[1] First, the president is chosen directly by a relatively small number of specially selected presidential electors, not by the general citizenry. Citizens cast votes in November for electors to represent them in the formal presidential election conducted in the various states in December. Although citizens are formally voting for electors, most ballots now show only the names of the presidential candidates in order to minimize voter confusion and ease printing. Electors are generally loyal activists of the political parties who are "pledged" to vote for their party's candidate. Some states have attempted to bind electors to their pledges through the threat of small sanctions for voting unfaithfully, but there is no constitutional barrier to electors voting independently. A handful of electors, for one reason or another, have broken their pledge, though this has never affected the outcome of an election. In 2000, for example, one Gore elector from Washington, D.C., cast a blank ballot as a protest against the District's limited representation in Congress. By common practice, the presidential electors do not vote by secret ballot.

Second, the number of electors, or seats in the Electoral College, is apportioned to the states in a number equal to the number of members in the House of Representatives plus the number of senators to which each state is entitled. This apportionment slightly favors the small states, relative to population, reflecting both the equal representation of the states in the U.S. Senate and the minimum representation guaranteed to each state in the U.S. House. Thus, even the smallest states are entitled to no fewer than three electors. In 1961 the Twenty-third Amendment awarded the District of Columbia the same number of electors as the least populous states.

Third, the Constitution specifies that the electors will be chosen in a manner determined by the state legislatures.[2] The states experimented with a variety of methods for choosing electors in the early years of the Republic. South Carolina was the last state to adopt statewide popular election as the means for choosing presidential electors—in 1868, more than three decades after the rest of the states had settled on that method of selection.[3] By 1836 every state had also chosen to award its electors on a winner-take-all, or unit, basis. States that award their electoral votes as a unit to a single candidate have greater weight than states that divide their electoral votes among multiple candidates, which creates an incentive for each state to adopt the unit-vote approach. Large states are also disproportionately benefited over small states by this system as they have a larger bloc of votes to swing behind a favored candidate no matter how small the vote differential between the candidates. Since 1836 there have been periodic experiments by some states with district-based apportionment of electors, that is, awarding electors by the popular vote in each congressional district. Maine and Nebraska have employed this system most recently. Some states have allowed citizens to vote for electors individually rather than as a single-party slate. This also creates the possibility of dividing electoral votes among different parties.

Fourth, candidates must win the votes of a majority of the electors appointed. The ballots of the presidential electors are opened and counted by the president of the Senate before a joint session of the House and the Senate.[4] If no candidate wins a majority of the electoral votes, then the House, voting by state, chooses a president from among the top three candidates. Originally, the presidential candidate with the second highest number of electoral votes became the vice president. The development of political parties made that system problematic, as the election of 1800 demonstrated. The Twelfth Amendment separated the ballots for president and vice president. The Senate chooses the vice president from the top two candidates if no candidate wins a majority of the electoral votes.

The presidential selection system has developed importantly since the Founding, but the bare constitutional bones of the Electoral College were put together with a combination of choice and happenstance. In Federalist No. 68, Alexander Hamilton concluded that the Electoral College scheme was "at least excellent" if "not perfect." No doubt the system seemed pleasing in part because it at least resolved the thorny problem of presidential selection that had bedeviled the Framers throughout the Philadelphia Convention.[5] The Convention initially considered following the example of the majority of the states at that time and giving the power of choosing the chief executive to the legislature. That proposal was never satisfying, however. Congressional selection of the president undermined the independence of the president and gave too much power to the legislature. At the same time, if the president could serve for more than one term, then the system also encouraged intrigue and the corruption of the legislature by an ambitious president seeking reelection. The obvious alternative, direct popular election of the president, had its own problems. Although everyone expected George Washington to be the first president, many of the Founders doubted that the people in a country as large as the United States would be able to know and evaluate the average presidential candidate. The most populous states could also expect to dominate a presidency selected by general election.[6] With only one chief executive, the Constitution needed to ensure that the president would represent the whole nation if states with diverse interests were to be expected to join the union. In the legislature, a balance of interests could be achieved by adding more representatives. The Founders' desire to vest executive power in only one person closed that route. Balance would have to be achieved through the mode of selecting the president.

The Electoral College was a useful compromise for the Philadelphia drafters that seemed to solve several of their problems at once. It replicated the carefully negotiated scheme of representation embodied in the Congress, without actually using Congress to choose a president. The temporary and diffuse nature of the Electoral College eliminated the concern with intrigue and corruption in the presidential selection while ensuring the appropriate independence of both the legislative and the executive branch. The presidential electors would be more likely to be able to evaluate the less famous candidates than would the people themselves, and the most democratic chamber of the national legislature could still serve as a backstop if no candidate could win the support of an electoral majority.[7]

The Founders' concerns are not our own. Even if the Electoral College was an essential compromise that helped to secure the success of the early Constitution and Union, it may no longer be particularly valuable. The rise of mass political parties and, later, modern campaign fund-raising and media have provided new routes by which lesser known presidential candidates can gain national and popular attention and renown. Unsurprisingly, the role of the constitutionally prescribed presidential electors became merely ministerial as soon as political parties emerged to nominate presidential candidates and mobilize popular support on their behalf. An informal network of party operatives, campaign consultants, political donors, and journalists has replaced the electors as the preferred mediators between the candidates and the people. We are also more likely to think of ourselves as part of a single nation than did Americans living during the first several decades of the Constitution's operation. We do not live under the threat that an outlying state may refuse to join or may secede from the Union if its interests are not sufficiently represented in the government. Citizens are now generally integrated into the polity individually rather than territorially, and so we may not share the Founders' solicitude for small states and geographic minorities. If we are to retain the Electoral College, we will do so for our own reasons, not for theirs.

The history and continuing development of the mode of presidential selection should not be irrelevant to our current judgments, however. On the one hand, the system has proven remarkably adaptive to changing social and political conditions, and that has minimized the need for changing it. On the other hand, the very unpredictability of the historical developments that have surrounded the Electoral College should caution us against unnecessary tinkering or wholesale reform. It could not have been expected that the presidential selection system would have to handle the rise of political parties or the expansion of the nation across the continent or the creation of modern media campaigns. It was not foreseen that states would game the system by packaging their electors as a bloc or that Congress would become so responsive to public opinion. The Founders adopted a scheme to solve their problems, and we have been fortunate that their mechanism has proven sufficient for later generations as well. It is difficult to predict the course of future events or the influence of basic constitutional changes on the shape of politics. Unless the existing system is significantly and irredeemably broken, we should hesitate to attempt to fix it with untested schemes of our own. It is difficult to sustain the case that the Electoral College is importantly broken, and we should respect its modest virtues, including adaptability and durability.

SOME POTENTIAL PROBLEMS, REAL AND IMAGINED

Some of the potential problems with the Electoral College are more theoretical than real. Despite our current concern about divided government and the periodic appeal of parliamentary systems to some scholars, there does not appear to be any popular desire to reconsider the basic constitutional choice of removing presidential selection from the hands of the legislature. The question is simply how best to institutionalize a system of popular presidential selection. The potential problem of the faithless elector can likewise be laid aside as unimportant. The electors lost their effective agency as soon as that agency lost its legitimacy. Constitutional practice has adjusted to changing political beliefs, rendering formal change in the constitutional text extraneous. Precisely because the office of presidential elector has lost its importance, it is occupied by those known more for loyalty than for constitutional savvy or political judgment. The very ordinariness of the individuals who serve as presidential electors discourages them from attempting to seize a more independent role, and those psychological inclinations are reinforced by layers of ritual and public oversight at the moment of electoral balloting. Electoral margins are rarely so small as to make a single idiosyncratic elector important, and the Founders' design is supplemented by strong social norms against any candidate attempting to tamper with the Electoral College and influence the electors or profiting from such actions. No aspect of the Electoral College seems so strange, and indefensible, as the existence of the human electors themselves, and yet no aspect is so unimportant in practice.

The 2000 election has called our attention to other potentially troubling but still fairly minor features of the Electoral College: state specification of the manner of choosing electors and congressional arbitration of the results. They should be briefly addressed. All the states fairly quickly adopted popular election as the method of choosing presidential electors (usually as a party slate), but there remains the potentially problematic condition of state electoral laws and the possibility of state legislatures reversing that decision. As for the first, there is no defense for flawed electoral laws, but the remedy is clear and readily available through state statute. It should be noted, however, that complaints about state electoral systems often arise out of substantive disputes rather than mere technical errors. Although some might prefer to impose a single vision of how elections should be conducted, a decentralized system has the virtue of allowing experimentation and reflecting genuine disagreement over the proper form of democracy. Over the course of American history, this decentralization has nurtured a variety of reform movements and made the system as a whole more adaptable. If some states have seemed behind the curve, others have been pushing ahead in testing new voting technologies, advancing progressive ballot designs, or varying the awarding of electors. As for the second, it seems clear that state legislators are generally in no hurry to take over the responsibility of choosing presidents from the voters—whom the legislators themselves will have to face in short order. Nonetheless, there are times when such measures may be appropriate. The Founders' electoral design is admirably filled with contingencies leading to timely resolution. Over the course of a nation's history, things can go wrong in unforeseeable ways, and it is sensible to plan for such contingencies in a manner that optimizes both democratic accountability within the states and the orderly transition of power in the nation.

Among the contingencies for which the Founders planned is the possibility that no presidential candidate will win the support of a majority of electors. Given the large expanse of the new nation and the lack of organized political parties, the Founders thought this contingency quite likely. Rather than accept a president with less, perhaps substantially less, than majority support, they preferred that the most democratically accountable body in the national government, the House of Representatives, choose a winner. This has been necessary only twice, in 1800 and 1824. On the first occasion, the need arose from an unforeseen complication of the rise of political parties that was corrected by the Twelfth Amendment; on the second, from the collapse of all political parties and the absence of any obvious presidential candidates around which a majority could rally. It is notable that the only other elections that have threatened to go to the House (in 1876 and 2000) did so as a result of disputes over the counting of the votes rather than because of the failure of any candidate to win an electoral majority. The need for such an election judge can be minimized, but it cannot be eliminated. It is not clear what institution we would prefer to arbitrate a disputed presidential election if not the electorally accountable House (the Supreme Court perhaps?).

Even the election of 1824 was not the notable failure for the presidential selection system that it is often portrayed as. The election of 1824 marked the end of the so-called Era of Good Feelings after the disintegration of the first political parties and before the rise of new parties. As a consequence it came closer to the Founders' expectations, with four regional candidates splitting the popular and electoral vote between them. Andrew Jackson won a plurality of the electoral and popular votes, but on the first ballot the House chose John Quincy Adams to serve as the nation's sixth president. Adams was limited to one term, as Jackson soundly defeated him in 1828. The Jacksonians harassed Adams throughout his term with charges of a "corrupt bargain" between the president and his new secretary of state, Henry Clay, who was both Speaker of the House and the trailing fourth presidential candidate in 1824. The charges leveled by the frontier military hero of the common man against the aristocratic son of a former president, cemented by Jackson's subsequent electoral triumph, have long tarred the constitutional role of the House in the presidential selection process. We should not be unduly swayed by results of the Jackson-Adams rematch, however. The Adams administration was a political disaster, plagued by policy errors and internal backbiting. Adams's reelection bid was doomed on its own merits, and Jackson took advantage. The existence of the "corrupt bargain" itself is dubious. Clay and Adams were in fact in substantial agreement on policy, and Adams actually carried fewer state delegations in the House than might have been expected based purely on the legislative voting records of the House members. Congressmen who voted for an Adams presidency actually fared better in their own reelection bids than did those who voted for Jackson. It also bears remembering that in 1824 Jackson managed to win only 42 percent of the popular vote, and several states did not yet choose presidential electors by general election and thus could not be included in those totals, including the large and pro-Adams state of New York. It is not evident that the House has performed badly when it has been called into service to resolve closely contested presidential elections.

The question of the Electoral College ultimately turns on its principle of apportioning the vote and the relative desirability of its primary alternative, direct popular election. The Electoral College replicates the representational scheme of the Congress. Both the president and the Congress speak for the same metaphorical people, and there is a pleasing symmetry in grounding both the executive and the legislative branches in the same electoral base. But, it is charged, that mode of presidential election is undemocratic. It is possible for the "wrong person" to win the presidency, as the loser of the popular vote can nonetheless win a majority of the electoral vote. This defect can of course be remedied simply by eliminating the Electoral College and choosing the president strictly on the basis of the popular vote. This is the central challenge to the Electoral College, and it must be addressed at somewhat greater length.

Democratic elections are a deceptively simple concept. In practice, there are a wide variety of electoral procedures serving a variety of competing goals, including interest representation, legitimization, securing accountability of government officials, provision of good government, and the orderly transition of power. There is no singly correct formula for institutionalizing democracy. Democratic elections may be at-large or within districts, divide power proportionally or in accord with majority rule, organize around parties or around individual candidates, conclude with a single ballot or require multiple ballots, or be structured in a variety of other ways. Laying aside the in-practice trivial fact that electoral votes are registered through human electors rather than automatically, the Electoral College is democratic.

The political winner is not a natural phenomenon. It is a creature of political institutions. The Electoral College cannot produce the "wrong winner." The right winner is defined by the electoral rules. The national total of the popular voting for president is literally meaningless, though easily calculated and widely reported. The Electoral College does not fail to accurately translate the national popular vote into an electoral winner.

It determines the winner based on an entirely different standard, the state-based electoral vote.

One difficulty with the wrong winner thesis is that it ignores the effects of campaigns on electoral outcomes. Candidates understand the rules of the game when they enter the contest and map their strategies for victory accordingly. As a result, historic national popular vote totals are not particularly meaningful. Successful presidential candidates do not run a single, national campaign designed to maximize their popular vote. They run fifty state campaigns designed to secure an electoral majority. Resources dedicated to maximizing voter turnout in states that are already safely in a candidate's column would have been wasted and could have been more effectively used in mobilizing supporters in a handful of pivotal swing states, and thus candidates do not use their limited resources in that fashion. If a candidate happens to win a majority of the national popular vote in a closely contested election, it is essentially an accident. From the organization of the political parties to the selection of party nominees to the purchase of campaign advertising, American electoral politics is shaped by the strategic expectations built into the Electoral College. It is not possible to convert the actual results of presidential elections under the Electoral College into hypothetical results under alternative systems because it is not possible to know how the campaigns would have developed under those alternatives. Elected officials gain democratic legitimacy not from winning hypothetical elections under alternative electoral schemes but from winning actual elections conducted according to known rules.

The logic of the wrong winner thesis is not usually applied in other, similar contexts. It is only the transparency of the national popular vote that lends it credibility, not its intrinsic merit as a theory of elections or democratic legitimacy. In fact, there is some discrepancy between popular votes cast and electoral outcomes in most electoral systems, and it is not necessarily the primary goal of electoral systems to minimize that discrepancy. This is most obviously the case in legislative assemblies. It is never reported and never a point of concern what the national vote total might be for the majority party in the House of Representatives, for example. It is well recognized and fully accepted that what matters are votes cast within congressional districts and that political power within the House is distributed according to the number of seats won by a party, not the number of votes cast for that party. If some congressional candidates of the Democratic Party win by landslides, the "extra" Democratic votes in those congressional districts have no consequence for total Democratic power in the House of Representatives. Because seats (whether in a legislative assembly or in the Electoral College) come in chunkier increments than do votes, there is always a "votes-seats gap," though the districting structure of the U.S. House creates a larger gap than a variety of alternative electoral arrangements.

Vote totals must be translated into an allocation of seats, or political power, and there are many formulas for making that translation consistent with democratic norms.

Even in the context of the elections of individuals it is not obvious how else to evaluate whether a candidate deserves to win other than by the fact that he or she did. It cannot be that the fear of the wrong winner reflects a fear of a president who did not receive the support of a popular majority. Nearly half of the presidents in American history received less than a majority of the votes cast in their elections. President Bill Clinton, for example, never won a majority of the votes cast in his two presidential elections and first won office with the support of only 43 percent of the voters. To the extent that voters can choose from more than two candidates, it would not be surprising if a majority voted for someone other than the eventual winner—or, to put it more forcefully, voted against the winner. Of course, it is also true that a large number of potential voters choose not to vote at all, and thus the registered popular support for any successful presidential candidate is actually substantially below a majority of the citizenry. To continue the 1992 example, Bill Clinton's measured share of support among registered voters was a mere 34 percent and only 24 percent of the voting age population. How should such citizens be incorporated into the calculation of the right winner, if not simply by determining the winner by following the established electoral rules? The question is of immediate interest because voter turnout is partially related to the nature of the campaigns. If the campaigns could have chosen to mobilize more of their supporters but did not for a variety of strategic reasons, then it is not clear why these strategically unmobilized voters are any more or less relevant to determining the right winner of the election than the "excess" voters who helped to create a popular but not an electoral majority.

Politics is all about match-ups. As social choice theory has amply demonstrated, voting outcomes crucially depend on the voting rules, including those rules determining the set of choices available to voters. Electoral outcomes would look different if voters were to choose from a set of six viable candidates rather than a set of two, or if they were offered a different pairing of candidates (e.g., John McCain vs. Al Gore rather than Bush vs. Gore). We do not generally regard successful candidates as suffering from a lack of democratic legitimacy if we know that a stronger opponent was waiting in the wings but did not enter the contest, or more provocatively was not able to win the nomination of a major party. Such possibilities are particularly telling because the available choice set is largely a function of the established electoral rules. The Electoral College discourages third-party candidates, and the party primary system is designed to mirror the Electoral College—resulting in the selection of party nominees who are more likely to succeed in a general election in the Electoral College. The importance of the electoral rules does not come into play only at the end of the process, when we compare national popular votes and electoral votes. It infuses the entire electoral process. Not only is it arbitrary to discount those rules only at one stage in the process, but it is also incoherent to imagine democratic legitimacy as separable from the electoral rules. It is always possible to claim that some silent or silenced majority really favored some other candidate. Every winner is the "wrong winner" from the perspective of some alternative set of electoral rules. For that reason, democracy exists only within electoral institutions, and the only correct democratic winner is the candidate who is successful according to the existent electoral rules.

THE ELECTORAL COLLEGE AND CONSTITUTIONAL GOVERNMENT

It is, of course, possible to give up on the wrong winner thesis while still holding that this is the wrong electoral system and should be changed. The Electoral College, like the rest of the U.S. Constitution, embraces popular government but is skeptical of mere majoritarianism. A central problem of constitutional government is the difficulty of checking political power and holding political leaders accountable. Elections are an important mechanism for securing accountability, but they do not fully solve the problem of political power. Though elected political leaders are less likely to use their power to abuse the citizenry broadly than those not subject to electoral accountability, they and their supporters may still safely use their power to abuse a segment of the citizenry. The Founders were deeply concerned about this problem of "majority tyranny." The Constitution is filled with a wide variety of mechanisms for channeling political power toward productive ends and containing the threat of majority tyranny. The most prominent of these to modern commentators is judicial review, frequently if not entirely accurately regarded as "countermajoritarian." But many others—including separation of powers, bicameralism, federalism, and representative government—are not at all countermajoritarian. Rather, they affect how majorities are constituted. The basic structure of Congress reflects that principle, and it is likewise built into the constitutional mode of electing a president. To the extent that the president would be a powerful government official, the Founders wanted him to be responsive to the broad needs of the nation as a whole. But there is a trade-off between responsibility and capability, and the Founders wanted at least to ensure that the president would not be responsive only to narrow majorities. The Electoral College is designed to broaden the president's constituency. In doing so, it seeks to be simultaneously democratic and constitutional.

The Electoral College requires presidents to win what might be called a federal majority. It is not enough to win a simple national majority to win the presidency. A successful candidate must also win a geographically broad majority. The design of the Electoral College is a variation on the principle of government by concurrent majorities. The great antebellum politician and political theorist John C. Calhoun usefully argued that this was the central principle of the U.S. Constitution, requiring that not just one but several popular majorities approve of government actions. James Madison doubted the effectiveness of judicial review and the "parchment barriers" of a Bill of Rights precisely because there was no other base of political power in a republican government other than popular majorities. In a mixed system, such as the earlier British government, representatives of the aristocracy or monarchy checked popular representatives. In a republican government, there is only the people. The Constitution's attempt to get around this problem, without violating democratic principles, was to create multiple institutions with different terms of office and different electoral districts that represented different aspects of the people. Government could take action only when these multiple majorities were in agreement. The Electoral College is not the most important instantiation of the principle of government by concurrent majorities, but it is one instantiation of it and it is an important principle for ensuring that democratic government is also constitutional government. The rejection of the Electoral College precisely because it embodies that principle is a rejection of the central commitments of the Constitution as a whole.

The Electoral College is a modest check on national majoritarianism. The Founders judged that, all things considered, it would be preferable for the president to have not merely popular support but popular support widely distributed. The Electoral College favors candidates who have supporters broadly distributed across the country. The Electoral College does not reward candidates for being able to win extraordinarily large majorities in only a small part of the nation. Any votes won beyond a plurality in any given state are wasted from the perspective of the Electoral College. It is not enough for a presidential candidate to have the deep support of a handful of large states or of a particular region of the country. Under the Electoral College, a successful presidential candidate must be, or must become, a national candidate.

The Electoral College does not create an absolute barrier against regional or favorite-son candidates gaining the presidency, but it makes it more difficult for them to succeed. Sectionalism was an obvious threat to the future of the Union in 1787. The states were not yet politically, socially, or economically integrated, and state independence was a real possibility. The small states feared that the big states would dominate the new national government to their detriment. Various regions of the country feared that the others would gain dominance and turn the national government to their disadvantage. The Electoral College reduces the problem of sectional animosity and state favoritism. When it has been unable to do so sufficiently, national politics and American society have suffered. At the extreme, when a strictly Northern candidate who was not even on the ballot in most Southern states was nonetheless able to win the presidency in a four-way race in 1860, disunion and civil war were the nearly inevitable results.

It is shortsighted to imagine that such sectional animosities are of only historic interest. Constitutions must not only address the problems of the present moment, but must also be capable of forestalling the problems of the future. It is often too late to reform the constitutional arrangements when those new problems make themselves evident. By then, the competing interests have hardened and the stakes of reform are too visible; compromise and accommodation become too difficult to manage. Nations across the globe give evidence that regional conflicts are a perennial political problem. If the United States is currently relatively free of such conflicts, we should not readily assume that this will still be the case a few decades or a century into the future, when, we hope, our Constitution will still be operating. Taking down our constitutional protections in the political good times may only lead to regrets in the political bad times. But we should not be too complacent about the problem of regionalism even now. Without question, the country is more integrated and more completely a nation now than it was in the middle of the nineteenth century, but there are still important regional differences in the United States rooted in economics, demographics, culture, and even the weather. Although fortunately not torn by an issue such as slavery, the country is still differentially affected by a host of more mundane issues, from energy policy to natural resources conservation and use to industrial and agricultural policy to transportation policy and even international trade and foreign policy. In part because of these differences, the political parties usually have a core regional base. The Electoral College creates incentives for the parties to reach beyond that base in order to be successful. When parties are insufficiently attentive to the interests of some regions, their hold on the presidency is endangered. Starting with the election of 1896, the Democratic Party embraced Populism and retreated into the South. Compared to a national popular vote, the Electoral College devalued the overwhelming support the Democratic Party had in the one-party South and overvalued more evenly divided swing states. The Democrats were not competitive for the presidency until they broadened their coalition beyond the solid South by nominating New York's Franklin Roosevelt and reaching out to the urban North. Similarly, the modern Democratic Party has been most successful when it has nominated candidates from the South, which is now central to the Republican presidential calculation. Geography is not destiny, but it is often politically relevant. The American constitutional system encourages political officials to overcome such differences of interests through compromise and coalition building and encourages presidential candidates to incorporate into their coalition concern for a broad range of states and interests.

The primary incentives of the Electoral College relate to regions and breadth of constituencies. This is related to but not quite the same as federalism and its particular concern for differentiating the responsibilities of the states and the national government. Both constitutional structures—the Electoral College and federalism—address the problem of geographic diversity of political interests, but the Electoral College tries to make national officials more responsive to those interests and federalism tries to devolve political power to state and local officials who are likely to be the most responsive to those interests. To the extent that federalism constraints on national power have eroded over the course of the twentieth century, the Electoral College may in some ways have become even more important to the constitutional system than it was when the national government had fewer responsibilities. The more policies are made at the national level, the more important it is that national political officials are sensitive to local differences and concerns.

The structure of the Electoral College may also play a modest role in helping to preserve federalism constraints. The Supreme Court has occasionally attempted to enforce the federalism constraints imposed by the Constitution on national power, but the "political safeguards of federalism" historically have been more important if not completely reliable. The representative structure of the national government is built on the backs of the states. The presidency itself can be won only by waging numerous state campaigns. To win presidential electors, candidates must obtain popular majorities within individual states. To do so, they have relied on the local knowledge and resources of state party officials. The national political parties developed as federations of state political parties, which every four years are collectively mobilized for the sake of winning presidential elections. The Electoral College encourages presidential candidates to nurture local party connections, which serves the twin values of strengthening the political parties as organizations and preserving federalism. The ties that presidential candidates must, out of electoral necessity, develop with state and local political officials can make those candidates sensitive to the interests of local political institutions and officials as well as to those of state and local constituencies. By forcing presidential candidates to win elections one state at a time rather than one voter at a time, the Electoral College nurtures the development of relationships between presidents and state leaders, a political safeguard of federalism. To this extent, the Electoral College is a countervailing force against the prevailing modern trend of independent presidential campaigns run through the media by national political consultants. In doing so, it makes a modest contribution to the maintenance of grassroots democracy and the institutions of federalism.

The Electoral College does not affect whether presidential candidates construct national popular majorities. It affects how those majorities are constructed. It encourages candidates to build broad coalitions rather than deep but narrow coalitions. It encourages candidates to be responsive to the diverse interests of different parts of the nation rather than the particular interests of only the most populous or naturally supportive areas. It encourages them to build local relationships rather than rely on national affiliations. The effects of the Electoral College are more modest than overwhelming. It creates incentives, but it cannot force candidates to behave in particular ways. Those incentives also have different particular implications in different historical circumstances. If a single region of the country is small enough and isolated enough, candidates may still ignore it, as when the nineteenth-century Republican Party abandoned the solidly Democratic South. If some areas of the country have stable and overwhelming preferences for a single party, then presidential candidates may actively compete only for a smaller number of swing states, as the two parties did in the late nineteenth century. If partisan support is more evenly distributed, then candidates may be forced to compete more actively in most of the states, as is more true in the modern era. The incentives of the Electoral College run counter to the general tendencies of contemporary politics, with its emphasis on national opinion polls, media campaigns, candidate-centered elections, and plebiscitary government. Eliminating or substantially reforming the Electoral College may only strengthen features of contemporary politics that many already find troubling.

COMPARED WITH WHAT?

The contribution of the Electoral College to the American constitutional system can also be seen through a brief consideration of some of the alternatives to it. It should be noted that the Electoral College is not the only electoral approach possible for advancing the principle of concurrent majorities. Even at the time of the Founding and certainly now, many issues divide citizens within the states as much as they divide citizens between the states. Individual citizens may well feel more of a connection with their fellow partisans in other states than with some of their fellow citizens within a state, and geographic representation may not reflect those intrastate divisions. The principle of concurrent majorities could be used in support of an electoral system empowering a variety of potential political communities, including those formed on race, class, occupation, or the like. But such alternatives are in many ways less appealing and more rigid than the Electoral College's geographic approach and are certainly far less consistent with American political culture and historic practices. Although such proposals are of theoretical interest, none is currently politically significant. It may also be noted that even though the Electoral College does not encourage candidates to mobilize some voters within particular states, it does not necessarily follow that it does not encourage candidates to appeal to their interests and mobilize voters with the same or similar interests in other states.

The most prominent alternative to the Electoral College system is simply the national popular vote. This alternative, of course, abandons the principle of concurrent majorities in favor of simple majoritarian democracy. In doing so, it eliminates any distinctive constitutional consideration from the selection of the president and simply recognizes the president as a national officer selected by a simple majority of the national populace. It reinforces and to some degree formalizes the development in twentieth-century politics of regarding the president as the sole and direct representative of the national majority in the U.S. government.

The national popular vote highlights the contribution of the Electoral College to maintaining the two-party system. National popular vote proposals often include a provision for a runoff election if no candidate crosses some minimum threshold of popular support, sometimes set at 50 percent, sometimes at 40 percent. The runoff provision is obviously designed to ensure that the winning candidate in fact has the support of a large proportion of the population and again to prevent the possibility of a "wrong winner" as a multicandidate election fractures what might otherwise have been a majority coalition, as when the socialist Salvador Allende won the Chilean presidency in 1970 with less than 37 percent of the vote in a three-way race. Allende was later deposed in a coup. On its face, such a runoff provision seems like a mere safety measure, since no winning presidential candidate other than Abraham Lincoln in 1860 has polled less than 40 percent of the popular vote. But that assumes that elections are unaffected by the structure of the electoral system and thus that historic experience under the Electoral College can be readily extrapolated into a future under a national popular vote. Such an assumption is unwarranted. Electoral systems affect the incentives and strategic calculations of potential candidates, and campaigns and elections under such a proposed system could look quite different from current presidential campaigns.

Political systems with a presidency tend to encourage the formation of a two-party system. There is only one presidency. The office is winner-take-all. Losing candidates—and parties—are shut out and gain nothing. As a consequence, aspirants for the presidency are encouraged to form as large a coalition as possible before the election in order to ensure an electoral plurality. By contrast, the numerous seats in a legislature allows for the sharing of power by multiple parties. Even parties with relatively limited popular support can win some seats in the legislature. Narrowly focused political parties can thrive in parliamentary systems because legislative majorities, which may be formed by the coalition of several small parties, select the prime minister. A political party need not win a popular majority to have a share of political power in a parliamentary system, and thus parties do not necessarily seek popular majorities. Governing coalitions are formed after rather than before the election. The American constitutional system, in which control of the executive branch must be contested separately from legislative elections, will make the survival of significant third parties difficult regardless of the exact procedures by which the president is elected.

In the context of a presidential system, however, electoral systems that provide for runoffs create incentives for more than two candidates to enter the race. An electoral system in which the candidate with the most votes wins (even if that is less than a majority of the votes) tends to drive out candidates and political parties that do not have a reasonable chance of securing a majority of the votes. Votes for someone other than one of the two most popular candidates are effectively wasted. Knowing that, voters are unlikely to waste their votes. Presidential aspirants with any prospects for a future political career are unlikely to want to damage those prospects by playing the spoiler in a single election. Political activists and donors will recognize the greater likelihood of having political influence working within an existing and stable political party than attempting to create a new one. The political parties that form under such rules will generally tend to produce centrist candidates capable of appealing to the middle of the electorate.

The possibility of a second ballot—a runoff—radically changes that calculation. Candidates and parties who cannot win on a first ballot may be able to win on the second, after the field of candidates has been narrowed. In a single-ballot system, there is only one path to victory: winning a plurality of the votes. A second-ballot system opens a second path to victory: forcing a runoff and winning a majority on the second ballot. Someone is guaranteed to win a majority of the votes on the second ballot, but the choice may well be between two narrowly focused or extremist candidates. Neither of the final candidates may have been capable of winning a single-ballot contest, and yet they may be fully capable of securing a place on the second ballot. Centrist candidates, for example, may be outflanked in both directions on the first ballot and thereby fail to draw enough support to contest the runoff.

Formally, the Electoral College is a three-ballot majority-rule system. In practice, it has operated as a particularly strong single-ballot plurality system. Although the presidential electors cast a "second" ballot, they do not exercise independent choice in casting that ballot. Presidential candidates must win a majority of the electoral vote in order to avoid sending the contest into the House for a runoff (or "third" ballot), but this has not been a real threat in practice. Because the Electoral College magnifies popular vote victories, it is usually only necessary for a candidate to win a plurality of the popular vote in order to win a majority of the Electoral College. In addition, the Constitution moves any presidential runoffs to a different electorate, the members of the House of Representatives voting by state delegation. These two considerations make strategic calculations based on the House contingency extremely difficult, and almost no candidate since the early nineteenth century entered the race expecting or hoping to send the election into the House. Although presidents elected without a popular vote majority are common, elections without an electoral vote majority are extremely rare, having occurred only in 1824. The practice of awarding states' presidential electors as a single unit makes third-party candidacies even more difficult. Candidates must be able to win a plurality within a state in order to win any electoral representation. Third-party candidates may be able to affect which major-party candidate wins a state's electors, but they have not been able to prevent some major-party candidate from gaining an electoral majority. Whereas major-party candidates are rewarded for having their supporters evenly distributed across the country, third-party candidates may be rewarded for having geographically concentrated support. A regional candidate may be able to win a plurality and thus some electors in a small number of states, as George Wallace did in 1968. In a closely divided contest, this could throw the election into the House. Even so, the election within the House is not structured to favor regional candidates, and thus this remains a poor electoral strategy for a serious presidential aspirant. Unsurprisingly given these incentives, third-party candidacies have either been trivial or extremely short-lived in American history.

Abandoning the Electoral College for a national popular vote may have unintended, and undesired, consequences for the party system. Whereas the Electoral College discourages third-party candidates, a national popular vote with runoff provisions encourages them. This could encourage independent runs for the White House, for example by presidential aspirants disappointed in the party primaries or emboldened by the profile of existing candidates. The major parties would no longer be the only viable vehicle for a presidential candidate, and thus the costs to the individual candidate of defecting from the party will be lower. Over the longer term, political parties may develop to take advantage of the new electoral incentives. Although some parties may continue to pursue a broad-based effort to win a large plurality on the first ballot, some parties may instead opt for the runoff strategy. The effect would not only be to create more parties but also to create very differently structured parties with narrower constituencies. Such a system makes it more likely that presidents will be elected with only extremist, narrow, or regional constituencies. Even those parties continuing to pursue victory on the first ballot would likely select their candidates quite differently than they do at present. Rather than maintain a nomination process currently designed to select candidates capable of winning the Electoral College, the parties would be likely to develop new selection procedures better capable of identifying candidates who can compete in the national popular vote. Such future strategic developments are unpredictable, but they will almost certainly lead to a further nationalization and weakening of the political parties and an even greater emphasis on fund-raising skills and political consultants. The current political primary system, with its series of state elections, would almost certainly be replaced by a more purely national system with even greater emphasis on money and the media in determining the nominees. The presidentialist political system will continue to constrain the degree to which parties can multiply in the United States, but a national popular vote is likely to create more political instability and greater division between the legislative and executive branches.

Ironically, the 2000 presidential election may highlight another advantage of the Electoral College over some alternative systems of presidential selection. The Electoral College tends to minimize the chances of a close election that may create election disputes, and when such disputes arise the Electoral College tends to contain them within a single state. A primary goal of any system of choosing political officials and managing the transitions of government power must be rapid and certain resolution. Unfortunately, every election runs the risk of uncertainty and disorder because every election is subject to disputes. Any close election is likely to be disputed since fraud, mistakes, or the intrinsic margin of error in the voting technology could alter the outcome. If the winning margin is small, measured as a percentage of the total votes, then it may be possible to reverse the initial outcome of the election through legal challenges.

The Electoral College minimizes the probability of such disputes arising in the first place because it minimizes the odds of a close election. The Electoral College tends to magnify the margin of victory for the winning candidate, making protracted disputes pointless because they are unlikely to affect the final results. In reality, every presidential election involves not one election but fifty-one elections, as votes are tallied in each state and the District of Columbia. Although the results in some states may be close and readily contestable, such individual results are unlikely to be pivotal. Close elections under the Electoral College are more likely to resemble New Mexico in 2000 than Florida in 2000—that is, irrelevant to determining who will be the next president. In order for a candidate to find it worthwhile to contest the results of an election, there must be a state that is both closely divided in the popular vote and pivotal to the electoral vote.

Such a convergence is extremely rare. It is our bad luck that those factors happened to converge in the state of Florida in the year 2000, but the important issue for evaluating the system as a whole is overall probabilities and the central tendencies of the system. The Electoral College minimizes the odds of election disputes. By contrast, the national popular vote increases the chances of a close election and subsequent disputes, making it more likely that the postelection struggles of the 2000 election will recur. Effectively, any national popular vote decided by a margin of 1 or 2 percent, as seven of our presidential elections have been, could be worth challenging. Whereas close elections are most likely to be irrelevant and hard to challenge under the Electoral College, any close election under a national popular vote will be readily subject to challenge and perhaps even a national recount.

The Electoral College also tends to contain election disputes when they do arise. Because the relevant popular elections and tight margins occur at the state level under the Electoral College, election challenges will also be limited to the states. In many cases, challenges can be pursued at the state level without affecting the national electoral outcome at all. Such was the case in 1960 when the margin of victory in Hawaii between Richard Nixon and John F. Kennedy was less than two hundred votes and recounts dragged out the process. In the end, Hawaii was given the time to finish the recounts and the legal challenges because the results did not matter. Although at best Kennedy defeated Nixon by only one-fifth of 1 percent of the national popular vote, his electoral margin of eighty-four votes easily swamped Hawaii's three contested electoral votes. Such outcomes also minimize the incentives to engage in fraud. Because no one state or locality is likely to be pivotal to the overall outcome, vote fraud must be organized across several closely contested states in order to be effective in altering the results of the election under the Electoral College. The difficulty of successfully organizing such a conspiracy or of affecting the results through isolated action discourages anyone from tampering with the integrity of the presidential vote. If crucial election disputes are unavoidable, as when a single pivotal state is also closely divided, then the Electoral College at least contains the dispute to a single state, focusing resources and publicity on a single set of disputed ballots. Rather than encourage candidates and their supporters to search for, or invent, electoral irregularities across the nation, the Electoral College concentrates the dispute and makes an appropriate and timely resolution more likely.

The contributions of the Electoral College to the American constitutional system are modest. The Electoral College has smaller effects on the political system than do other features of the constitutional structure, such as the separation of powers or bicameralism and the structure of representation in Congress. It is consistent with the rest of the constitutional structure, however, in encouraging compromise and consensus building and in discouraging the success of narrow factions. The Electoral College also has the often-underestimated virtue of being long established and well understood. Its implications are woven into the fabric of American politics, and it has proven remarkably adaptable and functional. For those who desire multiparty politics or majoritarian democracy, the Electoral College may appear less valuable than it does to those who value political compromise and consensus, but such goals run contrary to many aspects of the Constitution and they are unlikely to be realized in any coherent form without more radical constitutional reform. It would seem unwise to abandon such a serviceable electoral mechanism and invite substantial political unpredictability for such limited and largely hypothetical gains.

NOTES

The author thanks Christopher Eisgruber and Patrick Deneen for their helpful comments.

1. Useful overviews of the Electoral College include Lawrence D. Longley and Neal R. Peirce, *The Electoral College Primer 2000* (New Haven: Yale University Press, 1999); Neal R. Peirce and Lawrence D. Longley, *The People's President* (New Haven: Yale University Press, 1981).

2. The Constitution bars federal officeholders from serving as presidential electors.

3. In rare and isolated instances after 1836, state legislatures outside of South Carolina have directly chosen presidential electors.

4. In 1877 Congress adopted procedures for resolving disputes over the counting of electoral ballots.

5. See Shlomo Slonim, "The Electoral College at Philadelphia: The Evolution of an Ad Hoc Congress for the Selection of a President," *Journal of American History* 73 (1986): 35.

6. This concern allied the slave states and the small states, as even the large slave states had a relatively small number of voters.

7. Allowing the House to choose the president from a large list of candidates and voting by state likewise balanced the interests of democratic representation and geographic diversity. Before the Twelfth Amendment, the House was to choose from the top five candidates.

22

POPULAR ELECTION OF THE PRESIDENT
WITHOUT A CONSTITUTIONAL AMENDMENT

Robert W. Bennett

In the wake of the 2000 presidential election, it is certain that there will be debate about whether a nationwide popular vote should be substituted for the Electoral College mechanism for choosing the president. But that debate may be stifled to a degree because of the widespread assumption that constitutional amendment is the only way to effect this change.[1] Amendment of the United States Constitution basically requires the agreement of two-thirds of each house of Congress and three-fourths of the states. For a variety of reasons, those hurdles are likely to prove insuperable, at least initially. But in fact a constitutional amendment may not be necessary. For it is entirely possible that just a few states—conceivably just one or two—could bring about de facto direct election. And if that were to occur, opposition to a constitutional amendment might just melt away.

Each state's Electoral College delegation is equal to its total representation in the House and Senate, with the District of Columbia given the state minimum of three Electoral College votes by the Twenty-third Amendment. It is usually assumed that this apportionment favors the less populous states by virtue of the two electors that each state receives on account of its senators. This assumption is, however, questionable. All states but two (Maine and Nebraska) have adopted a winner-take-all system for selecting their electors. In those forty-eight states, no matter how close the statewide popular vote among presidential candidates, the entire Electoral College delegation goes to the winner. A voter in a populous state thus helps to determine more Electoral College votes than a voter in a less populous state. The net result of the two-elector "bonus" for less populous states and the winner-take-all rule is that voters in the states with very large delegations cast a mathematically weightier vote than do those in other states.[2] And of even more significance is that, holding the size of the state's electorate constant, a voter in a state that is closely divided among presidential candidates effectively casts a weightier vote than does one in a lopsided state.

Despite the complications, a substantial number of states would lose electoral clout from a move to a nationwide popular vote. And because of the complications, many more might worry that they would lose some of their electoral say. There are, in addition, less noticed stumbling blocks on the way to an amendment that would provide for a nationwide popular vote. Such a straightforward move to direct election would pose the question of how eligibility to vote in that election is defined. The original constitutional scheme gave each state the power to set voter qualifications. That discretion is now greatly hemmed in by constitutional and statutory restrictions. States cannot discriminate with regard to the vote on the basis of race or sex or against those over seventeen. They cannot impose poll taxes or English literacy tests or onerous residence requirements. But states retain the formalities of control over voter qualifications, and a number have exercised that discretion, most notoriously to withhold the vote from classes of felons and ex-felons. The ex-felon disenfranchisement in particular is inexcusable, but any move to direct election would arouse opposition from those who do not see it that way and more generally from those who view state authority here as a principled and important part of the system.

Another eligibility question that would be hard to avoid in a straightforward move to direct popular election is that of U.S. citizens in the overseas territories. At the present time this population has no vote that counts in a presidential election. The bulk of these American citizens reside in Puerto Rico, and any move that might enfranchise them would no doubt attract partisan controversy. There is also a relatively small population of U.S. citizens ineligible to vote for president that resides permanently in foreign countries. If those foreign residents have a substantial prior attachment to a state, they are allowed to vote in that state in federal elections. This is accomplished by a federal statute that is, in this respect, of dubious constitutionality.[3] But those U.S. citizens who are foreign residents without prior attachment to a state are not eligible to vote in presidential (or other federal) elections. Their number is not large, and they seem less likely than the population of the territories to arouse partisan concerns, but the uncertainty they inject into a move to change presents another political obstacle to amendment.

For these various reasons, early adoption of direct election by constitutional amendment is very unlikely. But there is a simple way to skirt the necessity of amendment. Some lessons about how this might be done are provided by the history of senatorial elections.[4]

The Constitution originally provided for selection of U.S. senators by state legislatures—the same bodies still charged with determining the "manner" in which presidential electors are to be chosen. The Seventeenth

Amendment now provides for direct popular election of senators, but that amendment was not the simple result of convincing a reluctant Congress and then lining up the requisite number of states. Instead a number of states forced the issue well before the amendment was passed, by insinuating direct election into their own processes.

Some of the pressure built spontaneously. In the 1858 Illinois senatorial battle between Lincoln and Douglas, for instance, the two political parties had made their senatorial favorites known before the state legislative elections. The fabled statewide debates between the two took on their electoral significance as arguments for state legislative candidates who, once seated, would cast their votes for the one senatorial "candidate" or the other. As populism and the progressive movement gained steam toward the end of the century, a number of states then experimented with measures that would draw the electorate into the process in more formal ways. With Oregon often taking the lead, states experimented with nonbinding senatorial primary or even general elections and various forms of pressure on state legislators to accede to the popular choice.[5] By one estimate, the result was that by 1910—three years before adoption of the Seventeenth Amendment—fourteen of the thirty newly chosen senators had been the product of de facto popular election.[6]

Now what does this teach about the Electoral College? One of the many things that the nation learned about the Electoral College from the 2000 election is that state legislatures have "plenary" power in establishing the manner of appointment of electors.[7] I seriously doubt that this means that the Florida legislature could appropriately have preempted the electoral process that it had originally chosen. But I see no obstacle to a state legislature's providing beforehand that its Electoral College delegation would be pledged to the winner of the nationwide popular vote. If states with just 270 electoral votes adopted such an approach, the popular vote winner would perforce win the presidency. Under the Electoral College allocations that were produced by the 1990 census, a mere eleven states—those with the largest populations, of course—control 270 electoral votes. That number falls well below the three-fourths required for a constitutional amendment (to say nothing of the requirement of congressional approval).[8]

To be sure, those populous states might be reluctant. We have seen that arguably some of them have the most to lose. But de facto popular election could be accomplished by fewer than eleven states. If just California and Texas—the two states that starting with the next election will have the largest Electoral College delegations, and which have opposed party inclinations at the present time—would adopt such a rule, the chances of a disparity between the Electoral College and the popular vote would be pretty close to the vanishing point.

To begin with, California and Texas had eighty-six electoral votes between them in the last election and seem likely to have even more after the congressional reapportionment worked by the census now being completed. There have been very few instances in our history when the popular vote winner lost outright in the Electoral College. Most typically the electoral vote exaggerates the victory of the popular vote winner. If the popular vote loser started out eighty-six or more votes behind, he would thus be exceedingly unlikely to win.[9]

Political dynamics would make it even less likely. At the present time, candidates employ "Electoral College" strategies, targeting states with sufficient Electoral College votes to win. They can do this basically without independent concern about the nationwide popular vote. With the suggested move by California and Texas, presidential candidates would be forced to radically alter that approach, devoting energy and resources to getting out the vote in all states. Deprived of the ability to single-mindedly pursue an Electoral College strategy they would be even less likely than they have been historically to secure an Electoral College win without winning the popular vote. There would still be a mathematical chance of their doing so, of course, but much less of a real-world chance.

Indeed it seems quite likely that even states less populous than California and Texas could turn the trick. For both substantive purposes and those of political acceptability, it would probably be important that the move be made by one or more states that are closely divided politically, or by some combination across the political divide. Adoption by the swing (and occasionally adventuresome) state of Wisconsin—with eleven electoral votes in the last election—would tilt the system decidedly toward popular election. Combinations of states across the political divide and with a larger total of electoral votes—Colorado and Oregon with a total of fifteen votes, for instance, or Missouri and Minnesota with twenty-one—would increase the odds even more.

There are a large number of variations on the theme. The initial states might move more cautiously at first, by tying their electoral votes to the nationwide popular vote only if a stated number of other states (or of states with a given number of electoral votes) followed suit. Or, as suggested to me by Dan Farber of the University of Minnesota Law School, a state could assign its electoral votes on the basis of the pooled popular vote from a group of states that adopted similar pooling laws. Too much inventiveness might, however, be the enemy of success. Adoption of a variety of devices by different states might weaken the chances of any one of them catching on. Still, if a few states took the plunge in one form or another, others might well follow, just as the movement for popular senatorial elections gained momentum over time. Opposition to a constitutional amendment could then quickly dissolve, just as it did back then.

This route to change would bring a degree of an advantage often cited for direct election. The winner-take-all rule provides political parties with no incentive to increase turnout in politically lopsided states. If electoral votes that could prove decisive were dependent on the nationwide popular vote, turnout would become important in every state. This route to change also finesses—initially at least—some tricky subissues. It avoids the question of whether a popular vote winner need obtain a majority of the vote or only a stated plurality instead. Each state could define its own popular vote trigger and provide for contingencies if that trigger proved indecisive. In addition, the popular vote trigger leaves untouched state prerogatives to define eligibility to vote. And it steers clear of the overseas territory and foreign resident voter questions. But it would also be possible for aggressive states to confront at least the territory and foreign resident issues. The pioneer states might provide that their electors would go to the winner in a vote that included citizens currently ineligible, if Congress would pass the necessary implementing legislation for tallying the votes in an effective and timely fashion.

I do not mean to suggest that this would be easy to accomplish. There are important differences between the senatorial and presidential election contexts. State legislators were susceptible to popular agitation for popular involvement in senatorial selection, because they had to stand for election themselves. In the presidential elector context, in contrast, state legislators would be asked to institute a system by which the choice of their own voters would not be dispositive in directing the state's electors. It is hard to see why a state's voters would agitate in large numbers for such a move.

There are other problems. At the present time, there is relatively little pressure for states that go decisively for one candidate or another to get a precise count of the popular vote. A state that opted for a nationwide count would want some assurance that the count was accurate. The same problem would be posed by a constitutional amendment, of course, and related concerns have been advanced as reasons not to abandon the Electoral College. Balloting reform could do a lot to allay this concern, but federal legislation might be necessary to assure a degree of integrity for the nationwide popular vote totals.

Despite the problems, the nationwide popular vote mechanism is actually more enticing in some ways than was the insinuation of popular voting into senatorial selection. The action of one state in moving toward popular election of senators brought no leverage on other states, save as the example might persuade on the merits. In the presidential context, in contrast, a very few states have the capacity to dramatically tilt the entire system toward direct election. The appeal to reformist zeal could prove tempting.

None of this is to suggest that a move to a nationwide popular vote is obviously a good thing, even in theory. The complex American system serves ends other than straight-out "majoritarianism," whatever that might mean. Neither the Senate nor the House of Representatives need be representative of a nationwide majority, and it is not obvious that the president must be. But there clearly is a good measure of dissatisfaction with the possibility of a disparity between the popular and electoral vote outcomes. A full-fledged debate on the merits of a change should not be pushed off the nation's agenda because of the difficulty of constitutional amendment.

NOTES

1. For just one example, albeit from the pen of one not deterred from the fight, see Ronald Dworkin's "A Badly Flawed Election," chap. 4, this volume.

2. See Lawrence D. Longley and Neal R. Peirce, *The Electoral College Primer 2000* (New Haven: Yale University Press, 1999), 149–54 (based on the 1990 census apportionment of the Electoral College).

3. Uniformed and Overseas Citizens Absentee Voting Act, 42 U.S.C. §§ 1973ff–1 to 1973ff–6 (1994).

4. The story is related in David A. Strauss, "The Irrelevance of Constitutional Amendments," 114 *Harv. L. Rev.* 1457, 1496–99 (2001).

5. See George H. Haynes, *The Election of Senators* (New York: Henry Holt & Co., 1906), 133–48.

6. George H. Haynes, *The Senate of the United States* (Boston: Houghton Mifflin, 1938), 104 (citing *Boston Herald* of December 26, 1910).

7. The characterization comes from McPherson v. Blacker, 146 U.S. 1, 7, 10 (1892).

8. It seems likely that eleven states will still suffice to get up to the required majority under the apportionment to be dictated by the 2000 census.

9. There have been at most four instances in our history—two clear and two not so clear—where the outright winner in the Electoral College lost the popular vote. In 1888, Cleveland won the popular vote but lost in the electoral college by sixty-five votes. The other clear case was in the disputed election of 1876, and the electoral vote margin there was one vote. The 2000 election is one of the unclear instances, and it too resulted in a razor-thin Electoral College margin. The final example was the 1960 election, in which it is impossible to know who won the popular vote, because the Alabama ballots listed only the electors and the political situation in Alabama makes it by no means clear how to ascribe votes for the various Democratic electors to Kennedy. Kennedy's margin in the Electoral College was eighty-four votes. See Longley and Peirce, *supra* note 1, at 46–59.

CONTRIBUTORS

BRUCE ACKERMAN is Sterling Professor of Law and Political Science at Yale University. He is a member of the American Law Institute and the American Academy of Arts and Sciences.

SHLOMO AVINERI is Herbert Samuel Professor of Political Science and Director of the Institute for European Studies at the Hebrew University of Jerusalem. He is a former director-general of Israel's Ministry of Foreign Affairs. Among his books are *The Social and Political Thought of Karl Marx, Hegel's Theory of the Modern State,* and *The Making of Modern Zionism.*

ROBERT W. BENNETT is Professor of Law at the Northwestern University School of Law, where he was dean from 1985 to 1995. His book, tentatively titled *Puzzles of American Democracy and Their Conversational Solution,* is scheduled for publication in 2002 by Cornell University Press.

JUDITH BEST is Distinguished Teaching Professor of Political Science, State University of New York, Cortland. She is the author of *The Choice of the People? Debating the Electoral College* and *The Case against Direct Election of the President: A Defense of the Electoral College.* At the request of committees of the U.S. Senate and House of Representatives, she has served several times as an expert witness on the Electoral College system. She has addressed the Twentieth Century Fund's Task Force on the Reform of the Presidential Election Process and the Freedom Forum's Symposium on Presidential Selection.

HENRY E. BRADY is Professor of Political Science and Public Policy and Director of the Survey Research Center at the University of California, Berkeley. He is coauthor of *Voice and Equality: Civic Voluntarism in American Politics* and *Letting the People Decide: The Dynamics of a Canadian Election.* He has written articles on elections and political participation in America, Canada, Estonia, and Russia. He is also coauthor of a monograph on disabled children in poor families titled *Expensive Children in Poor Families.*

RICHARD BROOKHISER is a senior editor of the *National Review* and a columnist for the *New York Observer*. His books include *Founding Father: Rediscovering George Washington, America's First Dynasty: The Adamses, 1735–1918,* and *Alexander Hamilton, American.*

RONALD DWORKIN is Frank Henry Summer Professor at the New York University School of Law and formerly Professor of Jurisprudence at Oxford University. His works include *Taking Rights Seriously, A Matter of Principle, Law's Empire,* and, most recently, *Sovereign Virtue.* He is a regular contributor to the *New York Review of Books.* He was cochair of the Democratic Party Abroad.

GEORGE P. FLETCHER is Cardozo Professor of Jurisprudence at the Columbia University Law School. He is the author of *Rethinking Criminal Law, A Crime of Self-Defense: Bernhard Goetz and the Law on Trial, With Justice for Some: Protecting Victims' Rights in Criminal Trials, Loyalty: An Essay on the Morality of Relationships, Basic Concepts of Legal Thought,* and *Our Secret Constitution: How Lincoln Redefined American Democracy.*

CHARLES FRIED is Beneficial Professor at the Harvard University Law School. He was President Reagan's solicitor general from 1985 to 1989 and an associate justice on the Massachusetts Supreme Judicial Court from 1995 to 1999. He was counsel to the Florida legislature during the disputes surrounding the presidential election in Florida. He is the author of *An Anatomy of Values: Problems of Personal and Social Choice Right and Wrong, Contract as Promise: A Theory of Contractual Obligation,* and *Order and Law: Arguing the Reagan Revolution, a Firsthand Account.*

DIETER GRIMM was a justice on the German Constitutional Court from 1987 to 1999. After completing his term, he joined the Law Faculty of Humboldt University in Berlin, where he teaches constitutional law. He is also a permanent fellow of the Institute for Advanced Study in Berlin, a distinguished member of the Global Law Faculty of New York University, and a visiting professor at the Yale Law School.

MICHAEL C. HERRON is Assistant Professor in the Department of Political Science, Northwestern University. His research on the butterfly ballot was carried out while he was a Postdoctoral Research Fellow at Harvard University. His current research interests include voting anomalies in the 2000 general election, legislative politics, and the properties of legislator preference measures.

ARTHUR J. JACOBSON is Max Freund Professor of Litigation and Advocacy at the Benjamin N. Cardozo School of Law.

MATTIAS KUMM is Assistant Professor of Law at the New York University School of Law. His research and teaching interests are in the areas of the law of the European Union, constitutional law, and legal and political philosophy. He has studied law, philosophy, and political science in Germany, France, and the United States.

NOËLLE LENOIR is a justice on the Conseil d'État (Administrative Supreme Court) of France. From 1992 to 2001 she was a justice on the Conseil Constitutionnel (Constitutional Supreme Court), which, among other tasks, supervises and certifies the results of national elections, including presidential and parliamentary elections. Justice Lenoir is also president of the European Group on Ethics of the European

Union, an independent multidisciplinary body advising the European Commission. She has been a visiting professor of law at Columbia University, Yale University, and University College, London.

LAWRENCE D. LONGLEY is Professor of Government at Lawrence University of Wisconsin. Among his many works on the Electoral College in presidental elections are *The People's President* and *The Electoral College Primer 2000*. He has testified before Congress on numerous occasions and has twice served as a presidential elector.

NELSON LUND is Professor at the George Mason University School of Law, where he has served as coeditor of the *Supreme Court Economic Review*. He served as law clerk for the Hon. Patrick E. Higginbotham of the United States Court of Appeals for the Fifth Circuit and for the Hon. Sandra Day O'Connor of the United States Supreme Court. In addition to experience at the U.S. Department of Justice in the Office of the Solicitor General and the Office of Legal Counsel, Lund served in the White House as associate counsel to President George H. W. Bush from 1989 to 1992.

WALTER R. MEBANE JR. is Associate Professor of Government at Cornell University. He is the former editor of *Political Analysis*. His research interests include American politics, elections, voting behavior, representative institutions, statistical methods, nonlinear and dynamic models, empirical and formal theory, and political methodology.

FRANK I. MICHELMAN is Robert Walmsley University Professor at Harvard University. He is the author of *Brennan and Democracy*.

BURT NEUBORNE is John Norton Pomeroy Professor of Law and Legal Director of the Brennan Center for Justice at New York University.

PASQUALE PASQUINO is Director of Research at the Centre National de la Recherche Scientifique in Paris and Professor in the Global Law School Program at the New York University School of Law. He is writing a book on comparative constitutional adjudication with John Ferejohn of Stanford University and the New York University School of Law.

RICHARD H. PILDES is Professor of Law at the New York University School of Law. He is coauthor of *The Law of Democracy: Legal Structure of the Political Process*, the leading casebook in its field. He was a legal consultant to NBC News during Election 2000.

MICHEL ROSENFELD is Justice Sydney L. Robins Professor of Human Rights at the Benjamin N. Cardozo School of Law. He is the editor in chief of the *International Journal of Constitutional Law (ICON)* and president of the International Association of Constitutional Law. He is the author of *Affirmative Action and Justice: A Philosophical and Constitutional Inquiry* and *Just Interpretations: Law between Ethics and Politics*, which has been translated into French and Italian. He is editor and coeditor of several books in legal philosophy and constitutional law.

JASJEET SINGH SEKHON is Assistant Professor of Government and an associate of the Center for Basic Research in the Social Sciences at Harvard University. His research interests include political methodology, computational methods, biostatistics, political economy, and American politics. He is also a partner at Lamarck, Inc.

KENNETH W. SHOTTS is Assistant Professor of Political Science at Northwestern University. His primary research interest is game theoretic models of political institutions. Among the topics he studies are racial gerrymandering, executive leadership, term limits, ecological inference statistical methodology, and the role of information in elections.

JONATHAN WAND is a Ph.D. candidate at Cornell University, currently writing a dissertation on the dynamics of campaign contributions and election forecasting. His research interests include comparative electoral behavior and political methodology, focusing on dynamic discrete-choice models. He is also a partner at Lamarck, Inc.

KEITH E. WHITTINGTON is Assistant Professor of Politics and John Maclean Jr. Presidential Preceptor at Princeton University. He is the author of *Constitutional Construction: Divided Powers and Constitutional Meaning* and *Constitutional Interpretation: Textual Meaning, Original Intent, and Judicial Review,* as well as articles and book chapters on constitutional theory and American constitutional and political development.

INDEX

Compositor: Binghamton Valley Composition, LLC
Text: 10/12 Baskerville
Display: Franklin Gothic and Baskerville
Printer and binder: Maple-Vail Manufacturing Group